saur

Nancy Schmidt

# Sub-Saharan African Films
# and Filmmakers:
# An Annotated Bibliography

# Films et Cinéastes Africains de la Région
# Subsaharienne:
# Une Bibliographie Commentée

## Hans Zell Publishers

an imprint of
Butterworths
London · München · New York · Paris 1988

British Library Cataloguing in Publication Data
    Schmidt, Nancy J.
    Sub-Saharan African films and filmmakers.
    an annotated bibliography.
    1. African cinema films. Bibliographies
    I. Title
    016.79143'096
    ISBN 0–905450–32–9

Hans Zell Publishers and K. G. Saur
are imprints of Butterworths.
Shropshire House, 2–10 Capper Street, London WC1E 6JA, England
Copyright © 1988 by Nancy Schmidt

Printed in Great Britain
at the University Printing House, Oxford
by David Stanford
Printer to the University

ISBN 0–905450–32–9

DEDICATED TO THE MEMORY OF

**PAULIN SOUMANOU VIEYRA**

Filmmaker, Film Critic and
Historian of African Film


May this bibliography enable others
to continue his pioneering work in
film criticism and the study of the
history of African film.


A LA MEMOIRE DE

PAULIN SOUMANOU VIEYRA

cinéaste, critique et
historien du cinéma africain


Que cette bibliographie permette à d'autres
de continuer son travail initiateur de critique et
de chronique du cinéma africain

# TABLE OF CONTENTS

# TABLE DES MATIERES

Acknowledgments

No bibliography that relies heavily on materials published in
Africa could be compiled without the extensive resources held in
American libraries and the cooperative library projects by which
newspapers are collected and preserved for future use. This
bibliography, like all my other bibliographies, could not have been
compiled without the extensive collection of Africana at the
Northwestern University Library and the skilled bibliographers who
service it. Special thanks to Dan Britz, Hans Panofsky and Mette
Shayne for the assistance they gave me in locating citations and
obtaining uncatalogued materials at Northwestern University.

The African Archives Libraries Committee through its cooperative
projects has made many African published materials available to
Africanist scholars. Especially useful for compiling this
bibliography have been long runs of African newspapers which have been
collected, microfilmed and made available on loan from the Center for
Research Libraries and Library of Congress.

Even the most comprehensive library collection does not have
everything on any topic. Because of the wide dispersion of material
on African films and filmmakers in the literature of many disciplines
published in Africa, Europe, America and Asia, extensive use has been
made of interlibrary loan. The Reference and Interlibrary Borrowing
staffs at Indiana University have been very helpful, especially Tom
Glastras and Rhonda Stone, who have patiently tracked down obscure
materials from less than perfect bibliographic data.

Jim Ballantyne, Vicki Evalds, Karen Fung, Russell Hamilton,

Gerald Moser, Tony Olden, Lawrence Rupley, Yvette Scheven and Gretchen Walsh have helped me obtain citations. Murlin Croucher helped me by translating materials in Russian. Through her generous hospitality, Katharine Ehle has made all of my research at the Northwestern University Library possible. Thanks also to Hans Zell for believing that bibliographic research on African film can make a contribution to African Studies and for facilitating the publication of this bibliography.

Last, but by no means least, thanks to Sue Hanson for typing the bibliography and carefully scrutinizing it with a keen editorial eye. Even in the computer age, accurate typing is essential in producing reliable research tools.

REMERCIEMENTS

La rédaction d'une bibliographie se basant principalement sur des matériaux publiés en Afrique serait inconcevable sans l'accès aux vastes ressources documentaires des bibliothèques américaines et aux projets communs par lesquels les bibliothèques rassemblent et conservent les journaux pour les générations futures. La présente bibliographie, comme toutes mes bibliographies précédentes, n'aurait pu être rédigée sans l'accès à la vaste documentation africaine conservée à la bibliothèque de la Northwestern University, ni sans l'aide des bibliographes experts qui la gèrent. Je voudrais remercier tout spécialement Dan Britz, Hans Panofsky et Mette Shayne pour l'aide qu'ils m'ont fournie dans le repérage des citations et pour obtenir les matériaux non catalogués conservés à l'Université.

Par ses divers projets coopératifs, l'African Archives Libraries Committee a assuré aux savants africanistes la disponibilité de nombreuses publications africaines. Les longues séries de journaux africains qui ont été rassemblées, microfilmées et mises à la disposition des chercheurs par le Center for Research Libraries et la Library of Congress, m'ont été particulièrement utiles.

Si complète qu'elle soit, aucune collection de livres ne peut tout rassembler sur un thème particulier. Etant donné la dispersion, parmi les littératures des diverses disciplines en Afrique, Europe, Amérique et Asie, des matériaux sur le cinéma et les cinéastes africains, il s'est avéré nécessaire, à maintes reprises, d'avoir recours au système de prêts entre bibliothèques. Le personnel du département des ouvrages à consulter et des prêts entre bibliothèques de l'Indiana University m'a été d'un grand secours. Je voudrais

3.

remercier spécialement Tom Glastras et Rhonda Stone, qui ont passé des heures à localiser des documents peu connus, à l'aide de données bibliographiques souvent insuffisantes.

Jim Ballantyne, Vicki Evalds, Karen Fung, Russell Hamilton, Gerald Moser, Tony Olden, Lawrence Rupley, Yvette Scheven et Gretchen Walsh m'ont également aidée à repérer des citations. Murlin Croucher a fourni un travail très utile en traduisant la documentation russe. Sans l'hospitalité généreuse de Katharine Ehle, toutes les recherches que j'ai réalisées à la bibliothèque de la Northwestern University auraient été impossibles. Je voudrais aussi remercier Hans Zell, pour avoir fait sienne la conviction que les recherches bibliographiques sur le cinéma africain constituent un apport important au développement des études africaines, et pour avoir rendu possible la publication de la présente bibliographie.

En dernier lieu, mais non par ordre d'importance, je voudrais remercier Sue Hanson, qui a dactylographié le texte et l'a scruté de son oeil perçant de rédactrice. Même à l'âge de l'ordinateur, une dactylographie précise est essentielle à la production d'outils de recherche fiables.

INTRODUCTION

African filmmakers have been making documentary and feature films in Sub-Saharan Africa for over three decades. Filmmaking is considered very important in nation building, cultural preservation and fostering national identity in many nations including Burkina Faso, Mali, Angola and Mocambique. Despite the severe infrastructural limitations which constrain their work, hundreds of Sub-Saharan African filmmakers have made perhaps 1000 short and long documentary and feature films. Most of these films are shown only within the countries in which they are made. Some of them, especially feature films, are viewed more widely at African, European, Asian and American film festivals. A few of the first generation of Sub-Saharan African filmmakers including Souleymane Cissé, Ruy Guerra, Med Hondo and Sembéne Ousmane have achieved international acclaim for their work. A second generation of filmmakers is already showing their work at international festivals, and recently such filmmakers as Mustapha Diop, Idrissa Ouédraogo, Emmanuel Sanou and Cheick Oumar Sissoko have received recognition for the originality of their work.

Despite the importance of filmmaking in Sub-Saharan Africa today, very little research has been conducted either on the films themselves or on the contexts in which they are being made and viewed, both in Africa and elsewhere in the world. However, there is a substantial body of reportage on Sub-Saharan African films and filmmakers which includes primary data that could be used in research. Most of the news and magazine reports are published in Africa. Paris is the primary center of reportage outside of Africa. However, as the list of film festivals in the index indicates, the scope of reportage on

5.

African film is truly worldwide. Very little of the available primary data have been used in the research that has been conducted on Sub-Saharan African film. Perhaps this is not surprising, since the majority of the published sources on Sub-Saharan African films and filmmakers are bibliographically inaccessible.

## Purpose of the bibliography

The purpose of this bibliography is to call attention to the wealth of published information available on Sub-Saharan African films and filmmakers. Although I have more than doubled the number of entries that appeared in my Sub-Saharan African Films and Filmmakers: A Preliminary Bibliography (Bloomington: African Studies Program, Indiana University, 1986), the current bibliography makes no claim to completeness. It is not complete and cannot be complete until all African newspapers, news and cultural magazines in countries in which films are made and relevant publications in all countries in which African films are shown and studied have been systematically examined. This task is too large for one individual to complete.

This bibliography calls attention to the kinds of published resources that are available on African films and filmmakers and to their wide dispersion. Annotations are provided to indicate where primary data can be found and the major topics of secondary reports. For the countries in which publications have been covered in relatively greater depth, this bibliography aims to be exemplary of the kinds of resources which should be consulted for all countries in which films are produced and shown.

It is hoped that this bibliography will be useful to African filmmakers in learning about the work of other African filmmakers, to

reviewers of African films in obtaining information about the
background of specific African films and African filmmaking in
general, as well as to those who conduct research on African film. It
is further hoped that this bibliography will stimulate a cooperative
effort to gain bibliographic control over the literature on
Sub-Saharan African films and filmmakers and to establish an African
film archive where as many of the films and as much of the literature
as possible will be collected and preserved for future use by
scholars, filmmakers and other interested persons.

## Scope of the bibliography

The bibliography focuses on films made by Sub-Saharan African
filmmakers. It excludes films made by North African filmmakers and
South African mainstream filmmakers because the bibliographic control
of information about films in these two areas is adequate. Films
about Africa by non-African filmmakers are excluded, with a few
exceptions, namely when an African and European codirect a film made
by a European company (e.g. La vie est belle), when the filmmaker is
considered African even though not born in Africa (e.g. Sarah
Maldoror), when the cast is primarily African although the director is
European (e.g. Black Mic Mac), and when the film is of African
literature, shown in Africa and discussed by African reviewers (e.g.
L'aventure ambigue by Jacques Champreux).

The scope of the bibliography, method of its compilation and
primary characteristics of the resources included in it are discussed
in detail in my "Visualizing Africa: the Bibliography of Films by
Sub-Saharan African Filmmakers" (forthcoming). It should be noted
here that citations were sought in European languages written in Roman

scripts. The majority of citations are in French, but many other European languages are represented. The bibliography includes books, theses, monographs, pamphlets, articles and reviews of both films and books about films. Short news notes of a few lines have been excluded, as have photographs unaccompanied by an article. An attempt was made to include as many sources as possible published until September 1987. However, because of delays in publication and the receipt of publications not all materials published early in 1987 were available for examination before September. Where long runs of journals and newspapers were available for examination, 1960 was selected as the cut-off date, since few Sub-Saharan African films were made before this date.

Relationship to preliminary bibliography

An attempt was made to verify all of the unverified entries in my Sub-Saharan African Films and Filmmakers: A Preliminary Bibliography. As a result, some entries have been corrected and others have been deleted because they either were unverifiable as cited or when examined were found not to be about Sub-Saharan African films or filmmakers.

The cut-off date for entries in the preliminary bibliography was 1984. The new entries in this bibliography come from three primary sources: updating the preliminary bibliography, expanding the resources covered, especially those written in Portuguese, and retrospectively examining African newspapers available on microfilm. Thus this bibliography includes substantially more older, as well as newer citations than the preliminary bibliography.

The indexes in the preliminary bibliography have been corrected where it has come to my attention that the same film was listed under different titles, either because the preliminary and final titles were different or the film had different titles in an African and European language.  Names in the indexes have been corrected where an author or filmmaker uses more than one name and where I have learned of a preferred form for a person's name.  Cross references have been added for alternate titles of films and variant forms of names.

Entry form

Entries are listed alphabetically by author in two sections: the first for books, theses, monographs and film programs and the second for articles, reviews and pamphlets.  Since there are relatively few books, it seemed useful to list them separately, thereby calling attention to the materials with more substantive coverage.  In those cases where books are edited volumes of essays, the component essays are listed separately with the articles.  Where special issues of journals have been issued separately as books, this is noted in the book entry.

The majority of the sources were examined.  An asterisk (*) precedes the entry numbers for materials that I have not examined.  To avoid a long list of anonymous authors of articles, all unsigned articles are listed with the title of the periodical as the author. African authors' names often are spelled in different ways or appear in different forms.  I have chosen the most frequent spelling of an author's name and the most frequently used form of an author's name where articles appear under two or more variant forms of a name.

The citations are as complete as possible.  Where bibliographic data are missing in unverified sources, it is because they were not provided in the citation I found. Where bibliographic data are missing in verified sources, it is because the photocopies I received on interlibrary loan did not include the data. There are some inconsistencies in citation form for African newspapers because I did not provide cover dates in the preliminary bibliography and was unable to reexamine the newspapers to provide them in this bibliography.

Information about the content of citations is provided by symbols and short annotations. The symbol (I) is for interviews. The name of the person interviewed will be included in the annotation only if it does not appear in the title of the article. Interviews are highlighted by a symbol because they are an important source of primary data. The symbol (R) is for reviews of films. The name of the film and filmmaker appear in the annotation only if they are not included in the title of the review. Reviews are annotated only if they include some substantive background information about the film or filmmaker or make a theoretical contribution to the literature. The symbol (BR) is for reviews of books. The title and author of the book are included in an annotation if they do not appear in the title of the review. No other information is included in book review annotations, since annotations are provided for the books in the first section of the bibliography. Cross references link reviews to entries for the books reviewed.

Annotations are short because of limitations placed on the length of the bibliography by the publisher. The annotations are designed to add information to that provided in the title of the book or article so that the primary content is known. If the work is a unique or major contribution, this will be noted. Annotations are descriptive.

There is insufficient space to critically evaluate the materials.

Indexes

The indexes of actors/actresses, film festivals, film titles, filmmakers, countries subdivided by subject, and general subjects are linked to the entry numbers. Each citation is indexed in detail, with as many subject headings as are relevant. It has been difficult to establish the proper form for some personal names because of variant forms, variant spellings and inconsistencies in compounding surnames. I have provided cross-references between different forms of personal names.

Country names are used to identify both the content of articles and the nationality of filmmakers, actors and actresses. Country entries are subdivided by major subjects about which materials are written. The general subject section includes articles about Sub-Saharan Africa, regions of Africa or several countries. The material indexed by subject under specific countries is not repeated in the general subject section.

Materials on film theory are included under Ideology along with materials about the ideals of what films should be or what filmmakers should do. Materials about infrastructure in general or several aspects of infrastructure are listed under Infrastructure. Materials which focus on a specific aspect of infrastructure such as Distribution or Theaters are listed under the more specific heading. Since I have been unable to reexamine all of the citations in the preliminary bibliography, some of them are indexed by more general terms than are citations added or verified since the preliminary bibliography was completed. Were I starting the project at this point in time, I would use more specific subject terms. However, it is only after examining thousands of sources that the most appropriate subject terms are obvious. For the sake of consistency I have used the same general subject terms throughout the indexes and have provided more specific subject terms in the annotations.

An attempt has been made to compile an accurate bibliography. However, I am sure this bibliography includes errors. As I explain in "Visualizing Africa: The Bibliography of Film by Sub-Saharan African Filmmakers" (forthcoming), there are many inconsistencies and errors in the sources included in this bibliography. I have tried to reconcile inconsistencies and correct errors that I am aware of. However, there are some that I cannot correct because I do not have adequate information. For example, the nationality of Cheick Doukouré is listed in different sources as Guinean, Ivorian and Senegalese; there are two actors named Johnny Sekka (Secka) and it is impossible to distinguish materials about them written prior to the clarification that was published in Le Soleil. Undoubtedly there are some inconsistencies and errors that I have not discovered.

This bibliography is offered as a first step in gaining bibliographic control over the literature about Sub-Saharan African films and filmmakers. A cooperative effort by knowledgeable persons is needed if a truly comprehensive, accurate bibliography on African film and filmmakers is to be completed.

# INTRODUCTION

Il y a plus de trois décennies que les cinéastes africains de la région subsaharienne tournent des films de long métrage et des documentaires. Dans de nombreux pays tels que le Burkina Faso, le Mali, l'Angola et le Mozambique, le cinéma est considéré comme un élément très important dans le développement de la nation, dans la préservation des valeurs culturelles, et dans la promotion d'une identité nationale. Malgré les insuffisances d'infrastructures dont souffre leur travail, des centaines de cinéastes subsahariens ont, ensemble, tourné un total d'environ 1.000 films et documentaires de diverses longueurs. La plupart de ces films sont projetés uniquement dans les pays où ils sont tournés. Quelques-uns, surtout les films de long métrage, atteignent un public plus large, aux festivals du film en Afrique, Europe, Asie et Amérique. Une poignée de cinéastes subsahariens de la première génération, dont Souleymane Cissé, Ruy Guerra, Med Hondo et Sembène Ousmane, ont vu leur travail salué dans les forums cinématographiques internationaux. Une deuxième génération de cinéastes présente déjà ses productions aux festivals internationaux, et récemment des cinéastes tels que Mustapha Diop, Idrissa Ouédraogo, Emmanuel Sanou et Cheick Oumar Sissoko, ont été acclamés pour leur originalité.

Malgré la place importante actuellement accordée au cinéma dans la région subsaharienne, les recherches sur les films eux-mêmes et sur le contexte dans lequel ceux-ci sont tournés et projetés sont restées, tant en Afrique qu'ailleurs, très rares. Il existe, cependant, une masse importante de reportages sur le cinéma et les cinéastes subsahariens, y compris des données de base susceptibles d'être

13.

utilisées dans la recherche. La plupart des articles de presse concernés sont publiés en Afrique. En dehors de l'Afrique, Paris est le centre principal où l'on trouve de tels matériaux. Pourtant, comme le montre la liste des festivals du film figurant dans l'index du présent ouvrage, l'envergure éventuelle des reportages sur le cinéma africain est véritablement mondiale. Très peu de l'information de base disponible a été utilisée dans les recherches faites sur le cinéma subsaharien. Constatation peu étonnante, étant donné que la plupart des sources ayant trait au cinéma et aux cinéastes de la région subsaharienne sont bibliographiquement inaccessibles.

Objet de la bibliographie

L'objet de la présente bibliographie est d'attirer l'attention sur l'abondance d'informations publiées sur le cinéma et les cinéastes de la région subsaharienne. Bien que le nombre de notices ait doublé par rapport à ma précédente bibliographie - Sub-Saharan African Films and Filmmakers: A Preliminary Bibliography (Bloomington: African Studies Program, Indiana University, 1986) - je ne prétends aucunement que la présente liste soit complète. Elle ne l'est pas et ne pourra l'être tant que la presse africaine - journaux, magazines d'actualités et périodiques culturels - dans tous les pays où des films sont tournés, et tant que toutes les publications dans les pays où les films africains sont projetés et étudiés n'auront pas été systématiquement analysées. Cette tâche est trop immense que pour être réalisée par une seule personne.

La présente bibliographie attire l'attention sur les divers genres de matériaux publiés sur les films et cinéastes africains, ainsi que sur la large dispersion de ces matériaux. Chaque notice est assortie d'annotations indiquant les coordonnées des informations de base, ainsi que les thèmes principaux des rapports secondaires éventuels. Dans le cas des pays où les publications ont fait l'objet d'une analyse relativement approfondie, la présente bibliographie se propose comme modèle du type de ressources qui devraient être consultées pour tous les pays où des films sont tournés et projetés.

J'espère que cette bibliographie sera utile: aux cinéastes africains désireux d'apprendre plus sur le travail de leur collègues, aux critiques de cinéma voulant connaître davantage le contexte dans lequel des films particuliers sont tournés et le contexte général du cinéma africain, et aux personnes entreprenant des recherches sur le cinéma africain. J'espère également que cette bibliographie stimulera l'effort commun pour parvenir à une maîtrise bibliographique des sources sur le cinéma et les cinéastes subsahariens, et pour mettre sur pied des archives du cinéma africain réunissant et conservant pour les générations futures de savants, de cinéastes et d'autres personnes intéressées, le plus grand nombre possible de films et de documents.

## Envergure de la bibliographie

La bibliographie se concentre sur les films tournés par les cinéastes de la région subsaharienne. Les films réalisés par les cinéastes nord-africains, ainsi que ceux tournés par les principaux cinéastes sud-africains sont exclus, puisque la maîtrise bibliographique des documents relatifs au cinéma de ces deux régions est déjà adéquate. Les films sur l'Afrique tournés par les cinéastes non africains sont également exclus, à part quelques exceptions, notamment quand un film, financé par une compagnie européenne, est tourné conjointement par un cinéaste africain et un cinéaste européen (par exemple La vie est belle); quand le cinéaste concerné est considéré comme étant africain bien qu'il ne soit pas né en Afrique (par exemple Sarah Maldoror); quand la plupart des acteurs et actrices, bien que collaborant avec un réalisateur européen, sont africains (par exemple Black Mic Mac); et quand il s'agit d'un film basé sur la littérature africaine, tourné en Afrique et discuté par des critiques de cinéma africains (par exemple L'aventure ambiguë de Jacques Champreux).

L'envergure de la bibliographie, le méthode utilisée pour la rédiger, et le caractère des matériaux qui y sont inclus, sont expliqués en détail dans mon article 'Visualizing Africa: the Bibliography of Films by Sub-Saharan Filmmakers', qui sera publié dans un proche avenir. Il est à noter que seules les citations en langues européennes et en caractères romains ont fait partie de la recherche. La plupart des citations sont en français, mais de nombreuses langues européennes figurent dans la bibliographie. Celle-ci inclut les livres, les thèses, les monographies, les brochures, les articles et les critiques - non seulement de films mais aussi de livres sur les films.

Les informations brèves n'occupant que quelques lignes, ainsi que les photographies sans commentaires, ont été exclues. J'ai tenté d'inclure le plus grand nombre possible de sources publiées jusqu'à septembre 1987. Cependant, à cause des retards dans le calendrier des publications, et à cause de la réception tardive de divers articles, certains des documents publiés au début de 1987 ne m'étaient toujours par disponibles en septembre. En ce qui concerne les longues séries de périodiques et journaux, j'ai choisi 1960 comme point de départ, car très peu de films ont été tournés dans la région subsaharienne avant cette date.

## Changements par rapport à la bibliographie préliminaire

Pour la présente bibliographie, j'ai tenté de vérifier toutes les notices non vérifiées figurant dans Sub-Saharan African Films and Filmmakers: A Preliminary Bibliography. Certaines notices ont donc été corrigées, d'autres supprimées, ou bien parce qu'elles étaient non vérifiables dans leur forme actuelle, ou bien parce qu'il s'est avéré qu'elles n'avaient pas trait au cinéma ou aux cinéastes de la région subsaharienne.

La date limite pour les notices figurant dans la bibliographie préliminaire était 1984. Les nouvelles notices incluses dans la présente bibliographie proviennent de trois sources principales: l'actualisation de la bibliographie préliminaire; l'extension de l'éventail des matériaux couverts, en particulier les articles en langue portugaise; l'analyse rétrospective des journaux africains disponibles sur microfilms. Ainsi la bibliographie contient-elle non seulement des citations nouvelles supplémentaires, mais aussi un nombre accru de citations plus anciennes.

Dans les cas où un film figurait sous plusieurs titres dans l'index de la bibliographie préliminaire - soit que le titre original et le titre définitif étaient différents, soit que des titres différents existaient en langue africaine et en langue européenne - l'index a été corrigé. Les noms figurant dans les index ont également été corrigés là où un cinéaste utilise plus d'un nom et là où j'ai appris la forme préférée d'un nom. Des références ont été ajoutées indiquant les différents titres d'un film ou les variantes d'un nom.

## Les notices

Les notices sont présentées dans l'ordre alphabétique des noms d'auteurs. Elles sont réparties en deux sections: dans la première figurent les livres, les thèses, les monographies et les programmes des films; dans la deuxième, les articles, les critiques et les brochures. Etant donné le nombre relativement petit de livres, il m'a semblé utile d'en faire une liste séparée, attirant ainsi l'attention sur les documents fournissant une information plus importante. Dans les cas des livres réunissant une série de contributions, chaque contribution est classée séparément parmi les articles. Tout numéro spécial de périodique publié individuellement comme livre est classé dans la liste des livres.

La majorité des sources figurant dans la bibliographie ont été individuellement scrutées. Toute notice contenant des matériaux non examinés est précédée d'un astérisque. Afin d'éviter une longue liste d'auteurs anonymes, tout article non signé est classé sous le nom du périodique dans lequel il est publié. Les noms d'auteurs africians s'écrivent souvent de diverses façons ou paraissent sous différentes formes. Dans les cas où les articles paraissent sous deux, ou plus de deux, variantes d'un nom, je me suis tenue à l'orthographe ou à la forme la plus fréquemment utilisée.

Les citations sont aussi complètes que possible. S'il manque des données bibliographiques dans les sources non vérifiées, c'est parce que ces détails ne figuraient pas dans la citation localisée. Pour les sources vérifées, les absences de données bibliographiques éventuelles sont dues au fait que celles-ci ni figuraient pas sur les photocopies obtenue par le système de prêt entre bibliothèques. Le lecteur remarquera une certaine incohérence en ce qui concerne la forme des citations tirées des journaux africains: les dates de ces publications n'étaient pas fournies dans la bibliographie préliminaire, et je n'ai pu réexaminer les journaux pour le présent ouvrage.

L'information concernant le contenu des citations est fournie sous forme de symboles et de brèves annotations. Les interviews sont signalées par la lettre (I). Le nom de la personne interviewée est mentionnée dans l'annotation uniquement s'il ne figure pas dans le titre de l'article. J'ai accordé un symbole spécial aux interviews parce qu'elles constituent une source importante de données de base. Les critiques de films sont signalées par la lettre (R). Le nom du film et du cinéaste concernés sont mentionnés seulement s'ils ne figurent pas dans le titre de la critique. Seules les critiques contenant d'importantes informations de base sur le film ou le cinéaste concerné, ou faisant un apport théorique important à la littérature cinématographique, font l'objet d'une annotation. Les critiques de livres sont signalées par les lettres (BR). Le titre du livre et le nom de l'auteur ne sont mentionnés dans l'annotation que s'ils ne figurent pas dans le titre de l'article. Aucune autre information n'est incluse dans les annotations ayant trait aux critiques de livres puisque des annotations sont fournies pour les livres dans la première section de la bibliographie. Des références renvoient aux notices ayant trait aux livres qui font l'objet des critiques.

En ce qui concerne la longueur des annotations, les limites imposées par l'éditeur font que celles-ci sont très succinctes.

L'objet des annotations est de compléter l'information fournie dans le titre du livre ou de l'article concerné, afin de donner au lecteur une esquisse du contenu. S'il s'agit d'un document unique ou présentant une importance exceptionnelle, ce fait est signalé dans l'annotation. Les annotations se veulent descriptives. Le manque d'espace ne permet pas une évaluation critique des documents.

Les index

Les index d'acteurs/d'actrices, de festivals du film, de titres de films, de cinéastes, de pays et de matières générales renvoient aux notices individuelles numérotées. Chaque citation fait l'objet d'un classement détaillé sous autant de rubriques que nécessaires. A cause des variantes orthographiques et des inconsistances en qui concerne la formation des noms de familles, le choix de formes fixes pour les noms personnels m'a été très difficile. Des références spéciales renvoient aux diverses formes des noms personnels.

L'index des pays fournit des données sur le contenu des articles et sur la nationalité des cinéastes, acteurs et actrices. Les rubriques pour chaque pays sont subdivisées en thèmes principaux faisant l'objet d'un article ou autre texte. Dans l'index des matières générales figurent les articles concernant la région subsaharienne, d'autres régions d'Afrique, ou plusiers pays africains. Les sources classées sous la rubrique d'un pays spécifique ne sont pas répétées dans l'index des matières générales.

Les matériaux ayant trait à la théorie du film, ainsi que ceux concernant les idéaux cinématographiques, sont classés sous la rubrique 'Idéologie'. Les sources concernant l'infrastructure en général, ou plusieurs aspects de l'infrastructure, sont classées sous

20.

la rubrique 'Infrastructure'. Les documents ayant trait aux aspects plus spécifiques de l'infrastructure, tels que la Distribution ou les Théâtres, figurent sous ces rubriques plus spécifiques. Un réexamen de toutes les citations figurant dans la bibliographie préliminaire n'ayant pas été possible, le classement de certaines anciennes citations est plus général que celui des citations ajoutées ou vérifiées depuis la réalisation de la première bibliographie. Si j'avais à recommencer ce projet, j'utiliserais des rubriques plus spécifiques. Mais ce n'est qu'en examinant des milliers de sources que l'on se rend compte des rubriques les plus appropriées. Afin de préserver l'uniformité, j'ai utilisé les mêmes rubriques générales dans tous les index, et j'ai fourni des rubriques plus spécifiques dans les annotations.

Bien que je me sois efforcée de produire une bibliographie précise, des erreurs se sont certainement glissées dans le texte. Comme je l'explique dans 'Visualizing Africa: The Bibliography of Films by Sub-Saharan African Filmmakers' (à paraître), les sources figurant dans la présente bibliographie contiennent de nombreuses variations et erreurs. J'ai tenté de résoudre ou de corriger celles dont je me suis aperçue; il en reste cepedant plusieurs que je ne peux rectifier, faute d'information adéquate. A titre d'exemple: Cheick Doukouré est présenté comme étant de nationalité guinéenne, ivoirienne ou sénégalaise selon les différentes sources. Ou encore: il existe deux acteurs appelés Johnny Sekka (Secka), et il est impossible de les distinguer dans les textes écrits avant la publication de la clarification de ce problème dans Le Soleil. Sans doute d'autres variations et erreurs m'ont-elles échapée.

21.

La présente bibliographie ne constitue qu'une étape sur la voie conduisant à une maîtrise bibliographique de la littérature concernant le cinéma et les cinéastes de la région subsaharienne. L'établissement d'un bibliographie précise et complète exige un effort commun de toutes les personnes expertes en cette matière.

Periodicals Cited in the Bibliography

Action (Tunis)
Actuel développement (Paris)
Adhoua (Paris)
Africa (Dakar)
Africa (Lisbon)
Africa (London)
Africa (Madrid)
Africa (Paris)
Africa Events (London)
Africa Hoje (Lisbon)
Africa International (Dakar)
Africa Now (London)
Africa Quarterly (New Delhi)
Africa Report (New York)
Africa Research Bulletin: Political
  Series (Exeter)
Africa-Tervuren (Tervuren)
Africa Today (Denver)
African Arts (Los Angeles)
African Concord (London)
African Guardian (Lagos)
African Literature Association
  Bulletin (Edmonton)
African Studies Newsletter UCLA
  (Los Angeles)
African Studies Review (Los Angeles)
Africascope (Paris)
Africasia (Paris)
AfricAsia (Paris)
Africéchos (Paris)
Africom (Nairobi)
Afrika (Bonn)
Afrika Heute (Bonn)
Afrique (London)
Afrique - Asie (Paris)
Afrique Contemporaine (Paris)
Afrique Littéraire (Paris)
Afrique Littéraire et Artistique
  (Paris)
Afrique Nouvelle (Dakar)
Afriscope (Lagos)
Afterimage (London)
Agecop Liaison (Paris)
Algérie-Actualité (Algiers)
American Anthropologist
  (Washington, D.C.)
American Behavioral Scientist
  (Princeton)
American Cinematographer
  (Los Angeles)
American Film (Washington, D.C.)

Annales de l'Université
  d'Abidjan, Serie D. Lettres
  (Abidjan)
Annuaire du Tiers Monde (Paris)
Arts in Society (Madison)
Asia and Africa Today (Moscow)
Atlas (New York)
Aujourd'hui l'Afrique (Paris)
Avant-Scène-Cinéma (Paris)
Balafon (Abidjan)
Bantu Film (Dar es Salaam)
Baraza (Zomba)
Benin Review (Benin City)
Bianco e Nero (Rome)
Bingo (Dakar)
Black Art (Jamaica, New York)
Black Camera (Bloomington, Indiana)
Bulletin de Liaison du Centre
  d'Etudes Economiques et Sociales
  d'Afrique Occidentale
  (Bobo-Dioulasso)
Busara (Nairobi)
Cahiers du Cinéma (Paris)
Canadian Journal of African
  Studies (Montreal)
Carrefour Africain (Ouagadougou)
Catholic Film Newsletter (New York)
Celuloide (Rio Maior)
Chicago Tribune (Chicago)
Christian Science Monitor (Boston)
Cine Cubano (Havana)
Ciné Dossiers (Paris)
Ciné Qua Non (Lome)
Ciné Tracts (Montreal)
Cinéaste (New York)
Cinéma (Paris)
Cinema Journal (Chicago)
Cinéma Québec (Montreal)
CinémAction (Paris)
CinémArabe (Paris)
Cinématographe (Paris)
Cinewave (Calcutta)
CLA Journal (Baltimore)
Combat (Paris)
Congo-Afrique (Kinshasa)
Congo Magazine (Leopoldville)
Continent (Paris)
Coopération et Développement (Paris)
Courrier de Saint-Ex (Libreville)
Critical Arts (Johannesburg)

Croissance des Jeunes Nations
(Paris)
Cultural Events in Africa (London)
Culture Française (Paris)
Current Bibliography on African
Affairs (Westport, Connecticut)
CVA Newsletter (Montreal)
Daily Nation (Nairobi)
Daily Star (Enugu)
Daily Times (Lagos)
Dakar Matin (Dakar)
Demain l'Afrique (Paris)
Les 2 Ecrans (Algiers)
Development and Cooperation (Bonn)
Development Forum (Geneva)
Diario Popular (Lisbon)
Differences
Diogenes (Florence)
Djassin Foue (Abidjan)
Domingo (Maputo)
Dossiers Pédagogiques (Paris)
3 Welt Magazin (Bonn)
Droit et Liberté (Paris)
Eburnea (Abidjan)
Ecran (Paris)
Educational Broadcasting
International (London)
Entente Africaine (Abidjan)
Entr'act (Paris)
Esprit (Paris)
Essence (New York)
Essor (Bamako)
Ethiopiques (Dakar)
Etudes Cinématographiques (Paris)
Evergreen Review (New York)
Film a Doba (Prague)
Film Bulgarie (Sofia)
Film Dope (London)
Film en Televisie (Brussels)
Film Français (Paris)
Film Library Quarterly (New York)
Film Quarterly (Berkeley)
Film und Fernsehen (Berlin)
Film World (Bombay)
Filme Cultura (Rio de Janeiro)
Filméchange (Paris)
Filmmakers' Newsletter (New York)
Films and Filming (London)
Films et Documents (Paris)
Filmwissenschaftliche Beiträge
(Berlin)
Fonike Magazine (Conakry)
Framework (Norwich, England)
France Nouvelle (Paris)

Fraternité Hebdo (Abidjan)
Fraternité Matin (Abidjan)
French Review (Champaign, Illinois)
Frontline (Braamfontein)
Gazette Littéraire (Paris)
Guardian (Lagos)
Guardian (Manchester)
Happy Home (Ikeja)
Harper's (New York)
Herald (Harare)
Hollywood Reporter (Hollywood,
California)
Horn of Africa (Summit,
New Jersey)
ICA Information (Dakar)
ICAM Information (Dakar)
I.D. (Abidjan)
Independent Film Journal (New York)
Index on Censorship (London)
Informations UNESCO (Paris)
Ikoro (Nsukka)
Image et Son (Paris)
Interlink (Lagos)
International Development Review
(Rome)
International Film Guide (London)
International Journal of Women's
Studies (Montreal)
Interstages (Brussels)
Intrus (Ouagadougou)
Issue (Los Angeles)
Ivoire Dimanche (Abidjan)
Jamana (Bamako)
Jeune Afrique (Paris)
Jeune Afrique Magazine (Paris)
Jeune Afrique Plus (Paris)
Jeune Cinéma (Paris)
Journal of the New African
Literature and the Arts (New York)
Journal of the University Film and
Video Association (Carbondale,
Illinois)
Jump Cut (Chicago)
Kazel (Niamey)
Koloniale Rundschau (Berlin)
Komparatistische Hefte (Bayreuth)
Kosmorama (Copenhagen)
Lagos Week-end (Lagos)
Leadership (Johannesburg)
Les Lettres Françaises (Paris)
Los Angeles Times (Los Angeles)
Magill's Cinema Annual (Englewood
Cliffs, New Jersey)
Medium (Stuttgart)

Medu Art Ensemble Newsletter
  (Gaborone)
Millennium Film Journal (New York)
Le Mois en Afrique (Paris)
Le Monde (Paris)
Le Monde Diplomatique (Paris)
Monogram (London)
Monthly Film Bulletin (London)
Morning Post (Lagos)
Moto (Harare)
National Concord (Ikeja)
Nawadi Cinema (Tunis)
Network Africa (New York)
New Academy (Benin City)
New African (London)
New Culture (Ibadan)
New Nigerian (Kaduna)
New York Times (New York)
New Yorker (New York)
Newswatch (Ikeja)
Nigerama (Niamey)
Nigeria Magazine (Lagos)
Nigerian Observer (Benin City)
Nigrizia (Verona)
Notre Librarie (Paris)
Les Nouvelles Littéraires (Paris)
Novembro (Luanda)
Observateur (Ouagadougou)
OCIC Info (Brussels)
Our Pride Periodic Magazine (Jos)
Peuples Noirs/Peuples Africains
  (Paris)
Postif (Paris)
Présence Africaine (Paris)
La Presse (Tunis)
Prize Africa (Harare)
The Progressive (Madison)
Projet (Paris)
Quarterly Review of Film Studies
  (Pleasantville, New York)
Race and Class (London)
Republique Matin (Oran?)
Recherche, Pédagogie et Culture
  (Paris)
Research in African Literatures
  (Austin)
Revue Africaine de Communication
  (Dakar)
Revue Belge du Cinéma (Brussels)
Revue du Cinéma (Paris)
Revue du Cinéma International
  (Lusanne)
Screen (London)
Sentiers (Paris)

SeptièmArt (Tunis)
Seven Days (New York)
Sidwaya (Ouagadougou)
Le Soleil (Dakar)
South (London)
South China Morning Post (Hong Kong)
Spotlight on Zimbabwe (Harare)
Studies in Twentieth Century
  Literature (Manhattan, Kansas)
Sunday Concord (Ikeja)
Sunday Mail (Harare)
Sunday Post (Lagos)
Sunday Punch Magazine (Ikeja)
Sunjata (Bamako)
Télé-ciné (Paris)
Tempo (Maputo)
Third World Affairs (London)
Third World Book Review (London)
Tiers-Monde (Paris)
Times (London)
Times International (Ikeja)
Trade Winds (New York)
Transition (Kampala)
Tribune Africaine (Limete, Zaire)
UFAHAMU (Los Angeles)
UNESCO Courier (Paris)
UNESCO Features (Paris)
L'Union (Libreville)
Unir (Saint Louis, Senegal)
Unir Ciné-Media (Saint Louis, Senegal)
Unir Cinéma (Saint-Louis, Senegal)
Update (Urbana, Illinois)
Variety (New York)
Les Veterans Coloniaux (Brussels)
Village Voice (New York)
Wal Fadjri (Dakar)
Waraango (Dakar)
Washington Post (Washington, D.C.)
Weekly Review (Nairobi)
West Africa (London)
Young Cinema and Theater (Prague)
Zaire (Kinshasa)
Zaire-Afrique (Kinshasa)
Zebra's Voice (Gaborone)
Zone 2 (Dakar)

# ACRONYMS USED IN THE ANNOTATIONS

| | |
|---|---|
| ACCT | Agence de Coopération Culturelle et Technique (France) |
| ACG | Association des Cinéastes Gabonais |
| ACNA | Association du Cinéma Negro Africain |
| ACS | Association des Cinéastes Sénégalais |
| ASSECCI | Association Sénégalais des Critiques de Cinéma |
| CA | Cameroun Actualités |
| CAC | Comité Africain de Cinéastes (Gabon) |
| CEDAOM | Centre d'Etude et de Documentation sur l'Afrique d'Outre-Mer |
| CENACI | Centre National du Cinéma (Gabon) |
| CESTI | Centre d'Etudes des Sciences et Technique de l'Information (Senegal) |
| CIDC | Consortium Interafricain de Distribution Cinématographique |
| CINAFRIC | Société Africaine de Cinéma |
| CIPROFILM | Consortium Interafricain de Production de Films |
| CNA | Conseil National de l'Audio-Visuel (Senegal) |
| CNC | Centre National du Cinéma (Côte d'Ivoire) |
| CNPC | Centre National de Production Cinématographique (Mali) |
| COMACICO | Compagnie Africaine de Cinéma Commercial (France) |
| FEPACI | Fédération Panafricaine des Cinéastes |
| FESPAC | SEE FESTAC |
| FESPACO | Festival Panafricain du Cinéma d'Ouagadougou |
| FESTAC | World Black and African Festival of Arts and Culture |
| FIFEF | Festival International du Film d'Expression Française |
| FODIC | Fonds de l'Industrie Cinématographique (Cameroun) |
| IAEC | Institut Africain d'Education Cinématographique (Burkina Faso) |

26.

| | |
|---|---|
| ICA | Institut Culturel Africain (Burkina Faso) |
| INAFEC | Institut Africain d'Education Cinématographique (Burkina Faso) |
| INC | Institut Nacional du Cinema (Mocambique) |
| INSET | Institut National Supérieur de l'Enseignement Technique (Côte d'Ivoire) |
| JCC | Journées Cinématographiques de Carthage |
| MIFED | Marche International du Film de Télévision et du Documentaire |
| MOBRAP | Mouvement Burkinabé de Lutte Contre le Racisme, l'Apartheid et Pour l'Amitié Entre les Peuples |
| MOGPAFIS | Mogadishu Pan-African Film Symposium |
| OAU | Organization of African Unity |
| OCAM | Organisation Commune Africaine Mauricienne |
| OCIC | Organisation Catholique Internationale du Cinéma |
| OCINAM | Office Cinématographique National du Mali |
| ONACI | Office National du Cinéma (Congo) |
| RFI | Radio France Internationale |
| SADCC | Southern African Development Coordination Conference |
| SATPEC | Société Anonyme Tunisienne de Production et d'Expansion Cinématographique |
| SCINFOMA | Service Cinématographique du Ministère d'Information du Mali |
| SECMA | Société d'Exploitation Cinématographique Africaine (France) |
| SIC | Société Ivoirienne de Cinéma |
| SIDEC | Société d'Importation de Distribution et d'Exploitation Cinématographique (Senegal) |
| SNC | Société National de Cinéma (Senegal) |
| SNPC | Société Nouvelle de Production Cinématographique (Senegal) |
| SOGACI | Société Gabonaise du Cinéma |

| | |
|---|---|
| SOGAFILM | Société Gabonaise du Film |
| SONACI | Société Nationale de Cinématographie (Senegal) |
| SONAVOCI | Société Nationale Voltaique de Cinéma |
| SONEXCI | Société Nigérienne d'Exploitation Cinématographique |
| SOPACIA | Société de Participations Cinématographiques Africaines |
| UAC | Union Africaine de Cinéma |
| UCINA | Union Cinématographique Africaine |
| UCOA | Union Cinématographique Ouest-Africaine |
| UGC | Union Générale Cinématographique (France) |
| UNCB | Union Nationale des Cinéastes Burkinabé |
| UNIBEN | University of Benin (Nigeria) |
| UNIDA | Union Ivoirienne des Annonceurs |
| URTNA | Union des Radio Diffusions Télévisions Nationales d'Afrique |
| WAFCO | West African Film Corporation |

# BOOKS, MONOGRAPHS AND THESES

1. d'Almeida, Ayi Francisco. _Cinéma négro-africain: reflet ou distorsion de la réalité sociale africaine._ Grenoble: Institut d'études politiques, Université des Sciences Sociales, 1973-74.

   Discussion of political themes in Francophone Africa.

*2. d'Almeida, Ayi Francisco. _Les conditions d'émergence de cinématographies nationales africaines._ Paris: I.E.D.E.S., 1981.

3. Armes, Roy. _Third World film making and the West._ Berkeley: University of California Press, 1987.

   History of African film discussed in Third World context. Short history of African film pp. 214-225. Analysis of Sembène's films pp. 281-292.

*4. Aubert, A. _Place au nouveau cinéma africain._ Paris: Secrétariat d'Etat aux Affaires Etrangères, 1970.

*5. _L'audio-visuel en Côte d'Ivoire - Annuaire 1984._ Abidjan: Ministère de l'Education Nationale et Recherche Scientifique, 1984.

6. Awed, Ibrahim M., Hussein M. Adam and Lionel Ngakane, eds. _First Mogadishu Pan-African Film Symposium. Pan African cinema...which way ahead?_ Mogadishu: MOGPAFIS Management Committee, 1983.

   Official MOGPAFIS documents. Discussion of infrastructure and themes. Country reports: Ghana, Somalia, Tanzania and Zambia.

7. Bachy, Victor. _Le cinéma au Gabon._ Brussels: OCIC, 1986.

   Colonial films about Gabon. Development of film since independence, emphasis on presidential support. Major filmmakers. Filmography.

8. Bachy, Victor. _Le cinéma au Mali._ Brussels: OCIC, 1982.

   History and organization of filmmaking. Major filmmakers. Excerpts from film reviews.

9. Bachy, Victor. _Cinéma en Afrique noire. Rapport préparé pour le Congrès de l'O.C.I.C._ Manila, novembre 1980. s.1:n.p., 1980.

   Distribution in Francophone Africa. History of filmmaking and distribution in Zaire. Reprints of articles on infrastructure.

10. Bachy, Victor. _Le cinéma en Côte d'Ivoire._ Brussels: OCIC, 1982.

    History and organization of filmmaking. Major filmmakers. Excerpts from film reviews.

11. Bachy, Victor. La Haute-Volta et le cinéma. Brussels: OCIC, 1982.

   History and organization of filmmaking. Major filmmakers. FESPACO, INAFEC, CIDC, CIPROFILM, CINAFRIC. Excerpts from reviews.

12. Balogun, Françoise. Le cinéma au Nigeria. Brussels: OCIC, 1984.

   History and organization of filmmaking. Major filmmakers. Filmography. Excerpts from interviews and documents. English translation to be published late in 1987.

13. Baratte Eno-Belinga, Thérèse. Ecrivains, cinéastes et artistes camerounais. Yaounde: Centre d'Edition de la Production pour l'Enseignement et la Recherche, 1978.

   Biographical information on Jean-Pierre Dikongue-Pipa, Daniel Kamwa and Ambroise Mbia.

14. Ben el Haj, Bahir, ed. Une politique africaine de cinéma. Paris: Editions Dadci, 1980.

   Structure and ideology of filmmaking in Congo, Namibia and Senegal.

15. Binet, Jacques, ed. Cinémas noirs d'Afrique. Paris: L'Harmattan, 1983; CinémAction 26 (1983).

   History, infrastructure, major themes, audience, FESPACO. Dictionary of 250 filmmakers and their films.

16. Bonneau, Richard. Ecrivains, cinéastes et artistes ivoiriens. Abidjan: Nouvelles Editions Africaines, 1973.

   Biographical entries for Emmanuel Diaman, Henri Duparc, Désiré Ecaré, Roger Gnoan M'Bala, Etienne N'Dabian Vodio and Timité Bassori.

17. Carrière, P. Le marché du film dans les nouveaux états de l'Afrique tropicale atlantique. Paris: Unifrance Film, 1961.

18. Centre d'Etude sur la Communication en Afrique. Caméra Nigra. Brussels: OCIC, 1984. (I)

   History, themes, infrastructure, criticism. Interview with Mahamane Bakabé. Filmography of 100 films made 1960-1984. Focus on Francophone Africa.

19. Cheriaa, Tahar. Ecrans d'abondance...ou cinémas de liberation en Afrique? Tunis: Satpec, 1978.

   Infrastructure, especially distribution. Case studies: Burkina

Faso and Tunisia.

20. Chertok, Semen Markovich. Nachalo Kino Chornoi Afriki. Moscow: Soiuz Kinomatografistov SSSR. Biuro Propogandy Sovetskogo Kinoiskusstva, 1973.

Infrastructure, themes. Information on 12 filmmakers.

*21. Colloque international sur la production cinématographique en Afrique. Niamey, 1982.

*22. Dedi-di N'Zau Nenkazi. Regards sur la critique de cinéma dans la presse kinoise. Kinshasa: Mémoire ISTI, 1977.

*23. Dia-Moukouri, Urbain. Le cinéma africain authentique. Paris: Société Africane de Culture, 1970.

24. Diakité, Madubuko. Film, culture, and the black filmmaker. New York: Arno Press, 1980.

Themes of films by black filmmakers. Chapter on Sembène.

25. Diawara, Manthia. African cinema: the background and economic context of production. Ph.D. dissertation, Indiana University, Bloomington, 1984.

History and infrastructure. Focus on Francophone Africa, with chapters on Anglophone and Lusophone production. French support for production.

*26. Dimandja Mboko Wembi. Réflexions sur deux cinémas populaires de Kinshasa. Kinshasa: Mémoire ISTI, 1977.

27. Diop, Mohamed. Mass media et culture traditionnelle en Afrique noire: le cinéma. Thesis, Université de Droit d'Economie et de Sciences Sociales de Paris (Paris II), 1974.

History of visual images, colonial film, post-independence film in Francophone West Africa. Audience characteristics and preferences. Censorship. Themes and styles.

28. Duarte de Carvalho, Ruy. O camarada e a câmera. Luanda: INALD, 1984.

Role of anthropology in development of national film industry. Film theory. Analysis of Nelisita. Focus on Angola.

*29. Ekwuasi, Hyginus. Towards a film industry: the film in Nigeria. MA thesis, University of Ibadan, 1981.

30. FESPACO. Colloque sur la littérature et le cinéma africains 21 au 23 Février 1985, Ouagadougou. Mimeo.

Themes, ideology pertaining to relation of oral and written

31.

literature and film.

31. FESPACO. <u>10e FESPACO 18ans au service du cinéma africain</u>. Ouagadougou: FESPACO, 1987.

    Background of FESPACO, details of 1987 FESPACO program. ACCT and African film.

32. FESPACO. <u>FESPACO Programme 87</u>. Ouagadougou: FESPACO, 1987.

33. FESPACO. <u>Festival panafricain du Cinéma de Ouagadougou</u>. Paris: Présence Africaine, 1987.

    Proceedings of 1983 symposium on African film and its public, including official resolutions.

34. FESPACO. <u>Journal du 8ème FESPACO</u>. Ouagadougou: Secrétariat Général du FESPACO, 1983.

    Official program and essays on 1983 FESPACO.

35. FESPACO. <u>9ème FESPACO, Cinéma et libération des peuples</u>. Ouagadougou: Secrétariat Général des Festivals Cinématographiques, 1985.

    Official program. Essays on infrastructure and ideology.

36. FESPACO. <u>6ème Festival du Cinéma Africain Ouagadougou du 2 au 10 février 1979</u>. Ouagadougou: n.p.:1979 (I).

    Official program. Interviews with Sembène and Mahama Johnson Traoré.

37. <u>Festival de Films du Tiers-Monde</u>. Fribourg: Festival de Films du Tiers-Monde, 1986. (R)(I)

    Reviews of films shown. Essay on conference theme: dialogue of cultures. Excerpts from interviews with Souleymane Cissé, Mustapha Diop and Sembène.

38. Folami, Takiu. <u>Orlando Martins, the legend</u>. Lagos: Executive Publishers, 1983.

    Biography of Nigerian actor.

39. Fray, Delphine. Le cinéma en Afrique noire francophone. Thesis maitrise. Paris: Université Paris II, Institut français de presse, Centre de documentation, 1985.

    History of distribution, colonial period to 1985. Production activities of national and interafrican groups.

40. Fuglesang, Andreas. <u>Film-making in developing countries: the Uppsala Workshop</u>. Uppsala: Dag Hammarskjöld Foundation, 1975.

Africa discussed in context of developing world. Two essays on Tanzania.

*41. Gardies, André, ed. Touki-Bouki de Djibril Diop Mambety. Description et analyse filmique. Collection Communiation Audiovisuelle No. 5, Université Nationale de Côte d'Ivoire, 1980.

42. Haffner, Pierre. Essai sur les fondements du cinéma africain. Abidjan: Nouvelles Editions Africaines, 1978.

Summary of writings on film development in Mali.

43. Haffner, Pierre. Palabres sur le cinématographe: initiation au cinéma. Kinshasa: Presses Africaines, 1978.

General discussion of infrastructure with references to Africa and emphasis on Sembène.

44. Hennebelle, Guy. Les cinémas africains en 1972. Dakar: Société Africaine d'Edition, 1972; Afrique Littéraire et Artistique 20(1972).

Themes, aesthetics. Colonial film. Dictionary of 168 filmmakers and their work.

45. Hennebelle, Guy and Catherine Ruelle, eds. Cinéastes d'Afrique noire. Afrique Littéraire et Artistique 49(1978); CinémAction 3(1978).(I)

Themes, ethics, infrastructure. Interviews with 50 filmmakers.

*46. Jacquemain, Jean-Pierre. Comparison de l'écriture littéraire et cinématographique chez Sembène Ousmane. Kinshasa, Université Louvanium, 1970.

*47. Kalonda Kayinda Kiama. Cinéma missionaire au Congo. Maison Edisco Film. Kinshasa: Mémoire ISTI, 1977.

48. Kinda, Theophane. Le cinéma africain: une approche au travers du FESPACO. Paris: Université de Droit d'Economie et de Sciences Sociales Paris II, 1984.

Conditions in which films made. Infrastructural problems. Role of FESPACO, future of FESPACO.

49. Laaksonen, Satu, ed. Mustan Afrikan Elokuva. Helsinki: Helsigin yliopiston Kehitysmaainstituutti, 1978.

General discussion of Sub-Saharan film. Dictionary of 103 filmmakers and their work.

50. Maarek, Philippe J., ed. Afrique noire: quel cinéma? Paris: Association du Ciné-Club de l'Université Paris X, 1983.

Acts of University of Paris X colloquium, December 1981.
Structure of production. French assistance for production and
promotion.

51. Martin, Angela, ed. African films: the context of production.
London: British Film Institute, 1982.

History and infrastructure. Primarily articles translated from
French. Profiles of 12 filmmakers. Short list of feature films
in English or sub-titled in English.

52. Martin, Angela. Eleventh hour presents Africa on Africa: a
season of African cinema. London: Channel Four Television, 1984.

History. Films of Kwaw Ansah, Moussa Yoro Bathily, Souleymane
Cissé, Jean-Pierre Dikongue-Pipa, Haile Gerima, Med Hondo,
Sembène Ousmane and in Mocambique.

53. Mgbejune, Onyero. Film in Nigeria: development, problems and
promise. Ph.D. dissertation, University of Texas at Austin,
1978.

History of production 1947 to mid-1970s.

54. Moore, Carrie Dailey. Evolution of an African artist: Social
realism in the works of Ousmane Sembene. Ph.D. dissertation,
Indiana University, 1973.(I)

Discusses novels and films. Includes interviews with Sembène.

*55. Mpungu Mulenda Saidi. Les formes de participation des Zairois au
spectacle cinématographique. U.C.L. Comm Sociale, 1981.

*56. Munyakaki Injongi. La cinéthèque de "La Voix du Zaire" de 1940 à
1976. Kinshasa: Mémoire ISTI, 1977.

*57. Ngansop, Guy Jérémie. La crise du cinéma camerounais. Paris:
Harmattan, 1987.

58. N'Gosso, Gaston Samé and Catherine Ruelle. Cinéma et télévision
en Afrique: de la dépendance à l'interdépendance. Paris: UNESCO,
1983.

History, infrastructure, audience, interafrican cooperation.
Focus on Francophone Africa.

*59. Nouvelles Editions Africaines. Le cinéma. Abidjan: Nouvelles
Editions Africaines, 1976.

*60. Ntahombaye, Philippe. Sembène Ousmane romancier sénégalais,
poète et cinéaste. Mémoire de licence en philologie romane.
Bruxelles: Université Libre de Bruxelles, 1970.

*61. Okioh, François Sourou. Le cinéma au Bénin. Brussels: OCIC, 1988 (forthcoming).

Excerpts from manuscript appear in No. 2917.

62. Okore, Ode. The film world of Ousmane Sembene. Ph.D. dissertation, Columbia University, 1982.

Description of major films. Sembène's philosophy and aesthetics.

63. Opubor, Alfred E. and Onuora E. Nwuneli, eds. The development and growth of the film industry in Nigeria. Lagos: Third Press, 1979.

Proceedings of seminar. Status and role of film in Nigeria. Role of film in cultural identity, role of music in film. Relation of film to theater. Production problems.

64. Otten, Rik. Le cinéma dans les pays des grands lacs Zaire, Rwanda, Burundi. Brussels: OCIC, 1984.

History and production. Major Zairois filmmakers. Filmography for Zaire.

*65. Otten, Rik and Marc Vanderleyden. Film in Zaire situatie in 1980. Leuven: Mémoire de licence K.U.L., 1981.

66. Pfaff, Françoise. The cinema of Ousmane Sembene, a pioneer of African film. Westport, Conn: Greenwood, 1984.

Analysis of 6 major films. General background on culture, narrative and filmic style. Excerpts from reviews.

67. Pommier, Pierre, comp. Cinéma et développement en Afrique noire francophone. Paris: Pedone, 1974.

Emphasis on distribution and production.

68. Présence Africaine. Séminaire sur "le role du Cinéaste africain dans l'éveil d'une conscience de civilisation noire." Présence Africaine 90 (1974):3-203.

Ideals for production of film, relation of film to African culture and role of filmmakers.

69. Schmidt, Nancy J. Subsaharan African films and filmmakers: a preliminary bibliography. Bloomington: African Studies Program, Indiana University, 1986.

70. Serceau, Daniel, ed. Sembène Ousmane. Afrique Littéraire 76(1985); CinémAction 34 (1985). (I)

Biography, criticism, analysis. Filmography. Interviews with Sembène and Jean Rouch.

71. Sundgren, Nils Petter. Pa bio söder om Sahara. Stockholm: Bokförlaget Pan/Norstedts, 1972.

    General survey, focus on themes.

72. Traoré, Biny. La problematique du cinéma africain. Bobo-Dioulasso: Lycée Quézzin Coulibaly, n.d.

    Problem of defining African film apart from African filmmakers, quality of production of films, audience characteristics and responses, functions of African film.

*73. Vieyra, Paulin Soumanou. A la recherche du cinéma africain. Thesis, Nanterre, 1982.

    Short summary in No. 1313.

74. Vieyra, Paulin Soumanou. Le cinéma africain. Paris: Présence Africaine, 1975.

    History to 1973. Focus on Francophone Africa.

75. Vieyra, Paulin Soumanou. Le cinéma au Sénégal. Brussels: OCIC, 1983. (I)

    History and structure of filmmaking. Major filmmakers discussed chronologically. Filmography. Excerpts from interviews with filmmakers.

76. Vieyra, Paulin Soumanou. Le cinéma et l'Afrique. Paris: Présence Africaine, 1969.

    Role of film in Africa, ideology, infrastructure, relation of African to Third World film.

77. Vieyra, Paulin Soumanou. Ousmane Sembène cinéaste. Paris: Présence Africaine, 1972.

    Biography, description and analysis of films made 1961-1972. Excerpts from film reviews.

ARTICLES, REVIEWS AND PAMPHLETS

78. A.B.   A Keur-Massar, A. Samb tourne "Codou": la possédée des
djinns.  Le Soleil Apr. 14 (1971):1-2.

Making of the film at Keur Massar; impact of filmmaking on the
village.

79. A.B.   "Adjatio" sur les écrans abidjanais.  Ivoire Dimanche 530
(1981):46. (R)

80. A.B.   La délégation ivoirienne a été très remarquée.  Fraternité
Matin Feb. 25 (1987):7.

Ivorian delegation to FESPACO. Activities of ACS.

81. A.B.   Les ivoiriens Célestine Bova Aiyi et N'Guessan Gretti
Sylvain, membres du jury.  Fraternité Matin June 15 (1987):13.

Ivorians on jury for Festival du film de la jeunesse, Paris.

82. A.B.   Le ministre Fologo: "Nyamanton" mérite tous les lauriers.
Fraternité Matin Apr. 3 (1987):10. (R)

83. A.B.B.   "Borom Xam Xam" de Maurice Dores (Sénégal...!) Action
(Tunis) NS7279 (1976):12. (R)

84. A.B.B.   Samba Tali (le petit cireur) de Ben Diogaye Bèye
(Sénégal).  Action (Tunis) NS 7277 (1976):13. (R)

85. A.C.  La lumiète.  Cinéma 400 (1987):6. (R)

Souleymane Cissé, Yeelen.

86. A.D.   CIDC-CIPROFILM ou la difficle reconquête du marche
africain.  Unir Cinéma 17 (1985):23-24.

87. A.D.  FESPACO 85.  Unir Cinéma 17 (1985):15-22.

88. AFP.  Le cinéma africain au creux de la vague.  L'Union June 6
(1986):8.

Crisis in filmmaking, few films being made, lack of financial
support, poorly chosen scripts.

89. AFP.  L'étalon de Yennega à Med Hondo.  Fraternité Matin Mar. 2
(1987):8.

FESPACO prize for Sarraounia.  Need to restructure CIDC, for more
attention to short films.

90. AFP.  L'OCINAM "gère provisoirement" les salles de cinéma de la
COMACICO.  Le Soleil Feb. 9 (1971):6.

Nationalization of theaters in Mali.

91. AFP. Semaine de la critique. Les révélations. Le Soleil May 18 (1987):6.

   Cannes film festival. Most comments on Idrissa Ouédraogo, Yam Daabo.

92. A.G. Ouverture le 1er janvier du cinéma "Amitié" Le Soleil 3507 (1982):14.

   New theater opens in Senegal.

93. AIB/PANA. Xe FESPACO. Au summum de la fête. Le Soleil Feb. 24 (1987):9.

94. AIB/PANA. Un prix Paul Robeson au FESPACO. Le Soleil Feb. 11 (1987):11.

95. A.J.B. Festival du Film Francophone. La tunisie en ouverture. Le Soleil June 30 (1986):7.

   FIFEF.

96. A.J.B. Ola Balogun un sens a l'avenir. Le Soleil Jan. 9 (1987):8.

   Suggestions for UCOA film festival that differs from FESPACO. Balogun's views on relation of film to cultural development.

97. A.J.B. Vraies et fausses difficultés du cinéma. Le Soleil Apr. 30-May 1-3 (1987):14.

   Overview of infrastructure in Senegal. Need for more coproductions and film clubs.

98. A.K.N. Des vedettes du cinéma français à Dakar. Le Soleil Apr. 5 (1978):10.

   African film week in Dakar.

99. A.M. Le cinéma africain se cherche. Afrique Nouvelle 836 (1963):15. (R)

   Sembène Ousmane, Borom Sarret.

100. A.P.N. Le cinéma africain aujourd'hui. Afrique Nouvelle 1088 (1968):15; 1089 (1968):15.

   Themes of films.

101. A.P.S. Ababacar Samb. "L'Afrique du Sud ne participera pas au festival du film de Teheran." Le Soleil June 29 (1973):5.

102. A.P.S. "Camp de Thiaroye" les droits de scenario signes. Le Soleil Jan. 15 (1987):10.

 Background on making of film. Information on actors. Changes in script from "Thiaroye 44".

103. A.P.S. Cheikh Ngaido Bah a réalisé son premier film "La Brosse." Le Soleil June 19 (1973):5. (R)

104. A.P.S. Des films sénégalais au festival Korlovy-Vary. Le Soleil Feb. 19 (1976):8.

105. A.P.S. Festival du film agricole une "oreille de bronze" au Sénégal. Le Soleil Feb. 23 (1986):8.

 West Berlin agriculture film festival. Abdoulaye Koita, Alimentaire face à la dépendance alimentaire.

106. A.P.S. Première de "Xala" à Paris. Le Soleil Nov. 14 (1974):1. (R)

107. A.P.S. Sembène fait un exposé sur la conscience aux cinéastes sénégalais. Le Soleil Dec. 5 (1974):2.

 Role of filmmaker in expressing national consciousness. Discussion of long and short films produced in Senegal.

108. A.P.S. 30 ans de cinéma sénégalais. Le Soleil Mar. 17 (1986):7.

 History of film, especially those produced in 1960s and early 1970s.

109. APS/ALG/PANA. "Thiaroye 44." Signature de la convention Algero-Sénégalaise. Le Soleil Jan. 30 (1987):7.

 Coproduction arrangements made with Algeria and Tunisia.

110. Abdelkader, Allolo. La commission nationale de censure cinématographique. Nigerama 3(1975?):15-16.

 Role of censorship commission in Niger.

111. Abdelkrim, Christine. Mozambique: la politique de ses moyens. Afrique-Asie 398(1987):48-50.

 Main priorities and roles of INC. Comments on recently produced films.

112. Abdu, Ali. Future of film distribution in Nigeria. New Nigerian Aug. 1 (1973):12.

113. Abdul-Shamoos, Adeiza. Daniel Imoudu: the tyrant of Village Headmaster. Guardian (Lagos) Nov. 9 (1986):4.

Daniel Imoudu actor in Nigerian television film series.

114.  Abdul-Shamoos, Adeiza.  Oghene: acting, watching the drama of life.  Guardian (Lagos) Jan. 25 (1987):3.

Melville Obriango, actor in Nigerian television film series.

115.  Abega-Mbarga, Mathieu.  Alphonse Beni: le cinéma africain manque de moyens.  Bingo 385 (1985):48-49.  (I)

Alphonse Beni discusses musical film, African Fever, made in Cameroun.

116.  Abega-Mbarga, Mathieu.    Larme  de  l'enfant.    Bingo 393(1985):64-65.  (I)

Hamadou Ouédraogo discusses how he became a filmmaker, his first film and the future of African film.

117.  Abiade, Folami.  Freedom and the independents.  Essence 11, 3 (1980):10, 12, 15.

Background about Musindo Mwinyipembe, co-director of Blacks Britannica; how film reedited for American television.

118.  Abubakar, Saddik.    The battle for film.    Concord Weekly 21 (1984): 34-35.  (I)

Ola Balogun and Eddie Ugbomah discuss real and ideal roles of government in filmmaking in Nigeria.

119.  Abubakar, Saddik.  A boost for Nigerian film.  Concord Weekly 21 (1984):34-35.

Review of 9 Nigerian films shown at Commonwealth Institute, London; comments on symposium on Nigerian film industry.

120.  Abudah, Usman.  Now, film producers this is your hour.  New Nigerian Apr. 3 (1976) Saturday Extra p. 1, 4.

Production and distribution in Nigeria.

121.  Ackermann, Jean Marie.    Films that ask.    International Development Review 18, 4(1976):28-32.  (R)

Sembène Ousmane, Xala

122.  Ackermann, Jean Marie.  New "national" cinemas.  International Development Review 13, 3(1971):38-40.

Film development in Senegal and Brazil.

123.  Ackermann, Jean Marie.  Protest with elegance.  International Development Review 12, 3(1970):36-37.  (R)

Sembène Ousmane, Mandabi.

124. Ackermann, Jean Marie.  A shattering of myths.  International Development Review 13, 4(1971):36-38.

Sembène Ousmane's techniques discussed among those of non-African filmmakers.

125. Action.  Acquisition des droits culturels des films projetés en compétition officielle.  L'Action Oct. 31 (1982):6.

J.C.C. activities regarding film distribution.

126. Action.  "L'appât du gain".  L'Action Oct. 23 (1982):13.  (R)

127. Action.  Assemblée générale des cinéastes africains.  L'Action Oct. 26 (1986):15.

J.C.C., activities of general assembly.

128. Action.  "Le bracelet de bronze."  L'Action Oct. 31 (1974):7.  (R)

129. Action.  Clôture hier soir des lXè J.C.C. en présence de M. Mohamed Mzali.  L'Action Oct. 31 (1982):1, 5.

J.C.C. prizes.

130. Action.  Conference de presse sur les 5èmes J.C.C.  L'Action Oct. 19(1974):8.

J.C.C. Speech by Mahmoud Messadi, participants, kinds of films shown.

131. Action.  Les Xèmes J.C.C. en plein.  L'Action Oct. 16 (1984):24.

132. Action.  En compétition: "Ablakon."  L'Action Oct. 15 (1986):24. (R)

133. Action.  Entretien avec M. Hamadi Essid, President des J.C.C. L'Action Nov. 8 (1979):3.  (I)

Discussion of innovations at J.C.C.

134. Action.  Entretien avec Sarah Maldorer (sic) cinéaste engagée. L'Action Oct. 7 (1972):7.  (I)

Background on Maldoror, her opinions of FESPACO and J.C.C.

135. Action.  Entretien avec Tewfik Salah, réalisateur égyptien membre du jury international des 5e J.C.C.  L'Action Nov. 2 (1974):12. (I)

Criteria for judging films.

136. Action. La femme au couteau (Côte d'Ivoire). L'Action (Tunis) Sept. 18 (1970):7. (R)

137. Action. Garantir une large audience aux cinémas arabe et africain. L'Action Oct. 27 (1982):12.

J.C.C. promotion of African films.

138. Action. Grande première d'Ayouma le second film de Mme Bongo. Union 609(1978):1.

Opening ceremony for Pierre-Marie Dong, Ayouma, in Libreville.

139. Action. Hommage au cinéma nigerien. Action (Tunis) NS 7288 (1976):16.

Films from Niger shown at J.C.C.

140. Action. J.C.C. Aujourd'hui en compétition le Liban, le Cameroun et le Maroc. L'Action Oct. 17 (1984):12. (R)

Jean Claude Tchuilen, Suicides.

141. Action. J.C.C. Aujourd'hui en compétition: "Missing person," "L'émigrant" et "L'aube noire." L'Action Oct. 18 (1984):24. (R)

142. Action. J.C.C. les derniers films en compétition. L'Action Oct. 19 (1984):24. (R)

Kitia Touré, Comédie exotique.

143. Action. Les J.C.C. 80 ont demarre. L'Action Nov. 18 (1980):11. (R)

Safi Faye, Fad jal; Med Hondo, West Indies; Jean-Claude Rahaga, Fitampoha.

144. Action. Les J.C.C. 78 au jour le jour. L'Action Nov. 21 (1979):10.

Brief comments on films to be shown.

145. Action. J.C.C. 78 evénments de la 4ème journée L'Action Nov. 22 (1978):3.

Brief comments on films to be shown.

146. Action. Les Journées Cinématographiques de Carthage 1970. L'Action (Tunis) Sept. 18 (1970):7.

J.C.C. Round table on Afroarab film. Brief comments on films to be shown.

147. Action. Kaddu Beykat ou Lettre paysanne (Sénégal). L'Action
     Oct. 18 (1975):6. (R)

148. Action. M. Béchir Ben Slama: "Les Xèmes J.C.C. prouvent que la
     production cinématographique arabo-africaine est sur la bonne
     vie." L'Action Oct. 23 (1984):24.

     Closing address on high level of film production and future of
     J.C.C.

149. Action. Une manifestation utile à l'essor des cultures arabes et
     africaines. L'Action Oct. 15 (1986):24.

     J.C.C. taking place despite organizational problems. Films to be
     shown.

150. Action. Mohamed Hondo: du theâtre au cinéma. L'Action Oct. 31
     (1974):7.

     Personal background, education, experience as actor.

151. Action. Ouverture aujourd'hui des IIIes journées
     cinématographiques de Carthage. L'Action Oct. 11 (1970):5.

     Brief review of previous J.C.C. Participants 1970.

152. Action. Palmarès du festival. L'Action Oct. 20 (1970):5.

     J.C.C. prizes.

153. Action. Le prix de la liberté. L'Action Nov. 23 (1979):3. (R)

154. Action. "La rançon d'une alliance." L'Action Oct. 31 (1974):7.
     (R)

155. Action. "Sambizanga." L'Action Oct. 5 (1972):7. (R)

156. Action. La SATPEC distribuera les films africains. L'Action
     Oct. 7 (1972):1,4.

     Protocol drawn up for film distribution at J.C.C.

157. Action. VIémes Journées cinématographiques de Carthage. Action
     NS 7273 (1976):12-13.

     J.C.C. program and jury.

158. Action. Soleil O une production française. L'Action Oct. 16
     (1970):7. (R)

159. Action. Special J.C.C. L'Action Nov. 19 (1980):5.

     Unique features of 1980 J.C.C.

160. Action. "Le Vent". L'Action Oct. 26 (1982):11. (R)

Souleymane Cissé, Finyé.

161. Actuel développement. Les grandes réalisations africaines. Actuel développement 25(1978):32-37.

History of African film.

162. Adam, Hussein, M. Introduction in First Mogadishu Pan-African Film Symposium. Pan African Cinema...Which Way Ahead. Ibrahim Awed et al. eds. Mogadishu: MOGPAFIS Management Committee, 1983. pp. vii-xiii.

MOGPAFIS. History, highlights of 1983 meeting.

163. Adams, Hector. Hier au ciné Volta. L'Observateur Jan. 29-30 (1977):4.

Opening of new theater in Burkina Faso. Need for improved infrastructure.

164. Adelugba, Dapo. Wole Soyinka's Kongi's Harvest: production and exegesis, in Colloque sur littérature et esthetique négro-africaines. Christophe Dailly, ed. Dakar: Nouvelles Editions Africaines, 1979. pp. 257-275.

Emphasizes cinematic aspects of play script; urges study of filmscript.

165. Adelugba, Segun. We need a film development board. Daily Times (Lagos) Mar. 25 (1974):32.

Need for film development corporation in Nigeria.

166. Adesanya, Afolabi. Across the stage and screen. Guardian (Lagos) Mar. 25 (1984):B6.

Joy Lemoine, Nigerian theater and television actress.

167. Adesanya, Afolabi. Clarion's call. Guardian (Lagos) Aug. 19 (1984):B7.

Clarion Chukwurah, Nigerian theater and film actress; opinion of Ola Balogun and Wole Soyinka as directors.

168. Adesanya, Afolabi. Dreams for real. Guardian (Lagos) Aug. 12 (1984):B6.

Tunde Kelani, Nigerian cameraman.

169. Adesanya, Afolabi. The film industry: staring or starring? Guardian (Lagos) Jan. 29 (1984):B1, B4-B5.

History and infrastructure of Nigerian film. List of feature filmmakers.

170. Adesanya, Afolabi. A fine adaptation. Guardian (Lagos) Apr. 8 (1984):B6. (R)

Adewale Adenuga, Papa Ajasco.

171. Adesanya, Afolabi. In search of freedom. Africa (London) 100(1979):78-79. (R)

Jean-Pierre Dikongue-Pipa, Le prix de la liberté.

172. Adesanya, Afolabi. Lady in the mirror. Guardian (Lagos) May 6 (1984):B7. (R)

Lola Fani-Fayode, Mirror in the Sun, Nigerian television series.

173. Adesanya, Afolabi. The making of a President. Guardian (Lagos) Sept. 25 (1983):21. (R)

Eddie Ugbomah, Death of a Black President.

174. Adichie, Chuma. 12 Nigerian films for C'wealth festival. Sunday Concord 5, 193 (1984):16.

Nigerian film week, Commonwealth Institute, London.

175. Adinoyi-Ojo, Shaibu. A one-way mirror in the sun. Guardian (Lagos) Oct. 28 (1984):B7. (R)

Lola Fani-Kayode, Mirror in the Sun, Nigerian television series.

176. Adissoda, Pascal O. Money Power un film simpliste qui exprime des idées sérieuses. Ehuzu Aug. 31 (1984):3. (R)

177. Administrateur de Rotabillets. A propos des billets de cinéma. Le Soleil Jan. 28 (1975):3.

Ticket prices in Senegal. Reply to No. 2752.

178. Africa. 'Awake the Morning'. Africa (London) 121(1981):79-80. (R)

Documentary made by women in Soweto.

179. Africa. The Cannes Film Festival and Africa. Africa (London) 73(1977):88-89.

180. Africa. No excitement from Carthage festival. Africa (London) 160(1984):50.

181. Africa. "Pousse-Pousse"...parisien. Africa (Dakar) 81(1976):26. (R)

182. Africa.   Sembene Ousmane and the censor.   Africa  (London)
     86(1978):85.

     Censorship of Ceddo and Xala in Senegal.

183. Africa.   Top award for Nigerian filmmaker.   Africa  (London)
     112(1980):70-71.

     Segun Oyekunle wins Samuel Goldwyn creative writing award for
     screenplay in pidgin, The Broken Cells.

184. Africa Events.   Celebrating joy.   Africa Events 2, 1(1986):66-67.
     (R)

     Désiré Ecaré, Visages de femmes, shown at London film festival.

185. Africa Now.   Cameraman honoured for famine pictures.   Africa Now
     48(1985):33.  (R)

     Mohamed Amin, African Calvary.

186. Africa Research Bulletin.   Panafrican film festival.   Africa
     Research Bulletin, Political Series 22, 4(1985):7629.

     FESPACO.

187. Africa Research Bulletin.   10th film festival (Ouagadougou).
     Africa Research Bulletin, Political Series 24, 3(1987):8453.

     FESPACO.

188. African Arts.   African film festival.   African Arts 4,
     3(1971):76-77.

     Films shown at Brandeis University, U.S.A.

189. African Guardian.   Book on celluloid.   African Guardian
     1,28(1986):36.  (R)

     David Orere, Things Fall Apart, Nigerian television series.

190. African Studies Center Newsletter.   Tanzania, Mulvihill reap
     FESPACO benefits of their co-production.   African Studies Center
     Newsletter (UCLA).   Spring (1985):28-29. (R)

     Arusi ya Mariamu.

191. Africasia.   Emitai, un long métrage sénégalais de Sembène
     Ousmane.   Africasia 44(1971):62-63. (R)

192. Africom.   Film equipment for Kenya.   Africom 8, 1(1986):7-8.

     Gift of equipment from Friedrich Ebert Foundation.

193. Afrika. Film. <u>Afrika</u> 26, 7-8(1985):39-41.

Review of filmmaking in Burkina Faso.

194. Afrika. Ninth Panafrican Film Festival. <u>Afrika</u> 26, 5(1985):26-27.

Films shown at FESPACO.

195. Afrika. Senegalese cinema stages a comeback. <u>Afrika</u> 25, 6(1984):25.

Government announces support of filmmaking.

196. Afrika. Third World Film Festival. <u>Afrika</u> 24, 1(1983):25.

Films shown at J.C.C.

197. Afrika Heute. Die afrikanische Filmkunst nach Cannes. <u>Afrika Heute</u> 12(1967):187.

198. Afrika Heute. Kongi's Ernte: Erster grosserer Spielfilm in Nigeria. <u>Afrika Heute</u> 11, 4(1973):44. (R)

Francis Oladele, <u>Kongi's Harvest</u>.

199. Afrique. Bako. L'echec de qui? <u>Afrique</u> 13(1978):104-105. (R)

200. Afrique. Le cinéma du président ... <u>Afrique</u> 19(1979):66. (R)

Pierre-Marie Dong, <u>Identité</u>. Acting by Doura Mané.

201. Afrique. Ouaga: VIe Fespaco. <u>Afrique</u> 20(1979):52-53.

202. Afrique. Sortir du ghetto. <u>Afrique</u> 23(1979):76-77.

FESPACO.

203. Afrique. Y-a-t-il un éclipse nigérien? <u>Afrique</u> 33(1980):43-44. (I)

Oumarou Ganda discusses film in Niger.

204. Afrique-Asie. "Dan Iyo Xarago" le premier film somalien. <u>Afrique-Asie</u> 36(1973):48. (R)

205. Afrique-Asie. Des cinéastes sahraouis pour la première fois au FESPACO. <u>Afrique-Asie</u> 397(1987):57.

Western Sahara films at FESPACO.

206. Afrique-Asie. Un film phare. <u>Afrique-Asie</u> 320(1984):51. (R)

Haile Gerima, Harvest 3000 Years.

207. Afrique-Asie. "Touki-Bouki" offert aux enfants d'Afrique. Afrique-Asie 197(1987):57.

Djibril Diop has created foundation for children supported by money earned from Touki-Bouki.

208. Afrique Contemporaine. Ceddo de Sembène Ousmane. Afrique Contemporaine 105(1979):36-37. (R)

209. Afrique Contemporaine. Festival panafricain du cinéma. Afrique Contemporaine 66(1973):17.

Aims of FESPACO, films shown.

210. Afrique Contemporaine. Le Festival panafricain du cinéma de Ouagadougou. Afrique Contemporaine 134(1985):52-53.

FESPACO prizes, administration.

211. Afrique Contemporaine. Ouagadougou capitale du cinéma. Afrique Contemporaine 126(1983):57.

FESPACO.

212. Afrique Nouvelle. A Ouagadougou, a lieu le premier Festival de Cinéma Africain. Afrique Nouvelle 1122(1969):5.

FESPACO.

213. Afrique Nouvelle. A propos du 1er festival de cinéma africain tenu en Haute-Volta. Afrique Nouvelle 1128(1969):15.

FESPACO.

214. Afrique Nouvelle. Après Carthage le cinéma africain. Afrique Nouvelle 1213(1970):15.

J.C.C.

215. Afrique Nouvelle. Au Festival de Dinard. Afrique Nouvelle 1198(1970):14.

FIFEF.

216. Afrique Nouvelle. Au Festival international du film à Moscou. Afrique Nouvelle 1148(1969):11.

Moscow film festival.

217. Afrique Nouvelle. Cannes 1980 le palmarès. Afrique Nouvelle 1613(1980):19.

218. Afrique Nouvelle. Carthage 78: décentralisation. <u>Afrique Nouvelle</u> 1514(1978):17.

   J.C.C.

219. Afrique Nouvelle. Cinéma. <u>Afrique Nouvelle</u> 1619(1980):19. (R)

   Gaetan Essoo, <u>Pik-Nik</u>.

220. Afrique Nouvelle. Cinéma africain à Ouagadougou. <u>Afrique Nouvelle</u> 1176(1970):15.

   FESPACO.

221. Afrique Nouvelle. Le cinéma africain dans le monde. <u>Afrique Nouvelle</u> 1156(1969):15.

   Film festivals in Europe and America where African films shown.

222. Afrique Nouvelle. Cinéma: une vocation africaine. <u>Afrique Nouvelle</u> 1382-1383(1975-1976):31.

   SONAVOCI.

223. Afrique Nouvelle. Codou. <u>Afrique Nouvelle</u> 1237(1971):14. (R)

224. Afrique Nouvelle. Déclaration de l'association des cinéastes sénégalais. <u>Afrique Nouvelle</u> 1073(1968):14.

   Statement on role of film in Senegalese society.

225. Afrique Nouvelle. "L'Effort Camerounais" pour la création d'un Office africain du Cinéma. <u>Afrique Nouvelle</u> 1186(1970):15.

   Office set up to control distribution of films and reduce number of violent films shown.

226. Afrique Nouvelle. Emitai, "Dieu du tonnerre." <u>Afrique Nouvelle</u> 1229(1971):14. (R)

227. Afrique Nouvelle. Mandabi: nouveau film tourné par O. Sembène. <u>Afrique Nouvelle</u> 1076(1968):14. (R)

228. Afrique Nouvelle. Ousmane Sembène à l'honneur. <u>Afrique Nouvelle</u> 1254(1971):11. (R)

   <u>Emitai</u>.

229. Afrique Nouvelle. Ousmane Sembène: "L'Afrique est un marché important qui n'a pas sa propre création cinématographique." <u>Afrique Nouvelle</u> 1033(1967):15. (I)

230. Afrique Nouvelle. Prise en charge pour l'Etat des salles de cinéma en Haute-Volta. <u>Afrique Nouvelle</u> 1171(1970):5.

Nationalization of theaters in Burkina Faso.

231. Afrique Nouvelle. Le prix de la francophonie à un français. Afrique Nouvelle 1260(1971):11.

FIFEF.

232. Afrique Nouvelle. Quarante-six pays au Festival de Carthage. Afrique Nouvelle 1204(1970):11.

233. Afrique Nouvelle. Les réalisations au festival de Carthage. Afrique Nouvelle 1196(1970):14.

234. Afrique Nouvelle. Résolutions du colloque sur le cinéma. Afrique Nouvelle 975(1966):15.

FESTAC resolutions on film.

235. Afrique Nouvelle. Les travaux des experts de l'OCAM sur le cinéma africain. Afrique Nouvelle 1274(1972):3.

FESPACO.

236. Afriscope. Ghana: the jubilee film. Afriscope 12, 1(1982):26.

Documentary on Ghana since independence.

237. Agbeyegbe, Fred. Facts, depth lost. Guardian (Lagos) Dec. 4 (1983):B7. (R)

Eddie Ugbomah, Death of a Black President.

238. Agblemagnon, Ferdinand N'Sougan. La condition socio-culturelle négro-africaine et le cinéma. Présence Africaine 55(1965):32-41.

239. Agecop Liaison. L'A.C.C.T. et le cinéma: incitation a la création et multiplication des échanges. Agecop Liaison 79(1985):20-21.

Review of 15 years of ACCT support for African film. FESPACO. J.C.C.

240. Agecop Liaison. L'Action cinématographique de l'ACCT. Agecop Liaison 57-58(1981):20.

241. Agecop Liaison. Bilan moral de "caméra négra." Agecop Liaison 77(1984):31.

Louvain film festival. Colloquium and films shown.

242. Agecop Liaison. Cinéma. Agecop Liaison 60(1981):26-27.

Films awarded ACCT prizes 1970-1981.

243.  Agecop Liaison.  Le cinéma.  <u>Agecop</u> <u>Liaison</u> 61(1981):26.

Television films in Gabon.

244.  Agecop Liaison.   Cinéma  et  solidarité.   <u>Agecop</u>  <u>Liaison</u>
46(1979):1-48.

245.  Agecop Liaison.   Concours  cinématographiques  de  l'ACCT,
règlements  et  dossiers  de  candidature.   <u>Agecop</u>  <u>Liaison</u>
75-76(1984):i-xvi.

Rules for ACCT film awards.

246.  Agecop Liaison.   Concours  internationaux  1982,  de  creation
cinématographique  et  littéraire  de  l'ACCT.   <u>Agecop</u>  <u>Liaison</u>
64-65(1982):i-xxxv.

Rules for ACCT film awards.

247.  Agecop Liaison.  Hommage au FESPACO à la cinémathéque Quebécoise
1982.  <u>Agecop</u> <u>Liaison</u> 63(1982):i-xvi.

FESPACO.  Quebec film festival.

248.  Agecop Liaison.   La  saison  des  festivals.   <u>Agecop</u>  <u>Liaison</u>
42(1978):45-47.

FESPACO, J.C.C., Namur film festival.

249.  Agecop Liaison.   Sembène  Ousmane  contra  la  "génération
commerciale"  du cinéma africain.  <u>Agecop</u> <u>Liaison</u> 43(1978):40-41.
(I)

Excerpted from <u>Afrique</u> <u>Littéraire</u> <u>et</u> <u>Artistique</u> No. 49, see No.
45.

250.  Agecop Liaison.   Vlle Festival Panafricain du Cinéma  de
Ouagadougou.  <u>Agecop</u> <u>Liaison</u> 57-58(1981):23-25.

251.  Agecop Liaison.   Vle FESPACO: un nouveau prix.  <u>Agecop</u> <u>Liaison</u>
45(1979):48.

252.  Agecop Liaison.   Special cinéma.   <u>Agecop</u> <u>Liaison</u> May-June
(1975):1-28.

ACCT involvement in African filmmaking.   Short overview of films
in French-speaking West Africa.

253.  Ahekoé, Joseph.  Cinéma: "Visages de femmes" de Désiré Ecaré.
<u>Balafon</u> 72(1985):46. (I)

254.  Ahmed, Mahmoon Baba.  Rising cost of gate fees at cinema houses.
<u>New</u> <u>Nigerian</u> Mar. 19 (1977) Saturday Extra pp. 1,2.

Need for regulation of ticket prices in Nigeria.

255. Ahmed, Saleh. "Cinema in Africa is like witchcraft." _Africa Events_ 1,4(1985):64. (I)

Interview with Haile Gerima.

256. Ahmed, Saleh. Fraternity against the odds. _Africa Events_ 1,4(1985):62-63.

FESPACO.

257. Ahua, B. Désiré Ecaré :le cinéaste ivoirien est un homme seul. _Fraternité Matin_ 4408(1979):20. (I)

258. Ahua, B. Le film "Bako" en présence de Sidiki Bakaba. _Fraternité Matin_ 4934(1981):19. (R)

Sidiki Bakaba, Ivorian actor in _Bako_.

259. Ahua, B. Le retour de Désiré Ecaré. _Fraternité Matin_ 4390(1979):21.

260. Ahua, B. Tous les films du FESPACO. _Fraternité Matin_ 4928(1981):81.

261. Aig-Imoukhede, Frank. Cinéma et télévision au Nigeria. _Présence Africaine_ 58(1966):91-96.

262. Aig-Imoukhuede, Frank. 'The film industry: staring or starring'? Yes, but...Guardian (Lagos) Feb. 19(1984):B5, B7.

Reply to No. 169, citing errors. Work of Federal Film Unit in 1960s. Recommended solutions to Nigerian infrastructure problems.

263. Ajao, Toyin. Wole Soyinka's blues for a prodigal. _Guardian_ (Lagos) Jan. 12(1985):9 (R)

264. Ajao, Toyin and Ben Tomoloju. Wind of change at the National Theatre. _Guardian_ (Lagos) Aug. 17(1985):11.

Desired role for National Theater in supporting Nigerian film.

265. Ajao, Wale. The rib breaker. _Newswatch_ 4, 1(1986):38. (R)

Moses Olaiya, _Mosebolatan_. Includes background on Olaiya.

266. Akanda, Jacques. Cinéma: la culture ou le besoin d'évasion. _L'Union_ Apr. 3(1985):11.

Criteria for film criticism.

267. Akanni, Fred. Ogun Idile: a jaded cliche. _Guardian_ (Lagos) Apr. 4(1987):11. (R)

268. Akhaze, Ricky. Baba Sala's latest film coming soon. _Guardian_ (Lagos)May 3 (1986):15.

Cast and cost of Moses Olaiya, _Mosebolatan_.

269. Akinosho, Toyin. Cinekraft: images of the wonder-lens. _Guardian_ (Lagos) Oct. 12(1985):10.

Films by Cinekraft, an independent Nigerian film production company.

270. Akinosho, Toyin. Mosebolatan aspiring to great heights in movie. _Guardian_ (Lagos) June 22 (1986):3. (R)

271. Akinosho, Toyin. Nigeria's arts and the tortuous sojourn. _Guardian_ (Lagos) Aug. 26 (1985):11.

Overview of film production and infrastructure.

272. Akinosho, Toyin. NTA plans to screen Achebe's 'Things Fall Apart.' _Guardian_ (Lagos) July 14 (1985):1, 12.

Production of _Things Fall Apart_, screen play, sponsors.

273. Akinosho, Toyin. Television producer screens political contributions of Nigerian women. _Guardian_ (Lagos) June 23 (1985):3. (R)

Gold Oruh, _Away from the Sidewalk_.

274. Akpederi, Joni. New movie on screen. _African Guardian_ 1, 32(1986):38.

Outline of Danladi Bako, _SPACS_, Nigerian television film series.

275. Akrout, Hassen. Pour un consolidation de la production cinématographique arabo-africaine. _Le Soleil_ Nov. 29-30 (1980):13.

Underdevelopment of film since colonial period. Technical and financial problems.

276. Akselrad, Maleleine. Ola Balogun. _Afrique Littéraire et Artistique_ 8(1969):26-27.

277. Akue, Miwonvi. O.C.T.C. Office Catholique Togolaise du Cinéma. _Unir Cinéma_ 17(1985):27-29.

278. Alain, Yves. "Codou" d'Ababacar Samb, un film que l'on n'attendait plus. _Soleil_ 217(1971):58-59. (R)

279. Alain, Yves. Diegue Bi, le film de Johnson Traoré, rélève la femme sénégalaise. _Bingo_ 213(1970):38-39. (R)

280. Alain, Yves. Le festival de Ouagadougou. _Jeune_ _Afrique_ 478(1970):51.

281. Alain, Yves. "F.V.V.A." le film de Moustapha Alassane dénonce un certain laisser-aller. _Bingo_ 214(1970):48-49. (R)

282. Alain, Yves. Karim film de Momar Thiam. _Bingo_ 215(1970):60-61. (R)

283. Alain, Yves. Mouna de Henri Duparc être artiste et improviser. _Bingo_ 221(1971):58-59. (R)

284. Alain, Yves. "Le roi mort en exil" un film de Richard de Medeiros pour quel publique? _Bingo_ 216(1971):58-59. (R)

285. Alaja-Browne, Akin. Cries of a movie director. _New_ _Nigerian_ Mar. 11(1978) Saturday extra. p. 3. (R)

     Eddie Ugbomah, _Rise_ _and_ _Fall_ _of_ _Dr._ _Oyenusi_.

286. Alavo, Yves. Johnson Traoré "Le revenant." _Bingo_ 330(1980):64. (R)

287. Alegbe, Ohi. Story without end. _African_ _Guardian_ 26, 2(1987):33. (R)

     Moyo Ogundipe, _Olohun_ _Iyo_.

*288. Algérie-Actualité. Les structures des cinémas africains. _Algérie-Actualité_ numero spécial (1971).

289. Alhaji, Mu'azu. Film on Kebbi Empire to be launched in Argungu. _New_ _Nigerian_ Feb. 13 (1979):11; Feb. 19 (1979):7.

     Article does not give title of film or name of filmmaker. Same article on both dates.

290. Alibi, Idang. A festival of sight and sound. _Daily_ _Times_ (Lagos) Sept. 18 (1986):5.

     Poor attendance of big name filmmakers at film week at Center for Continuing Education. Need for Nigerian film policy and to break monopoly of multinational distributors.

291. Alibi, Idang. ...state of Nigeria's filmcraft. _Daily_ _Times_ (Lagos) Sept. 18 (1986):5.

     Film festival at Center for Continuing Education long on sound and short on sight. Evaluation of films shown, primarily documentaries.

292.  Allan, Elkan, ed.  Guide to World Cinema.  London: Whittet Books, 1985.  pp. 13, 27, 55, 79, 89, 160, 201, 371, 483, 515, 613, 636. (R)

Films by Ola Balogun, Haile Gerima, Med Hondo, Sarah Maldoror and Sembéne Ousmane shown at National Film Theater, London.

293.  Allaux, J.P.  Le festival de Cannes et le cinéma oublié. Croissance des jeunes nations 137-138(1973):33.

294.  Alleins, Madeleine.  Une révélation: "La femme au couteau." Les Lettres Françaises 1302(1969):15-16. (R)

295.  Allen, Tom.  The Third World Oracle.  The Village Voice 23, 8(1978):40. (R)

Sembéne Ousmane, Ceddo.

296.  d'Allonnes, Fabrice Revault.  Le Médecin de Gafiré.  Cinéma 336(1986):2. (R)

297.  d'Allonnes, Fabrice Revault.  Touki-Bouki.  Cinéma 346(1986):4. (R)

298.  Allou.  M'Bissine Diop l'émouvante interprète du film de Sembène Ousmane "La Noire de".  Bingo 168(1967):10-13.

Senegalese actress.

299.  d'Almeida, Ayi Francisco.  Publics oubliés, publics absents. CinémAction 26(1983):142-148.

300.  d'Almeida, Fernando.  David Endéné vedette de "Muna Moto" premier long métrage de Dikongue Pipa.  Bingo 269(1975):70. (I)

Camerounian actor.

301.  d'Almeida, Fernando.  Dikongue Pipa: "Je me refuse à être le chantre d'une cause à laquelle je ne crois pas.  Bingo 269(1975):70-71. (I)

302.  d'Almeida, Fernando.  Dikongue Pipa, le premier long métrage camerounais.  Bingo 260(1974):63. (I)

Discusses L'enfant de l'autre.

303.  Al-Moufraji, Ahmed F.  The Afro-Arab cooperation, in First Mogadishu Pan-African Film Symposium.  Pan African Cinema...Which Way Ahead?  Ibrahim Awed et al eds.  Mogadishu: MOGPAFIS Management Committee, 1983.  pp. 27-28.

Ideals for cooperation through OAU and Arab League.

304.  Amadangoleda, L.B.  Cameroun: vers un "cinéma novo."  Africa

(Dakar) 155(1983):47-48.

Problems since independence. Functions of CA and FODIC. List of films made in Cameroun.

305. Amah, Stanley. How far so far? African Guardian 1,2(1986):43.

Background about and views of Ola Balogun.

306. Amboka, Andere. Kolormask. Unir cinéma 136(1987):15-16. (R)

307. Ambroise, Koffi Brou and Grah Boua Pascal. Le cinéma à l'heure de l'ivoirisation. Ivoire Dimanche 578(1982):44-45.

308. Amengual, Barthelemy. Ceddo. Positif 195-196(1977):83. (R)

309. American Cinematographer. Ousmane Sembène at the Olympic Games. American Cinematographer 53, 11(1972):1276, 1322. (I)

310. Amiel, Mireille. A nous deux, France. Cinéma 71 152(1971):138-140. (R)

311. Amiel, Mireille. Baara de Souleymane Cissé. Cinéma 311(1984):39-40. (R)

312. Amiel, Mireille. Ceddo. Cinéma 249(1979):92-93. (R)

313. Amiel, Mireille. Festival de Royan, Afrique ou Panafrique? Cinema 77 220(1977):111.

FIFEF.

314. Amiel, Mireille. Qui peut, en France, parler de l'Afrique. Cinema 77 219(1977):112-113.

FIFEF.

315. Amig. O Tempo dos Leopardos. Variety 321, 9(1985):14. (R)

316. Amon, Lanou. François Okioh: convaincre avec des films. Bingo 388(1985):56. (I)

317. Amupitan, Ola. London hosts Nigerian film week. National Concord 5, 1493(1984):5.

10 films shown at Commonwealth Institute, London.

318. Andere, Amboka. Director cautions educated Africans. Daily Nation (Nairobi) Dec. 10 (1986):15. (I)

Background about Kwaw Ansah.

319. Andere, Ambrose. A movie of Kenyans by Kenyans and for Kenyans. Daily Nation (Nairobi) Dec. 5 (1986):6. (R)

Sao Gamba, Kolormask.

320. Andma. CIPROFILMS: ca rebouge. Intrus Mar. 27 (1987):2.

Special meeting to revive CIPROFILM.

321. Andma. FESPACO: demain, le premier tour de manivelle. Intrus Feb. 20 (1987):2.

322. Andrews, Nigel. Mandat, Le (The Money Order). Monthly Film Bulletin 40(1973):31. (R)

323. Andriamirado, Sennen. "Les cinéastes africains sont paresseux." Jeune Afrique 1377(1987):48-49. (I)

Cheick Ngaido Ba discusses film in Senegal and militant African films.

324. Ano, N. Abusuan...un film et des préjugés. Fraternité Matin 2446(1973):8. (R)

325. Ano, N. "Abusuan": un film qui nous concerne tous. Fraternité Matin 2435(1972):7. (I)

Henri Duparc comments on his film.

326. Ano, N. Aujourd'hui, le cinéaste Emmanuel Diaman. Fraternité Matin 2424(1972):10. (I)

Discussion of Djanmagade.

327. Ano, N. "Le cri du muezzin", un film qui fait peur. Fraternité Matin 2463(1973):9. (R)

328. Anthony, David H. Clandestine filming in South Africa. Cinéaste 7,3(1976):18-19, 50. (I)

Nana Mahomo discusses Last Grave at Dimbaza and Phela Ndaba.

329. Anthony, David H. Nana Mahomo un Sud-Africain contra l'"apartheid". Afrique-Asie 120(1976):65-66. (I)

330. Araka, John. Destroying Nigeria with imported films. Daily Times (Lagos) June 25(1984):3.

331. Arbois, Janik. Le Mandat. Avant-Scène-Cinema 90(1969):147-150. (R)

Biography of Sembène and synopsis of Mandabi.

332. Armah, Ayi Kwei. Islam and 'Ceddo'. West Africa 3503(1984):2031.

333. Armes, Roy. Black African cinema in the eighties. Screen 26,3-4 (1985):60-73.

Survey of infrastructure. Activities of CIDC, OCIC, FEPACI, ACCT.

334. Armes, Roy. Cameroon. International Film Guide (1986):87-88.

Feature films produced since 1975. Activities of FODIC.

335. Armes, Roy. Carthage film festival. New African 207(1984):34.

336. Armes, Roy. Congo. International Film Guide (1984):103.

Short summary of filmmaking since independence.

337. Armes, Roy. Gabon. International Film Guide (1984):140-141.

Television and feature films produced since the 1960s.

338. Armes, Roy. Ivory Coast. International Film Guide (1984):200-201.

Compares older and younger filmmakers. Activities of SIC.

339. Armes, Roy. Keeping Africa in the picture. New African 195(1983):51.

MOGPAFIS.

340. Armes, Roy. Mali. International Film Guide (1984):214-215.

Development of film influenced by U.S.S.R. and Eastern Europe. Major filmmakers.

341. Armes, Roy. Niger. International Film Guide (1984):247-248.

Influence of Jean Rouch on filmmakers. Major filmmakers. Increasing importance of television films.

342. Armes, Roy. Nigerian cinema's unrealised potential. New African 209(1985):43.

343. Armes, Roy. Ousmane Sembene: questions of change. Ciné-tracts 14(1981):71-77.

Summary of Sembène's life and films.

344. Armes, Roy. Senegal. International Film Guide (1985):266-268.

Forefront of African film, dominance of Sembène. Variation in feature films 1960s-1980s.

345. Armes, Roy. Upper Volta. International Film Guide

(1984):328-330.

Leader in support of African film. Activities of CINAFRIC, CIDC, CIPROFILM, INAFEC and SONAVOCI.

346. Arnold, Gary. 'Xala': a satire of social pretensions. Washington Post Sept. 29(1977):D9. (R)

347. Arogundade, Fola. Baba Sala talks about film industry. National Concord 4,1249(1984):12.

Moses Olaiya advocates Nigerian government support of filmmaking.

348. Arora, K.L. Africa speaks out. Film World 16, 3(1979):67-69. (I)

Sembène interviewed at International Film Festival of India discussed Third World Film, politics and film, relative freedom of filmmakers and journalists and importance of communicating with the masses.

349. Arseniev, Leonid. Deux questions à Paulin Vieyra. L'Essor July 30 (1971):4. (I)

Interview at Moscow film festival about history of African film.

350. Arthur, Kweku B. Film industry - a mine yet to be tapped. New Nigerian 6085(1985):12.

Infrastructure problems in Nigeria.

351. d'Arthuys, Jacques. Les indépendants du cinéma direct. Monde Diplomatique 317(1980):23.

Use of Super 8 in Mocambique.

352. d'Arthuys, Xavier. Les mensonges a peau d'elephant. Nouvelles Littéraires 2884(1983):47.

Themes of films in French-speaking West Africa.

353. Asawe, Pius N. Les multiples talents de Joseph Momo. Bingo 309(1978):61-62. (I)

Camerounian actor and choreographer.

354. Ashiwaju, Garba. Non-support for film-makers in Nigeria: National Theatre states its case. Guardian (Lagos) Feb. 1 (1984):9.

National Theater's treatment of Ola Balogun's films. General policies of National Theater on films. See related article No. 508.

355. Association des Cinéastes Sénégalais. Sénégal. Conference de presse. Unir Cinéma 12(1984):8-10.

356. Assogba, Bonaventure. Benin. Les premières journées cinématographiques du Bénin. Unir Ciné-Media 7(1985):34-36.

First festival of Beninois film held in Benin, Sept. 1985. Brief summaries of some films shown.

357. Assogba, Bonaventure. Conaissance avec un cinéaste béninois. Ehuzu July 6(1984):3,8.

Films by Thomas Akodjinou shown at Soviet Culture Center in Cotonou; brief comments on each film.

358. Ata, Afum. Black Goddess - a critique. New Culture 1, 5(1979):43-44. (R)

359. Atilade, David. Kongi's Harvest and the men who made the film. Interlink 6, 4(1970):4-15.

*360. Atta Koffi, Raphael. La femme au couteau...un coup d'épeé dans l'eau. Fraternité Hebdo 688(1972):15. (R)

*361. Attah, A.B. Haunted in black. Sunday Punch Magazine Nov. 11 (1973).

362. Aubert, Alain. Afrique et francophonie, Le FIFEF, Dinard/Beyrouth. Cinéma Québec 3, 1(1973):37-38.

363. Aubert, Alain. Ouagadougou. Ecran 82(1979):15-16.

FESPACO.

364. Aubry, Roger. Le cinéma au Cameroun. African Arts 2,3(1969):66-69.

Distribution problems. Activities of Film et Culture. Films by Thérèse Sita Bella, Urbain Dia-Moukouri, Jean-Pierre Dikongue-Pipa and Jean Paul N'Gassa discussed.

365. Augé, Simon. CENACI. Promouvoir et protéger la production nationale. L'Union May 26 (1986):7.

366. Augé, Simon. Le cinéma gabonais dans l'impasse. L'Union Jan. 14(1985):7.

Little filmmaking because CENACI inactive.

367. Aumont, Jacques. En marge de Hyères: Entretien avec Désiré Ecaré. Cahiers du Cinéma 203(1968):21-22. (I)

Discussion of Concerto pour un exile.

368. Aumont, Jacques and Sylvie Pierre. Huit fois deux. Cahiers du Cinéma 206(1968):30. (R)

Oumarou Ganda, Cabascabo and Sembène Ousmane, Mandabi.

369. Aw, E.R. Table ronde au CESTI sur le cinéma pour les futurs journalistes. Le Soleil Jan. 29(1974):4.

Senegalese journalists and filmmakers discuss domination of distribution by COMACICO and SECMA.

370. Awed, Ibrahim M. Country report on Somalia, in First Mogadishu Pan-African Film Symposium. Pan African Cinema...Which Way Ahead? Ibrahim Awed et al eds. Mogadishu: MOGPAFIS Management Committee. 1983 pp. 66-69.

Aims and activities of Somali Film Agency. Imported films.

371. Awed, Ibrahim M. Opening statement, in First Mogadishu Pan-African Film Symposium. Pan African Cinema...Which Way Ahead? Ibrahim Awed et al eds. Mogadishu: MOGPAFIS Management Committee. 1983 pp. 3-5.

Aims of MOGPAFIS, sources of financial support.

372. Ayachi, Amel. Rencontre avec Leila Alaoui, L'Action Oct. 26(1984):24. (I)

Egyptian actress discusses her discovery of African film at J.C.C.

373. Ayari, Farida. A bout de souffle. Jeune Afrique 987(1979):64-65.

FIFEF held in Dakar.

374. Ayari, Farida. Après l'espoir, le bilan. Continent 6(1980):9.

Problems of African filmmaking.

375. Ayari, Farida. Aux Journées cinématographiques de Carthage vif succès du film tunisien "Aziza". Continent 8(1980):12.

Films of Safi Faye and Jean-Louis Koula at J.C.C.

376. Ayari, Farida. Le bateau-île. Jeune Afrique 955(1979):36-39. (I)

Med Hondo discusses his work.

377. Ayari, Farida. "Cinéma contre racism" réflexions plurielles. Continent 144(1981):11. (BR)

378.  Ayari, Farida.   Le colloque de Niamey.   <u>Agecop</u> <u>Liaison</u>
      64-65(1982):34-36.

      Niamey conference on film distribution.  See No. 21.

379.  Ayari, Farida.   "Cry Freedom" d'Ola Balogun guérilleros sans
      âmes.  <u>Continent</u> 140(1981):11.  (R)

      <u>Ija</u> <u>Ominira</u>.

380.  Ayari, Farida.   De bon films...qu'on distribue pas.   <u>Jeune</u>
      <u>Afrique</u> 993(1980)52-53.

      Malian and Maghrebian films.

*381. Ayari, Farida.   Djéli...La légende au présent.   <u>Adhoua</u>
      4-5(1981):7-8.  (R)

*382. Ayari, Farida.   En résidence surveillée, de P.S. Vieyra.   <u>Adhoua</u>
      3(1981):22-23.  (R)

383.  Ayari, Farida.   Entretien avec Haile Gerima, réalisateur
      éthiopien.  <u>Carrefour</u> <u>Africain</u> 867(1985):28-29.  (I)

      Discussion of <u>Bush</u> <u>Mama</u>.

384.  Ayari, Farida.   Le festival des professionnels.   <u>Zone</u> <u>2</u>
      215(1983):15.

      Report of meeting of film professionals in Morocco.

385.  Ayari, Farida.   Le Festival des Trois Continents rendra hommage à
      Sembène Ousmane.  <u>Continent</u> 150(1981):10.

386.  Ayari, Farida.   Les films africains veulent être vus.   <u>Jeune</u>
      <u>Afrique</u> 947(1979):46-48.

      FESPACO.

387.  Ayari, Farida.   L'histoire du cinéma africain en images.   <u>Zone</u> <u>2</u>
      194(1983):19.  (R)

      Férid Boughedir, <u>Caméra</u> <u>d'Afrique</u>, on history of African film.

388.  Ayari, Farida.   Les hommes du refus.   <u>Jeune</u> <u>Afrique</u> 966(1979):66.
      (R)

      Sembène Ousmane, <u>Ceddo</u>.

389.  Ayari, Farida.   Les huitièmes Journées cinématographiques de
      Carthage, retour aux sources.  <u>Continent</u> 6(1980):8.

390.  Ayari, Farida.   The image of women in the African cinema, in
      <u>First</u> <u>Mogadishu</u> <u>Pan-African</u> <u>Film</u> <u>Symposium.</u>   <u>Pan</u> <u>African</u>

Cinema...Which Way Ahead? Ibrahim Awed et al eds. Mogadishu: MOGPAFIS Management Committee. 1983 pp. 37-38.

391. Ayari, Farida. Images de femmes. CinémAction 26(1983):136-139.

392. Ayari, Farida. Jacques Champreux: Ce n'est pas un film réaliste...c'est une tragédie lyrique. Carrefour Africain 868(1985):26-27. (R)

Aventure ambigue film of C.H. Kane's novel.

*393. Ayari, Farida. Le jeune cinéma sénégalais: la parole à l'image. Adhoua 3(1981):3-6.

Themes of Senegalese films.

394. Ayari, Farida. Jeune garde. Jeune Afrique 956(1979):80. (R)

Cheick Ngaido Ba, Rewo Daande Maayo.

395. Ayari, Farida. Journal du 8ème FESPACO. Agecop Liaison 69-70(1983):26-33.

396. Ayari, Farida. Négriers d'hier et d'aujourd 'hui. Jeune Afrique 976(1979):67.

Humor of Med Hondo's films.

397. Ayari, Farida. Les parents pauvres de la foire du cinéma. Jeune Afrique 960(1979):46-47.

Cannes film festival.

*398. Ayari, Farida. Poko, la mort au bout du chemin. Adhoua 4-5(1981):8. (R)

399. Ayari, Farida. Premier festival du Tiers monde. Jeune Afrique 957(1979):54-55.

400. Ayari, Farida. "Présent angolais/Le Temps des Mumuila" de Ruy Duarte. Continent 119(1981):11. (R)

*401. Ayari, Farida. Vers un renouveau du cinéma africain. Le Continent Mar. 9-10 (1981).

402. Ayari, Farida, Sylviane Kamara, Mohamed Maiga and Françis Soudan. Jeune Afrique fait parler Sembène Ousmane. Jeune Afrique 976(1979):71-75. (I)

403. Ayilla, Mever. Ugbomah's trouble with our film industry. New Nigerian May 10 (1986):2.

Need for funding of Nigerian films.

404. Ayissi-Essomba, Andre.    Un  amateur  courageux.    Bingo
     396(1986):53. (I)

     Films of Arthur Si Bita.  Filmmakers association in Cameroun.

405. B.A.  La cinéaste Sara Maldoror va tourner un long métrage sur la
     vie d'une militante.  Dakar Matin June 25 (1969):5.

     Film on armed struggle in Guinea Bissau, Fusils pour Banta.

406. B.A. Desiré Ecaré en grève.  Fraternité Matin 5095(1981):18.

407. B.A.  Maurice Sy, vedette du film "Séjour à N'Dakarou."  Dakar
     Matin June 7 (1969):3. (R)

     Actors Maurice Sy and Johnny Sekka.

408. B.A.  Sembène Ousmane.  Les cinéastes ne sont pas les martyrs.
     Fraternité Matin 5218(1982):16.

     Discussion of Ceddo.

409. B.A.  Sembène Ousmane pour la diversité.    Fraternité Matin
     5230(1982):17. (I)

410. B.A.  Timité Bassori "Réaliser un film est un combat."
     Fraternité Matin 5194(1982):18. (I)

411. BASS.  Les cinéaste panafricains souhaitent la tenue de festivals
     dans les pays anglophones.  Le Soleil Mar. 20 (1972):6.

     FESPACO.  Need for better distribution and more film labs.  Need
     films related to many ideologies.

412. BASS. Ousmane Sembène et Christian Lacoste tournent à Dakar "La
     Noire de...." Dakar Matin Dec. 14 (1965):3.

     The making of a scene in La Noire de.

413. BASS.  Seringe N'Diaye Gonzalès future vedette du cinéma Europo-
     Africain.  Dakar Matin Sept. 2 (1967):3.

     Senegalese actor comments on Italian audiences.

414. BASS.  Serigne N'Diaye Gonzalès va tourner un film en Italie.
     Dakar Matin June 30 (1967):3.

     Senegalese actor in Italian film.

415. Ba, Abdoulayé.  Les cinéastes d'Afrique ont etudié l'organisation
     du cinéma africain, mode d'expression moderne de la culture
     négro-africaine.  Dakar Matin Feb. 10 (1965):3. (I)

     Paulin Vieyra discusses conference in Italy on black African culture and film.

416.  Ba, Abdoulayé.  La semaine du cinéma africain.  <u>Dakar</u> <u>Matin</u> Jan.
18 (1967):3.

Films shown in Dakar: Moustapha Alassane, <u>Bague</u> <u>du</u> <u>roi</u> <u>Koda</u>;
Momar Thiam, <u>Sarzan</u>; Paulin Vieyra, <u>N'Diongane</u>.

417.  Ba, Abdoulayé.  Trop de vieux films.  <u>Le</u> <u>Soleil</u> Jan. 2 (1979):6.

Not enough recent films being shown in Senegal.

418.  Ba, Pape Samba.  Un champ non encore labouré.  <u>Le</u> <u>Soleil</u> Apr. 24
(1975):2.

Need to look at problems and perspectives of Senegalese film.
Film as art and conscience of people.

419.  Babatunde, Abdullamidi.  'Shehu Umar' - a breakthrough in
Nigeria's film industry.  <u>New</u> <u>Nigerian</u> Mar. 22 (1975) Saturday
extra p. 2.

Shooting of Adamu Halilu's film based on Balewa's novel in
northern Nigeria.

420.  Bachman, Gideon.  Carthage: des oeuvres majeures.  <u>Cinéma</u> <u>75</u>
194(1975):86-91.

J.C.C.

421.  Bachman, Gideon.  Film in black Africa.  <u>Variety</u> 295, 1(1979):68,
254-256.

Infrastructure and themes.

422.  Bachy, Victor.  Le cinéma au Cameroun.  <u>Revue</u> <u>du</u> <u>Cinéma</u>
351(1980):87-94.

423.  Bachy, Victor.  Le cinéma au Tchad.  <u>Revue</u> <u>du</u> <u>cinéma</u>
341(1979):52.

424.  Bachy, Victor.  Le cinéma en Haute Volta.  <u>SeptièmArt</u>
50(1984):15-17.

Excerpt from Bachy's book. See No. 11.

425.  Bachy, Victor.  Le cinéma en république populaire du Congo.
<u>Revue</u> <u>du</u> <u>cinéma</u> 341(1979):44-46.

Distribution problems.  Major filmmakers.

426.  Bachy, Victor.  Le cinéma sénégalais.  <u>Revue</u> <u>du</u> <u>Cinéma</u>
341(1979):38-43.

427. Bachy, Victor. Dictionnaire de deux cent cinquante cinéastes. CinémAction 26(1983):186-201.

   Filmography.

428. Bachy, Victor. La distribution cinématographique en Afrique noire. Filméchange 15(1981):31-44.

   Survey of distribution from colonial period to 1980s.

429. Bachy, Victor. Dossier. Unir Cinéma 19(1985):11-14. (R)

   Désiré Ecaré, Visages de femmes.

430. Bachy, Victor. Un film "a caractere historique": Si les cavaliers, in Caméra Nigra. C.E.S.C.A. ed. Brussels: OCIC, 1984. pp. 93-100. (I)

   Mahamane Bakabé discusses Si les cavaliers.

431. Bachy, Victor. Les moyens de communication sociale en Côte d'Ivoire. Interstages 68-69(1971):1-27.

   SIC discussed pp. 18-21.

432. Bachy, Victor. Ouagadougou establishes the vitality of Burkina's cinema. OCIC Info 1/2(1987):6-7.

   FESPACO. Film prizes, vitality of Burkinabe cinema, infrastructure.

433. Bachy, Victor. Panoramique sur les cinémas sud-sahariens. CinémAction 26(1983):23-43.

   Themes of films summarized country by country.

434. Bachy, Victor. Un (relativement) nouveau venu au cinéma: le Mali. Revue du cinéma 341(1979):47-51.

435. Bachy, Victor. Survol des cinémas noirs, in Caméra Nigra C.E.S.C.A. ed., Brussels:OCIC, 1984. pp. 13-21.

   History.

436. Baecque, Antoine and Stéphane Braunschweig. Pionnier en son pays. Cahiers du Cinéma 381(1986):vi. (I)

   Souleymane Cissé discusses making of Yeelen and his attitudes about African film.

437. Bailly, D. and J.S. Bakyono. Sidiki Bakaba le deuxième âge. Ivoire Dimanche 594(1982):30-31.

   Côte d'Ivoire actor.

438.  Bakary, Sanogo.  "Ablakon" à nouveau sur les écrans.  Fraternité
      Matin 6335(1985):5.  (R)

439.  Bakary, Sanogo.  "Ablakon" prime à Amiens: un autre succès du
      cinéma ivoirien.  Fraternité Matin 6341(1985):19.  (R)

440.  Bakary, Sanogo.  Les cinéastes demandent l'aide à la production.
      Fraternité Matin Dec. 26 (1986):11.

      UCOA meeting in Dakar, production and distribution problems
      discussed.

441.  Bakary, Sanogo.  "Comédie exotique" un coup de maître.
      Fraternité Matin 6204(1985):11.  (R)

442.  Bakary, Sanogo.  "Ironu" au Paris: tortures et tracasseries
      stigmatisées.  Fraternité Matin July 16 (1986):4.  (R)

443.  Bakary, Sanogo.  Issach de Bankolé vendu du cinéma français?
      Fraternité Matin Nov. 4 (1986):11.  (I)

      Discussion of Bankole's acting and filmmaking, differences
      between his and Sidiki Bakaba's acting.

444.  Bakary, Sanogo.  Issach de Bankolé vise loin ... le monde.
      Fraternité Matin Oct. 31, Nov. 1-2 (1986):12.  (I)

      Bankolé discusses his role in Black Mic Mac.

445.  Bakary, Sanogo.  N'Dabian Vodio inhumé a Grand-Bassan.
      Fraternité Matin Oct. 13 (1986):10.

      Obituary includes biographical information.

446.  Bakary, Sanogo.  Nous bricolons activement.  Fraternité Matin
      Jan. 8 (1987):9.  (I)

      Roger Gnoan Mbala discusses Ablakon, problems of distribution in
      France and Côte d'Ivoire, response of French audience.

447.  Bakary, Sanogo.  L'UCOA pour une exploitation industrielle
      cinématographique.  Fraternité Matin Feb. 5 (1986):9.

      Functions of UCOA.

448.  Bakary, Sanogo.  "Visages de femmes."  Le public unanime: c'est
      un bon film.  Fraterité Matin 6434(1986):14.

      Five viewers in Côte d'Ivoire express their opinions.

449.  Bakary, Sanogo.  "Visages de femmes".  L'hymne au feminisme.
      Fraternité Matin 6434(1986):13.  (R)

450. Bakayoko, Laman. CIDC pour une approche réaliste du cinéma africain. <u>Fraternité</u> <u>Matin</u> May 12 (1987):3.

451. Bakyono, J.S. Ablakon. <u>I.D.</u> 738(1985):40-41. (R)

452. Bakyono, J.S. Adja-Tio la révision du procès de l'héritage. <u>Ivoire</u> <u>Dimanche</u> 513(1980):38-39. (R)

453. Bakyono, J.S. Adjatio ou le procès de l'héritage. <u>Ivoire</u> <u>Dimanche</u> 511(1980):40-41. (R)

454. Bakyono, J.S. Cinéma africain de nouveaux espoirs. <u>I.D.</u> 736(1985):39.

   Infrastructure developments.

455. Bakyono, J.S. Le combat d'un humaniste. <u>Ivoire</u> <u>Dimanche</u> 497(1980):40. (R)

   Jean-Pierre Dikongue-Pipa, <u>La prix de la liberté</u>.

456. Bakyono, J.S. Comédie exotique. <u>I.D.</u> 746(1985):40-41. (R)

457. Bakyono, J.S. Les coopérants. <u>I.D.</u> 747(1985):40. (R)

458. Bakyono, J.S. De bons films, mais un public peu enthousiaste. <u>Ivoire</u> <u>Dimanche</u> 530(1981):46.

   Audience response in Côte d'Ivoire.

459. Bakyono, J.S. Xème FESPACO cinéma du rêve, cinéma du réveil. <u>I.D.</u> 839(1987):36-39.

460. Bakyonno, J.S. Donaldo Fofana, le briseur d'icônes. <u>Afrique</u> 4(1977):67-69. (I)

   Guinean actor discusses his work.

461. Bakyono, J.S. Donald Fonfana (sic), the iconoclast. <u>Africa</u> 75(1977):78-79. (I)

   Guinean actor discusses his roles in Henri Duparc's films.

462. Bakyono, J.S. Donaldo Fofana: une valeur africaine du cinéma. <u>Ivoire</u> <u>Dimanche</u> 323(1977):36-37.

   Guinean actor in Côte d'Ivoire films.

463. Bakyono, J.S. Un festival dominé par la politique. <u>Ivoire</u> <u>Dimanche</u> 422(1979):32-33.

   FESPACO.

464. Bakyono, J.S. "L'Herbe sauvage" dans le sillage de Henri Duparc.

Ivoire Dimanche 318(1977):34-35. (R)

465. Bakyono, J.S. L'histoire de l'Afrique écrite par trois cinéastes. Ivoire Dimanche 531(1981):43; 532(1981):45.

Oumarou Ganda, L'exile; Sembène Ousmane, Ceddo; Paulin Vieyra, En residence surveillée.

466. Bakyono, J.S. L'homme d'ailleurs...dans le manteau des ténèbres. Ivoire Dimanche 515(1980):42.

Work of Mory Traoré.

467. Bakyono, J.S. VIIIème FESPACO: un compétition serrée. Ivoire Dimanche 626(1983):44-45.

468. Bakyono, J.S. Idrissa Ouédraogo, cinéaste Burkinabé réalisateur de Yam Daabo (Le Choix) "Le Sahel n'est pas un fatalité." I.D. 849(1987):36-38. (I)

469. Bakyono, J.S. Le médecin de Gafiré. I.D. 700(1984):42-43. (R)

470. Bakyono, J.S. Momo Joseph, un artiste polyvalent. Ivoire Dimanche 548(1981):44.

Camerounian actor.

471. Bakyono, J.S. Naitou. I.D. 740(1985):40. (R)

472. Bakyono, J.S. "Notre fille" de Daniel Kamwa, les moeurs de l'Afrique d'aujourd'hui. Ivoire Dimanche 527(1981):43. (R)

473. Bakyono, J.S. IXème FESPACO. Des actes pour une renaissance. I.D. 736(1985):36-38.

474. Bakyono, J.S. IXème FESPACO. La fête de l'espérance. I.D. 735(1985):36-38.

475. Bakyono, J.S. Ouagadougou, capitale du cinéma africain. Entente africaine 52(1983):24-27.

FESPACO. Background, films shown, prizes.

476. Bakyono, J.S. Ousmane Sembène parle... Ivoire Dimanche 597(1982):46.

Use of African languages in film.

477. Bakyono, J.S. Pétanqui (Le droit a la vie) honoré a Tachkent. Ivoire Dimanche 698(1984):38-40. (R)

478. Bakyono, J.S. 40ème Festival de Cannes l'Afrique noire est la fête avec "lumière." I.D. 848(1987):40-41.

479. Bakyono, J.S.    Le réveil des cinéastes ivoiriens. <u>I.D.</u>
840(1987):42.

Discussion of films in process.

480. Bakyono, J.S.    Sarraounia, un résistante à la pénétration
colonial.   <u>Ivoire</u> <u>Dimanche</u> 666(1983):40-43.  (R)

481. Bakyono, J.S.    Sidiki Bakaba le fou du théâtre.   <u>Ivoire</u> <u>Dimanche</u>
635(1983):44-45.

Ivorian actor.

482. Bakyono, J.S.    Sidiki Bakaba, un comédien affamé de liberté.
<u>Ivoire</u> <u>Dimanche</u> 544(1981):44.

Ivorian actor.

483. Bakyono, J.S.    6e FESPACO le festival du compromis.   <u>Ivoire</u>
<u>Dimanche</u> 419(1979):36.

484. Bakyono, J.S.    Timité Bassory.   <u>Ivoire</u> <u>Dimanche</u> 258(1976):36-37.
(I)

Discussion of national promotion of film.

485. Bakyono, J.S.    "Visages de femmes" interdit par la censure.   <u>I.D.</u>
743(1985):39.

Banned in Côte d'Ivoire.

486. Bakyono, J.S., D. Bailly and Paulus.   Comédie exotique (un film
de Kitia Touré).   Le public ne suit pas.   <u>I.D.</u> 751(1985):36-38.
(I)

487. Bakyono, J.S. and J. Carlos D. Bailly.   Désiré Ecaré et les
femmes.   "Visions (sic) de femmes" censuré.   <u>I.D.</u> 743(1985):36-37.
(I)

488. Bakyono, J.S. and Paulus.   Une cinéaste camerounais juge la
coopération.   <u>I.D.</u> 748(1985):36-38.  (I)

Arthur Si Bita discusses infrastructure of Camerounian film.

489. Balafon.   Ablakon, l'aviateur-ESCROC.   <u>Balafon</u> 71(1985):47.  (R)

490. Balafon.   Noir c'est noir.   <u>Balafon</u> 77(1986):40-41.

Films made by Dingarey Maiga.

491. Balafon.   On en parle.   <u>Balafon</u> 63(1984):42.  (R)

Arthur Si Bita, <u>Les</u> <u>Coopérants</u>.

492. Balafon. Le roi du fric. Balafon 67(1984):50. (R)

   Ola Balogun, Money Power.

493. Balde, Thierno. Djingaré Maiga: l'autre dimension. Bingo
   319(1979):31-32. (I)

   Discussion of Moustapha Alassane, FVVA.

494. Balde, Thierno. La nouvelle étoile du cinéma nigérien. Bingo
   319(1979):32. (I)

   Dorothée Dousso, actress.

495. Balewa, Saddik. Nigeria's film industry. West Africa
   3513(1984):2583-2584. (I)

   Adamu Halilu discusses infrastructure.

496. Balliet Bleziri, Camile. "Le seul espoir du cinéma africain est
   dans la coopération interafricaine" déclare M. Babacar Samb.
   Africascope (Paris) 7(1971):55.

   FEPACI. Problems of filmmaking.

497. Ballo, Bi. "L'Espoir" ou l'autopsie des travailleurs immigrés.
   Ivoire Dimanche 354(1977):38-39. (R)

498. Balogun, Françoise. Un cinéma au stade de l'adolescence. Le
   Monde Diplomatique 333(1981):31.

   History and infrastructure of Nigerian film.

499. Balogun, Françoise. A hymn to dignity. West Africa Nov. 11
   (1986):2406-2407. (R)

   Med Hondo, Sarraounia.

500. Balogun, Françoise. Putting Africa in the picture. Times
   (London) Jan. 18 (1977):iv.

   Finance and distribution. Themes.

501. Balogun, Françoise. Sarraounia ou le triomphe de la dignité.
   Présence africaine 139(1986):213-215. (R)

502. Balogun, Ola. Africa, in The Education of the Film-maker: an
   International View. Paris:UNESCO, 1975, pp. 33-41.

   Training needed by African filmmakers.

503. Balogun, Ola. Cinema, reality and the dream world: film language
   as the inheritor of visual and oral tradition, in Cinema and
   Society. International Film and Television Council, ed.

Paris:IFTC, 1981, pp. 41-47.

Film as opium of the people and as stimulating influence. Ideals for African film.

504. Balogun, Ola. 'The film industry: staring or starring?' No. Guardian (Lagos) Feb. 19 (1984);:B5, B7.

Reply to No. 169. Errors in No. 169. Need for genuine cultural policy covering all aspects of film and television.

505. Balogun, Ola. The film maker's travails. Guardian (Lagos) Mar. 6 (1986):9.

Reply to No. 2538. General strategy needed for development of Nigerian film industry.

*506. Balogun, Ola. The menace of Nigerian telly. Guardian (Lagos) July 6 (1983).

507. Balogun, Ola. Nigeria needs a film industry. Daily Times (Lagos) Mar. 25 (1974):32.

Need to eliminate trashy foreign films and invest theater profits in local film industry.

508. Balogun, Ola. Ola Balogun unreels own tape. Guardian (Lagos) Feb. 12 (1984):B7.

Background on making of Balogun's films; his view of Eddie Ugbomah's films. Reply to No. 354.

509. Balogun, Ola. Paths to a Nigerian film industry. Guardian (Lagos) Mar. 10 (1985):B1-B2, B4.

New national priorities needed. Film village irrelevant. More infrastructure needed to reduce dependence on foreign exchange. New means of financing and distribution suggested.

510. Balthazar, A.G.L. Le prix de quelle liberté? Afrique 18(1978):74. (R)

Jean-Pierre Dikongue-Pipa, La prix de la liberté.

511. Bamouni, Babou Paulin and B. Hubert Pare. Regard retrospectif sur le cinéma burkinabé et perspectives d'avenir. Carrefour Africain 871(1985):18-22.

Infrastructure of Burkinabe film.

512. Bandiera, Monique. Le cinéma africain. Ciné Qua Non 2(1972):3-6.

History.

513. Banfield, Jane. Film in East Africa. <u>Transition</u> 13(1964):18-21.

History, attendance, locally made propaganda films.

514. Banjoko, Akin. Mike Enahoro's 'Martial Force.' <u>Daily</u> <u>Times</u> (Lagos) Sept. 6 (1984):18. (R)

*515. Baptista, Cristina. Discutir-se Sambizanga é um sinal de vitalidade do filme. <u>Diário</u> <u>Popular</u> Oct. 24 (1974):3. (I)

Luandino Vieira discusses Sarah Maldoror's, <u>Sambizanga</u>, based on his fiction.

516. Barbou, Pierre-Andre. Semaine du cinéma angolais à Luanda. <u>Afrique-Asie</u> 250(1981):44.

Film festival in Luanda of Angolan films made since 1975. Short descriptions of several films.

517. Baroncelli, Jacques de. Un film canadien l'emporte è Dinard. <u>Le</u> <u>Monde</u> July 15 (1971):5.

FIFEF. Failure of African film to establish its own language.

518. Barrat, Patrice. Souleymane Cissé: v'la l'bon vent. <u>Nouvelles</u> <u>Littéraires</u> 2884(1983):46. (I)

Discussion of <u>Finyé</u>.

519. Barrett, Eseoghene. Ajani Ogun: a film for all seasons. <u>New</u> <u>Nigerian</u> June 19 (1976) Saturday extra. n.p. (R)

520. Barrett, Eseoghene. Worthwhile effort in film making. <u>Daily</u> <u>Times</u> (Lagos) June 24 (1976):7. (R)

Sanya Dosunmu, <u>Dinner</u> <u>with</u> <u>the</u> <u>Devil</u>.

521. Barrett, Lindsay. Cry Freedom: an image of a people's struggle. <u>Sunday</u> <u>Times</u> (Lagos) Mar. 29 (1981):n.p. (R)

<u>Ija</u> <u>Ominira</u>.

522. Barry, Aliou. Débat sur le cinéma. <u>Le</u> <u>Soleil</u> 3439(1981):4.

Filmmaking in Senegal.

523. Barry, Aliou. Inauguration du cinéma "Amite" et de la recette principale. <u>Le</u> <u>Soleil</u> Nov. 17 (1982):13.

New cinema complex in Thies, Senegal. Need for renovation of theaters and more money for SIDEC.

524. Barry, Aliou. "Médecins des hommes" en tournage au Sénégal. <u>Le</u>

Soleil Mar. 25 (1987):12.

Senegalese actors in film being made for television: Aliou Cissé, Abdoulaye Diop, Lamine Ndiaye, Ndiaye Mour Ndiaye and Oumar Seck.

BART, ANNE JEAN, See JEAN-BART, ANNE.

525.  Bassan, Raphaël.  Amiens, festival des différences.  Afrique Asie 363(1985):78-79.

526.  Bassan, Raphaël.  A breakthrough in black cinema.  AfricAsia 11(1984):86-87. (R)

Review of Haile Gerima's films.

527.  Bassan, Raphaël.  Cannes 83 et la création tiers-mondiste: un sismographe.  Afrique-Asie 298(1983):64-66.

528.  Bassan, Raphaël.  Cannes 85: le festival et le monde. Afrique-Asie 350(1985):52-53.

529.  Bassan, Raphaël.  Carthage.  Revue du cinéma 424(1987):88-89.

Brief history of J.C.C., problems in funding films 1986, intolerant attitudes toward Visages de femmes and Homme de cendres.

530.  Bassan, Raphaël. Carthage ne sera pas détruite.  Afrique-Asie 387(1986):70-71.

J.C.C. films shown.

531.  Bassan, Raphaël.  Ceddo.  Ecran 83(1979):62-63. (R)

532.  Bassan, Raphaël.  Comment filmer l'Afrique?  Afrique-Asie 320(1984):50-52.

Problems in filmmaking, recent successful films.

533.  Bassan, Raphaël.  L'écran. à R.F.I.  Afrique-Asie 327(1984):67.

Importance of R.F.I. program, Cinémas l'aujourd'hui, for African filmmakers; kinds of programs broadcast.

534.  Bassan, Raphaël.  Festival de Nantes: turbulences asiatiques. Avant-scène-cinéma 356(1987):105-106.

Three Nigerian films shown at Trois Continents film festival: Bayo Aderohunmu, Kannakanna; Adeyemi Afoloyan, Kadara and Adamu Halilu, Shehu Umar.

535.  Bassan, Raphaël.  Images d'Afrique.  Ecran 72(1978):8-9.

Themes of films shown at AFCAE seminar.

536. Bassan, Raphaël. 'Kukurantumi': The Road to Accra. AfricAsia
16(1985):58. (R)

537. Bassan, Raphaël. Les mille et un regards. Afrique-Asie
348(1985):50-51.

Trois Continents film festival.

538. Bassan, Raphaël. Nantes: carrefour des trois continents.
Afrique-Asie 365(1986):62-64.

Trois Continents film festival; commments on Mustapha Diop,
Médecin de Gafiré.

539. Bassan, Raphaël. Peut-on guérir du savoir? Afrique Asie
371(1986):49-50. (R)

Mustapha Diop, Médecin de Gafiré. Includes biographical
information on Diop.

540. Bassan, Raphaël. Quand "nourriture" rime avec "culture".
Afrique-Asie 338(1984):129. (R)

Safi Faye, Ambassades nourricières.

541. Bassan, Raphaël. Sembène Ousmane, griot de la culture africaine.
Afrique-Asie 362(1985):46-47.

Excerpt from No. 70.

542. Bassan, Raphaël. Two African ambassadors. AfricAsia
38(1987):74-75.

Med Hondo as actor and filmmaker.

543. Bassan, Raphaël. Le vent de l'esprit souffle sur le Mali.
Afrique-Asie 288(1983):56-57. (R)

Souleymane Cissé, Finyé.

544. Bassan, Raphaël. Vers une unité de la diaspora noire.
Afrique-Asie 347(1985):54-56.

Racines noires festival, Paris.

545. Bassolé, A. La censure a été levée. Fraternité Matin
6426(1986):8.

Censorship of Désiré Ecaré, Visages de femmes.

546. Bassolé, A. Le CIDC, un an après... Fraternité Matin
5260(1982):17.

Distribution.

547. Bassolé, A. Cinéma Ivoirien un marché anarchique. Fraternité
Matin 5265(1982):24.

Infrastructure, Côte d'Ivoire.

548. Bassolé, A. Désiré Ecaré. Le coureur de fond. Fraternité Matin
6434(1986):11-12.

Censorship of Visages de femmes. Ecaré's goals as filmmaker.

549. Bassolé, A. Fadika Kramo Lanciné, nous avons besouin d'un cadre
de travail. Fraternité Matin 5125(1981):27. (I)

550. Bassolé, A. "Un homme, des femmes" de Ben D. Bèye. La polygamie
au banc des accusés. Fraernité Matin 5217(1982):3. (R)

551. Bassolé, A. "Jom" (de Ababacar Samb), un hymne è la dignité.
Fraternité Matin 5300(1982):19. (R)

552. Bassolé, A. "Pétanqui" de Yeo Kozoloa. Le premier tour de
manivelle a été donné au Niger. Fraternité Matin 5288(1982):21.

Pétanqui shown in Niger.

553. Bassolé, A. Un problème de structures. Fraternité Matin
6141(1985):12.

Recent films made in Côte d'Ivoire.

554. Bassolé, A. Sidiki Bakaba. Un combat de tous les jours.
Fraternité Matin 6428(1986):11-12.

Biographical information on Côte d'Ivoire actor.

555. Bassolé, A. Structure inexistante pour des créateurs doués.
Fraternité Matin 6367(1986):16-17.

Lack of production facilities in Côte d'Ivoire. Comments about
Ivorian films by Désiré Ecaré, Roger Gnoan Mbala and Kitia Touré.

556. Bassono, Emile. Cinéma: Au Carrefour de la toute puissance de
l'imagination africaine. Carrefour Africain 710-711(1981):1, 16.

FESPACO.

557. Bastide, R. Faire mieux connaître l'Afrique par le cinéma.
L'Essor July 12(1973):1, 4.

Course on filmmaking by Ministry of Information, Mali.

558. Bathily, Moussa Yoro. Badou Boy. Le Soleil Aug. 30 (1972):2.
(R)

559. Bathily, Moussa Yoro.  Kodou d'Ababacar Samb.  Le Soleil Mar. 28 (1973):2.  (R)

560. Bathily, Moussa Yoro.  La production du film de qualité en Afrique, in FESPACO 1983.  Paris; Présence Africaine, 1987.  pp. 33-41.

Needs for production and promotion of films.

561. Bathily, Moussa Yoro and Paulin S. Vieyra.  Silence! on (de) tourne.  Africa International 180(1985):35.

Differences in these filmmakers' views of what kinds of films should be made.

562. Baudin, N'Diaye.  Création d'une société nationale d'importation et de distribution des films.  Le Soleil Jan. 5 (1974):2.

Distribution of films in Senegal, cooperation with other countries.

563. Baudin, N'Diaye.  Première monteuse sénégalaise N'Dèye Guèye veut faire des films.  Le Soleil July 1 (1972):5.

Biographical information on N'Dèye Guèye, Senegalese scriptwriter and maker of television and educational films.

564. Bayili, Justin B.  La directrice de Faso Dan Fani: "La cotonnade revalorise notre patrimonie vestimentaire."  Sidwaya Feb. 27 (1987):5.  (I)

FESPACO.  Cultural events.

565. Bayoh Cissey, Moussa.  Barron: après le théatre, le cinéma.  Bingo 265 (1975):68-69.  (I)

Camerounian actor discusses his work.

566. Bazie, Godefroy.  Clôture du FESPACO sur notes melodieuses.  Sidwaya Mar. 5 (1985):4.

567. Bazie, Jacques Prosper.  Le fin du FESPACO, le retour des Shaolin.  Sidwaya June 25 (1987):11.

Western films shown in theaters in Burkina Faso after FESPACO undermine value of FESPACO.

568. Bebey, Francis.  The awakening African cinema.  Unesco Courier 30,5 (1977):30-33.

Problems of filmmaking.  Films of prolific filmmakers discussed.

569. Bekele, Solomon.  Zur Lage des Films in Nigeria.  Afrika Heute

4(1973):45. (I)

Francis Oladele discusses Kongi's Harvest.

570.  Belko, Kambou.  FESPACO (fin).  Intrus Mar. 6 (1987):2.

571.  Belko, Kambou.  Pourquoi le CIDC-CIPROFILM est malade? Intrus May 8 (1987):5.

572.  Bellow, Ledji.  Du nouveau au FESPACO.  Jeune Afrique 1363(1987):61.

BEMBA, KABINE See DIAKITE, KABINE BEMBA.

573.  Ben Ammar, Mustapha.  Plus qu'une réussite une victoire. L'Action Oct. 17 (1986):12.

J.C.C. support and sponsorship.

574.  Ben Idriss, Z.  FESPACO.  L'Observateur 2034(1981):11.

575.  Ben Idriss, Z.  Vlle FESPACO.  Visite d'un complexe de production.  L'Observateur 2036(1981):1, 10-11.

576.  Ben Salama, Mohand.  De la Fepaci.  Recherche, pédagogie et culture 17-18(1975):60-61.

577.  Ben Salama, Mohand.  Journées cinématographiques de Carthage: un Festival stratégique.  Recherche, pédagogie et culture 17-18(1975):59.

578.  Benabdessadok, Cherifa.  L'Afrique à la première personne. Afrique-Asie 355(1985):52-53.

Themes of films about Africa shown on French television.

579.  Benabdessadok, Cherifa.  "Baara": les héros du quotidien. Afrique-Asie 336(1984):63-64. (R)

580.  Benabdessadok, Cherifa.  La baraka cinématographique. Afrique-Asie 331(1984):60-61. (I)

Gaston Kaboré and Paul Zoumbara discuss their filmmaking.

581.  Benabdessadok, Cherifa.  Le choix d'Idrissa.  Afrique-Asie 395 (1987):50-51. (R)

Idrissa Ouédraogo, Yam Daabo.

582.  Benabdessadok, Cherifa.  C.I.D.C.:une drôle de gestion.  Afrique-Asie 341(1985):56-57. (I)

Interview with Raoufi Badirou, director of FEPACI.

583. **Benabdessadok, Cherifa.** Cinémas noirs en revue. <u>Afrique-Asie</u> 397(1987):58-59.

Short history of 25 years of filmmaking.

584. **Benabdessadok, Cherifa.** 10e FESPACO, Ouaga grand écran. <u>Afrique-Asie</u> 396(1987):50-51.

585. **Benabdessadok, Cherifa.** Entretien avec Tahar Chériaa. <u>Afrique-Asie</u> 396(1987):51-53. (I)

Discussion of criteria for judging films at FESPACO and film distribution.

586. **Benabdessadok, Cherifa.** La maladie honteuse. <u>Afrique-Asie</u> 397(1987):56-57.

Problems of distribution, failure of CIDC.

587. **Benabdessadok, Cherifa.** Pleins feux sur Ouaga. <u>Afrique-Asie</u> 345(1985):73-75.

FESPACO.

588. **Benabdessadok, Cherifa.** Visages de femmes. <u>Afrique-Asie</u> 353(1985):57. (R)

589. **Benabdessadok, Cherifa.** Wend Kuuni le don de dieu. <u>Afrique-Asie</u> 319(1984):56-57. (I)

Gaston Kaboré discusses <u>Wend Kuuni</u>.

590. **Benayoun, Robert et al.** Entretien avec Ruy Guerra. <u>Positif</u> 86(1967):3-15. (I)

Discussion of <u>Os Cafajestes,</u> <u>Os Fuzis</u> and cinema novo.

591. **Benon, B. Richard.** VIe Festival Panafricain du Cinéma de Ouagadougou ou la concrétisation du cinéma africain. <u>Carrefour Africain</u> 688(1979):5.

*592. **Benson, Precious.** Dosunmu's dinner with the devil. <u>Times International</u> June 21 (1976).

Sanya Dosunmu, <u>Dinner with the Devil</u>.

593. **Bentsi-Enchill, Nii K.** Fair deal for film. <u>West Africa</u> 3509(1984):2319-2320. (I)

Kwaw Ansah discusses raising money to make a new film.

594. **Bentsi-Enchill, Nii K.** Money, power and cinema. <u>West Africa</u> 3393(1982):2093-2094. (R)

Ola Balogun, Money Power.

595. Bentsi-Enchill, Nii K. Surviving in a hostile society. West Africa 3360(1981):3062, 3067.

Films shown at London film festival.

596. Bere Aib-Sanmatenga, Grégoire. Construction d'une salle de cinéma provincale à Kaya. Sidwaya Jan. 21(1985):5.

New theater in Burkina Faso.

*597. Berghoff, Gert. Afrikas Filmer Haben Ideen, aber kein Geld. Régisseur Babacar Samb besucht Köln. Koloniale Rundschau Oct. 13 (1971).

598. Berman, Abrao. Entretien avec Ruy Guerra. Image et son May (1969):66-68. (I)

Biographical background; discussion of Os Cafajestes, Os fuzis and film provisionally titled Appat.

599. Bernard, Jean. Les agressions d'un village d'autrefois. Afrique Nouvelle 1401(1976):16-17. (R)

Sembène Ousmane, Ceddo.

600. Bernard, Jean. De festival en festival. Afrique Nouvelle 1372(1975):16-18. (R)

Safi Faye's, Kaddu Beykat shown in Geneva and at FESPACO.

601. Bernard, Jean. Un film africain: Touki Bouki. Afrique Nouvelle 1347(1975):24. (R)

602. Bernard, Jean. Un film de Mahama Traoré. Afrique Nouvelle 1350(1975):16-17. (R)

Njangaan.

603. Bernard, Mariama and Yves Bernard. Le cinéma au Niger. Septièm Art 49(1984):5-7.

604. Berrah, Mouny. Carthage 82 en marge. 2 écrans 51(182):26-30.

605. Berthome, Jean-Pierre. Festival des Trois Continents de Nantes. Positif 315(1987):57-59. (R)

606. Bertin, Akaffou. Le cinéma et la télévision ivoirienne. Unir Cinéma 23-24(1986):8.

Television program in Côte d'Ivoire on history of African film.

607. Bertin-Maghit, Jean-Pierre. Nice 5 Octobre-19 Octobre 1979.

Revue du Cinéma 345(1979):30-32.

FIFEF.

608. Beti, Mongo. Cameroun, in Le tiers monde en films. Guy
Hennebelle, ed. Paris: CinémAction Tricontinental, 1982. pp.
105-107.

609. Bèye, Ben Diogaye. "Baks" le nouveau film du Momar Thiam, le
triste univers de la drogue. Bingo 260(1974):64-65. (R)

610. Bèye, Ben Diogaye. "Communication et jeuness" une conférence du
Pére Jean Vast. Unir Cinéma 15(1984):26-29.

Report on conference held in Dakar by Ministre Sénégalais de la
Jeunesse et des Sports on role of audio-visual communication.

611. Bèye, Ben Diogaye. Momar Thiam: "Je suis satisfait de mon film."
Bingo 260(1974):65-66. (I)

612. Bèye, Ben Diogaye. lXe FESPACO a mains d'une surprise. Unir
Cinéma 16(1985):5-6.

613. Bèye, Ben Diogaye. Pour que vive la FEPACI. Unir Cinéma
16(1985):10-11.

Report on third FEPACI congress.

614. Bèye, Ben Diogaye. Une réelle dialectique dans le dialogue des
cultures. Cinéma 77 221(1977):64-69.

FIFEF.

615. Bèye, Ben Diogaye. Le 3e congres FEPACI aura-t-il lieu? Unir
Cinéma 16(1985):7-9. (I)

Momar Thiam discusses work of FEPACI.

616. Bhêly-Quénum, Olympe. La voie étroite de jeune cinéma africain.
Croissance des jeunes nations 67(1967):39-40. (I)

Blaise Senghor discusses infrastructure and themes of films.

*617. Bif. Nouveau départ pour le film national. Filméchange
5(1979):102-103.

618. Bikoko, Ngoyo Moussavou. Sembène Ousmane: "Le cinéma africain
est à l'image de nos indépendances. L'Union Jan. 19-20(1980):7.
(I)

Sembène discusses his training, ideology of filmmaking, role of
governments and FEPACI, distribution and censorship of Ceddo at
colloquium in Libreville.

619. Bilal, Badra.   L'Afrique a Cannes.   <u>Africa</u> <u>International</u>
195(1987):37-38.

620. Bilal, Badra.   Angers fait écho a Ouaga.   <u>Africa</u> <u>International</u>
195(1987):39.

Angers film festival.

621. Bilal, Badra.   "Chacun cherche la lumière."  <u>Africa</u> <u>International</u>
195(1987):38-39. (I)

Souleymane Cissé discusses <u>Yeelen</u> and his ideology of making
fiction films.

622. Bilal, Badra.   Le choix D'Issa.   <u>Africa</u> <u>International</u>
193(1987):42-43. (I)

Idrissa Ouédraogo discusses making <u>Yam</u> <u>Daabo</u> and aims of film.

623. Bilal, Badra.   Jean Rouch: "Je ne fais pas du cinéma africain."
<u>Africa</u> <u>International</u> 196(1987):55-57. (I)

Rouch discusses making film of Fifi Niane's play, <u>Bac</u> <u>ou</u> <u>mariage</u>
and comments on films by Souleymane Cissé, Miriama Hima and
Idrissa Ouédraogo.

624. Bilal, Badra.   Une malade honteuse.   <u>Africa</u> <u>International</u>
193(1987):44.

FESPACO.

625. Bilal, Badra.   Med Hondo censure.   <u>Africa</u> <u>International</u>
192(1987):37-38.

<u>Sarraounia</u> shown in Paris for limited period, problems in its
distribution.

626. Bilal, Badra.   Sigiri Bakaba le Bambara.   <u>Africa</u> <u>International</u>
194(1987):35-37.

Biographical background and acting career of Sidiki Bakaba.

627. Bilé, Emmanuel.   Mory Traoré, l'homme d'ailleurs.   <u>Afrique</u>
42(1980):70-71.

628. Bilé, Emmanuel.   Le Projet Vert.   <u>Afrique</u> 46(1981):36-38.

FESPACO.

629. Biloa, Marie-Roger.   La consécration de l'enfant de Treichville.
<u>Jeune</u> <u>Afrique</u> 1334(1986):64.

Issach Bankolé, actor, roles in films and plays.

630. Biloa, Marie-Roger. Fespaco: beaucoup de prix, trop de prix?
Jeune Afrique 1366(1987):30.

631. Biloa, Marie-Roger. Issach de Bankolé: son enfance, sa vie, son
métier. Jeune Afrique Magazine 36(1987):24-25. (I)

632. Biloa, Marie-Roger. Lumières d'Afrique à Cannes. Jeune Afrique
1378(1987):46-49.

633. Biloa, Marie-Roger. Polémiques autour d'un massacre. Jeune
Afrique 1384(1987):64-65.

Sembène Ousmane and Thierno Faty Sow, Camp de Thiaroye; problems
with script, financing and filming scene of massacre.

634. Biloa, Marie-Roger. Sacré Charlemagne! Jeune Afrique
1349(1986):82-83. (R)

Roger Gnoan Mbala, Ablakon.

635. Biloa, Marie-Roger. Souleymane Cissé, Prix du Jury au 40e
festival de Cannes. Jeune Afrique Magazine 38(1987):22-23. (I)

636. Biloa, Marie-Roger. Vieux guérisseur contre jeune médecin.
Jeune Afrique 1313(1986):68. (R)

Mustapha Diop, Médecin de Gafiré.

BILOA-LEHMANN, MARIE ROGER See BILOA, MARIE-ROGER.

637. Bim Yéti, K.M. Décollage ou faux départ? Fraternité Matin
6145(1985):23.

Themes of recent films in Côte d'Ivoire.

638. Bim Yéti, K.M. Festival de Carthage. La Côte d'Ivoire
représentée par deux films. Fraternité Matin 6008(1984):26.

Films by Yeo Kozoloa and Kitia Touré shown at J.C.C.

639. Bim Yéti, K.M. Kitia Touré un "petit génie." Fraternité Matin
6186(1985):17.

640. Bim Yéti, K.M. Kodjo Ebouclé: déjà 12 ans d'expérience.
Fraternité Matin 6141(1985):13.

Actor in Roger Gnoan Mbala, Ablakon.

641. Binet, Jacques. L'A.C.C.T. et les cinémas africains.
CinémAction 26(1983):202-204.

ACCT support for African filmmaking.

642. Binet, Jacques. L'argent dans les films africains. Afrique

Littéraire et Artistique 43(1977):90-93.

Problem of financing films.

643. Binet, Jacques. Bilan de la rétrospective organisée par le C.E.D.A.O.M. Afrique Contemporaine 83(1976):27-30.

Short summary of films shown at CEDAOM retrospective in Paris.

644. Binet, Jacques. La cinéma africain. Afrique Contemporaine 123(1982):5-8.

Film production, educational functions of film.

645. Binet, Jacques. Le cinéma africain a la documentation française. Afrique Contemporaine 81(1975):7-8.

Film festival at University of Paris.

646. Binet, Jacques. The contribution and the influence of black African cinema. Diogènes 110(1980):66-82.

Themes of films.

647. Binet, Jacques. Les cultures africaines et les images. CinémAction 26(1983):16-26.

Early history of African film.

648. Binet, Jacques. Le fonction de l'action. CinémAction 26(1983):96-99.

Themes, especially type of action (or non-action) in films.

649. Binet, Jacques. Le langage des cinéastes africains. CinémAction 26(1983):84-89.

Structure of films.

650. Binet, Jacques. Modernisme du cinéma africain? Projet 139(1979):1090-1096.

Themes, extent to which films create a new world.

651. Binet, Jacques. La nature dans le cinéma africain. Afrique Littéraire et Artistique 39(1976):52-58.

Themes.

652. Binet, Jacques. La place du héros. CinémAction 26(1983):94-95.

Heroes of films.

653. Binet, Jacques. Le sacré, in Caméra Nigra. C.E.S.C.A. ed.

Brussels: OCIC, 1984. pp. 45-75.

Religious themes.

654. Binet, Jacques. Le sacré dans le cinéma négro-africain. *Positif* 235(1980):44-49.

Religious themes.

655. Binet, Jacques. Le sacré dans le cinéma négro-africain, Post-scriptum sur Ceddo. *Positif* 235(1980):53. (R)

656. Binet, Jacques. Le sacré, l'extase, la folie et leur expression dans les films. *CinémaAction* 26(1983):118-123.

Religious themes and symbolism.

657. Binet, Jacques. Temps et espace dans le cinéma africain. *Positif* 198(1977):57-63.

Themes, use of time and space.

658. Binet, Jacques. Le travail et l'argent. *CinémAction* 26(1983):104-108.

Themes, "traditional" and "modern" economy.

659. Binet, Jacques. L'utilisation du son. *CinémAction* 26(1983):90-93.

Use of words, noise, music and dance in films.

660. Binet, Jacques. Violence et cinéma africain. *Afrique Littéraire et Artistique* 44(1977):73-80.

Themes, violence.

661. Binet, Jacques. La vision de l'Etat. *CinémAction* 26(1983):109-112.

Themes, role of national governments.

662. Bingo. Acteur et metteur en scène Ibrahima Seck. *Bingo* 121(1963):14-15.

Senegalese actor.

663. Bingo. L'Afriqiue à Paris. *Bingo* 397(1986):55.

Actors in *Black Mic Mac*: Issach Bankolé, Cheick Doukouré, Khoudia Seye, Francois Villeret and Félicité Wouassi.

664. Bingo. Après Cannes. *Bingo* 332(1980):48-49.

665. Bingo. Bambo des lycéens malien tournent un court métrage. Bingo 201(1969):21. (R)

666. Bingo. Le CENACI. Bingo 397(1986):59.

CENACI support for filmmaking in Gabon.

667. Bingo. Le cinéma africain couronne "Sarraounia" le film du realisateur mauritanien Med Hondo. Bingo 411(1987):10.

FESPACO prizes.

668. Bingo. Le cinéma africain de A à Z. Bingo 195(1969):30-31.

Filmography.

669. Bingo. Daniel Kamwa un talentueux camerounais. Bingo 200(1969):45.

Activities as actor and writer.

670. Bingo. De la faim à la gloire ou la vie due grand acteur Orlando Martins. Bingo 90(1960):9,44.

Nigerian actor.

671. Bingo. Diakhabi un film de Johnson Traoré ou du ciné-club à la mise en scène. Bingo. 197(1969):26-27. (R)

672. Bingo. 18 millions de Fr CFA à Sarah Maldoror. Bingo 234(1972):53.

Funding to make Sambizanga.

673. Bingo. Un film camerounais? Bingo 299(1977):77. (R)

Jean-Claude Tchulien, Claudo.

674. Bingo. Le grand Moussa. Bingo 377(1984):27. (R)

675. Bingo. Le griot des temps modernes. Bingo 310(1978):67.

Discussion of Sembène's films at symposium in Los Angeles.

676. Bingo. Un jeune cinéaste nigérien Moustapha Alassane "réinvente" le cinéma. Bingo 201(1969):48-49.

677. Bingo. Liberté un film écrit et joué par des africains. Bingo 69(1958):22-23. (R)

678. Bingo. M'Bissine Diop: perfectionner son art. Bingo 292(1977):62-64.

Senegalese actress.

679. Bingo. "Me voici" de François Okioh. <u>Bingo</u> 335(1980):84. (R)

680. Bingo. Le miroir des réalitiés locales. <u>Bingo</u> 316(1979):72.

FESPACO.

681. Bingo. La mort de Doura Mané: une grande vedette disparaît. <u>Bingo</u> 308(1978):55.

Obituary, Guinean actor.

682. Bingo. "Le nouveau venu" Richard de Medeiros jeune cinéaste béninois corrige les moeurs en riant. <u>Bingo</u> 289(1977):32-35. (I)

Interview with Medeiros and two actors in <u>Le</u> <u>nouveau</u> <u>venu</u>: Michel Julien Djondo and Ogounjobe Adéboyé Sikirou.

683. Bingo. Ola Balogun révélé à Venise. <u>Bingo</u> 234(1972):53. (R)

<u>Shango</u>.

684. Bingo. Ou en est le cinéma africain? <u>Bingo</u> 127(1963):21, 44-45.

Actors and actresses in films of French-speaking West and Central Africa.

685. Bingo. Ousmane Sembène et "Samory." <u>Bingo</u> 386(1985):48.

686. Bingo. Ousmane Sembène l'affirme: le cinéma est la plus grande école du soir d'Afrique noire. <u>Bingo</u> 176(1967):24.

687. Bingo. Pourquois allons-nous au cinéma? <u>Bingo</u> 91(1960):34-35. (I)

Summary of interviews with 11 persons about audience responses to films.

688. Bingo. Un prix pour Johnson Traoré. <u>Bingo</u> 304(1978):50-51.

His films shown in New York.

689. Bingo. Quatre jeunes cinéastes ont fonde le groupement africain du cinéma. <u>Bingo</u> 52(1957):9-13.

Group of Senegalese filmmakers formed in Paris.

690. Bingo. "Le signe du Vodoun" premier long métrage du dahoméen Pascal Abikanlou. <u>Bingo</u> 252(1974):39. (R)

691. Bingo. "Synapse" premier film du nigerien Moustapha Diop. <u>Bingo</u> 231(1972):62. (R)

692. Biodan, Idrissou S. Alphonse Beni. <u>Bingo</u> 395(1985):17.

Actors and actresses in <u>African</u> <u>Fever</u>.

693. Biondi, Jean-Pierre. Le Conseil National de l'Audio-Visuel du Sénégal. <u>Ethiopiques</u> 10(1977):13-18.

BITA, ARTHUR SI See SI BITA, ARTHUR.

694. Bitégué, Evouang. CENACI: Objectif largement atteint. <u>L'Union</u> May 8(1986):5.

African film week held in Port-Gentil, Gabon.

695. Biyick, Ruben G. Les cinéastes africains condamnés à la mendicité professionnelle. <u>Bingo</u> 354(1982):52-53. (I)

Jean-Claude Tchuilen discusses problems of filmmaking.

696. Biz. Après Ouagadougou "Désébagato" fait un tabac à Bobo et Banfora. <u>Sidwaya</u> June 19 (1987):4.

697. Bleicher, Thomas. Filmische Literatur und literarischer Film - Peter Handkes Erzählung "Die linkshändige Frau" und Sembène Ousmanes Film Xala als Paradigmata neuer Kunstformen. <u>Komparatistische</u> <u>Hefte</u> 5/6(1982):119-137. (R)

698. Böhl, Michael. <u>Entwicklung des ethnographischen Films</u>. Göttingen: Edition Herodot, 1985. pp. 158-162, 169-172.

Short history of filmmaking in French-speaking West Africa. Filmography for 16 filmmakers.

*699. Bolen, Francis. Cinéma au long cours. <u>Ciné-Dossiers</u> Apr. 13 (1969):1-17.

*700. Bolen, Francis. Cinéma au long cours (1952-1962) <u>Ciné-Dossiers</u> Apr. 30 (1972):1-18.

*701. Bolen, Francis. Dans un congo en guerre. <u>Ciné-Dossiers</u> Dec. 17 (1969):1-6.

702. Bolwell, Edwin. Tarzan's Africa may be up a tree. <u>New</u> <u>York</u> <u>Times</u> July 15 (1967):15.

Production of <u>Kongi's</u> <u>Harvest</u>.

703. Bombote, Diomansi. Deux jeunes acteurs-amateurs maliens: Fernande Coulibaly et Moussa Sidibé. <u>L'Essor</u> Dec. 10(1970):3. (I)

Actor and actress in Djibril Kouyaté, <u>Retour</u> <u>de</u> <u>Tiéman</u>.

704. Bombote, Diomansi. Recontre avec Djibril Kouyaté le réalisateur de "Le retour de Tiéman". <u>L'Essor</u> Dec. 8(1970):3. (I)

705. Bonakolo, Moyo A.   Quel cinéma pour des millions! _Afrique_ _Asie_
379(1986):18-19.

Government support for filmmaking in Cameroun.

706. Bonitzer, Pascal.   L'argent-fantôme. _Cahiers_ _du_ _Cinéma_
209(1969):57-58. (R)

Sembène Ousmane, _Mandabi_.

707. Bonkane, Chouaibou.   Du festival du film au forum de la jeunesse.
_L'Essor_ July 27 (1967):3.

Moscow film festival.

708. Bonner, Lesley.   Nigeria's Hollywood hero.   _New_ _African_
186(1983):44-45. (R)

Segun Oyekunle, _Parcel_ _Post_.

709. Bonnet, Jean-Claude.   Ceddo.   _Cinématographe_ 28(1977):44. (R)

710. Bonnet, Jean-Claude.   Ousmane Sembène.   _Cinématographe_
28(1977):43-44. (I)

Discussion of _Ceddo_.

711. Boolamou, A. and B. Dosso.   Yéo Kozoloa: cinéaste ivoirien.
_Ivoire_ _Dimanche_ 480(1980):26-27. (I)

712. Borrak, Omar.   Soudan: L'ère du marasme.   _Afrique-Asie_
58(1974):50-51.

713. Borsten, Joan.   Lights, camera, Africa.   _Chicago_ _Tribune_ July 7
(1985):Sect. 10, 25-27.

FESPACO.

714. Bosséno, Christian.   A Carthage: l'entente arabo-africaine.
_Afrique-Asie_ 283(1982):52-53.

J.C.C.

715. Bosséno, Christian.   Afrique, continent des origines.   _Revue_ _du_
_Cinéma_ 424(1987):62-68.

History, infrastructure, films that have won prizes, major
themes, style.

716. Bosséno, Christian.   Ceddo.   _Revue_ _du_ _Cinéma_ 342(1979):114-118.
(I)

Sembène discusses _Ceddo_.

717. Bosséno, Christian. Fêtes biennales des cinémas d'Afrique. Recherche, Pédagogie et Culture 53-54(1981):69-73.

FESPACO, J.C.C.

718. Bosséno, Christian. Ouagadougou 81: le festival des caméras d'Afrique. Afrique-Asie 236(1981):57-59.

FESPACO.

719. Bossy, Magda. Le communique officiel du jury. Unir Cinéma 23-24(1986):29-30.

Tiers Monde film festival. Prize to Wend Kuuni; importance of film in Burkina Faso.

720. Botan, Ahmed Ashkir. Closing statement, in First Mogadishu Pan-African Film Symposium. Pan African Cinema...Which Way Ahead? Ibrahim Awed et al eds. Mogadishu: MOGPAFIS Management Committee, 1983. pp. 82-83.

Accomplishments of MOGPAFIS.

*721. Botombele Ekanga Bokoga. Le cinéma et la télévision au Zaire. Ciné-Dossiers 74(1979):14-18; 75(1979):15-18.

722. Bouabid, Hamadi. Vllle J.C.C., l'an XIV de Carthage. Agecop Liaison 55-56(1980):48-51.

723. Bouchard, Dady. Quand regardera-t-on nos propres films? L'Union 1319(1980):3.

Distribution of films in Gabon.

724. Boudhina, Slah. Les films africains ou la force d'écrire la réalité de tous les jours. L'Action Nov. 21 (1980):9.

J.C.C. Themes of films shown.

725. Boudhina, Slah. J.C.C.: Une course contra la montre. L'Action Nov. 19 (1980):16.

726. Boudhina, Slah. Palmarès des J.C.C. 80. L'Action Nov. 25 (1980):9.

727. Boudhina, Slah. Une soirée fort réussie. L'Action Oct. 24 (1982):7.

J.C.C.

728. Boudjengui, Antoine. Une nouvelle salle de cinéma. L'Union 1377(1980):2.

New theater in Gabon.

729. Boughedir, Férid. A Cannes, le Tiers monde est présent. Jeune Afrique 802(1976):56-57.

730. Boughedir, Férid. A l'est du nouveau. Jeune Afrique 1088(1981):83.

MOGPAFIS.

731. Boughedir, Férid. Adieu au fesitval francophone. Jeune Afrique 1059(1981):72.

FIFEF.

732. Boughedir, Férid. L'Afrique à la une chez les "francophones" à Namur. Jeune Afrique 926(1978):44-45.

733. Boughedir, Férid. Afrique-sur-Gange. Jeune Afrique 1205(1984):52-53.

Bombay film festival.

734. Boughedir, Férid. Alger deuxième congrès du cinéma africain. Cinéma 75 197(1975):18-19.

735. Boughedir, Férid. Ancien cuisinier et débardeur, l'émigre Med Hondo exprime sa vérité de l'éxil. Jeune Afrique 725(1974):60-63. (I)

736. Boughedir, Férid. L'année des dupes? Jeune Afrique 1095(1981):166-169.

Need for African control of film distribution.

737. Boughedir, Férid. Avec des bouts de ficelle. Jeune Afrique 1040(1980):68-69.

J.C.C.

738. Boughedir, Férid. The blossoming of the Senegalese cinema. Young Cinema and Theater 3(1974):14-20.

Themes of Senegalese films.

739. Boughedir, Férid. Cabourg ou le français en sous-titre. Jeune Afrique 871(1977):38-39.

FIFEF.

740. Boughedir, Férid. Caméra d'Afrique 20 years of African cinema. SeptièmArt 48(1983):14-15.

Author discusses his film on history of African film.

741. Boughedir, Férid.   Caméras de tous les pays... Jeune Afrique
     1136(1982):62-63.

     J.C.C.

742. Boughedir, Férid.   Cannes... et après.   Pour un cinéma
     non-aligné.  SeptièmArt 57(1986):10-12.

743. Boughedir, Férid.   Cannes, victime de l'Afrique.   Jeune Afrique
     1116(1982):100-101.

744. Boughedir, Férid.   Carthage 1978: une grande fête du cinéma.
     Jeune Afrique 893(1978):48.

745. Boughedir, Férid.   Carthage 78: pari tenu pour les Africains et
     les Arabes.   Jeune Afrique 936(1978):91-93.

746. Boughedir, Férid.   Le cinéma africain a quinze ans.   Filméchange
     4(1978):75-80.

     History of African film since making of Borom Sarret, emphasis on
     themes and distribution.

747. Boughedir, Férid.   Cinéma africain et francophonie.   Culture
     française  29,2(1980):33-37.

     Themes, use of French and African languages in films.

748. Boughedir, Férid.   Cinéma africain le temps de l'immobilisme.   2
     écrans 42-43(1982):15-19.

     Problems of film production.

749. Boughedir, Férid.   Le cinéma africain, problèmes et solutions.
     7e Art 41(1981):16-18.

750. Boughedir, Férid.   Le cinéma camerounais: les premiers pas.
     Cinéma Québec 3, 9-10(1973):42-43.

751. Boughedir, Férid.   Le cinéma dahoméen: un cinéma quise libère.
     Cinéma Québec 3, 9-10(1973):38-39.

752. Boughedir, Férid.   Cinéma: David et Goliath.   Jeune Afrique
     626(1973):48-50.

     Problems of filmmaking in 1973.

753. Boughedir, Férid.   A cinema fighting for its liberation, in
     Journey Across Three Continents.   Renee Tajima, ed. New York:
     Third World Newsreel, 1985. pp. 22-25.

     Short history of African film since 1963.

754. Boughedir, Férid. Le cinéma gabonais: à la recherche d'une "identité." Cinéma Québec 3, 9-10(1973):34-35.

755. Boughedir, Férid. Cinéma: Idi Amin vedette d'un festival. Jeune Afrique 701(1974):58-65.

Cannes film festival.

756. Boughedir, Férid. Le cinéma ivoirien: de riches possiblitiés. Cinéma Québec 3, 9-10(1973):30-32.

757. Boughedir, Férid. Le cinéma malgache: une vision sociale réaliste. Cinéma Québec 3, 9-10(1973):36-37.

758. Boughedir, Férid. Le cinéma malien: premiers balbutiements. Cinéma Québec 3, 9-10(1973):33.

759. Boughedir, Férid. Le cinéma nigérien: l'authenticité de l'autodidacte. Cinéma Québec 3, 9-10(1973):28-29.

Short summaries of Nigerien films.

760. Boughedir, Férid. Le cinéma sénégalais: le plus important d'Afrique noire. Cinéma Québec 3, 9-10(1973):24-26.

Short summaries of Senegalese films.

761. Boughedir, Férid. Le cinéma voltaique: un symbole de libération. Cinéma Québec 3, 9-10(1973):40-41.

762. Boughedir, Férid. Le colonialisme ordinaire. Jeune Afrique 646(1973):74-75. (R)

Sarah Maldoror, Sambizanga.

763. Boughedir, Férid. Le conte de l'enfant muet. Jeune Afrique 1125(1982):56-57. (R)

Gaston Kaboré, Wend Kuuni.

764. Boughedir, Férid. Cuvée 79. Jeune Afrique 947(1979):47.

FESPACO.

765. Boughedir, Férid. Dalida, Tanit et les autres. Jeune Afrique 1345(1986):82-83.

J.C.C.

766. Boughedir, Férid. Dans le monde arabe et en Afrique: "une convergence assez nette." Tiers-Monde 20, 79(1979):638-641.

Themes and impact of Third World film.

767. Boughedir, Férid. Dans une Afrique d'opérette. Jeune Afrique 803(1976):56-57. (R)

Daniel Kamwa, Pousse-Pousse and Sembène Ousmane, Xala.

768. Boughedir, Férid. Déception à Carthage. Jeune Afrique 828(1976):60-61.

J.C.C. Few new films, lack of enthusiasm.

769. Boughedir, Férid. Derrière la fête, la crise. Jeune Afrique 1367(1987):48-51.

FESPACO. Problems in film selection and distribution. Comments by 20 participants.

770. Boughedir, Férid. Derrière l'écran l'apartheid. Jeune Afrique 1196(1983):66-67.

Films about southern Africa.

771. Boughedir, Férid. Des Africains sans complexes. Jeune Afrique 1142(1982):61.

J.C.C.

772. Boughedir, Férid. Des armes et des larmes. Jeune Afrique 1145(1982):56-57.

Trois Continents film festival.

773. Boughedir, Férid. Des films dans "le vent." Jeune Afrique 1172(1983):76-77.

Themes of African films shown in France.

774. Boughedir, Férid. Les deux visages du cinéma africain. Jeune Afrique 586(1972):46-49.

FESPACO.

775. Boughedir, Férid. Dinard: le triomphe du cinéma africain. Jeune Afrique 604(1972):56-59.

FIFEF.

776. Boughedir, Férid. Les dix ans de Carthage. Jeune Afrique 823(1976):63.

Films shown at J.C.C.

777. Boughedir, Férid. Dix-huit bougies pour Carthage. Jeune Afrique 1241(1984):68-69.

J.C.C.

778.  Boughedir, Férid.  L'eclosion du cinéma sénégalais.  <u>Jeune</u>
      <u>Afrique</u> 699(1974):46-50.

      Review of 10 years of filmmaking in Senegal.

779.  Boughedir, Férid.  L'effet Balogun.  <u>Jeune</u> <u>Afrique</u> 1138(1982):65.
      (R)

      Ola Balogun, <u>Money</u> <u>Power</u>.

780.  Boughedir, Férid.  L'émigration vue par émigré.  <u>Jeune</u> <u>Afrique</u>
      787(1976):52.  (R)

      Sidney Sokhona, <u>Nationalité</u> <u>émigré</u>.

781.  Boughedir, Férid.  Et maintenant, que la fête commence!  <u>Jeune</u>
      <u>Afrique</u> 1151(1983):53-54.

      FESPACO.

782.  Boughedir, Férid.  FEPACI, fais pas ça.  <u>Jeune</u> <u>Afrique</u>
      1107(1982):58-59.

783.  Boughedir, Férid.  La FEPACI: pour libération du cinéma en
      Afrique.  <u>Cinéma</u> <u>Québec</u> 3, 9-10(1973):49.

784.  Boughedir, Férid.  FESPACO: cap sur l'an 2000.  <u>Jeune</u> <u>Afrique</u>
      1364(1987):60-61.

785.  Boughedir, Férid.  FESPACO: le 8e festival panafrican du cinéma
      de Ouagadougou.  <u>Recherche,</u> <u>pédagogie</u> <u>et</u> <u>culture</u> 62(1983):89-92.

786.  Boughedir, Férid.  Festival de Cannes: les surprises du tiers
      monde.  <u>Jeune</u> <u>Afrique</u> 649(1973):62-66.

787.  Boughedir, Férid.  Les films africains à lâge adulte.  <u>Jeune</u>
      <u>Afrique</u> 791(1976):44-45.

      FESPACO.

788.  Boughedir, Férid.  Le fin de l'amateurisme.  <u>Jeune</u> <u>Afrique</u>
      1149(1983):60-62.

      Reduction in foreign financial support for African filmmaking.

789.  Boughedir, Férid.  Francophonie en plusieurs langues.  <u>Jeune</u>
      <u>Afrique</u> 708(1978):68-69.

      FIFEF.

790.  Boughedir, Férid.  Les grandes dates cinéma africain.  <u>Jeune</u>
      <u>Afrique</u> 1303-1304(1986):89.

History, list of major dates when important films made.

791. Boughedir, Férid. Les grandes tendances du cinéma en Afrique noire. CinémAction 26(1983):48-57.

Major themes of films.

792. Boughedir, Férid. Les grands absents du festival. Jeune Afrique 1017(1980):67.

Lack of African films at Cannes film festival.

793. Boughedir, Férid. Les hériters d'Oumarou Ganda. Jeune Afrique 1053(1981):62-63.

FESPACO.

794. Boughedir, Férid. L'heure de l'indépendance? Jeune Afrique 1051(1981):70-71.

FESPACO.

795. Boughedir, Férid. Un Hollywood africain? Jeune Afrique 1054(1981):63.

Role of CINAFRIC.

796. Boughedir, Férid. Hollywood sur Volta. Jeune Afrique 1153(1983):62-63.

Ouagadougou, capital of African filmmaking.

797. Boughedir, Férid. Le 8éme Festival Panafricain de Cinéma de Ouagadougou. SeptièmArt 48(1983):8-10.

798. Boughedir, Férid. Il n'y a pas que le sport. Jeune Afrique 1234(1984):72-73.

African and American filmmakers participate in a conference in Hollywood.

799. Boughedir, Férid. L'image apprivoisée. Jeune Afrique 914(1978):185-188.

Survey of African filmmaking talent and economic problems.

800. Boughedir, Férid. La longue marche des Africains. Jeune Afrique 1298(1985):46-47.

MOGPAFIS.

801. Boughedir, Férid. 1975, l'année des grandes victoires. Jeune Afrique 782-783(1976):60-61.

Themes of films made in 1975.

802. Boughedir, Férid. 1982-83: de Carthage IX à Ouagadougou VIII, nouvelle génération, nouveaux espoirs. CinémAction 26(1983):178-185.

803. Boughedir, Férid. Le nouveau credo des cinéastes africains: le Manifeste de Niamey. CinémAction 26(1983):168-172.

Resolutions of conference on production held in Niamey in 1982.

804. Boughedir, Férid. Un nouveau souffle sur Cannes. Jeune Afrique 858(1977):62-64.

805. Boughedir, Férid. Une nouvelle génération. Jeune Afrique 1064(1981):67.

Cannes film festival.

806. Boughedir, Férid. Une nouvelle vague de cinéastes. Jeune Afrique 1156(1983):78-80.

FESPACO.

807. Boughedir, Férid. Une oasis en Somalie. Jeune Afrique 1191(1983):72-73.

MOGPAFIS.

808. Boughedir, Férid. Où sont passés les films africains? Jeune Afrique 1220(1984):54-55.

Cannes film festival.

809. Boughedir, Férid. Une parabole des privilégiés. Jeune Afrique 795(1976):56-58. (R)

Sembène Ousmane, Xala.

810. Boughedir, Férid. Paris découvre l'Angola et Sarah Maldoror. Jeune Afrique 646(1973):76.

811. Boughedir, Férid. Parler français? Jeune Afrique 709(1974):45.

Language of films shown at FESPACO.

812. Boughedir, Férid. Petit guide des cinéastes africains. Cinéma Québec 3, 9-10(1973):44-45.

Filmography.

813. Boughedir, Férid. La petit soeur de "Boubou-cravate." Jeune Afrique 1091(1981):78-79. (R)

Daniel Kamwa, Notre fille.

814. Boughedir, Férid. Pleins feux sur Carthage. Jeune Afrique 1036(1980):71.

J.C.C.

815. Boughedir, Férid. Le plus productif des cinéastes africains. Jeune Afrique 1065(1981):65-66.

Ola Balogun.

816. Boughedir, Férid. Pour une critique africaine décolonisée. Unir Cinéma 14(1984):4-6.

817. Boughedir, Férid. Pour une production indépendante. Jeune Afrique 1056(1981):66.

CIPROFILM.

818. Boughedir, Férid. Pour une theorie du cinéma africain. Ecran 30(1974):46-48.

819. Boughedir, Férid. Présence africaine. Recherche, pédagogie et culture 17-18(1975):43-45.

Summary of FESPACO seminar on role of African filmmaker.

820. Boughedir, Férid. Qu'on l'admire ou qu'on le dénigre... Afrique littéraire 76(1985):4; CinémAction 34(1985):4.

Work of Sembène Ousmane.

821. Boughedir, Férid. Reflections on African cinema industry, in First Mogadishu Pan-African Film Symposium. Pan African Cinema...Which Way Ahead? Ibrahim Awed et al. eds. Mogadishu: MOGPAFIS Management Committee, 1983. pp. xiv-xvii.

Reasons why African film industry has not developed.

822. Boughedir, Férid. Report and prospects, in Cinema and Society. International Film and Television Council, ed. Paris: IFTC, 1981. pp. 99-112.

Roles of film in post-colonial Africa.

823. Boughedir, Férid. Retour aux sources. Jeune Afrique 1221(1984):52-53.

Cannes film festival.

824. Boughedir, Férid. Le rôle de la presse et de la publicité dans la préparation du public à l'accueil du film africain, in FESPACO

_1983_.  Paris: Présence Africaine, 1987. pp. 49-60.

Promotion and criticism of film.

825.  Boughedir, Férid.  Sept films africains à Cannes.  _Jeune Afrique_
1009(1980):71.

826.  Boughedir, Férid.  Le septième art entre deux mondes.  _Jeune
Afrique_ 808(1976):56-57.

Cannes film festival.

827.  Boughedir, Férid.  Six cavaliers pour le septième art.  _Jeune
Afrique_ 1157(1983):60-61.

Films by Joseph Akouissone, Moussa Yoro Bathily, Souleymane
Cissé, Gaston Kaboré, Taieb Louhichi and Mweze Ngangura.

828.  Boughedir, Férid.  VIe FESPACO la critique ou la politique du
grain du sable.  _L'Observateur_ Feb. 7(1979):1,6-7.

Report on FESPACO colloquium on the role of the critic.

829.  Boughedir, Férid.  Tanits d'or et d'argent.  _Jeune Afrique_
725(1974):59-60.

Films shown at J.C.C.

830.  Boughedir, Férid.  Le tiers monde de Paris à Cannes.  _Jeune
Afrique_ 957(1979):55.

831.  Boughedir, Férid.  Un tiers monde sur mesure.  _Jeune Afrique_
1117(1982):68-69.

Cannes film festival.

832.  Boughedir, Férid.  35 bougies pour un festival. _Jeune Afrique_
1112(1982):91.

Cannes film festival.

833.  Boughedir, Férid.  La(trop) longue marche des cinéastes africains
vers la rentabilité économique.  _CinémAction_ 26(1983):152-159.

834.  Boughedir, Férid.  La Tunisie entre sectarisme et tolérance.
_Jeune Afrique_ 1350(1986):82-83.

J.C.C.

835.  Boughedir, Férid.  "Le vent" en poupe.  _Jeune Afrique_
1141(1982):100-101.

J.C.C.

836. Bourboune, Mourad.    Le lVe  Festival  des  journées cinématographiques de Carthage.    Nos mutuelles différences. Nouvelles Littéraires 2353(1972):16.

837. Boussida, Abdelhafidh.    Les manifestations marginales des J.C.C. Action (Tunis) NS 7276(1976):12.

838. Boussida, Abdelhafidh.    Muna Moto ou l'art du silence musical. Action (Tunis) NS7276(1976):13. (R)

839. Boussida, Abdelhafidh.    La participation étrangère aux J.C.C. 1976.  Action (Tunis) NS 7274(1976):17.

840. Boyd, William.    Twitching townie.    Times Literary Supplement May 14 (1982):533. (R)

Michael Raeburn, The Grass Is Singing.

841. Bouzid, Dorra.    J.C.C. 1982 un flash biennal dans une obscurité opaque.  L'Action Nov. 2 (1982):9.

842. Bouzid, Dorra.    J.C.C. 1982 unième colloque sur le même desarroi afro-arabe.  L'Action Nov. 2 (1982):8.

J.C.C. colloquium on creation and creativity.

843. Bouzid, Dorra.    J.C.C. 82 la douloureuse double question biennale.  L'Action Nov. 8 (1982):8-9.

Problems of distribution of films.

844. Bragaglia, Cristina.    Rui Guerra, in Dizinario universale del cinema.  Fernaldo Di Giammatteo, ed.  Rome: Editori Riuniti, 1985.  Vol. 2, pp. 711-712.

Biographical information, comments on each of Guerra's films.

845. Branco, Paulo. Entretien avec Ruy Duarte de Carvalho.  Cahiers du Cinéma 274(1977):59-60. (I)

Discussion of filmmaking in Angola 1974-1976.

846. Brandli, Sibylle.    Festival panafricain du cinéma (FESPACO) CVA Newsletter Aug. (1986):11-12.

847. Brathier, Léon.    "Visages de femmes."  La femme africaine sans fard ni paravent.  Ehuzu June 12 (1987):3. (R)

848. Braucourt, Guy.    Cinémas africains.    Nouvelles Littéraires. 2319(1972):30. (BR)

Guy Hennebelle, Les cinémas africains en 1972.  See No. 44.

849. Braucourt, Guy.    Les cinémas arabes et africaines.    Nouvelles

_Littéraires_ 2459(1974):8.

J.C.C.

850. Braucourt, Guy. Festival de Dinard. La conscience francophone. _Nouvelles Littéraires_ 2339(1972):24.

FIFEF.

851. Brauer, Dieter. Film and national development. _Development and Cooperation_ 3(1986):23-24.

Workshop for Third World filmmakers held at Mannheim film festival.

852. Brooks, Philip. Africa's film men are looking for heroes. _Herald_ Apr. 10(1985):6.

FESPACO.

853. Brossard, Jean-Pierre. Brève histoire du cinéma au Mozambique (1975-1980). _2 écrans_ 33(1981):21-23.

*854. Browne, A. Alpha: an African revolution. _New Nigerian_. May 12 (1973).

Ola Balogun, _Alpha_.

855. Broz, Martin. The birth of African cinema. _Young Cinema and Theater_ 1(1968):37-43.

Role of film in Africa. Ideas of Sembène.

856. Bruneau, Jean-Pierre. Le film africain s'exporte de plus en plus. _Jeune Afrique_ 1359(1987):64-65.

Distribution of African films in France.

857. Bruneau, Jean-Pierre. Ni riches ni célèbres...plutôt marginaux. _Jeune Afrique_ 1361(1987):56.

Roles of actors and actresses in 1986: Sidiki Bakaba, Issach Bankolé, Cheick Doukouré, Sotigui Kouyaté and Felicité Wouassi.

858. Bruno, D.S. Ruy Duarte de Carvalho, O Camarada e a Câmera. _Africa_ (Lisbon) 14(1986):81-82. (BR)

See No. 28.

859. Buana Kabue. Le cinéma zairois: un bon départ. _Zaire_ 195(1972):14-17.

860. Budiak, Ludmila Mikhailovna. _Kinematograf razvivaiuschcikhsia stran_. Moskva: Izdvo Znanie, 1981. pp. 18-23.

Problems of filmmaking in Africa.

861. Bunce, Alan N.   African films start unusual series.   Christian
     Science Monitor Jan. 17 (1969):4. (R)

     Sembène Ousmane, Borom Sarret and La Noire de.

862. Bureau Social Urbain, Caritas.   Cinémas et vidéo à Kigali.
     Kigali: Bureau Social Urbain, Caritas, 1985. (pamphlet)

     Kinds of films shown, behavior in theaters.

863. C.L.   Ni trop long, ni trop court.   Africa (Dakar)
     167(1984):43-44.

     Critique of short documentary films being made in Senegal.

864. C.V.   Un film dont on parle et dont on parlera longtemps: "Le
     mandat" d'Ousmane Sembène.   Bingo 195(1969):41-42. (I)

865. Cakpo, Barthélémy.   Cinéma dahoméen.   Afrique Nouvelle
     1367(1975):17. (R)

     Richard de Medeiros, Le Nouveau venu.

*866. Calao. Le cinéma à Ouagadougou.   Calao 50(1983):6.

     FESPACO.

867. Camille, Balliet Bléziri.   Entretien avec Tahar Chéria.   Sentiers
     48(1974):14-16. (I)

     Discussion of FEPCAI and problems of distribution.

868. Camacho, Martine.   Les écrans français et les films africains.
     Ehuzu Jan. 23 (1987):3.

     African films shown in Paris.

869. Camacho, Martine.   FESPACO 87 sous le thème "Cinéma et identité
     culturelle." Ehuzu Feb. 20 (1987):3.

870. Camacho, Martine.   Panorama de 25 ans de cinéma africain au sud
     du Sahara.   Ehuzu Apr. 10 (1987):3; Apr. 17 (1987):3; May 8
     (1987):3.

     History, focuses on distribution and fiction films in
     French-speaking Africa.

871. Camy, Gérard.   Entretien avec Ruy Guerra.   Jeune Cinéma
     175(1986):3-8. (I)

     Reasons for making Opera do Malandro.

872. Camy, Gérard. Gangster ou Malandro: un opéra sur fond de dictature. Jeune Cinéma 175(1986):3-8. (I)

Ruy Guerra discusses Opera do Malandro.

873. Camy, Gérard. Italie et Russie sous le Soleil de Satan. Jeune Cinéma 182(1987):20-23.

Cannes film festival.

874. Canby, Vincent. Are black films losing their blackness? New York Times Apr. 25 (1976):II, 15. (R)

Ross Devenish, Boesman and Lena.

875. Canby, Vincent. Film: 'Ceddo,' a pageant from Sembène's Africa. New York Times Feb. 17 (1978):C8. (R)

876. Canby, Vincent. Film: 7 stories by Nadine Gordimer. New York Times May 18 (1983):C26. (R)

Manie Van Rensburg, Country Lovers.

877. Canby, Vincent. Screen: Amin's rise and fall. New York Times Mar. 19 (1982):C13. (R)

Sharad Patel, Amin the Rise and Fall.

878. Canby, Vincent. Screen: 'Wend Kuuni.' New York Times Mar. 27 (1983):I, 55. (R)

879. Cancel, Robert. Epic elements in Ceddo. Current Bibliography on African Affairs 18, 1(1985-86):3-19.

880. Capdenac, Michel. La "francophonie" en question et d'heureuses surprises. Les Lettres francaises July 21 (1971):14-15.

FIFEF.

881. Carbonnier, Alain. Le Vent de Souleymane Cissé. Cinéma 33(1985):10. (R)

Finyé.

882. Carrefour Africain. L'africanisation du cinéma vient de franchir une étape important. Carrefour Africain 687(1979):8.

CIDC, CIPROFILM.

883. Carrefour Africain. L'assemblée générale de la SONAVOCI. Carrefour Africain 647-648(1977):4.

884. Carrefour Africain. Le Burkina était à l'honneur. Carrefour

Africain 986(1987):21.

Film week in Perouse, Italy, attended by African filmmakers and critics.

885.  Carrefour Africain.  Le ciné-club de Ouagadougou a clôturé ses travaux.  Carrefour Africain 520(1972):3.

Film club activities in Burkina Faso.

886.  Carrefour Africain.  Cinéma et identité culturelle.  Carrefour Africain 975(1987):6-7.

FESPACO theme, film and cultural identity.

887.  Carrefour Africain.  Clôture du premier festival du cinéma africain francophone de Ouagadougou.  Carrefour Africain 357(1969):1,3.

FESPACO, aims and predictions for development of African film.

888.  Carrefour Africain.  Colloque sur la littérature et le cinéma africains.  Carrefour Africain 872(1985):12.

Report on FESPACO colloquium on literature and film.

889.  Carrefour, Africain.  Conférence extraordinaire des Ministres Africains chargés du cinéma.  Carrefour Africain 687(1979):3.

CIDC, CIPROFILM.

*890.  Carrefour Africain.  Le deuxième festival de Ouagadougou. Carrefour Africain 409(1969).

891.  Carrefour Africain.  Du 1er au 15 Février: 1er Festival du Cinéma Africain à Ouagadougou.  Carrefour Africain 350-351(1969):8.

Reasons for FESPACO.

892.  Carrefour Africain.  Fin du 11ème Congrès de la FEPACI. Carrefour Africain 872(1985):11.

893.  Carrefour Africain.  "Mandabi (le Mandat)."  Carrefour Africain 346(1968):8. (R)

894.  Carrefour Africain.  Palmarès 10ème FESPACO Ouagadougou 21-28 février 1987.  Carrefour Africain 976(1987):14-15.

895.  Carrefour Africain.  Palmarès du 9ème FESPACO.  Carrefour Africain 872(1985):9-10.

896.  Carrefour Africain.  Pour la première fois, un film de langue Djerma est présenté au festival de Cannes.  Carrefour Africain 371(1969):8. (R)

Information about Oumarou Ganda and his <u>Cabascabo</u>.

897. Carrefour Africain.   Prochain festival du Cinéma Africain.
<u>Carrefour</u> <u>Africain</u> 352(1969):1.

FESPACO.

898. Carrefour Africian.   Un salon de matériel cinématographique pour
le 10ème FESPACO. <u>Carrefour</u> <u>Africain</u> 924(1986):6.

Council of ministers meet to plan FESPACO.

899. Carrefour Africain.   Séance d'ouverture  de  l'Assemblée
Constitutive du CIPROFILMS et du CIDC.   <u>Carrefour</u>  <u>Africain</u>
666-667(1978):1, 7.

900. Carrefour Africain.   Selon M. Emile Bassono le cinéma ne doit pas
être un simple moyen de divertissement.   <u>Carrefour</u>  <u>Africain</u>
614-615(1976):9.

Activities of SONAVOCI.

901. Carrefour Africain.   Séminaire de l'Afrique francophe (sic) sur
cinéma et Audo-Visuel (sic) dans l'Evangélisation.   <u>Carrefour</u>
<u>Africain</u> 638-639(1977):16.

Report on OCIC conference.

902. Carrefour Africain.   VIIéme FESPACO: participation record.
<u>Carrefour</u> <u>Africain</u> 710-711(1981):1-8.

903. Carrefour Africain.   SONAVOCI: Construire 10 nouvelles salles
dans 5 ans.  <u>Carrefour</u> <u>Africain</u> 710-711(1981):3.

904. Carrere, Charles.  Nous sommes tous des délinquants.  <u>Le</u> <u>Soleil</u>
Apr. 19 (1975):2. (R)

Momar Thiam, <u>Baks</u>.

905. Carvalho, Sol.  XII Festival cinematográfico de Moscovo, um
festival diferente.  <u>Tempo</u> 564(1981):20-23. (I)

Interview with Samuel Matola, director of INC, at Moscow film
festival.

906. Carvalho, Sol.  Jornadas Cinematográficas de Cartago: Orio e a
margem de um festival.  <u>Tempo</u> 530(1980):48-51.

Mocambiquan films shown at J.C.C.

907. Carvalho, Sol and Labi Mendonça.  A magia do cinema.  Como se faz
un filme? <u>Tempo</u> 606(1982):56-60.

Film course at INC, Mocambique.

908. Casas, Arlette. L'Afrique de papa à "Confrontation XIX." Afrique-Asie 296(1983):54-55.

FIFEF.

909. Casas, Arlette. Images de femmes. Afrique-Asie 386(1986):54-55.

Themes of films shown at Constantine film festival.

910. Catholic Film Newsletter. Emitai. Catholic Film Newsletter 37,23(1972):116. (R)

*911. Cauvin, André and Jean Leyder. Le cinéma au Congo Belge. Les Vétérans coloniaux Oct. (1967):3-12.

912. Celi, C. La realtà del cinema africano. Nigrizia 94,7(1976):8-9.

FESPACO.

913. Celuloide. Angola e Moçambique fazem cinema a meias. Celuloide 330(1981):2. (R)

João Costa and Carlos Henriques, Pamberi ne Zimbabwé.

914. Celuloide. Cinema Angolano. Celuloide 350(1983):6.

Review of films made 1975-1982.

915. Celuloide. Cinema Angolano. Celuloide 355-356(1983):20.

Fiction films to be made in 1984.

916. Celuloide. Cinema Moçambicano. Celuloide 357(1984):19.

Films made 1979-1983.

917. Celuloide. Cinema Moçambicano. Celuloide 363-365(1984):7.

Films made 1981-1983.

918. Celuloide. Cultura cinematográfica em Moçambique. Celuloide 310/311(1981):17.

Report on Polish delegation to Mocambique and films shown.

919. Celuloide. A festa da vida/Duarte Carvalho. Celuloide 227(1976):18. (R)

920. Celuloide. Semanas de cinema cubano, africano e bulgaro em Moçambique. Celuloide 298-299(1980):20-21.

921. Cervoni, Albert. Caméra et fusil. Cinéma 72 162(1972):20. (R)

   Sembène Ousmane, Emitai.

922. Cervoni, Albert. Le cinéma et l'Afrique. France Nouvelle 1033(1965):17-19.

   Discussion between Sembène Ousmane and Jean Rouch.

923. Cervoni, Albert. Le Mandat. Cinéma 69 134(1969):119-121. (R)

924. Cervoni, Albert. Touki Bouki. Cinéma 73 177(1973):39. (R)

925. Challard, Jean-Pierre. "Raphia": l'etoffe d'un film. Africa International 194(1987):36-37. (R)

926. Challard, Jean-Pierre. Le second souffle. Africa International 179(1986):39-40. (R)

   Henri-Joseph Koumba, Singe fou and background on filmmaking in Gabon.

927. Challouf, Mohamed. E festa di popolo. Nigizia 103, 5(1985):44-45.

   FESPACO.

928. Challouf, Mohamed. Vince la cenere. Nigrizia 104, 12(1986):40-41.

   J.C.C. participants and prizes.

929. Cham, Mbye Baboucar. Art and ideology in the work of Sembène Ousmane and Hailé Gerima. Présence Africaine 129(1984):79-91.

   Slightly edited version of No. 930.

930. Cham, Mbye Baboucar. Artistic and ideological convergence: Ousmane Sembène and Hailé Gerima. UFAHAMU 11,2(1981-1982):140-152.

931. Cham, Mbye Baboucar. The creative artist, state and society in Africa. Current Bibliography on African Affairs. 17,1(1984-1985):17-28.

   Role of filmmakker in society.

932. Cham, Mbye Baboucar. Film producton in West Africa: 1979-1981. Présence Africaine 124(1982):168-189.

   Ghana, Nigeria and French-speaking West Africa.

933. Cham, Mbye Baboucar. Islam in Senegalese literature and film. Africa (London) 55,4(1985):447-463.

107.

934. Cham, Mbye Baboucar. Ousmane Sembène and the aesthetics of African oral traditions. Africana Journal 13(1982):24-40.

935. Chansou, A.B. Ousmane Sembène: L'état doit aider les cinéastes. Le Soleil July 27(1970):3. (I)

Need for African film festival, problems of film distribution and criticism.

936. Chapier, Henry. A la recherche d'un cinéma d'expression française. Combat (Paris) July 12 (1971):9. (R)

Simon Augé, Ou vas-tu Koumba shown at FIFEF.

937. Charbonnier, Georges, ed. Découpages d'Afrique noire. Cinéma et Tiers-Monde. Poitiers: Collectif Tiers-Monde, 1984. pp. 13-16.

CIDC, CIPROFILM. Role of Burkina Faso in African filmmaking.

938. Charbonnier, Georges, ed. Scénario et monologue d'imperialism. Cinéma et Tiers-Monde. Portiers: Collectif Tiers-Monde, 1984. pp. 7-10.

Distribution, production.

939. Charbonnier, Jean. Quel cinéma, pour qui? Ciné Qua Non 2(1972):1-3.

940. Charensol, Georges. Cabascabo par Oumarou Ganda, Concerto pour un exil par Désiré Ecaré. Nouvelles Littéraires 2194(1969):14. (R)

941. Charensol, Georges. L'enfant de l'autre de Dikongue-Pipa. Nouvelles Littéraires 2535(1976):29. (R)

942. Charrier, Sylvie. Lettre paysanne de Safi Faye. Balafon 35(nd):37. (R)

Kaddu Beykat.

943. Charrier, Sylvie. Muna Moto de Dikongue Pipa. Balafon 35(nd):37. (R)

944. Cheikh, Ben. 9 films sénégalais vont être achetés par l'état. Le Soleil 3227(1981):5.

945. Chergui, Halim. Inoussa Ousseini "Les films africains trop influencés par le cinéma européen." Afrique-Asie 66(1974):30-32; Nigerama 3(1975?):23, 33, 35; Recherche, pédagogie et culture 17-18(1975):57-58. (I)

Biographical background on Ousseini; European influence on African films; characteristics of African audiences.

946. Chériaa, Tahar. Der afrikanische Film. <u>Filmwissenschaftliche Beiträge</u> 21,3(1981):31-35.

Themes of films.

947. Chériaa, Tahar. L'artiste et la révolution. <u>Cinéma Québec</u> 3, 9-10(1973):12-17. (I)

Sembène Ousmane discusses roles of African filmmakers.

*948. Chériaa, Tahar. Carthage et le chemin de la dignité africaine et arabe. <u>CinémArab</u> 4-5(1976):15-17. (I)

Interview with Sembène Ousmane.

949. Chériaa, Tahar. Carthage et le cinéma africain. <u>Cinéma Québec</u> 3,9-10(1973):51-52. (I)

Sembène Ousmane discusses J.C.C.

950. Chériaa, Tahar. Cinéastes d'Afrique noire. <u>Afrique-Asie</u> 175(1978):60-62. (BR)

Guy Hennebelle and Catherine Ruelle, <u>Cinéastes d'Afrique noire</u>. See No. 45.

951. Chériaa, Tahar. Le cinéma en afrique francophone. <u>Cinéma Québec</u> 1, 10(1972):23-27.

Infrastructure.

952. Chériaa, Tahar. Cinéma et distribution. <u>Recherche pédagogie et culture</u> 17-18(1975):33-38.

Economic, political, social and cultural reasons for distribution problems.

953. Chériaa, Tahar. Distribution cinématographique et nationalisation. <u>Ethiopiques</u> 1(1975):142-150.

954. Chériaa, Tahar. Entretien avec M. Bila Zacre. <u>Cinéma 73</u> 175(1973):26-29. (I)

Discussion of FESPACO by Burkinabe Minister of Information.

955. Chériaa, Tahar. Le groupe et le héros, in <u>Caméra Nigra</u>. C.E.S.C.A. ed. Brussels: OCIC, 1984. pp. 109-111.

Heroes in African films.

956. Chériaa, Tahar. Un mecanisme grippe: le commerce du film en Afrique, in <u>Caméra Nigra</u>. C.E.S.C.A. ed. Brussels: OCIC, 1984. pp. 23-41.

Distribution problems.

957. Chériaa, Tahar.   Policies, politics and films in the Arab and African countries.   Young Cinema and Theater 4(1971):27-33.

Translation of No. 958.

958. Chériaa, Tahar.   La politique et le cinéma dans les pays arabes et africains.   Cinéma 71 154(1971):99-109.

Ideology and infrastructure.

959. Chériaa, Tahar.   Une prise de conscience.   Cinéma 72 165(1972):37.

Ideology.

960. Chériaa, Tahar and Férid Boughedir.   Jeune Afrique fait parler Sembène Ousmane.   Jeune Afrique 795(1976):54-56.

Sembène discusses Xala.

961. Chevallier, Jacques.   Sarraounia, le mouvement de l'histoire. Revue du cinéma 422(1986):25-26.   (R)

962. Chifunyise, Stephen.   Africa fights the film war.   Moto 1,7(1982):36-37.

Distribution problems.   Solutions in Ghana, Zambia and Zimbabwe.

963. Chiremba, George.   The film scene in a Zimbabwean perspective. Moto 20(1984):29-30.

Audience responses to Western films; ways to change audience values.

964. Chiriseri, Elliot.   Films with racial bias out-Chigorimbo. Sunday Mail Nov. 9(1986):11.

Steve Chigorimbo, Zimbabwean actor, dicusses his film and theater roles.

965. Choisey, Jean-Pierre.   Des cinéastes africains à Alger.   Jeune Cinéma 41(1969):26-29.

Algiers film festival.

966. Chorfi, Abdelmajid.   "Abusuan" (Côte d'Ivoire) L'Action Oct. 29 (1974):8.   (R)

967. Chorfi, Abdelmajid.   Ajani Ogun (Nigeria), un échec dans le cinéma musical.   Action NS 7276(1976):13.   (R)

968. Chorfi, Abdelmajid. La beauté du film indien nous a fait oublier les déceptions ivoriennes. L'Action Oct. 15 (1970):7. (R)

Désiré Ecaré, A nous deux France and Timité Bassori, Femme au couteau.

969. Chorfi, Abdelmajid. "Les Bicots-Nègres, vos voisins" du Mohamed Abid Hondo. L'Action Oct. 31 (1974):7. (R)

970. Chorfi, Abdelmajid. Entente afro-arabe autour de la distribution et de la production cinématographique. L'Action Nov. 6 (1974):6.

Discussion of distribution and production at J.C.C.

971. Chorfi, Abdelmajid. Le festival est mort! Vive le festival! L'Action Nov. 6 (1974):6.

J.C.C. Few actors and actresses present; prize winning films.

972. Chorfi, Abdelmajid. FIFEF: Festival du film francophone. L'Action Oct. 18 (1975):6.

Danger of concept "francophone." Film prizes.

973. Chorfi, Abdelmajid. Interview express: M. Tahar Guiga, Président de J.C.C. L'Action Oct. 27 (1974):7. (I)

Aims of J.C.C. Procedures for entering films in competition.

974. Chorfi, Abdelmajid. Interview Mohamed Abid Hondo. L'Action Nov. 4 (1974):7. (I)

Discussion of Hondo's film philosophy, financing of his films.

975. Choupaut, Yves Marie. Le cinéma africain devient un art populaire. Balafon 31(1975):40-41.

Short history.

976. Choupaut, Yves Marie. "Codou" bientôt sur les écrans sénégalais. Le Soleil Oct. 7 (1971):4. (R)

977. Choupaut, Yves Marie. Deux générations de cinéastes africains au Festival de Ouagadougou. Carrefour Africain 616(1976):4.

978. Choupaut, Yves Marie. Emile Bassono (Haute-Volta) le troisième journaliste de l'Ouest-africain qui devient ministre. Carrefour Africain 616(1976):4.

SONAVOCI.

979. Choupaut, Yves Marie. Filmfestival von Dinard. Afrika Heute 15/16(1972):319.

FIFEF.

980. Choupaut, Yves Marie. Les pays africains producteurs de films progressent. Carrefour Africain 616(1976):3.

FIFEF.

981. Chronique de Yennenga. Le cinéma gabonais. Le Courrier de Saint Ex 18(1979):3.

Gabonais films shown at FESPACO. Excerpts from press conference with Pierre-Marie Dong.

*982. Chuna, Adichie. Money Power. A celluloid portrait of Nigeria 1983. Sunday Concord Jan. 8 (1984).

983. Ciira, Wanjiru. Film bonanza in Kenya. Weekly Review 607(1986):46.

Film festival supported by FEPACI.

984. Ciira, Wanjiru. Is Kenya ready to go into film production? Weekly Review 544(1985):13.

Activities of Kenya Film Corporation.

985. Ciira, Wanjiru. Too many stereotypes. Weekly Review 607(1986):47. (R)

Sao Gamba, Kolormask.

986. Ciment, Michel. Concerto pour un exil. Entretien avec Désiré Ecaré. Positif 97(1968):32-36. (I)

987. Ciment, Michel. Le Dieu, le diable et les fusils. Positif 84(1967):25-32. (R)

Ruy Guerra, Os fuzis.

988. Ciment, Michel. Entretien avec Ruy Guerra. Positif 116(1970):33-42. (I)

989. Ciment, Michel. Mandabi (Le mandat). Positif 100-101(1968-1969):45. (R)

990. Ciment, Michel. Ruy Guerra, in Ian Cameron et al. Second Wave. New York: Praeger, 1970. pp. 99-109.

Discussion of Guerra's films in context of cinema novo.

991. Ciment, Michel and Jacques Demeure. Entretien avec Ruy Guerra. Positif 123(1971):3-9. (I)

Discussion of Sweet Hunters.

992. Ciment, Michel and Paul-Louis Thirard.    Entretien avec Med Hondo.
      Positif 119(1970):22-26.  (I)

      Discussion of Hondo's acting, problems of making Soleil O and
      style of African films.

993. Ciment, Michel, François Maurin, Albert Cervoni and Gérard
      Langlois.  Ruy Guerra, êtes-vous un tendre?  Avant-Scène-Cinéma
      112(1971):9-38.

      Comments on and script of Sweet Hunters.

994. Cine Cubano.    La influencia del cine mudo sovietico en los
      cineastas africanos.  Cine Cubano 93(1979):14-16.  (R)

      Sembène Ousmane, Ceddo.

995. Cinéma Québec.    Le cinéma africain en 1974: longue marche et
      grandes manoeuvres.  Cinéma Québec 3, 9-10(1973):46-48.

      Themes.

996. Cinéma Québec.    Problematique du cinéaste africain: l'artiste et
      la révolution.  Cinéma Québec 3, 9-10(1973) special issue.

997. Cinespectadora.    Cinema  activo  contra  o  racismo  pela
      solidaridade.  Domingo (Maputo) May 9 (1982):13.

      Themes of Mocambiquan and Angolan films.

998. Cissé, A.S.  On prend trop de "libertés" au Liberté.  Le Soleil
      Apr. 17 (1977):4.

      SIDEC.

999. Cissé, Ben.  Barry Adboulaye: la jeunesse turbulent.  Bingo
      399(1986):55.  (I)

      Côte d'Ivoire actor in television films discusses his roles and
      views of films.

1000. Cissé, Lanciné O.  Le IX Festival de Tachkent.  Fonike Magazine
      6(1986):25-26.

      History of Tashkent film festival; African films shown.

1001. Cissé-Koné, Awa.  Dans la capitale du cinéma africain.  Balafon
      64(1984):22-25.

      FESPACO.

1002. Cissoko, Véronique.  Le premier César Nègre.  Jeune Afrique
      1369(1987):48-50.  (I)

Issach Bankolé, Côte d'Ivoire actor, discusses his career.

1003. Clarke, Robert H. and Cynthia Grant Shoenberger. Filming the African revolution. International Development Review 18, 2(1976):28-31. (R)

Nana Mahomo, Last Grave at Dimbaza and Sarah Maldoror, Sambizanga.

1004. Cluny, Claude Michel. A chacun ses urgences. Cinéma 242 (1979):62-64.

J.C.C.

1005. Cluny, Claude Michel. Cinéma africain: le festival de Ouagadougou. Cinéma 72 165(1972):36-42.

FESPACO. Short reviews of some films shown.

1006. Cluny, Claude Michel. Ouagadougou, un cinéma africain libre s'affirme. Cinéma 73 175(1973):22-25.

FESPACO.

1007. Cluny, Claude Michel. 4ème Festival de Ouagadougou, l'Afrique se délivre de ses conventions. Afrique-Asie 26(1973):45-47.

1008. Cluny, Claude Michel. Victoire d'un cinéma de combat. Cinéma 75 194(1975):92-96.

J.C.C.

1009. Coad, Malcolm. Ousmane Sembène and Ceddo. Index on Censorship 10,4(1981):32-33.

Censorship in Senegal.

1010. Cohn, Bernard. Soleil O. Positif 119(1970):18-20. (R)

1011. Collins, John. A wealth of film. West Africa 3513(1984):2585-2586. (I)

Interview with Haruna Attah about Ghana film archive.

1012. Collombet, Boris. Ablakon. Cinéma 377(1986):3. (R)

1013. Combs, Richard. Jodorowsky's carnival of cruelty. Times (London) Oct. 26 (1973):15. (R)

Sembène Ousmane, Mandabi.

1014. Comité. "Lamb" un film de luttes sénégalais et "Le train sifflera trois fois." Dakar Matin Feb. 23 (1965):3.

Vieyra's film to be shown at film club in Dakar.

1015. Comte, Phillippe. "Pousse-Pousse" de Daniel Kamwa. <u>L'Union</u> Oct. 3 (1975):7. (R)

1016. Condé, Maryse. Maldoror change de veste. <u>Afrique</u> 47(1981):47. (R)

<u>Un</u> <u>dessert</u> <u>pour</u> <u>Constance</u>.

1017. Condé, Maryse. Med Hondo ouvre une ère nouvelle. <u>Demain</u> <u>l'Afrique</u> 33-34(1979):72-74.

1018. Condé, Maryse. Politique et póetique "Bako,l'autre rive." <u>Demain</u> <u>l'Afrique</u> 19(1979):11. (R)

1019. Condé, Maryse. Portrait flash Jean-Claude Courrent réalisateur. <u>Africascope</u> (Paris) 11(1971):51. (I)

Problems of making films about Africa.

1020. Condé, Maryse. Quatre siècles d'oppression. <u>Demain</u> <u>l'Afrique</u> 22(1979):68-70. (R)

Med Hondo, <u>West</u> <u>Indies</u>.

1021. Condé, Maryse. Souleymane Cissé le coup d'oeil... <u>Demain</u> <u>l'Afrique</u> 11(1978):84-85.

<u>Baara</u>.

1022. Condé, Maryse. "Les tams tams se sont tus" un film de Philippe Mory. <u>Bingo</u> 232(1972):82-83. (I)

Mory discusses his film.

1023. Condé, Maryse. La tentation de l'occident. <u>Bingo</u> 232(1972):83-84. (R)

Philippe Mory, <u>Les</u> <u>tams</u> <u>tams</u> <u>se</u> <u>sont</u> <u>tus</u>.

1024. Conference episcopale de la ouest afrique francophone. Les crétiens et le cinéma. <u>Unir</u> 16(1970):4-5.

Selections from declarations on film regarding need for authentic African films, theaters and financial support.

1025. Congo, Eric. Djim Kola: le cinéma voltaique en crise. <u>Carrefour</u> <u>Africain</u> 710-711(1981):3. (I)

1026. Conseil d'administration. "Thiaroye 44" sera réalisé. <u>Le</u> <u>Soleil</u> Feb. 14 (1986):9.

Reasons why filming of <u>Camp</u> <u>de</u> <u>Thiaroye</u> suspended.

1027. Cook, Allen. Filming the victory over barbarity. <u>Third</u> <u>World</u>
<u>Book</u> <u>Review</u> 2, 1-2(1986):106. (R)

Barry Feinberg, <u>Anvil</u> <u>and</u> <u>the</u> <u>Hammer</u>.

1028. Copans, Jean. Contrepoint: Ceddo entre l'histoire et les mythes.
<u>Afrique</u> <u>Littéraire</u> 76(1985):57-59; <u>CinémAction</u> 34(1985):57-59.
(R)

1029. Copans, Jean. Non à ethnocinéma! <u>Afrique-Asie</u> 154(1978):48-49.

Ideology of Sembène and other West African filmmakers.

1030. Coq, Peter de. Mandabi. <u>Afrika</u> <u>Heute</u> 8(1973):46. (R)

1031. Correa, Edom. Le jeune cinéma africain a l'honneur du Ciné-Club
avec Vieyra et Sembène. <u>Dakar</u> <u>Matin</u> May 12 (1965):3.

Film club in Dakar shows <u>Niaye</u>, <u>Borom</u> <u>Sarret</u> and <u>Lamb</u>.

1032. Correa, Marie-Rose, Bernard Assanvo and Venance Bouhina. A
propos de quelques films africains. <u>Revue</u> <u>africaine</u> <u>de</u>
<u>communication</u> 5(1984):43-45. (R)

Cheick Ngaido Ba, <u>Xew</u> <u>Xew</u>; Jean-Louis Koula, <u>Pétanqui</u>; and Momar
Thiam, <u>Sa</u> <u>Dagga</u>.

1033. Correspondent. African cinema in London. <u>West</u> <u>Africa</u>
2923(1973):801.

Themes of films shown in London.

1034. Correspondent. Beirut hosting French language film festival.
<u>New</u> <u>Nigerian</u> Sept. 5 (1973):16.

FIFEF.

1035. Correspondent. The birth of the Volta cinema. <u>New</u> <u>Nigerian</u> Apr.
4 (1973):12.

Pierre-Marie Dong, <u>Identité</u> and Djim Kola, <u>Sang</u> <u>des</u> <u>parias</u>.

1036. Correspondent. Cameroun seen through an exile's eyes. <u>New</u>
<u>Nigerian</u> Sept. 12 (1973):15. (R)

Urbain Dia-Moukouri, <u>Soleil</u> <u>d'avril</u>.

1037. Correspondent. Controversy over Senegal film. <u>West</u> <u>Africa</u>
3248(1979):1881. (R)

Sembène Ousmane, <u>Ceddo</u>.

1038. Correspondent.  Developing Africa's cinema.  <u>West</u> <u>Africa</u>
3358(1981):2911-2914.

Souleymane Cissé, <u>Baara</u>.

1039. Correspondent.  Festival debates cinema's future.  <u>New</u> <u>Nigerian</u>
Apr. 10 (1976) Saturday extra, pp. 2-3.

FESPACO, discussion of future of African film.

1040. Correspondent.  Film art and monetary profit.  <u>West</u> <u>Africa</u>
3277(1980):828-829. (I)

Ola Balogun discusses <u>Ajani</u> <u>Ogun</u>.

1041. Correspondent.  Films out of Cameroon.  <u>West</u> <u>Africa</u>
3212(1979):207.

Films by Jean-Pierre Dikongue-Pipa, Daniel Kamwa, Philip Moumie
and Sab Stephens.

1042. Correspondent. Kongi on film. <u>West</u> <u>Africa</u> 2775(1970):950. (R)

Francis Oladele, <u>Kongi's</u> <u>Harvest</u>.

1043. Correspondent. Laments of a wasted generation. <u>National</u> <u>Concord</u>
5,1523(1985):5.  (R)

Wole Soyinka, <u>Blues</u> <u>for</u> <u>a</u> <u>Prodigal</u>.

1044. Correspondent.  Mali's first colour film ready shortly.  <u>New</u>
<u>Nigerian</u> Nov. 16 (1974) Saturday extra p.3. (R)

Alkaly Kaba, <u>Walanda</u>.

1045. Correspondent.  Med Hondo: film-maker.  <u>West</u> <u>Africa</u>
3434(1983):1348-1349.

1046. Correspondent.  Political cinema.  <u>West</u> <u>Africa</u> 2926(1973):911.

Themes of West African films.

1047. Correspondent.  Relevant love story out of Ghana.  <u>West</u> <u>Africa</u>
3277(1980):824-825. (R)

Kwaw Ansah, <u>Love</u> <u>Brewed</u> <u>in</u> <u>the</u> <u>African</u> <u>Pot</u>.

1048. Correspondent.  School for African TV producers.  <u>West</u> <u>Africa</u>
3211(1979):159-160.

West German assistance for training television filmmakers and
actors in Ghana.

1049. Correspondent.  Taiwo Ajai-actress with eyes on Nigeria.  <u>New</u>

Nigerian Jan. 9 (1974):12.

1050. Correspondent. Xala, by Sembène Ousmane. West Africa 3099(1976):1748. (R)

1051. Correspondent à Bamako. Le premier film malien. Jeune Afrique 433(1969):37. (R)

Bambo.

1052. Correspondent à Dakar. Traoré ne manque pas de culot. Jeune Afrique 439(1969):51. (R)

Mahama Johnson Traoré, Diankha-Bi.

1053. Costandoni, Gian Carlo. Vento maliano. Nigrizia 102,1(1984):44. (R)

Souleymane Cissé, Finyé.

1054. Coulibaly, Abdou Latif. Ouaga et Carthage au pays de l'hiver. Le Soleil May 5 (1987):10.

Canadian festival of African films, comments on films shown.

1055. Coulibaly, Abdou Latif. ...Senegal une présence plutôt discrète. Le Soleil May 5 (1987):10.

Senegalese films shown at Canadian festival of African films.

1056. Coulibaly, Ibrahim Brin. Duel sur les falaises. Bingo 390 (1985):57. (R)

1057. Courant, Gérard. Fad, jal. Cinéma 247-248(1979):27. (R)

1058. Courrier de Saint-Ex. Le cinéma: un art, une technique. Le Courrier de Saint-Ex. 11(1978):3; 13(1979):3.

Development of filmmaking in Gabon.

1059. Courrier de Saint-Ex. Entretien avec Pierre-Marie Dong. Le Courrier de Saint-Ex 17(1979):6. (I)

Discussion of development of filmmaking in Gabon and Dong's philosophy of filmmaking.

1060. Courrier de Saint-Ex. Entretien avec Simon Augé. Le Courrier de Saint-Ex 17(1979):5. (I)

Discussion of roles of African filmmakers, kinds of films that should be made.

1061. Courrier de Saint-Ex. Huit ans de cinéma gabonais. Le Courrier de Saint-Ex 17(1979):2-3.

Discussion of 8 films made in Gabon and excerpts from reviews of them.

1062. Couturon, Janine. Le dixième festival du cinéma africain de Ouagadougou: la prise de conscience. Aujourd'hui l'Afrique 34(1987):21-22.

1063. Craig, Patricia. Not like that. Times Literary Supplement Dec. 4 (1981):1417. (R)

Michael Raeburn, The Grass Is Singing.

1064. Crane, Louise. Entertainment films and video in Africa. Update (Urbana) nd [Feb. 1987]:5-8.

Short history of African film since 1960s. Major themes of films.

1065. Crowdus, Gary. Un cinéaste noir en exil: Lionel Ngakane. L'Afrique littéraire 78(1986):99. (I)

Discussion of Ngakane's films and ANC film unit in Lusaka.

1066. Crowdus, Gary. South African filmmaking in exile, an interview with Lionel Ngakane. Cinéaste 15,2(1986):16-17. (I)

Translation of No. 1065.

1067. Crowdus, Gary and Marvis Broullon. Cinema in Africa must be a school. Cinéaste 6,1(1973):32-35. (I)

Interview with Mahama Johnson Traoré.

1068. Cyclope. Baks de Momar Thiam. Le Solel Feb. 13 (1975):8. (R)

1069. Cyclope. Le cyclope a vu Diègue-Bi. Le Soleil Apr. 15 (1971):2. (R)

Mahama Johnson Traoré, Diègue Bi.

1070. Cyclope. Le cyclope a vu Njangaan. Le Soleil May 5 (1975):2. (R)

Mahama Johnson Traoré, Njangaan.

1071. Cyclope. Le cyclope a vu Sikasso à Sorano. Le Soleil May 22 (1975):6. (R)

1072. Cyclope. Le cyclope a vu Touki Bouki. Le Soleil Apr. 24 (1975):8. (R)

1073. Cyclope. Xala rut barre d'Ousmane Sembène. Le Soleil Feb. 27 (1975):11. (R)

1074. Cyr, Helen W. Filmography of the Third World. Metuchen, N.J.:Scarecrow Press, 1976 pp. 11,15,19,21,24,35,226,229,255.

Films by Ruy Guerra, Med Hondo, Sarah Maldoror, Sembène Ousmane and Mahama Johnson Traoré.

1075. Cyr, Helen W. Filmography of the Third World 1976-1983. Metuchen, N.J.:Scarecrow Press, 1985. pp. 27,29,31.

Kongi's Harvest, Last Grave at Dimbaza and Njangaan.

1076. D, J-L. "Djéli" vu par "sud-ouest." Fraternité Matin 5109(1981):11. (R)

1077. D.B. Djéli ou contes d'aujourd'hui. Ivoire Dimanche 487(1980):39. (R)

1078. D.B. La municipalité ferme le cinéma "l'Oguoué." L'Union Mar. 2 (1983):2.

Theater closed in Gabon.

1079. D.B. Les responsables de média africains chez le président du Faso. Sidwaya Feb. 25 (1987):7.

Review of activities of URTNA which has been invited to participate in FESPACO.

1080. Dabia, Amévi. L'Afrique au festival de moscou. Afrique Nouvelle 1882(1985):21.

Moscow film festival.

1081. Dabia, Amévi. l'OAU et le cinéma. Afrique Nouvelle 1883(1985):18.

OAU support of African film.

1082. Dabia, Amévi. Pétanqui: corrompu ou corrupteur. Afrique Nouvelle 1813(1984):19. (R)

1083. Dabia, Amévi. Pour une production africaine rentable. Film échange 23(1983):45-54.

Distribution and production of film. Brief review of all agencies involved.

1084. Dabia, Amévi. Week-ends du cinéma africain. Afrique Nouvelle 1858(1985):16-17.

African films shown in Togo.

1085. Dadson, Nanabanyin. African films come of age. AfricAsia

41(1987):59.

Film week in Nairobi December 1986.

1086. Dadson, Nanabanyin.   The bad old days.   West Africa Aug. 31
(1987):1693-1694.   (R)

Kwaw Ansah, Heritage.

1087. Dadson, Nanabanyin.   Ghana: Herzog and the Amazons.   AfricAsia
40(1987):56-67.

Ghanaian-German coproductions and new films by Kwaw Ansah.

1088. Dadson, Nanabanyin.   A positive view of Africa.   African Concord
141(1987):50.   (R)

Cobra Verde, Ghanaian-German coproduction.

1089. Dadson, Nanabanyin.   Production and co-production.   West Africa
3616(1986):2649-2650.

King Ampaw, Nana Akoto, shown on West German television.
Coproduction as solution to problem of financing films.

1090. Dagron, Alfonso Gumucio.   Cinéma du Mozambique.   Afrique-Asie
150(1977):61-63.

Films about FRELIMO, colonial films about Mocambique,
organization of INC and films made by INC.

1091. Dahmani, Abdelaziz.   Samory ou le couronnement.   Jeune Afrique
1045(1981):68.

Plans for making Samory by Sembène Ousmane.

1092. Daily Times.   African films at Tashkent fair.   Daily Times
(Lagos) June 14 (1984):8.

1093. Daily Times.   Agreement signed on filming of Kongi's Harvest.
Daily Times (Lagos) Aug. 26 (1969):6.

Difficulties in completing filmscript and involving Calpenny
Films.   Hopes for future coproductions.

1094. Daily Times.   Blues for a prodigal.   Daily Times (Lagos) Jan. 3
(1985):18.   (R)

1095. Daily Times.   Film corporation for Nigeria soon.   Daily Times
(Lagos) June 14 (1976):2.

Planned expansion of Federal Film Unit for producing films.

1096. Daily Times.   Film festival opens today.   Daily Times (Lagos)

Dec. 28 (1985):2.

Film week at National Arts Theater, Nigeria.

1097. Daily Times. Film review panel submits report. Daily Times (Lagos) Jan. 8 (1985):13.

Nigeria.

1098. Daily Times. Firms told to back the film industry. Daily Times (Lagos) Dec. 20 (1985):24.

Nigerian business asked to support film industry.

1099. Daily Times. Nigerian film festival in London. Daily Times (Lagos) Dec. 13 (1984):26.

Themes of films shown.

1100. Daily Times. Nigeria's film industry. Daily Times (Lagos) Sept. 23 (1986):8.

Ideals for support of filmmaking and content of films.

1101. Daily Times. The return of money power. Daily Times (Lagos) Dec. 22 (1984):5. (R)

Ola Balogun, Money Power.

1102. Daily Times. Why impact of films is limited. Daily Times (Lagos) Dec. 21 (1985):24.

Film Makers Association of Nigeria.

1103. Daja, Allarabaye. Carthage. Unir Cinéma 15(1984):7-11.

J.C.C.

1104. Daja, Allarabaye. Effervescence dans le cinéma sénégalais. Unir Cinéma 20-21(1985):31-32.

Activities of SNPC since 1984.

1105. Daja, Allarabaye. Entretien avec Idrissa Ouédraogo. Unir Cinéma 18(1985):6-9. (I)

Discussion of Issa le tisserand.

1106. Daja, Allarabaye. Entretien avec Mbala. Unir Cinéma 20-21(1985):9-12. (I)

Roger Gnoan Mbala discusses Ablakon, SIDEC, FEPACI and Ivorian government support of filmmaking.

1107.  Daja, Allarabaye.  FEPACI-FESPACO: la fête de la réconciliation.
       Unir Cinéma 16(1985):4.

1108.  Daja, Allarabaye and Martin Faye.  La parole aux cinéastes
       sénégalais.  Unir Cinéma 22(1986):3-14.

       Discussion about contributions of Fidele Dimé, Bara Diokhane,
       Serigne Ndiaye Gonzales, Joseph Sane and Momar Thiam to
       Senegalese filmmaking.

1109.  Dakar Matin.  A la grande quinzaine d'Alger, le cinéma africain
       démontre sa vitalité et la qualité de ses réalisateurs.  Dakar
       Matin July 31 (1969):6.

       Algiers film festival.

1110.  Dakar Matin.  A 7 km de Tivaouane, Ousmane Sembène tourne son
       nouveau film: "Véhe Thiossane."  Dakar Matin Dec. 21 (1964):6.

       Sembène Ousmane, Niaye.

1111.  Dakar, Matin.  Abdoulaye Faye, vedette du film "Un coeur gros
       comme ça" vient de publier "Le Débrouillard."  Dakar Matin Apr. 16
       (1964):3.

       Senegalese actor.

1112.  Dakar Matin.  L'Afrique au festival.  Dakar Matin Aug. 13
       (1969):4.

       Oumarou Ganda, Cabascabo, shown at Cannes film festival.

1113.  Dakar Matin.  Au festival du film d'expression française à
       Dinard.  Dakar Matin July 4 (1969):2.

       18 African films to be shown at FIFEF.

1114.  Dakar Matin.  Au "Lagon", un cliente anonyme: M'Bissine Diop, la
       vedette du nouveau film de Ousmane Sembène.  Dakar Matin Dec. 7
       (1965):3.

       Actress to play lead role in Sembène Ousmane, La Noire de.

1115.  Dakar Matin.  Ce soir le ciné-club de Dakar présente "La noire
       de" et "Et la neige n'était plus."  Dakar Matin Jan. 19 (1968):2.

       Dakar film club to give support to new Senegalese films.

1116.  Dakar Matin.  Le ciné club de Dakar reprend ses activitiés.
       Dakar Matin Nov. 3 (1967):3.

       Dakar film club membership regulations and list of forthcoming
       film programs.

1117.  Dakar Matin.  Un cinéaste qui croit encore a quelque chose: Sembène Ousmane.  Dakar Matin Aug. 15-16 (1966):5.

Discussion of Borom Sarret and Niaye.

1118.  Dakar Matin.  Les cinéastes sénégalais a l'honneur.  Dakar Matin Jan. 16 (1969):3.

Senegalese at Tashkent film festival.

1119.  Dakar Matin.  Le cinéma africain à l'honneur au Festival de Tours.  Dakar Matin Feb. 5 (1966):5.  (I)

Sembène Ousmane, Niaye, awarded prize at Tours film festival, different responses of African and European audiences.

1120.  Dakar Matin.  Le cinéma africain et la critique.  Dakar Matin Sept. 6 (1969):4.

African films shown at Algiers film festival.

1121.  Dakar Matin.  Cinéma africain et Malgache.  Dakar Matin Mar. 23 (1968):6.

African films shown in Chad for 3 weeks, sponsored by Ministry of Information.

1122.  Dakar Matin.  "Le cinéma doit être entièrement au service de la paix," a déclaré l'artiste sénégalaise Thérèse Diop.  Dakar Matin Aug. 7 (1969):6.  (I)

Mbissine Diop, Senegalese actress, interviewed at Moscow film festival, comments on African films shown in Moscow and film development in Senegal.

1123.  Dakar Matin.  "Le cinéma semble être le mode d'expression idéal pour rapprocher des hommes ayant en commun la langue francaise" a déclaré M. Yvon Bourges.  Dakar Matin July 8 (1969):6.

Senegalese participation in FIFEF.

1124.  Dakar Matin. 50 des 70 films annoncés sont déja parvenus à la section cinéma.  Dakar Matin Mar. 10 (1966):3.

FESTAC.  Films sent for competition, list of prizes to be given.

1125.  Dakar Matin.  "Concerto pour un exil" de Désiré Ecaré.  Dakar Matin Sept. 10 (1968):4.  (R)

1126.  Dakar Matin.  Deux films africains "Concerto pour un exil" et "Cabascabo."  Dakar Matin Nov. 6 (1969):6.  (R)

1127.  Dakar Matin.  Deux metteurs en scène africains.  Dakar Matin Jan. 2 (1969):6.

Jean Paul Ngassa and Moustapha Alassane, biographical background and films made.

1128. Dakar Matin. Djibril Diop vient de terminer le tournage de son film "Badou Boy." Dakar Matin Jan. 21 (1970):3. (I)

Discussion of making film, actors, and differences in two versions of the film.

1129. Dakar Matin. "Et la neige n'était plus" court métrage sénégalais présenté à Venise. Dakar Matin Sept. 5 (1966):3. (R)

1130. Dakar Matin. "Et la neige n'était plus" en cours de tournage par le jeune cinéaste Ababacar Samb. Dakar Matin May 14 (1965):3. (R)

Includes biographical information on Samb.

1131. Dakar Matin. L'exile et la mort, thème d'un film camerounais. Dakar Matin. Jan. 16 (1968):6. (R)

Urbain Dia-Moukouri, Fleur dans le sang.

1132. Dakar Matin. Festival Culturel Panafricain: avis aux cinéastes sénégalais. Dakar Matin May 23 (1969):1.

Senegalese participation in Algiers film festival.

1133. Dakar Matin. Le Festival de Madagascar du cinéma africain et Malgache. Dakar Matin May 24 (1965):4.

African and French films shown in Madagascar.

1134. Dakar Matin. Le Festival de Moscou ouvert par La Noire de... Dakar Matin Aug. 7 (1967):6.

1135. Dakar Matin. Un film en langue Djerma, Cabascado (sic). Dakar Matin June 6 (1969):4. (R)

Background on Oumarou Ganda included in review.

1136. Dakar Matin. Les films sélectionnés pour le Grand Prix au Cinéma. Dakar Matin Mar. 31 (1966):5.

FESTAC prizes.

1137. Dakar Matin. Les grands prix du cinéma du festival décernés hier. Dakar Matin Apr. 6 (1966):1.

Same information as No. 1136, but films organized by type.

1138. Dakar Matin. Johnson Traoré grand prix du Festival du film de Dinard de retour à Dakar. Dakar Matin Sept. 22 (1969):1.

FIFEF prize to Mahama Johnson Traoré, Diankha-Bi.

1139.   Dakar Matin.   Journées d'études du cinéma africain et malgache à
Fort-Lamy.   Dakar Matin Mar. 1 (1968):4.

Same article as No. 1121.

1140.   Dakar Matin.   Un livre de Paulin Vieyra, le doyen des cinéastes
africains: "Le cinéma et l'Afrique."   Dakar Matin Apr. 13
(1970):6.   (BR)

Review includes information about Vieyra's filmmaking.   See No.
76.

1141.   Dakar Matin.   "Mandabi" de Sembène Ousmane est le premier
long-métrage africain parlant oulouf.   Dakar Matin Nov. 8
(1968):6.   (I)

1142.   Dakar Matin.   Momar Thiam "La malle de Maka Kouli."   Dakar Matin
Nov. 8 (1969):6.   (R)

1143.   Dakar Matin.   Niaye de Sembène Ousmane.   Dakar Matin July 9
(1965):4.   (R)

1144.   Dakar Matin.   11 films sénégalais au festival.   Dakar Matin Mar.
30 (1966):4.

Senegalese films shown at FESTAC.

1145.   Dakar Matin.   Panorama de l'action cinématogrpahique au titre de
la coopération.   Dakar Matin Mar. 13 (1968):6.

Support for film production by Centre National Francais du
Cinéma.

1146.   Dakar Matin.   Pour le cinéaste sénégalais Sembène Ousmane le
cinéma est un moyen d'action.   Dakar Matin Jan. 23 (1970):6.

Summary of interview in No. 1866.

1147.   Dakar Matin.   Le primière société cinématographique la
Calpenny-Nigeria films.   Dakar Matin Apr. 15 (1970):6.

Plans for making Kongi's Harvest.

1148.   Dakar Matin.   Le semaine du cinéma africain au Centre Brottier.
Dakar Matin Jan. 16 (1967):2.

Films by Moustapha Alassane, Ababacar Samb and Sembène Ousmane to
be shown in Dakar.   See No. 416.

1149.   Dakar Matin.   Sembène Ousmane: "Le Mandat."   Dakar Matin Jan. 6
(1969):6.   (R)

1150. Dakar Matin. Le Sénégal au Festival de Venise. Dakar Matin Oct. 1 (1966):4. (R)

Same article as No. 1129.

1151. Dakar Matin. Le Sénégal participera au 11e festival international des tournées cinématographiques de Carthage. Dakar Matin Oct. 9 (1968):2.

Senegalese filmmakers and actors at J.C.C.

1152. Dakar Matin. Le sénégalais Johnson Traoré remporte le Grand Prix du Festival de Dinard avec le film "Diankha-Bi." Dakar Matin July 12 (1969):1.

FIFEF.

1153. Dakar Matin. Septième table ronde sur le cinéma africain. Dakar Matin Sept. 23 (1969):6.

Discussion on production, distribution and ideology at Venice film festival.

1154. Dakar Matin. Timiti Bassory: "La dune de la solitude." Dakar Matin Dec. 28 (1967):6.

1155. Damani, Shiraz. African autumn festival 77. Afrika 18, 12(1977):22-23.

Bochum film festival.

1156. Damassi, Ismaël. Au cinéma "Le Woleu" des réparations améliorent la qualité du son et de l'image. L'Union 1550(1981):2.

Films by Joseph Etoundi shown in Cameroun.

1157. Damiba, Béatrice. Les mailles de l'organisation. Carrefour Africain 766(1983):17.

FESPACO.

1158. Daney, Serge. Ceddo. Cahiers du Cinéma 304(1979):51-53. (R)

1159. Daney, Serge and Jean-Pierre Oudart. Entretien avec Sidney Sokhona. Cahiers du Cinéma. 285(1978):48-54. (I)

Discussion of Safrana, militant films, use of tradition in films, making films in France.

1160. Dare, Segun. Film review: Chinua Achebe's "Things Fall Apart." New Nigerian May 26 (1979) Saturday extra pp. 2-3. (R)

Francis Oladele, Bullfrog in the Sun.

1161. Datche, Simplice. La Côte d'Ivoire a l'honneur. <u>Ivoire</u> <u>Dimanche</u> 368(1978):36.

Roger Gnoan-Mbala, <u>Le</u> <u>chapeau</u> and Cissoko Moussa and Paul Doumerc <u>Village,</u> <u>villageois,</u> <u>cantons.</u>

1162. Davay, P. Ayouma. <u>Revue</u> <u>Belge</u> <u>du</u> <u>Cinéma</u> 11(1978):37. (R)

1163. Davay, P. Baara. <u>Revue</u> <u>Belge</u> <u>du</u> <u>Cinéma</u> 11(1978):18-19. (R)

1164. David, Colette. La danse, langage universal. <u>Jeune</u> <u>Afrique</u> 1094(1981):61.

Trois Continents film festival.

1165. David, Colette. Regards sur le Tiers Monde. <u>Jeune</u> <u>Afrique</u> 1042(1980):97.

Trois Continents film festival.

1166. Davier, Joseph. Film im Kongo. <u>Afrika</u> <u>Heute</u> 20(1970):359. (I)

Translation of article from <u>Tribune</u> <u>Africaine</u> (Kinshasa).

1167. Davis, Elliot. The making of Harvest. <u>Filmmakers</u> <u>Newsletter</u> 8, 6(1975):18-19, 38.

Haile Gerima, <u>Harvest</u> <u>3000</u> <u>Years.</u>

1168. Davis, Ossie. When is a camera a weapon? <u>New</u> <u>York</u> <u>Times</u> Sept. 20 (1970):II 17, 24.

Francis Oladele's experiences in making <u>Kongi's</u> <u>Harvest.</u>

1169. Deboste, Michel. "Les coopérants" ou les limites du dialogue nord-sud. <u>Africa</u> (Dakar) 158(1984):79-80. (R)

1170. Débrix, Jean Réné. Le cinéma africain. <u>Afrique</u> <u>Contemporaine</u> 38-39(1968):7-12.

Short history including colonial films and African-made films.

1171. Débrix, Jean Réné. Le cinéma africain. <u>Afrique</u> <u>Contemporaine</u> 40(1968):2-6.

Distribution, theaters.

1172. Débrix, Jean Réné. Dix ans de coopération Franco-Africaine ont permis la naissance du cinéma d'Afrique noire. <u>Sentiers</u> 43(1973):13-19.

French aid to African filmmaking 1962-1972.

1173. Débrix, Jean Réné. Le Festival cinématographique de Carthage. Coopération et développement 44(1973):40-46.

1174. Débrix, Jean Réné. Die Geburtshilfe Frankreichs für den Film in Schwarzafrika. Afrika Heute supp. to 19(1971):19-22.

   Support for film production. Review of recently made films.

1175. Débrix, Jean Réné. La quinzaine nigérienne de cinéma. Recherche, pédagogie et culture 17-18(1975):54-55.

1176. Débrix, Jean Réné. Sous le signe de la coopération cinématographe: naissance d'un cinéma négro-africain. Coopération et développement 29(1970):16-23.

   Problems of filmmaking. Experimental films.

1177. Dékou, Abotsi. Une semaine du cinéma africain. Afrique Nouvelle 1460(1977):16-17.

   African film week in Dakar.

1178. Delati, Abdou Achouba. Ecran 74. Recherche, pédagogie et culture 17-18(1975):46,64. (I)

   Interview with Med Hondo.

1179. Delati, Abdou Achouba. Mahama Johnson Traoré sur la voie d'une éthique négro-africaine. Cinéma 75 194(1975):92-96.

1180. Delcroix, Jacqueline. Prima visione. Nigrizia 100, 10(1982):18-20.

   Themes of films.

1181. Delcroix, Jacqueline. "West Indies." Nigrizia 99, 4(1981):40. (R)

1182. Delmas, Jean. La condition ouvrière, Turquie, Mali, Vénézuela. Jeune Cinéma 119(1979):10-14. (R)

   Souleymane Cissé, Baara.

1183. Delmas, Jean. Med Hondo: Soleil O. Jeune Cinéma 48(1970):32-38. (I)

1184. Delmas, Jean. Muna Moto. Jeune Cinéma 99(1976-1977):18-19. (R)

1185. Delmas, Jean. La noire de... Jeune Cinéma 22 (1967):20-22. (R)

1186. Delmas, Jean. Ousmane Sembène: "Un film est un débat." Jeune Cinéma 99(1976-1977):13-17. (I)

   Discussion of Xala.

1187. Delmas, Jean. Situation du cinéma d'Afrique noire. Jeune Cinéma 99(1976-1977):1-2.

1188. Delmas, Jean. Le tiers monde à Cannes. Jeune Cinéma 96(1976):39-41. (R)

Haile Gerima, Harvest 3000 Years.

1189. Delmas, Jean. Xala. Jeune Cinéma 93(1976):30-32. (R)

1190. Delmas, Jean and Ginette Delmas. Mahama Traoré... "au service du peuple." Jeune Cinéma 99(1976-1977):3-7. (I)

Discussion of N'Diangane.

1191. Delorme, Christine. "Certificat d'indigence" de Moussa Bathily. Afrique-Asie 306(1983):55-56. (I)

1192. Delorme, Christine. Mory Traoré, "Homme d'ailleurs?" Afrique-Asie 316(1984):56. (I)

1193. Demeure, Jacques. Pour un réalisme magique. Positif 123(1971):10-13. (R)

Ruy Guerra, Os Deuses e os mortos.

1194. Deschler, Hans P. An African film school? Educational Broadcasting International 9,4(1976):175-177.

Kenya Institute of Mass Communications.

1195. Deschler, Hans P. Film training in Kenya. Educational Broadcasting International 13,3(1980):149-151.

1196. De Smedt, Thierry and Ndianga Moctar Ba. Les éléments sonores, in Caméra Nigra. C.E.S.C.A. ed. Brussels: OCIC, 1984. pp. 187-213.

Sound in Moussa Yoro Bathily, Certificat d'indigence.

1197. Desouches, Dominique. Le cinéma en Côte d'Ivoire. Eburnea 48(1971):36-39.

Production, distribution.

1198. Devin, Jean. A Senegalese film and French-Algerian cooperation. Young Cinema and Theater 2(1969):26-27. (R)

Sembène Ousmane, Mandabi.

1199. Dhab, Nefla. L'éternel refrain. SeptièmArt 52(1984):30-31.

Financial problems of filmmakers.

1200. Dia, Alioune Touré. The African film is true to itself. <u>Afrika</u>
22,2-3(1981):40-41. (I)

Oumarou Ganda discusses filmmaking in Niger.

1201. Dia, Alioune Touré. La dernier grande oeuvre de Sembène Ousmane.
<u>Bingo</u> 406(1986):52-57. (I)

Plans for making <u>Samory</u>.

1202. Dia, Alioune Touré. La grandeur de Dieu. <u>Bingo</u> 335(1980):77.
(I)

Akhya Alpha Dia discusses <u>Allahou</u> <u>Akbar</u>.

1203. Dia, Alioune Touré. "Jom" ou la dignité. <u>Bingo</u> 333(1980):58-59.
(I)

Ababacar Samb-Makharam discusses <u>Jom</u>.

1204. Dia, Alioune Touré. Shadows over Senegalese screens? <u>Afrika</u>
24,1(1983):24-26.

1205. Dia, Alioune Touré. Threats to African cinema. <u>Afrika</u>
23,1(1982):25.

Problems of distribution, financing and banal themes.

1206. Dia, M. Un prix pour Touki Bouky? <u>Le</u> <u>Soleil</u> Apr. 22 (1975):2.
(R)

1207. Dia, Mam Less. Des films sénégalais que nous voulons voir. <u>Le</u>
<u>Soleil</u> Oct. 22 (1974):2.

Activities of SNC and SIDEC.

1208. Dia, Mam Less. Entretien avec Doura Mané, "Je reviens sur la
scène cette année." <u>Le</u> <u>Soleil</u> Jan. 31 (1975):3. (I)

Mané discusses his acting in theater and film.

1209. Dia, Mam Less. Notre étoile cesse de brille à Carthage. <u>Le</u>
<u>Soleil</u> Nov. 7 (1974):4.

J.C.C. prizes since 1966.

1210. Dia, Mouhamadou M. "Bako": de Jacques Champreux, la calvaire de
la clandestinité. <u>Le</u> <u>Soleil</u> Dec. 23 (1983):8. (R)

1211. Dia, Mouhamadou M. "Den Muso" de Souleymane Cissé, La chute. <u>Le</u>
<u>Soleil</u> Sept. 13 (1983):2. (R)

<u>Den</u> <u>Muso</u> compared to <u>Baara</u> and <u>Finyé</u>.

1212. Dia, Oumar. L'envers du décor. Afrique 20 (1979):53-54. (I)

Interview with Safi Faye.

1213. Dia, Saidou. L'âge adulte du cinéma africain. Revue africaine de communication 8(1984-1985):3.

Recent history of African film.

1214. Dia-Moukouri, Urbain. Intuition d'un langage cinématographique africain. Présence Africaine 61(1967):206-218.

1215. Diack, Moktar. "Emitai" or Africa arisen. Young Cinema and Theater 4(1972):27-29. (R)

1216. Diagne, Moustapha S. Articulation télévision-cinéma. Le Soleil May 23 (1986):5.

Action of SIDEC to revitalize filmmaking in Senegal.

1217. Diagne, Moustapha S. Djibo Ka au Bureau Sénégalais du cinéma. Le Soleil Jan. 31-Feb. 1-2 (1986):5.

Minister of Communication discusses promotion of film as means of preserving cultural heritage.

1218. Diagne, Yves. Faisons le point! 7e Art 37(1980):6-8; 41(1981):19-22.

Overview of filmmaking in Senegal.

1219. Diakité, Kabiné Bemba. "Le bracelet de Bronze" une oeuvre actuelle dans la réalité Sahélienne. L'Essor Aug. 19 (1975):2. (R)

1220. Diakité, Kabiné Bemba. Le Mali sera-t-il absent du FESPACO? L'Essor Jan. 12-13 (1985):5.

FESPACO prizes for Malian films. Falaba Issa Traoré unable to finance completion of Duel sur la falaise.

1221. Diakité, Kabiné Bemba. Ou va l'argent du cinéma? L'Essor Apr. 26-27 (1985):6-8.

Ticket prices, distribution in Mali.

1222. Diakité, Kabiné Bemba. Peu de personnel, peu de matériel, pas d'argent. L'Essor Feb. 2-3 (1985):7.

Reasons for few feature films being made in Mali.

DIALLO, A.B. See DIALLO, ABDOULAYE BAMBA.

132.

1223. Diallo, Abdoulaye Bamba.   A l'école indienne.   <u>Zone</u> <u>2</u>
      236(1984):17.

      Bombay film festival.

1224. Diallo, Abdoulaye Bamba.   L'Afrique à Cannes 80.  <u>Zone</u> <u>2</u>
      69(1980):23.

      Short description of 7 African feature films shown at Cannes.

1225. Diallo, Abdoulaye Bamba.   L'année cinématographique.   <u>Zone</u> <u>2</u>
      122(1982):19.

      Themes of films.

1226. Diallo, Abdoulaye Bamba.   L'année de tous le regrets?   <u>Zone</u> <u>2</u>
      226(1984):15. (R)

      Souleymane Cissé, <u>Finyé</u>.

1227. Diallo, Abdoulaye Bamba.   Avec le film "Xala" ou en sommes-nous?
      <u>Le</u> <u>Soleil</u> Feb. 1 (1975):5.

      Problems of film projection and poor equipment.

1228. Diallo, Abdoulaye Bamba.   Bako ou l'autre rive.   <u>Zone</u> <u>2</u>
      224(1983):18. (R)

1229. Diallo, Abdoulaye Bamba.   Ben Diogaye Bèye cinéaste.   <u>Zone</u> <u>2</u>
      64(1980):21. (I)

      Discussion of <u>Seye</u> <u>Seyeti</u>.

1230. Diallo, Abdoulaye Bamba.   "Bidasse" Le dernier.   <u>Bingo</u>
      347(1981):85-86.

      Sidney Koto, Beninois actor.

1231. Diallo, Abdoulaye Bamba.   Carthage fait peau neuve.   <u>Zone</u> <u>2</u>
      137(1982):20.

1232. Diallo, Abdoulaye Bamba.   "Ceddo" pour les beaux yeux de Dior
      Yacine.   <u>Zone</u> <u>2</u> 253(1984):19. (R)

1233. Diallo, Abdoulaye Bamba.   Ceddo sur les écrans.   <u>Zone</u> <u>2</u>
      246(1984):19. (R)

1234. Diallo, Abdoulaye Bamba.   "Ceddo" sur les écrans.   <u>Zone</u> <u>2</u>
      252(1984):17. (R)

1235. Diallo, Abdoulaye Bamba.   Les cinéastes africains à Bombay.   <u>Zone</u>
      <u>2</u> 236(1984):17.

      Bombay film festival.

*1236.  Diallo, Abdoulaye Bamba.   Cinéma sénégalais.   Quelque chose
        cloche.  Zone 2 (1981):23.

1237.   Diallo, Abdoulaye Bamba.   Cinéma sénégalais.   Silence...on ne
        tourne plus.  Le Soleil Magazine 3305(1981):5,7.

        Infrastructure, themes.

1238.   Diallo, Abdoulaye Bamba.   "Code électoral" de Maguette Diop.
        Zone 2 172(1982):18.  (R)

1239.   Diallo, Abdoulaye Bamba.   Coup de balai chez les cinéastes.  Zone
        2 222(1983):16.

        Interministerial council discusses problems of filmmaking in
        Senegal.

1240.   Diallo, Abdoulaye Bamba.   Deux tanits de bronze au Sénégal.  Zone
        2 97(1980):18.

        J.C.C. prizes to Safi Faye and Ousmane Mbaye.

1241.   Diallo, Abdoulaye Bamba.   "Djéli."  Zone 2 162(1982):18.  (R)

1242.   Diallo, Abdoulaye Bamba.   Entretien avec Mahama Johnson Traoré.
        Zone 2 238(1984):15-16.  (I)

        Discussion of infrastructure in Senegal.

1243.   Diallo, Abdoulaye Bamba.   Un état si généreux.   Zone 2
        222(1983):15-16.

        Films made in Senegal.

1244.   Diallo, Abdoulaye Bamba.   L'état s'y met.  Zone 2 173(1982):18.

        Senegalese filmmaking during 1982.

1245.   Diallo, Abdoulaye Bamba.   Festival de Berlin.   German connection
        pour nos cinéastes Zone 2 168(1982):17.

1246.   Diallo, Abdoulaye Bamba.   Festival du film du tiers-monde. Zone 2
        132(1982):22.

        Film festival in Paris.

1247.   Diallo, Abdoulaye Bamba.   Finyé, le vent.  Zone 2 178(1983):18.
        (R)

1248.   Diallo, Abdoulaye Bamba.   Fousseyny Cissokho, l'amoureux de
        "Finyé."  Zone 2 216(1983):13.

        Malian actor.

1249. Diallo, Abdoulaye Bamba.   La geste de Ngaido Ba.   Zone 2
      63(1980):20.

      Music in Kattan.

1250. Diallo, Abdoulaye Bamba.   La grande Royale a perdu...son pari.
      Zone 2 250(1984):18. (R)

      Aventure ambigue based on novel of C.A. Kane.

1251. Diallo, Abdoulaye Bamba.   "Gros lot," le nouveau film de Fadika
      Kramo Lanciné.   Zone 2 117(1981):22. (R)

1252. Diallo, Abdoulaye Bamba.   Johnson est blanc de toutes
      accusations.   Zone 2 179(1983):15. (I)

      Mahama Johnson Traoré discusses FEPACI.

1253. Diallo, Abdoulaye Bamba.   Johnson Traoré directeur general.   Zone
      2 235(1984):17.

      Activities of SNPC.

1254. Diallo, Abdoulaye Bamba.   "Jom" de Ababacar Samb Makharam.   Zone
      2 140(1982):18. (R)

1255. Diallo, Abdoulaye Bamba.   "Kattan" de Ngaido Ba.   Zone 2
      65(1980):19. (R)

      Kattan compared to Ceddo.

1256. Diallo, Abdoulaye Bamba.   Mahama Johnson Traoré secrétaire
      général du FEPACI.   Le Soleil Magazine 3305(1981):7.

1257. Diallo, Abdoulaye Bamba.   "Ndigël" le film.   Zone 2 259(1984):19.
      (R)

1258. Diallo, Abdoulaye Bamba.   Patrice Toto producteur de "Xew-Xew."
      Zone 2 232(1984):116.

1259. Diallo, Abdoulaye Bamba.   Petit blanc à la sauce au gombo ou au
      manioc.   Zone 2 282(1985):18-19. (I)

      Moussa Yaro Bathily discusses her film.

1260. Diallo, Abdoulaye Bamba.   Le poète qui parle avec ses doigts.
      Bingo 366(1983):57.

      Film about Francis Bebey by Mathieu Abega Mbarga.

1261. Diallo, Abdoulaye Bamba.   Pourvu que ça tourne!  Zone 2
      276(1984):14-15.

Films supported by SNPC.

1262. Diallo, Abdoulaye Bamba. Samory selon Sembène. Zone 2 265(1984):13.

1263. Diallo, Abdoulaye Bamba. Le Sénégal à l'honneur. Zone 2 97(1980):19.

Senegalese participation at Philip Morris Foundation colloquium.

1264. Diallo, Abdoulaye Bamba. "Sey Seyeti" de Ben Diogaye Bèye. Zone 2 64(1980):23. (R)

1265. Diallo, Abdoulaye Bamba. Xllle edition des Journées Cinématographiques de Carthage. Zone 2 96(1980):18.

Films to be shown at J.C.C.

1266. Diallo, Abdoulaye Bamba. 35e festival de Cannes. Participation africaine. Zone 2 143(1982):20.

1267. Diallo, Abdoulaye Bamba. Les voies du renouveau. Zone 2 229(1984):17.

Review of Senegalese films.

1268. Diallo, Abdoulaye Bamba. "Xew, Xew": la fête commence. Le Soleil Aug. 21-22 (1982):5.

1269. Diallo, Abdoulaye Bamba. "Xew-Xew" le cinéma des acteurs. Zone 2 220(1983):20. (R)

1270. Diallo, Assiatou. Le culot de Sidney Koto. Bingo 322(1979):67.

Beninois actor.

DIALLO, LAYE See DIALLO, ABDOULAYE BAMBA.

1271. Diallo, Samba. Projections. Unir Cinéma 8(1983):3-4.

Amateur projection of films.

1272. Diallo, Siradiou. Jeune Afrique fait parler Sembène Ousmane. Jeune Afrique 629(1973):44-49. (I)

Discussion of Sembène's filmmaking and fiction writing.

1273. Diarra, Isack B. Le panier de crabes d'"Adja Tio." L'Essor Sept. 5-6 (1981):8. (R)

1274. Diatta, Esther. Emitai ou la résistance collective. Jeune Afrique 860(1977):90-91. (I)

Sembène discusses his film.

1275.  Diatta, Esther.  Par la peuple et pour le peuple.  Jeune Afrique
       867-868(1977):56-57.

       Conference in Maputo on cooperation in filmmaking.

1276.  Diaw, Fara.  Un fouineur objectif.  Le Soleil Mar. 18 (1986):7.

       Meeting of ASSECCI on film criticism.

*1277. Diawara, Manthia.  African cinema: FESPACO, an evaluation.  Third
       World Affairs (1986):404-411.

1278.  Diawara, Manthia.  The cinema of Ousmane Sembene, a pioneer of
       African film.  Framework 32/33(1986):218-222. (BR)

       Françoise Pfaff, The Cinema of Ousmane Sembene. See No. 66.

1279.  Diawara, Manthia.  Images  of  children.  West  Africa
       3599(1986):1780-1781. (R)

       Cheick Oumar Sissoko, Nyamanton.

1280.  Diawara, Manthia.  The 9th Pan-African Film Festival.  Black
       Camera 1,1(1985):4.

       FESPACO.

1281.  Diawara, Manthia.  Oral literature and African film: narratology
       in "Wend Kuuni."  Présence Africaine 142(1987):36-49.

1282.  Diawara, Manthia.  Sub-Saharan African film production
       technological paternalism.  Jump Cut 32(1987):61-65.

       Colonial and post-colonial films in Ghana, Nigeria and Zaire.

1283.  Diawara, Manthia.  Who is in control?  West Africa Feb. 17
       (1986):348-349.

       Problems of distribution.

1284.  Dickson, Alain.  La crise du cinéma africain.  Le Courrier de
       Saint Ex 17(1979):5.

       Problems of distribution.

1285.  Diédhiou, Djib.  L'aide de l'Etat se poursuivra assure M. Assane
       Seck.  Le Soleil 3334(1981):3.

       Meeting of Senegalese filmmakers.

1286.  Diédhiou, Djib.  Un certain regard sur l'Afrique profonde.  Le
       Soleil 3270(1981):8.

FESPACO.

1287.  Diédhiou, Djib.  Le cinéma sénégalais s'afficher à l'extérieur. Le Soleil Nov. 8-9 (1975):1-3.

Distribution problems. No Senegalese feature films made in 1975.

1288.  Diédhiou, Djib.  Conference de presse des cinéastes sénégalais. Le Soleil Dec. 10-11 (1983):4.

Summary of press conference by Mahama Johnson Traoré on activities of SIDEC, relationships between filmmakers and SIDEC, and criteria for selecting films to produce.

1289.  Diédhiou, Djib.  "Cry Freedom" hymne à la liberté.  Le Soleil Oct. 22-23 (1983):4. (R)

Ola Balogun, Ija Ominira.

1290.  Diédhiou, Djib.  Des charges fiscales trop lourdes.  Le Soleil 3271(1981):9.

FESPACO.

1291.  Diédhiou, Djib.  Des cinéastes africains et antillais aux U.S.A. Le Soleil Oct. 15-17 (1983):6.

African filmmakers on USIA visit in U.S.A. to several universities, to attend the African Studies Association meetings and visit the Smithsonian Institution.  Finyé shown at the New York film festival.

1292.  Diédhiou, Djib.  Des films de fracture moyenne.  Le Soleil 3269(1981):7.

FESPACO.

1293.  Diédhiou, Djib.  Des mesures de survie proposées à l'Etat.  Le Soleil 3337(1981):2.

Need for national film center in Senegal.

1294.  Diédhiou, Djib.  Des spectateurs d'accord pour un seul film.  Le Soleil May 26 (1977):3.

SIDEC.

1295.  Diédhiou, Djib.  "Le Désert des Tartares" "Repérages."  Le Soleil Apr. 18 (1978):2. (R)

Daniel Kamwa, Pousse-Pousse.

1296.  Diédhiou, Djib.  "La distribution est mal assurée" estiment les réalisateurs.  Le Soleil 3335(1981):3.

138.

Distribution problems in Senegal.

1297. Diédhiou, Djib. "Djéli" contre le système des castes. Le Soleil
Oct. 9-10 (1982):8. (R)

1298. Diédhiou, Djib. Dotor les salles du confort idéal. Le Soleil
June 1 (1977):3. (I)

Mahama Johnson Traoré discusses distribution.

1299. Diédhiou, Djib. "Dundee Yaakar" les tribulations d'un jeune
chômeur. Le Soleil Mar. 4 (1983):2. (R)

1300. Diédhiou, Djib. "Finyé" de Souleymane Cissé, le souffle des
ancêtres. Le Soleil Jan. 31-Feb. 1 (1983):10. (R)

1301. Diédhiou, Djib. "Geti Tey" et "Rewo Daande Mayo"; 2 nouveaux
films sénégalais. Le Soleil Mar. 21 (1979):2. (R)

1302. Diédhiou, Djib. Hommage à Doura Mané. Le Soleil July 1
(1980):2.

Memorial service held by Senghor Foundation.

1303. Diédhiou, Djib. Interview de Seex Ngaido Ba. Le Soleil Jan. 12
(1984):6. (I)

1304. Diédhiou, Djib. Interview: M. Salgebery du Festival de Berlin.
Le Soleil Nov. 19 (1982):5. (I)

Comments on SIDEC and film awards at Berlin film festival.

1305. Diédhiou, Djib. Mbissine Diop: De l'écran à la tapisserie. Le
Soleil 3513(1982):2.

Senegalese actress.

1306. Diédhiou, Djib. Momar Thiam, réalisateur de "Sadagga"; un regard
sur la tradition. Le Soleil Sept. 10 (1982):4. (I)

1307. Diédhiou, Djib. Moussa Bathily termine un film sur la polio. Le
Soleil 3370(1981):2.

Siggi ou la poliomelite.

1308. Diédhiou, Djib. Muna Moto (l'enfant de l'autre). Le Soleil Apr.
15 (1978):2. (R)

1309. Diédhiou, Djib. "Nuages noirs" on attendait mieux. Le Soleil
Nov. 17-18 (1979):2. (R)

1310. Diédhiou, Djib. L'ombrage du fromager géant. Le Soleil July 20
(1978):3.

Senegalese delegation to Doura Mané's funeral.

1311. Diédhiou, Djib.    L'ombre d'Oumarou Ganda.    <u>Le</u> <u>Soleil</u>
3268(1981):8.

FESPACO.

1312. Diédhiou, Djib.    Patrice Toto prepare "le feu dans le sang."  <u>Le</u>
<u>Soleil</u> Feb. 8 (1984):5.

1313. Diédhiou, Djib.    Paulin S. Vieyra a recontré le cinéma africain.
<u>Le</u> <u>Soleil</u> Dec. 27-28 (1982):7.

Vieyra's thesis, <u>A</u> <u>la</u> <u>recherche</u> <u>du</u> <u>cinéma</u> <u>africain</u>.

1314. Diédhiou, Djib.    Pour une écriture originale.    <u>Le</u> <u>Soleil</u>
3336(1981):2.

Themes of Senegalese films.

1315. Diédhiou, Djib.    Promotion du court-métrage.    <u>Le</u> <u>Soleil</u> Jan.
15-16 (1983):7.

Production and distribution of documentaries in Senegal.

1316. Diédhiou, Djib.    "Rewo Dande Mayo" poésie, symbolisme.  <u>Le</u> <u>Soleil</u>
Nov. 16 (1979):2. (R)

1317. Diédhiou, Djib.    La semaine franco-africaine prend fin.    <u>Le</u>
<u>Soleil</u> Mar. 25 (1979):2.

Films of 5 Senegalese filmmakers.

1318. Diédhiou, Djib.    "Tiyabu Biru" n'est pas un film ethnographique.
<u>Le</u> <u>Soleil</u> June 2-4 (1979):2. (I)

Moussa Yoro Bathily discusses her film.

1319. Diédhiou, Djib.    "Touki-Bouki" a la soirée Yaadikone.  <u>Le</u> <u>Soleil</u>
Feb. 7-8 (1987):8.   (R)

1320. Diédhiou, Djib.    Tournage d'un film sur "la médecine
traditionelle en Afrique."  <u>Le</u> <u>Soleil</u> May 31 (1983):9.

Mahama Johnson Traoré, <u>Médecin</u> <u>traditionelle</u> <u>en</u> <u>Afrique</u>, film
series for television.

1321. Diédhiou, Djib.  Un tremplin pour "Xew Xew" de Cheick Ngaido Ba.
<u>Le</u> <u>Soleil</u> Nov. 23 (1983):6.

Promotion and distribution of <u>Xew</u> <u>Xew</u>.

1322. Diédhiou, Djib.    Trouver une place dans la politique économique.

Le Soleil Nov. 10 (1975):3.

Activities of SNC.

1323. Diédhiou, Djib. "West Indies" grand prix de FIFEF. Le Soleil Nov. 19 (1979):1-2. (R)

Jean-Pierre Dikongue-Pipa Prix de la liberté and Muna Moto also discussed.

1324. Diédhiou, Djib. "Xew-Xew" une fête ratée. Le Soleil Jan. 11 (1984):4. (R)

1325. Diene, Doudou. Cinéma et le Tiers Monde. Annuaire du Tiers Monde 8 (1975-1976):388-396.

Comparison of film and dependence in Tunisia and Senegal. Distribution problems. Ways of decolonizing films.

1326. Diene, Doudou. Vers un écriture cinématographique africaine. Annuaire du Tiers Monde 3(1977):321-324.

Distribution problems. Japan and Brazil good examples of production. Need for more creativity in filmmaking. Comparisons between oral tradition and film.

1327. Dieng, Mansour. La voie de l'engagement. Le Soleil Apr. 12 (1975):2.

Film as tool of decolonization.

1328. Dieng, Mansour and Nis Dakar. Sey-Seyeti "Un travail bâclé". Le Soleil 3246(1981):2. (R)

1329. Dienguessé, Louis de Dravo. Cinéaste gabonais cherche sponsor. L'Union Aug. 10 (1984):3.

Filmscript, Conflits des générations by Antoine Dacky Mondendé.

1330. Differences. Cinéma et apartheid. Differences 28(1983):supplement 1-68.

Amiens film festival. Focus on Mocambique pp. 51-60, Angola. pp. 61-68.

1331. Dimas, Atanásio. Três documentários sãotomenses montados nos laboratorios do INC. Domingo (Maputo) Sept. 5 (1982):13.

Film production facilities in Mocambique, cooperation with São Tome and Principe.

1332. Diop, Abdou Aziz. Lecture de film: "Touki-Bouki" de Djibril M. Diop. Unir Cinéma 16(1985):27-29; 17(1985):25-26. (R)

1333.   Diop, Baba.   Amour a mort.   Afrique Nouvelle 1979(1987):16-17.

Films shown in Dakar for Commauté-Economique Europeenne meeting.

1334.   Diop, Baba.   Ce qui fait courir nobila.   Afrique Nouvelle
1965(1987):20. (BR)

Festival Panafricain du Cinéma de Ouagadougou. See No. 33.

1335.   Diop, Baba.   Etalon d'or de Yennenga.   Afrique Nouvelle
1963(1987):16-17. (R)

Med Hondo, Sarraounia.

1336.   Diop, Baba.   Etre cinéaste en 1985.   Unir Cinéma 17(1985):50-52.

Problems of filmmaking.   Excerpt from article in Waraango (Dakar)
No. 10.

1337.   Diop, Baba.   Un festival de la coproduction.   Afrique Nouvelle
1961(1987):13.

FESPACO.

1338.   Diop, Baba.   Goree sur les écrans.   Afrique Nouvelle
1957(1987):18. (I)

Interview with Souhel Ben Barka on problems of filmmaking in
Senegal.

1339.   Diop, Baba.   "Pour un cinéma africain vrai et sans complexe."
Afrique Nouvelle 1970(1987):18-19. (I)

Interview with Haile Gerima on making of Nunu and his views of
African filmmakers and ideal content of films.

1340.   Diop, Baba.   Une recompense a "Yeelen" de Souleymane Cissé.
Afrique Nouvelle 1976(1987):18-19. (R)

1341.   Diop, Babacar.   Le collage de Ouagadougou.   Unir Cinéma
19(1985):4-9.

FESPACO.

1342.   Diop, Barbara.   Notre cinéma d'hier et d'aujord'hui, Revue
africaine de communication 4(1984):45-47. (BR)

Paulin Vieyra, Le cinema au Sénégal. See No. 74.

1343.   Diop, Boubacar.   Littérature et cinéma.   Unir Cinéma
20-21(1985):5-8.

Report on FESPACO colloquium.

1344. Diop, Edge. Hommage à Doura Mané. Le Soleil July 14 (1978) arts & lettres 1,4.

Guinean actor.

1345. Diop, Mody. "Baara" un film qui honore le cinéma africain. Le Soleil Oct. 2 (1979):2. (R)

1346. Diop, Mody. "Le Certificat" de Tidiane Aw. Le Soleil 3229(1981):2. (R)

1347. Diop, Mody. Le courts métrages de "Moseka" à "Bambo." Le Soleil Apr. 17 (1978):2. (R)

Bambo; Moustapha Alassane, Bon voyage sim Niger and Kwami N. Zinga, Moseka.

1348. Diop, Mody. Démarrage du "Certificat" de Tidiane Aw. Le Soleil Aug. 11 (1978):3.

Background on making Certificat.

1349. Diop, Mody. Le "Festac 77" à l'écran. Le Soleil Oct. 16 (1979):2. (R)

1350. Diop, Mody. L'herbe sauvage de Henri Duparc. Le Soleil July 11 (1978):2. (R)

1351. Diop, Mody. Momar Thiam adapte "Sa Dagga" de Birago Diop. Le Soleil July 19 (1979):2. (R)

1352. Diop, Mody. "Mon film sortira." Le Soleil July 2 (1979):2.

Ben Diogaye Bèye, Seye Seyeti.

1353. Diop, Mody. "Le pacte" de Sylva de Condé. Le Soleil Jan. 3 (1979):2. (R)

1354. Diop, Mody. Un scenario contre la drogue "Les Destructeurs." Le Soleil Aug. 30 (1979):2.

Abdou Karim Fofana, Senegalese actor.

1355. Diop, Mody. "Tiyabu Biru" de Moussa Bathily. Le Soleil May 22 (1979):2. (R)

1356. Diop, Mohamed. Approche africaine de la critique. Unir Cinéma 15(1984):4-5.

Criteria for film criticism.

1357. Diop, Mohamed. Cinéma négro-africain hymne à la femme noire. Afrique Nouvelle 1311(1974):12-15.

Films about African women.

1358. Diop, Mohamed. Congrès d'Alger: un charte pour les cinéastes africains. Afrique Nouvelle 1335(1975):22-24.

Report on FEPACO Congress, charter of African filmmakers.

1359. Diop, Mohamed. Terre d'élection du cinéma l'Afrique noire consomme les pires navets en forgeant son industrie du 7e art. Recherche, pédagogie et culture 17-18(1975):29-32.

Audience responses to Western films.

1360. Diop, Moustapha. Les carpet-baggers. Sidwaya Feb. 27 (1987):13.

Distribution problems. Benefits of coproduction with French companies.

1361. Diop, Ndiogou. Le choc des cultures. Le Soleil Feb. 27 (1986):10. (R)

Massène Niang, Europa Mein Traw.

1362. Diop, Pierre. La comèdie exotique. Africa (Dakar) 169(1985):37. (R)

1363. Diop, Raymond. Un contribution au développement. Le Soleil Apr. 24 (1975):2.

How themes of films can contribute to development in Senegal.

1364. Diop, Sidy Guissé. L'impact des mediats sur la jeunesse sénégalaise. Unir Cinéma 16(1985):35-37.

Senegalese audiences responses to films.

1365. Diop, Yandé Christiane. Lecture du palmarès du Grand Prix FESPACO 87. Présence Africaine 143(1987):195-197.

Text of speech announcing FESPACO prizes.

1366. Diop Buuba, Babacar. Malaise autour de Ceddo. Revue africaine de communcation 7(1984):45-52.

Responses of Senegalese audiences and critics.

1367. Diouf, Bara. Avec "Emitai" Sembène restitue l'Afrique dans sa pureté originelle. Le Soleil Jan. 21 (1972):4. (R)

1368. Diouf, Bara. La Mandat, film d'Ousmane Sembène. Dakar Matin Dec. 7 (1968):1,8. (R)

1369. Diouf, Latyr Mbassou. A la recherche du souffle libérateur. Le Soleil Apr. 14 (1975):2.

Criticism of weaknesses of Senegalese films.

1370. Diouf, Moustapha. Les meilleurs du continent. Le Soleil Apr. 22 (1975):2.

Criticism of Senegalese films should take into account personal nature of filmmaking and youth of Senegalese cinema.

1371. Direction générale de la culture - service du cinéma. Concours cinématographiques de l'ACCT, réglements et dossiers de candidature. Agecop Liaison 75-76(1984):i-xvi.

Regulations for entering films in ACCT competition.

1372. Djire, Dembele Sata. Video in the village. Development Forum 11,4(1983):1,12.

Film used for development training in Mali.

1373. Doherty, Folake. Soyinka's coming attraction: "Blues for the Prodigal." Guardian (Lagos) Dec. 23 (1984):5. (I)

Discussion of problems in making this political film.

1374. Dokoui, Pol. Sidiki Bakaba au bout du tunnel. Ivoire Dimanche 510(1980):36-37.

Actor; role in Dessert pour Constance.

1375. Dolo, Guimogo. Le club, un cinéma, de luxe, mais... L'Essor Oct. 6 (1971):1,4.

New theater in Mali, program on opening night.

1376. Domancich, Micheline. Abusuan le film de Duparc. Ivoire Dimanche 94(1972):4-5.

Natou Kolly, actress, and Jean-Baptiste Tiémélé, actor, personal background and roles in Abusuan.

1377. Domancich, Micheline. Le cri du muezzin: un film sensible et intelligent. Ivoire Dimanche 103(1973):8. (R)

1378. Domancich, Micheline. Les films malsains. Ivoire Dimanche 74(1972):4-7.

Problems of filmmaking, goals in filmmaking.

1379. Domingo. "Canta meu irmão" no Festival de Tachkent. Domingo (Maputo) Apr. 15 (1984):4. (R)

1380. Domingo. "Canta meu irmão" premiado em Tashkent. Domingo (Maputo) June 17 (1984):4.

1381. Domingo.   Cartago:  a arte dos Cineastas Africanos e Arabes. Domingo (Maputo) Nov. 21 (1982):19.

Pamberi ne Zimbabwé shown at J.C.C.

1382. Domingo.  Cinema: arte, industria ou comércio?  Domingo (Maputo) Nov. 20 (1983):10-11.

Ruy Guerra represents Mocambique at Madeira film festival. Summary of discussions on infrastructure.

1383. Domingo.  O cinema da Africa Austral.  Domingo (Maputo) Dec. 25 (1983):2.

Ruy Duarte de Carvalho, Nelisita, shown at Amiens film festival.

1384. Domingo.   Cinema homenageia Samora.  Domingo (Maputo) Jan. 25 (1987):1.  (R)

Brief comments on documentaries on Samora Machel: Papa Samora, Porque Alguma Voz São Todas as Vozes and Samora Vive, made in Mocambique.

1385. Domingo.   Conhecer todos os segredos da máquina.  Domingo (Maputo) May 30 (1982):12.

Work of Antonio Chiure, projectionist for INC.

1386. Domingo. Um festival e uma competiçao.  Domingo (Maputo) Sept. 30 (1984):4.

Film festival on national liberation organized by INC.

1387. Domingo.  Filmagens do "Mayombe" em Angola.  Domingo (Maputo) Nov. 27 (1983):4.

Mocambiquan/Cuban coproduction of film based on José Luandino Vieira's novel.

1388. Domingo.  Filmes moçambicanos em ciclo na Itália.   Domingo (Maputo) Dec. 7 (1986):2.

Mocambiquan films shown in Italy.

1389. Domingo.  INC promove retrospectiva do cinema moçambicano. Domingo (Maputo) June 27 (1982):13.

Films shown to commemorate 20th anniversary of FRELIMO.

1390. Domingo. Moçambique no Festival de Aveiro.  Domingo (Maputo) May 6 (1984):2.

1391. Domingo.  O nosso primeiro filme.  Domingo (Maputo) Jan. 20

(1985):1.

Madrugada dos Imbomdeiros.

1392. Domingo. Novo documentario em estreia. Domingo (Maputo) Jan. 25
(1987):4. (R)

Rodrigo Gonçalves, Papa Samora.

1393. Domingo. Novo filme de Med Hondo adiado. Domingo (Maputo) July
29 (1984):13.

Sarraounia to be filmed. Films completed by Hondo.

1394. Domingo. Para uma história da cinematografia em Moçambique.
1.Filme sobre nosso país data de 1941. Domingo (Maputo) July 11
(1982):13.

Colonial films about Mocambique, films on the independence
struggle including Mocambiquan coproductions with Angola, Cuba,
Korea and Portugal.

1395. Domingo. Pintura moçambicana em filme. Domingo (Maputo) Feb. 2
(1986):4.

Films by Rodrigo Gonçalves, including new film on Mocambiquan
painting.

1396. Domingo. Da poesia para a imagem... da imagem para a poesia.
Domingo (Maputo) Jan. 8 (1984):16 (I)

Camilo de Sousa discusses personal background and filmmaking
philosophy.

1397. Domingo. Prepara-se em Maputo filme Moçambicano-Soviético.
Domingo (Maputo) July 4 (1982):12.

Mocambique, no caminho das tranformaçoes economicas to be made.

1398. Domingo. Próximo filme de Rui Guerra. Domingo (Maputo) Nov. 13
(1983):6.

Ruy Guerra to make Opera do Malandro.

1399. Domingo. Quem pode ser actor de cinema? Domingo (Maputo) Mar. 2
(1986):2.

Importance of careful selection of actors.

1400. Domingo. Semanca do filme moçambicano em Sófia. Domingo
(Maputo) Oct. 23 (1983):11.

Mocambiquan films shown in Sofia.

1401. Do.meyer, James. Pour un cinéma africain... "il n'y a pas de temps à perdre." Afrique Nouvelle 852(1963):9.

Need for African made films to counteract such films as La pyramid humaine.

1402. Dorsinville, Roger and Nabil Haidar. P.S. Vieyra: "pour les Africains, le prestige c'est d'être réalisateur." Africa (Dakar) 157(1984):55-57. (I)

History of Senegalese film, need for more short films, lack of scriptwriters and trained technicians, problem of distributing films in Africa.

1403. Douce, Anne-Marie. Repas et convivialité. CinémAction 26(1983):124-130.

Themes of eating, drinking, communication and related symbolism.

1404. Doucouré, Bandiougou Bidian. A quand la rénovation des cinémas prives? L'Essor July 3 (1970):1,4.

Need to renovate theaters in Mali.

1405. Doucouré, Bandiougou Bidian. "5 jours d'une vie." L'Essor June 5 (1971):4. (R)

1406. Doucouré, Bandiougou Bidian. Un film qui a du mérite mais... L'Essor Jan. 30 (1971):3. (R)

Djibril Kouyaté, Retour de Tiéman.

1407. Doucouré, Bandiougou Bidian. Non au minimum d'investissement pour le maximum de profit. L'Essor Jan. 5 (1971):1,4.

Profits of theaters in Mali.

1408. Doucouré, Bandiougou Bidian and Djibril Diallo. Pour un cinéma au service du peuple malien. L'Essor Mar. 4 (1971):1,4; Mar. 5 (1971):1,4,. (I)

Abdoulaye Sy, president of a Bamako film club, discusses its goals and briefly comments on history of African film.

1409. Doudou, Venance. "Maman, je veux vivre": le nouveau film d'éducation de Kitia Touré. Fraternité Matin June 18 (1987):9. (I)

Kitia Touré discusses film series on health, its financing and planned distribution.

1410. Doughan, Davina. Mohammed Amin film maker. Concord Weekly 32(1985):35.

1411. Dougoué, Michel. "Ousmane Sembène incarne l'âme du cinéma africain" nous déclare Sékou Camara. Dakar Matin Aug. 16 (1969):3. (I)

Sékou Camara, Guinean cameraman, discusses his work and comments on Algiers film festival.

1412. Douin, Jean-Luc. Entretien avec Ruy Guerra. Ecran 32(1975):80-81. (I)

1413. Doumbia, Boubakar. Les deux visages de l'économie dans les films africains. CinémAction 26 (1983):102-104.

Themes on subsistence and money economies.

1414. Drabo, G. Entretien Souleymane Cissé. Zone 2 175(1983):15. (I)

1415. Drame, Kandioura. Oyekunle on African film industry. Africscope 11,2(1981):27-33. (I)

Discussion of his background in theater, criteria of good African films, need for training of African film technicians.

1416. 3 Welt Magazin. Das Letzte Grab in Dimbaza. 3 Welt Magazin 314(1976):61. (R)

Nana Mahomo, Last Grave at Dimbaza.

1417. Drodzynski, Olivier. Issach de Bankolé: l'Ivoirien qui fait fureur en Europe. Fraternité Matin July 12-13 (1986):14.

Background on Ivorian actor, his roles in Black Mic Mac and Taxi Boy.

1418. Dubroux, Danièle. Exhibition (Xala). Cahiers du Cinéma 266-267(1976):72-74. (R)

1419. Duchâteau Effemba. Le couple présidentiel à la grande première d'Ayouma. L'Union Jan. 7-8 (1978):2. (I)

Pierre Marie Dong discusses Ayouma and Obali, relation of film to national development.

1420. Duchâteau Effemba. En grande première cet après-midi au Komo "Ayouma" sous le haute patronage du Chef de l'Etat. L'Union Jan. 5 (1978):2. (R)

1421. Duchâteau Effemba. Grande première d'"Ilombé" le nouveau film gabonais. L'Union June 16-17 (1979):3. (I)

Charles Mensah discusses problems in making Ilombé, philosophy of filmmaking and problems of distribution.

1422. Duchâteau Effemba. Institut culturel africain: un instrument de coopération culturelle intergovernmental. L'Union 1538(1981):7.

Role of ICA in Gabon.

1423. Duchâteau Effemba. Le nouveau film de Charles Mensah: "Ilombé, l'homme face à son destin. L'Union Feb. 21 (1978):2. (I)

Charles Mensah discusses plot and progress in making Ilombé.

1424. Duchâteau Effemba. Projection du film "Ilombé" au Komo. L'Union June 19 (1979):5. (R)

1425. Duparc, Henri. La longue marche. Afrique 1(1977):69-70.

Problems of production; major themes.

1426. Duparc, Henri. Sur le carnet de route de Duparc à Paris. Ivoire Dimanche 333(1977):37-38.

Music for Herbe sauvage.

*1427. Dupas, Jean. Ousmane Sembène et sa conception du cinéma africain. Nawadi Cinéma Aug. 1 (1968):64-68.

1428. Dura, Madeleine. Entretien avec Med Hondo. Jeune Cinéma 121(1979):21-28. (I)

1429. Durarte, Fernando. Breve história do cinema moçambicano. Celuloid 283-284 (1979): supp. 13-16.

Chronology of events in filmmaking and films made 1975-1979.

1430. Durarte, Fernando and Maria Fernanda Reis. 9° Festival de Santarém - Moçambique. Celuloide 285-286(1979):8.

Mocambiquan representation at Santarém film festival.

1431. Durarte, Fernando and Maria Fernanda Reis. 9° Festival de Santarém - Senegal. Celuloide 285-286(1979):9. (R)

Safi Faye, Fad jal.

1432. During, Ola. African women cineasts praised. Africa Now 69(1987):40.

Moussa Yoro Bathily, Certificate d'indigence and Safi Faye, Kaddu Beykat shown in London.

1433. Duteil, Christian. Le dernière tombe à Dimbaza. Jeune Cinéma 91(1975):31-33. (R)

Nana Mahomo, Last Grave at Dimbaza.

1434. E.B.S. L'image de marque nos salles. Le Soleil Oct. 1 (1975):2.

High cost of theater tickets in Senegal.

1435. E.J.M. West Indies, les Nègres marons de la liberté. Demain l'Afrique 33-34(1979):70. (R)

1436. E.R.A. Le cinéma sénégalais n'est plus un enfant. Le Soleil Dec. 7 (1974):2.

Legislation to facilitate filmmaking in Senegal.

1437. E.S. Indiscrétions sur le "Nouveau Venu." Afrique Nouvelle 1385(1976):17. (R)

1438. Ebenebo. Nigerian images on screen. Guardian (Lagos) Sept. 1 (1985):7.

Themes of Nigerian televison films.

1439. Ebony, Noël. "Abusuan":première ce soir au "Rex." Fraternité Matin 2432(1972):7. (R)

1440. Ebony, Noël. L'an 10 du cinéma africain. Demain l'Afrique 19(1979):80-81.

FESPACO.

1441. Ebony, Noël. L'herbe sauvage'. Afrique 7(1978):74-76. (R)

1442. Ebony, Noël. Journée ivoirienne: triomphe pour nos réalisateurs. Fraternité Matin 2473(1973):11.

Ivorian films shown at FESPACO.

1443. Ebony, Noël. Ousmane Sembène témoigne... Afrique 15(1978):92-95. (I)

Sembène discusses his training and filmmaking.

1444. Eburnea. Le consécration de Désiré Ecaré. Eburnea 37(1970):26. (R)

A nous deux France shown at Cannes film festival.

1445. Eburnea. Les débuts prometteurs du cinéma ivoirien. Eburnea 39(1970):26-27.

1446. Eburnea. Un livre de Guy Hennebelle fait le point sur le cinéma africain. Eburnea 58 (1972):38. (BR)

Guy Hennebelle, Les cinémas africains en 1972. See no. 44.

1447. Eburnea. La naissance du cinéma africain. Eburnea 37(1970):27-28.

1448. Eburnea. Roger M'Bala ou le triomphe d'un obscur. <u>Eburnea</u>
63(1972):34-35.

Survey of African films in 1972.

1449. Ecaré, Désiré. "Visages de femmes." <u>Unir</u> <u>Cinéma</u> 18(1985):10-12.

1450. Eder, Richard. 'Boesman and Lena' is at Film Forum. <u>New</u> <u>York</u>
<u>Times</u> Apr. 23 (1976):23. (R)

1451. Eder, Richard. Film festival: Cutting, radiant 'Xala.' <u>New</u> <u>York</u>
<u>Times</u> Oct. 1 (1975):62. (R)

1452. Edgar, John. The 'Doctor of Gafire.' <u>African</u> <u>Now</u> 59(1986):47.
(R)

Mustapha Diop, <u>Médecin</u> <u>de</u> <u>Gafiré</u>.

EFFEMBA, DUCHÂTEAU See DUCHÂTEAU EFEMBA.

1453. Egbuchulam, James. The film industry. Has it any hope in
Nigeria? <u>Daily</u> <u>Star</u> 1447(1977):13. (I)

Ola Balogun discusses his films and FESTAC.

1454. Egeonu, Dan. 'Ayanmo's still destiny.' <u>Daily</u> <u>Times</u> (Lagos) Aug.
2 (1987):16. (I)

Hubert Ogunde discusses his film and play, <u>Ayanmo</u>.

1455. Ehuzu. Festival de cinéma d'Afrique noire à Brussels. <u>Ehuzu</u>
Apr. 6 (1984):3.

Filmmakers present at Brussels film festival. Meeting of CIDC.

1456. Ehuzu. Le film "La vie est belle" plus d'um million de dollars.
<u>Ehuzu</u> Sept. 25 (1987):3.

1457. Ehuzu. Le triomple (sic) des films burkinabé. <u>Ehuzu</u> Mar. 6
(1987):3.

Prize winning films at FESPACO.

1458. Eichenberger, Ambros. <u>Dritte</u> <u>Welt</u> <u>kontra</u> <u>Hollywood</u>. Bremen:
Me-editon 5, 1981. pp. 17-38. (I)

Interviews with Souleymane Cissé, Safi Faye, Gadalla Gubara and
Jean Claude Rahaga.

1459. Ekoga, Ollomo. "Bako" ou l'autre rive. <u>L'Union</u> Apr. 11
(1986):3. (R)

1460. Ekoga, Ollomo. CENACI. Bientôt "Raphia" sur nos écrans.

L'Union Apr. 10 (1986):3.

Production of Paul Mouketa's, Raphia.

1461. Ekoga, Ollomo. CENACI. Le renouveau du cinéma gabonais. L'Union Nov. 18 (1985):3.

Problems in making Henri Joseph Koumba's, Singe Fou.

1462. Ekoga, Ollomo. CENACI. Le renouveau du cinéma gabonais. L'Union Mar. 2 (1986):5.

Filming of Henri Joseph Koumba's, Singe fou.

1463. Ekwu, Oga. 'Kannakanna" for the North. New Nigerian July 26 (1986):2. (R)

1464. Ekwuazi, Hyginus O. The colonisation of the Nigerian film industry. West Africa 3532 (1985):883-884. (R)

Francis Oladele, Kongi's Harvest.

1465. Ekwuasi, Hyginus O. Towards a development scheme for the Nigerian film culture. Nigeria Magazine 54, 2(1986):56-57.

History of filmmaking since the colonial period. List of feature films 1962-1984. Discussion of seminar on film and cultural identity.

1466. El-Djillali. Festival cinématogrpahique des Etats sahariens, un act de naissance. Afrique-Asie 259(1982):50-51.

Saharan States film festival.

1467. El Kara, Ki. La sécurite des cinéastes. L'Observateur Feb. 27-28, Mar. 1 (1981):1, 5, 8.

Closing ceremonies of FESPACO. Meeting of FEPACI.

1468. El Kara, Ki. Vlle FESPACO c'est parti. L'Observateur Feb. 23 (1981):1, 11, 12. (R)

Oumarou Ganda, Exile.

1469. El Kara, Ki. Vlle FESPACO les langues et la fiscalité. L'Observateur Feb. 25 (1981):1, 10.

Report on colloquium on distribution.

1470. El Kara, Ki. Vle FESPACO qui remportera l'étalon de Yennenga? L'Observateur Feb. 9-11 (1979):1, 5, 9.

Film jury, film prizes and discussion of colloquium on film and liberation.

1471. Elegbede, Wole. Afro-Asian film festival kicks off next week. Guardian (Lagos) May 17 (1986):11.

Tashkent film festival.

1472. Ellovich, Risa. Review of Black Girl. American Anthropologist 79, 1(1977):198-200. (R)

Sembène Ousmane, La noire de.

1473. Elsaesser, Thomas. Erendira. Monthly Film Bulletin 53(1986):208-209. (R)

1474. Elsaesser, Thomas. Interview Ruy Guerra. Monogram 5(1974):27-33. (I)

1475. Ephson, Ben. "Kukurantumi" hits Ghanaian screens. Concord Weekly 34(1985):27. (R)

1476. Ephson, Ben. 'Kukurantumi-Road to Accra.' West Africa 3488(1984):1303-1304. (R)

1477. Esso, Christiane. "Nyamanthon" (sic) ou la "leçon des ordures." Fraternité Hebdo 1460(1987):31. (I)

Cheick Oumar Sissoko discusses making of Nyamanton, response of Malian audiences.

1478. Essomba, Philippe. Bhime: de la mode au cinéma. Bingo 315(1979):17-20. (I)

Bama Souaré, Guinean actor, discusses his work.

1479. Essomba, Philippe. "Bugo de Subo" le passé et le présent. Bingo 367(1983):58-59. (R)

1480. Essomba, Philippe. Le cinéma africain manque de structure d'accueil. Bingo 361(1983):56-58. (I)

Paulin Vieyra discusses infrastructure of African film.

1481. Essomba, Philippe. En quête d'auteurs. Bingo 319(1979):7.

Need for better scriptwriters.

1482. Essomba, Philippe. Gérard Essomba pour un retour aux sources. Bingo 346(1981):68.

Camerounian actor.

1483. Essomba, Philippe. "Notre fille" Nicole Okala. Bingo 334(1980):18-19.

Camerounian actress.

1484. Essor. "Ba Bemba," un cinéma la mesure de notre dignité. L'Essor Apr. 17 (1967):4.

New theater in Mali financed by China.

1485. Essor. Le cinéma africain au septième festival de Moscou. L'Essor July 29 (1971):1,4.

Moscow film festival.

1486. Essor. Le cinéma africain selon Paulin Vieyra. L'Essor Nov. 13 (1975):3. (BR)

Le cinéma africain. See No. 74.

1487. Essor. Le cinéma documentaire, une force probante. L'Essor July 31, (1971):1,4.

Documentaries shown at Moscow film festival.

1488. Essor. Les cinémas privés doivent penser a la modernisation de leurs salles vétustés. L'Essor June 24 (1970):1,4.

Need for more theaters in Mali.

1489. Essor. Le couple présidentiel assiste à la projection de "Sarraounia." L'Essor June 13-14 (1987):2.

Special showing of Sarraounia for Malian government officials.

1490. Essor. Des difficultés persistantes malgré des efforts louables de la Direction. L'Essor Mar. 5-6 (1983):3.

Activities of OCINAM.

1491. Essor. Développer le cinéma africain pour que rayonne la culture africaine. L'Essor Feb. 6 (1973):4.

FESPACO. Problems of African filmmaking.

1492. Essor. Don d'une chaîne de production cinématographique au Ciné-club Askia Nouh. L'Essor Dec. 6-7 (1975):5.

New film club in Mali.

1493. Essor. Festival cinéma tunisien. L'Essor Oct. 20 (1970):4.

J.C.C. prizes.

1494. Essor. Le festival du film francophone de Dinard. L'Essor July 11 (1974):2.

FIFEF. African films shown not well made.

1495. Essor. Le film "Bambo" mérite la diffusion la plus large possible. L'Essor Apr. 5(1969):4. (R)

1496. Essor. Le gouvernement exerce desormais le monopole de l'exploitation du cinéma. L'Essor Feb. 28 (1974):4.

Government control of film distribution in Benin.

1497. Essor. Hôtels et cinémas guinéens reviennent au secteur privé. L'Essor Feb. 16 (1972):4.

Government role in film distribution in Guineé.

1498. Essor. Inauguration du cinéma d'état "Babemba." L'Essor June 12 (1967):1-2,7.

Text of speech by Mamadou Gologo on role of film in Mali on occasion of opening of a new theater.

1499. Essor. Ismaila Sarr n'est plus. L'Essor June 22-23 (1985):5.

Malian actor who appeared in Baara and Finyé.

1500. Essor. Ouverture de la cinquième semaine du cinéma français. L'Essor Jan. 29 (1975):1,4; Feb. 1-2 (1975):1,5.

French influence on Malian film, film as conveyor of culture. Same article on two days.

1501. Essor. La "première cinématographe" du film "Bambo" aura lieu aujourd'hui a L'E.N.I. L'Essor Apr. 3 (1969):4.

Background on making of Bambo by students at Lycée de Bamako.

1502. Essor. Prochain festival du film africain à Los Angeles. L'Essor Oct. 31 (1970):4.

Film festival at University of California, Los Angeles.

1503. Essor. Une reussite complète déclare le Director Général de l'OCINAM. L'Essor Feb. 24-25 (1979):4.

Prizes at FESPACO.

1504. Essor. "Sambizanga" symbole d'un cinéma africain engagé. L'Essor Apr. 25 (1973):13. (R)

1505. Essor. "Yeelen": c'est bientôt parti! L'Essor Nov. 13 (1984):6. (R)

1506. Estève, Michel. Note sur Sweet Hunters (Tendres Chasseurs) ou la poésie de l'imaginaire. Etudes cinématographiques 93-96

(1972):139-144. (R)

1507. Esu, Boniface. The influx of western films into Nigeria. Guardian (Lagos) Aug. 29 (1986):9.

Influence of western films on Nigerian television. Need for Nigerian-produced television films.

1508. Esu, Boniface. Things Fall Apart: a mixture of goodness and filth. Guardian (Lagos) Aug. 12 (1986):13. (R)

1509. Even, Martin. Un africain à Paris. Le Monde Jan. 5 (1973):11. (I)

Med Hondo discusses making Soleil O and his views on African film.

1510. Even, Martin. Le cinéma africain entre Paris et Ouagadougou. Le Monde June 15 (1973):21.

Distribution problems. Need for an African distribution company.

1511. Ewande, Félix. L'Afrique des caméras. Dakar Matin July 3 (1967):6.

Summary of article in Connaissance de l'Afrique on relation of African films to African audiences, and criticism of colonial and ethnographic films.

1512. Ewande, Félix. Afrique des caméras. Jeune Afrique 386-387(1968):71.

Development of film in Africa late 19th century to mid-1960s.

1513. Ewande, Félix. Causes du sous-développement africain en matière de cinéma. Présence Africaine 6(1967):199-205.

Historical conditions for development of African film and ideals for African filmmaking.

1514. Ewande, Félix. Le cinéma africain? Dakar Matin July 3 (1967):6.

Cannes film festival. Responses to Third World films.

1515. Ewande, Félix. Festival du cinéma africain à Louvain. Sentiers 31 (1970):20.

1516. Expert africains. Afrique: longue marche et grandes manoeuvres. Afrique-Asie 57(1974):72-74.

Government role in making and distributing films.

1517. Ezeani, Andy. Things Fall Apart falls on TV screen every Saturday. Guardian (Lagos) July 12 (1986):1-2.

Final phase of filming. Beginning of new era in television film.

1518. Ezekiel, Esta. Allegation of fraud over film on Dan Fodio. Guardian (Lagos) Apr. 26 (1987):1,11.

Contract and script problems with Jihad.

1519. Ezzeddine, Haykel. Fadika Kramo Lanciné. SeptièmArt 51(1984):23.

FESPACO prize for Djéli.

1520. F.B. L'Afrique et le Festival. L'Union 131(1976):2.

Cannes.

1521. F.B. Le cinéma at la couture au Festival de Lagos. L'Union Feb. 7 (1977):5.

Biographical information and films made by Pierre-Marie Dong.

*1522. F.B.H. Ajani Ogun: un spectacle de la jungle. Presse (Tunis) Oct. 17 (1976).

1523. F.F.N. Que sera la société nationale de distribution de films? Zaire 316(1974):9.

Distribution of films in Zaire.

1524. Fadhloun, Essya. Clôture des travaux du 11e colloque de J.C.C. sur la production et la distribution des films arabes et africains. L'Action Nov. 18 (1978):3.

1525. Fadhloun, Essya. Libérer le psychisme africain colonisé en continuant d'importer des mauvais films? 7e Art 34(1979):26-28; 41(1981):12-15. (I)

Interview with Richard de Medeiros.

1526. Fadhloun, Essya. Ouagadougou-Carthage: vers la confrontation. 7e Art 42(1981):20-21.

1527. Falk Nzuji Madiya, Clémentine. Symbolisme et cinéma africain, in Caméra Nigra. C.E.S.C.A. ed. Brussels: OCIC, 1984. pp. 215-224.

1528. Falgayrettes, Ch. La réconciliation de la ville et de la brousse. Bingo 339 (1981):40. (R)

Kalifa Dienta, A Banna.

1529. Fall, Amadou. Relance de l'industrie cinématographique nationale. Le Soleil May 28-29 (1983):6-7.

Senegal's film budget for 1983-1984. Censorship of _Ceddo_, need for censorship of television films.

1530. Fall, Amedine. Journée du Cosapad-Présidence. _Le Soleil_ June 3 (1986):9.

Films on Islam made for Ramadan.

1531. Fall, Babacar. Le testament de Doura Mané. _Afrique_ 14(1978):87-89.

Guinean actor.

1532. Fall, Bilal and Jacques Polet. Le film africain: traits immanents et relation à son public, in _Caméra Nigra_. C.E.S.C.A. ed. Brussels: OCIC, 1984. pp. 175-186.

Themes of films, audience response.

1533. Fall, Elimane. Cinéma: plus de colloques que de films. _Jeune Afrique_ 1303-1304(1986):87-89.

Historical overview of 25 years of filmmaking.

1534. Fallet, Pierre. L'éclatante revanche d'Henri Duparc. _Eburnea_ 68(1973):13-15. (R)

_Abusuan_.

1535. Fanon, Josie. Au nom de la tolérance. _Demain l'Afrique_ 32(1979):72-73. (I)

Sembène discusses _Ceddo_.

1536. Fara Biram Lo, Andre. L'option: un film de Thierno Sow. Les mariages mixtes peuvent-ils durer? _Le Soleil_ 258(1974):60-61. (I)

1537. Farès, Twefik. Les gris-gris de Ousmane Sembène. _Jeune Afrique_ 602(1972):66. (R)

_Emitai_.

1538. Farfola, Juan. Festival Panafricano de Cine. _Africa_ (Madrid) 413(1976):19-20.

FESPACO.

1539. Faye, Birame. Le Bracelet... _Le Soleil_ Apr. 12 (1975):2. (R)

Tidiane Aw, _Bracelet de bronze_. Music by Wato Sita mentioned.

1540. Faye, Martin. L'Afrique et les nouveaux médias. _Unir Cinéma_ 16(1985):24-26.

Audiovisual revolution in Africa, including videocassettes, magnetoscope and television.

1541. Feinberg, Barry. The role of social documentary films in our struggle for national liberation. Young Cinema and Theater 3(1984):14-20.

Barry Feinberg, The Sun Will Rise; role of film in South African liberation.

1542. Felipe, Celso Nóbua. Festival de Tróia. Africa Hoje 19(1986):48-49.

Documentaries on Africa shown at Troia film festival.

1543. Fenuku, R.O. A brief outline on Ghana, in First Mogadishu Pan-African Film Symposium. Pan African Cinema... Which Way Ahead? Ibrahim Awed et al eds. Mogadishu: MOGPAFIS Management Committee, 1983. p.49.

Short description of Ghana Film Industry Corporation.

1544. FEPACI. Charte d'Alger du cinéma panafrican. Carrefour Africain 850(1985):21.

1545. FEPACI. III Congrès de la FEPACI des motions et recommendations. Carrefour Africain 873(1985):21.

1546. Férent, Catherine. Le premier long métrage éthiopien. Jeune Afrique 854(1977):60. (R)

Haile Gerima, Harvest 3000 Years.

1547. Ferrari, Alain. Le second souffle du cinéma africain. Télé-ciné 176(1973):2-9. (I)

Interview with Sarah Maldoror about Sambizanga. Review of filmmaking in early 1970's.

1548. Fieschi, Jean-André and Jean Narboni. Entretien avec Ruy Guerra. Cahiers du Cinéma 189(1967):52-56. (I)

Background for making Os Cafejestes and Os Fuzis, cinema novo and opinion of Glauber Rocha's and others' films.

*1549. Film Bulgarie. Echanges de semaines du film entre le Nigeria et la Bulgarie. Film Bulgarie 1(1983):2.

1550. Film Correspondent. 'Amadi' to be screened in northern states. New Nigerian Nov. 15 (1975): Saturday extra, pp. 2-3. (R)

1551. Film Correspondent. Cameroun work soon to be filmed. New Nigerian Aug. 23 (1975) Saturday extra, pp. 2-3.

Louis Balthazar Amadangoleda to make film of Bebey's novel, Fils d'Agatha Moudio.

1552. Film Correspondent. Can cinema bring a cultural revolution? New Nigerian Mar. 15 (1975) Saturday extra p. 3.

Report on second FEPACI congress.

1553. Film Correspondent. Film director working against odds. New Nigerian Oct. 23 (1976) Saturday extra pp. 3-4.

Problems in making Ola Balogun's Muzik Man; background on actors.

1554. Film Correspondent. Ola Balogun on a second film. New Nigerian Jan. 4 (1975) Saturday extra pp. 2-4.

Financing and plans for making Amadi.

1555. Film Correspondent. Sembène mixes sex, politics. New Nigerian May 1 (1976) Saturday extra, n.p. (R)

Xala.

1556. Film Cultura. A deusa negra. Film Cultura 33(1979):90. (R)

Ola Balogun, Black Goddess.

1557. Film Dope. Ruy Guerra. Film Dope 22(1981):21.

Biographical background, films made.

*1558. Film Français. Un festival en préparation à Lagos. Film Français Dec. 27 (1963):12.

1559. Filmsta 84. African cinema: in perspective, in Journey Across Three Continents. Renee Tajima, ed. New York: Third World Newsreel, 1985. pp. 60-61.

Chronology of films and film festivals 1955-1983. Reprinted from Filmsta (Bombay) Jan. 1984.

1560. Fiofori, Tam. Film realities. West Africa Apr. 27 (1987):820-822. (I)

Interview with Idrissa Ouédraogo, Rasman Ouédraogo (Burkinabe actor) and Sembène Ousmane.

1561. Fiofori, Tam. Growth of the film industry in Nigeria. Afriscope 11,9(1981):43-46.

1562. Fiofori, Tam. Memories of FESPACO '87. Guardian (Lagos) Apr. 19 (1987):B1-B2.

Nigerian representation at FESPACO. Burkinabe response to Nigerian films.

1563. Fiofori, Tam. 'There are many choices that can be taken...' Guardian (Lagos) Apr. 19 (1987):B2. (I)

Idrissa Ouédraogo discusses Yam Daabo and cultural and political roles of films.

1564. Fiofori, Tam. 'Young African film-makers are good...' Guardian (Lagos) Apr. 19 (1987):B1. (I)

Sembène discusses films of young filmmakers shown at FESPACO.

1565. Firk, Michele. Ruy Guerra: "J'ai fait 'Os fuzis' par nostalgie." Jeune Afrique 329(1967):78-79.

1566. Fischer, Lucy. Xala: a study in black humor. Millennium Film Journal 7-9(1980-81):165-172. (R)

1567. Flatley, Guy. Senegal is Senegal, not Harlem. New York Times Nov. 2 (1969):D17.

Sembène's attitudes toward coming to the U.S., his political views and film career.

1568. Flor, Paola and Luigi Elongi. L'Afrique et l'écran. Afrique Asie 379(1986):52-53.

Sidiki Bakaba's acting career.

1569. Flor, Paola and Luigi Elongi. Sarraounia une reine africaine. Afrique Asie 389(1986):54. (I)

Med Hondo discusses Sarraounia.

1570. Fofana, A. Allocution de Monsieur le Ministre de l'Information et des Postes et Télécommunications à la cérémonie d'ouverture, in FESPACO 1983. Paris: Présence Africaine, 1987. pp. 21-22.

FESPACO address on role of Burkina Faso in supporting African filmmaking.

1571. Follot, I. "Baara" un film réaliste. Bingo 306(1978):54. (R)

1572. Fomson, L.T. Documentary films in Nigeria. Our Pride Periodic Magazine (Jos)(1984):7-10.

History of documentary film in Nigeria.

1573. Fonike Magazine. Cinéma africain: Le CIDC et le CIPROFILM. Fonike Magazine 8(1987):22-23.

Review of activities 1971-1986.

1574.  Francis, Jeff.  The black man's burden.  *International Development Review* 14, 1(1972):40-42. (R)

James Nee-Owoo, *My Brother's Children* and *You Hide Me*.

1575.  Fraternité Matin.  Après le Sénégalais Sembène Ousmane, l'Ivoirien Désiré Ecaré voit son talent consacré à Cannes. *Fraternité Matin* 1061(1968):7.

1576.  Fraternité Matin.  Le cinéaste Henri Duparc et "Mouna ou le rêve d'un artiste." *Fraternité Matin* 2181(1972):8. (R)

1577.  Fraternité Matin.  Le cinéaste Timité Bassori et "La femme au couteau." *Fraternité Matin* 2175(1972):8. (I)

1578.  Fraternité Matin.  Le cinéma africain noir a perdue Oumarou Ganda. *Fraternité Matin* 4880(1981):19. (I)

Interview and necrology.

1579.  Fraternité Matin.  Crise du cinéma, des propositions concrètes des cinéastes professionnels. *Fraternité Matin* 5115 (1981):16.

Document by SIC.

1580.  Fraternité Matin. "Dalokan" un film de Moussa Dosso.  Tradition et modernisme en question. *Fraternité Matin* 5435 (1982):12. (R)

1581.  Fraternité Matin.  Désiré Ecaré: encore un nouveau film. *Fraternité Matin* 1260(1969):7. (R)

*Concerto pour un exil*.

1582.  Fraternité Matin.  "Dialogue avec le sacre": un exemple de coopération? *Fraternité Matin* 5458(1982):24.

1583.  Fraternité Matin.  Encore un dossier de "L'Afrique Littéraire sur Sembène Ousmane. *Fraternité Matin* 6376(1986):10. (BR)

Daniel Serceau, *Sembène Ousmane*.  See No. 70.

1584.  Fraternité Matin. Festival du film africain à Tokyo. *Fraternité Matin* 6009(1984):27.

1585.  Fraternité Matin. Festival du film publicitaire. *Fraternité Matin* 6185(1985):13-15.

1586.  Fraternité Matin.  Le film (Yeelen) du Malien Souleymane Cissé prix du jury. *Fraternité Matin* May 20 (1987):26. (R)

Cannes prize for *Yeelen*.

1587.  Fraternité Matin. Grande première de gala des films de Désiré

Ecaré. Fraternité Matin 1670(1970):7.

French responses to Ecaré's films.

1588.  Fraternité Matin. Un nouveau film sénégalais. Fraternité Matin Dec. 30-31-Jan. 1 (1978-1979):2. (R)

Ousmane William Mbaye, Domu Ngac.

1589.  Fraternité Matin. Une nouvelle étape dans le cinéma africain: la victoire au Festival d'Hyères du réalisateur ivoirien Désiré Ecaré. Fraternité Matin 1033 (1968):7.

1590.  Fraternité Matin. Le palmarès. Fraternité Matin Mar. 2 (1987):9.

FESPACO prize winning films.

1591.  Fraternité Matin. 1er festival francophone à la Martinique. Fraternité Matin Aug. 22-23 (1987):14.

Film festival to be held in Fort de France.

1592.  Fraternité Matin. Prix ICA au meilleur film documentaire. Fraternité Matin 5456(1982):20.

ICA prize for documentary film.

1593.  Fraternité Matin. Le 7ème art au Burkina. Fraternité Matin Jan. 30 (1987):11.

Short history of filmmaking in Burkina Faso.

1594.  Frazer, John. Mandabi. Film Quarterly 23, 4(1970):48-50. (R)

1595.  Fresu, Anna. Crianças e jovens escolhem as seus filmes. Domingo (Maputo) Sept. 12 (1982): 22-23.

Mocambiquan films shown at Giffoni Valle Piana film festival in Italy.

1596.  G.P. Ce qu'en pense un spectateur. Le Courrier de Saint-Ex 17(1979):1.

Films made in Gabon and public's awareness of them.

1597.  Gabriel, Teshome H. Ceddo: a revolution reborn through the efforts of womanhood. Framework 15-17(1981):38-39. (R)

1598.  Gabriel, Teshome H. Interview with Ousmane Sembene, in Third Cinema in the Third World. Ann Arbor: UMI Research Press, 1982. Appendix C. pp. 112-116. (I)

Interview at University of California, Los Angeles, 1975.

1599.   Gabriel, Teshome H.   "Let their eyes testify," an interview with
        Nana Mahomo.   UFAHAMU 7,1(1976):97-113. (I)

1600.   Gabriel, Teshome H.   Teaching Third World cinema.   Screen
        24,2(1983):60-64.

        Film criticism.

1601.   Gabriel, Teshome H.   Towards a critical theory of Third World
        films.   Third World Affairs (1985):355-369.

        Detailed outline of components of critical theory: texts,
        reception and production, which are discussed in relation to 3
        phases in historical development of film.

1602.   Gabriel, Teshome H.   "Xala": A cinema of wax and gold.   Présence
        Africaine 116(1980):202-214; Jump Cut 27(1982):31-33. (R)

1603.   Gachamba, Chece wa.   'Kolormask' opens tomorrow. Daily Nation
        (Nairobi) Dec. 4 (1986):4.

        Completion of film; expected attendance at opening.

1604.   Gagny Kanté, Amadou.   Moussa Sidibé s'est suspassé dans "Le
        retour de Tiéman."   L'Essor Nov. 25 (1970):3.

        Malian actor.

1605.   Gagny Kanté, Amadou.   La répression est la seule forme complète
        d'agissement.   L'Essor Dec. 18 (1971):1,4.

        Problems with behavior in theaters and screening of mediocre
        films in Mali.

1606.   Gallone, Annamaria.   Alzarsi in volo.   Nigrizia 105, 1(1987):51.

        Angolan films shown at Verona film festival.

1607.   Gallone, Annamaria.   Creare la propria immagine.   Nigrizia
        105,4(1987):56-58.

        FESPACO.

1608.   Ganda, Oumarou.   Menaces sur le cinéma nigérien.   Bingo
        319(1979):29-30.

        Problems in filmmaking in Niger.

1609.   Gansa Ndombasi.   Le cinéma zairois.   Unir Cinéma 137(1987):9-11;
        137(1987):5-6.

        Themes of 7 feature films made 1960-1983.   Negative images of
        cities dominant.   Music in films.

1610. Gansa Ndombasi. Cinéma zairois: bon vent a Ngambo 1. Unir Cinéma 27(1986):9-11.

Films of Kwami Mambu Nzinga: Moseka and Ngambo. (Unir Cinéma ceased numbering separately from Unir in 1987, which accounts for the numbering discrepancy between this and the preceding entry.)

1611. Gantie, Jacques. Le Ciné-club ferme ses portes. Le Soleil June 16 (1971):3.

Reasons film club closed in Senegal.

1612. Garb, Gill and Nii K. Bentsi Enchill. Ousman Sembene: the medium is the message. Africa Now 3 (1981):75-76. (I)

Discussion of filmmaking and creative writing.

1613. Garcia, Jean-Pierre, Marc Mangin and René Prédal. Afrique du sud, in Le tiers monde en films. Guy Hennebelle, ed. Paris: CinémAction Tricontinental, 1982. pp. 86-88.

Nana Mahomo, Last Grave at Dimbaza and Phela Ndaba.

*1614. Garcia Espinosa, Julio. For an imperfect cinema. Afterimage 3(1971).

1615. Gardies, André. Le cinéma africain à l'heure de la maturité. Ivoire Dimanche 629(1983):44-45.

FESPACO.

1616. Gardies, André. Cinéma et littérature. Notre Librarie 87(1987):102-107.

Films on oral and written literature; 20 Ivorian films mentioned.

1617. Gardies, André. 1981: regards sur le Vlle Fespaco, CinémAction 26(1983):173-177.

1618. Gardies, André. Notes sur un festival. Annales de l'Université d'Abidjan, Serie D Lettres 12(1979):283-298.

FESPACO.

1619. Garidou, R.M. Le symbolisme du masque dans "La Noire de..." Ciné Qua Non 2(1972):10-12. (R)

1620. Garreau, Gérard. Dikongue-Pipa: un visionnaire. Actuel développement 25(1978):33-38. (I)

1621. Gasperi, Anne de, Louis Marcorelles and Louis Skorecki. "Visages de femmes" primé à Cannes. Fraternité Matin 6181(1985):31. (R)

1622. Gauthier, Guy. Le cinéma en Afrique noire. <u>Image</u> <u>et</u> <u>Son</u>
173(1964):27-30. (I)

Interview with Jean Rouch, Sembène Ousmane and Momar Thiam.

1623. Gavigan, Patrick. Playing out the drama of apartheid. <u>Third</u>
<u>World</u> <u>Book</u> <u>Review</u> 2, 1-2(1986):85-91. (R)

Athol Fugard and Ross Devenish, <u>Marigolds</u> <u>in</u> <u>August</u>.

1624. Gavshon, Harriet. Levels of intervention in films made for
African audiences in South Africa. <u>Critical</u> <u>Arts</u>
2,4(1983):13-21.

1625. Gaye, Amadou. Un film sur la vie de Cheikh Ahmadou Bamba. <u>Le</u>
<u>Soleil</u> Nov. 3 (1977):2.

Film on the Mourides in Senegal.

1626. Gaye, Amadou. L'oeil ou l'hommage à l'Afrique combattante. <u>Le</u>
<u>Soleil</u> May 19 (1980):4. (R)

Thierno Faty Sow, <u>Oeil</u>.

1627. Gaye, I. Les films sénégalais à la quinzaine de Cannes: un test
positif. <u>Le</u> <u>Soleil</u> May 30 (1975):2.

Sembène Ousmane, <u>Xala</u> and Mahama Johnson Traoré, <u>Njangaan</u>.

1628. Gaye, I. Rétrospective pour un nouveau départ du cinéma
sénégalais. <u>Le</u> <u>Soleil</u> Dec. 3 (1974):4.

4 day retrospective of Senegalese film held in Dakar.

1629. Gayet, Anne. Deux approches de l'histoire africaine. <u>Croissance</u>
<u>des</u> <u>jeunes</u> <u>nations</u> 209(1979):37-39. (R)

Med Hondo, <u>West</u> <u>Indies</u> and Sembène Ousmane, <u>Ceddo</u>.

1630. Gbegnonvi, Marie-Louise. 'Pousse-Pousse'. <u>Afrique</u>
10(1978):92-93. (R)

1631. Gei, Mario. Le Retour d'un Aventurier. <u>Afrika</u> <u>Heute</u>
617(1973):77. (R)

1632. George, Susan. A film festival with a brain. <u>AfricAsia</u>
17(1985):62.

Onyeka Onwenu, <u>Nigeria:</u> <u>a</u> <u>Squandering</u> <u>of</u> <u>Riches</u> receives Geneva
International Television Film Prize.

1633. Gérard, Claude. Désiré Ecaré s'explique. <u>Fraterité</u> <u>Matin</u>
1947(1971):3. (I)

Discussion of Concerto pour un exil and A nous deux France.

1634. Gérard, Claude.  Festival à Ouagadougou.  Jeune Afrique 425(1969):44.

FESPACO.

1635. Gérard, Claude.  Panoramique sur la semaine.  Fraternité Matin 1932(1971):4.

Désiré Ecaré, A nous deux France and Concerto pour un exil.

1636. Gérard, Claude.  Venise à l'heure du Tiers-Monde.  Fraternité Matin 1455(1969):9; 1456(1969):9.

Roundtable on African film includes discussion of films by Désiré Ecaré.

1637. Gérard, Claude.  Le XXlle Festival du Cinéma Français: un enrichissement général.  Fraternité Matin 1125(1968):7.

FIFEF.  Brief comments by Désiré Ecaré on Concerto pour un exil.

1638. Gérard, Claude.  Visage du cinéma africain d'aujourd'hui II: avec Timité Bassori.  Fraternité Matin 1242(1969):7. (I)

Discussion of Femme au couteau.

1639. Gerima, Haile.  On independent black cinema, in Black Cinema Aesthetics, Gladstone L. Yearwood, ed. Athens: Ohio University Center for Afro-American Studies, 1982. pp. 106-113.

Discussion of African film in context of ideals for black filmmakers.

1640. Gervais, Ginette.  Hier et aujourd'hui même combat.  Jeune Cinéma 121(1979):21. (R)

Med Hondo, West Indies.

1641. Gervais, Ginette.  Jom.  Jeune Cinéma 144(1982):40-41. (R)

1642. Ghali, Noureddine.  Ousmane Sembène.  Cinéma 76 208(1976):83-95. (I)

Discussion of Emitai and Xala.

1643. Ghali, Noureddine.  Safi Faye.  Lettre paysanne.  Cinéma 76 205(1976):25. (R)

1644. Gharbi, Neila.  Le cinéma en Haute Volta.  SeptièmArt 50(1984):14.

1645. Gharbi, Neila.  Présence arabe et africaine à Cannes ou sont-ils?

SeptièmArt 59(1986):15-16.

1646. Gibbs, James. Climates of terror: an African writer's response. New African 215(1985):40. (R)

Wole Soyinka, Blues for a Prodigal.

1647. Gibbs, James. 'Yapping" and 'Pushing': notes on Wole Soyinka's 'Broke Time Bar' radio series of the early sixties. Africa Today 33,1(1986):19-26.

Origin of script for Wole Soyinka, Blues for a Prodigal.

1648. Gibbs, James and Jane Bryce. Soyinka's blues. New African 213(1985):44-45. (R)

Wole Soyinka, Blues for a Prodigal.

1649. Gilbert, Leah. Journée des films africains. Le Soleil Dec. 6-7 (1987):13. (R)

Med Hondo, Soleil O and Sembène Ousmane, La noire de.

1650. Gili, Jean A. Entretien avec Ruy Guerra. Etudes cinématographiques 93-96(1972):80-123. (I)

1651. Gili, Jean A. Fantastique magie et réalité dans l'oeuvre de Ruy Guerra. Etudes cinématographiques 93-96(1972):124-138.

1652. Gili, Jean A. Ruy Guerra. Etudes cinématographiques 93-96(1972):150-153.

1653. Gilliam, Angela. African cinema as new literature, in Journey Across Three Continents. Renee Tajima, ed. New York: Third World Newsreel, 1985. pp. 37-40.

Political themes of films.

1654. Ginesy-Galano, Mirielle. Qui s'intéresse au cinéma du tiers-monde? Croissance des jeunes nations 218(1980):36-37.

Tiers-Monde film festival.

1655. Gleeson, Mark. Attenborough's 'Trouble' wraps in Zimbabwe; stuntman assaulted. Variety 325, 1(1986):55.

Zimbabwean technicians gain experience working on Attenborough film, Asking for Trouble.

1656. Gleeson, Mark. Racial mixing starts at So. African sites. Variety 321, 2(1985):1, 92.

1657. Gningue, Abdou. Tachkent: fête de l'amitié entre les peuples. Le Soleil June 12-13 (1982):19.

African films shown at Tashkent film festival.

1658. Gnonlonfoun, Alexis.   L'Afrique à Cannes.   Afrique Nouvelle
1557(1979):3.

1659. Gnonlonfoun, Alexis.   L'Afrique à Tachkent.   Afrique Nouvelle
1721(1982):14-15.

1660. Gnonlonfoun, Alexis.   L'Afrique au rendez-vous de Cannes.
Afrique Nouvelle 1455(1977):23.

1661. Gnonlonfoun, Alexis.   Au chevet du FIFEF.   Afrique Nouvelle
1586(1979):14-15, 17.

1662. Gnonlonfoun, Alexis.   Au rendez-vous du FESPACO 81.   Afrique
Nouvelle 1653(1981):14-17.

1663. Gnonlonfoun, Alexis.   L'audio-visuel au service de tout l'homme.
Afrique Nouvelle 1435(1976-1977):12-15.

OCIC conference in Dakar.

1664. Gnonlonfoun, Alexis.   "Baara".   Afrique Nouvelle
1528(1978):16-17. (R)

1665. Gnonlonfoun, Alexis.   "Bako" à la recherche d'une nationalité.
Afrique Nouvelle 1548(1979):16-17. (R)

1666. Gnonlonfoun, Alexis.   Carthage 78 cinéastes et artistes ont la
parole. Afrique Nouvelle 1537(1978):12-15.

Marie-Thérèse Badgel, Camerounian actress, and filmmakers:
Jean-Pierre Dikongue-Pipa, Alkaly Kaba, Richard de Medeiros and
Ababacar Samb.

1667. Gnonlonfoun, Alexis.   Carthage 78 ou l'arabisation d'un festival.
Afrique Nouvelle 1536(1978):12-15.

1668. Gnonlonfoun, Alexis.   Ce que j'ai vu à Carthage.   Afrique
Nouvelle 1427(1976):12-15, 22.

1669. Gnonlonfoun, Alexis.   La chambre de l'évêque.   Afrique Nouvelle
1523(1978):19.

Themes of films in French-speaking West Africa.

1670. Gnonlonfoun, Alexis.   Cinéma africain au présent.   Afrique
Nouvelle 1706(1982):5.

Colloquium of African film production held in Niamey.   See No.
21.

1671. Gnonlonfoun, Alexis.   Le cinéma africain mérite encouragement et promotion. <u>Afrique</u> <u>Nouvelle</u> 1462(1977):16-17.

1672.  Gnonlonfoun, Alexis.    Ve FESPACO: qu'en penser?   <u>Afrique</u> <u>Nouvelle</u>
        1390(1976):12-15.

1673.  Gnonlonfoun, Alexis.    Con speranza e passione.   <u>Nigrizia</u>
        99,4(1981):26-30.

        Themes of films.

1674.  Gnonlonfoun, Alexis.    Décoloniser le cinéma.   <u>Afrique</u> <u>Nouvelle</u>
        1555(1979):3. (R)

        Pierre-Marie Dong, <u>Demain</u> <u>un</u> <u>jour</u> <u>nouveau</u>.

1675.  Gnonlonfoun, Alexis.    Diana Djingarèye: l'acteur est une valeur
        fragile.   <u>Afrique</u> <u>Nouvelle</u> 1454(1977):23.

        Nigerien actress.

1676.  Gnonlonfoun, Alexis.    En suivant la caméra.   <u>Afrique</u> <u>Nouvelle</u>
        1391(1976):12-15.

        FESPACO.

1677.  Gnonlonfoun, Alexis.    En tout franchise avec...   <u>Afrique</u> <u>Nouvelle</u>
        1453(1977):2.

        Arlette Din-Bell, Camerounian actress.

1678.  Gnonlonfoun, Alexis.    Entretien avec Safi Faye.   <u>Afrique</u> <u>Nouvelle</u>
        1562(1979):15. (I)

        Discussion of <u>Fad</u> <u>jal</u>.

1679.  Gnonlonfoun, Alexis.    Eux aussi nous ont dit.   <u>Afrique</u> <u>Nouvelle</u>
        1722(1982):17. (I)

        Moussa Diakité, Bakabé Mahamane, Falaba Issa Traoré and Bernard
        Yonli interviewed at Tashkent film festival.

1680.  Gnonlonfoun, Alexis.    FESPACO: rendez-vous à Ouaga en 1979.
        <u>Afrique</u> <u>Nouvelle</u> 1478(1977):22.

1681.  Gnonlonfoun, Alexis.    FESPACO 79 le rendez-vous du cinéma
        africain.   <u>Afrique</u> <u>Nouvelle</u> 1546(1979):12-17.

1682.  Gnonlonfoun, Alexis.    FESPACO 79 que s'est-il passé à Ouaga?
        <u>Afrique</u> <u>Nouvelle</u> 1547(1979):16-17.

1683.  Gnonlonfoun, Alexis.    FESPACO une femme aux commandes.   <u>Afrique</u>
        <u>Nouvelle</u> 1709(1982):18-19.

1684.  Gnonlonfoun, Alexis.    Festival de Namur, l'Afrique en vedette.

Afrique Nouvelle 1526(1978):16-17,24.

FIFEF.

1685. Gnonlonfoun, Alexis.   Le FIFEF à Dakar.   Afrique Nouvelle 1583(1979):16-17.

1686. Gnonlonfoun, Alexis.   FIFEF 1979 émergence des jeunes.   Afrique Nouvelle 1585(1979):22-23.

1687. Gnonlonfoun, Alexis.   Films vus à Namur.   Afrique Nouvelle 1533(1978):16-17.

FIFEF.

1688. Gnonlonfoun, Alexis.   "L'herbe sauvage".   Afrique Nouvelle 1519(1978):17. (R)

1689. Gnonlonfoun, Alexis.   Inoussa Ousseyni, un espoir.   Afrique Nouvelle 1394(1976):16.

3 short films by Ousseini shown at FESPACO, focus on Paris c'est joli.

1690. Gnonlonfoun, Alexis.   JCC 80 à quand l'ouverture africaine? Afrique Nouvelle 1641(1980):16-18.

1691. Gnonlonfoun, Alexis.   Un nouvel ordre?   Ce que j'en crois. Afrique Nouvelle 1539(1978-1979):31-33.

Problems of filmmaking.

1692. Gnonlonfoun, Alexis.   "Nuages noirs" de Djingarey Maiga du Niger. Afrique Nouvelle 1586(1979):15. (R)

1693. Gnonlonfoun, Alexis.   Ola Balogun a raté le coche.   Afrique Nouvelle 1438(1977):16-17.

Ajani Ogun.

1694. Gnonlonfoun, Alexis.   Ouagadougou: le rendez-vous de février. Afrique Nouvelle 1542(1979):17.

FESPACO.

1695. Gnonlonfoun, Alexis.   Ouagadougou, synonyme du cinéma africain. ICA Information 11/12(1980):57-58.

Films shown at FESPACO. Text also in English.

1696. Gnonlonfoun, Alexis.   Oumarou Ganda dans l'au-delà.   Afrique Nouvelle 1646(1981):21.

Obituary.

1697. Gnonlonfoun, Alexis. Oumarou Ganda: "Je préfère le vinaigre des critiques à la pommade des éloges." Afrique Nouvelle 1406(1976):17.

Review of Ganda's films.

1698. Gnonlonfoun, Alexis. Oumou Diarra vedette du cinéma malien. Afrique Nouvelle 1595(1980):18-19. (I)

Malian actress discusses how she became a film actress and her role in Baara.

1699. Gnonlonfoun, Alexis. Point de vue d'un dahoméen. Afrique Nouvelle 1341(1975):17, 23. (R)

Sembène Ousmane, Xala.

1700. Gnonlonfoun, Alexis. Première participation de l'O.C.I.C. Afrique Nouvelle 1536(1978):15.

OCIC assisted films shown at J.C.C.

1701. Gnonlonfoun, Alexis. "Le prix de la liberté." Afrique Nouvelle 1538(1978):16-17. (R)

1702. Gnonlonfoun, Alexis. Safrana ou "le droit à la parole." Afrique Nouvelle 1430(1976):2. (R)

1703. Gnonlonfoun, Alexis. Salomon Bekele: le cinéma africain doit s'imposer. Afrique Nouvelle 1447(1977):17. (I)

Bekele, interviewed at J.C.C., discusses his filmmaking philosophy.

1704. Gnonlonfoun, Alexis. Semaine franco-africaine à Dakar. Afrique Nouvelle 1504(1978):18.

1705. Gnonlonfoun, Alexis. 7e FESPACO. Afrique Nouvelle 1650(1981):5.

1706. Gnonlonfoun, Alexis. 7ème FESPACO en images. Afrique Nouvelle 1654(1981):14-17.

1707. Gnonlonfoun, Alexis. Sidney Sokhona j'aime le "flash-back." Afrique Nouvelle 1485(1977):16-17. (I)

Discussion of Safrana.

1708. Gnonlonfoun, Alexis. Six films africains à Namur. Afrique Nouvelle 1519(1978):17.

FIFEF.

1709. Gnonlonfoun, Alexis. Sous le signe du vodun. Afrique Nouvelle

1312(1974):24. (R)

Pascal Abikanlou, Vodun.

1710. Gnonlonfoun, Alexis. Tachkent 78, 84 états répresentés au 5e festival. Afrique Nouvelle 1514(1978):16-17.

1711. Gnonlonfoun, Alexis. Trois cinéastes nigériens ont la parole. Afrique Nouvelle 1490(1978):16-17.

Mahamane Bakabé, Oumarou Ganda and Inoussa Ousseini.

1712. Gnonlonfoun, Alexis. 25e F.I.F.E.F. à Cabourg. Afrique Nouvelle 1477(1977):12-17.

1713. Gnonlonfoun, Alexis. Vive FESPACO 83! Afrique Nouvelle 1751(1983):5.

1714. Gnonlonfoun, Alexis. Zalika Souley un vedette qui monte. Afrique Nouvelle 1398(1976):17.

Nigerien actress.

1715. Go, Mistral. Un professionnel visite le CENACI. L'Union Dec. 6 (1985):5.

Making of Henri-Joseph Koumba, Le singe fou.

1716. Gofa, L. Panafrikanisches Filmfestival Karthago 1972. Afrika Heute 23/24(1972):533.

J.C.C.

1717. Goffe, Anthony. Racial viewpoints. West Africa 3512(1984):2527-2528.

Kitia Touré, Comédie exotique, shown at Amiens film festival.

1718. Gogui, Désiré. Issaka Tihombiano (sic) doyen du cinéma burkinabé. L'itinéraire d'un autodidacte. Fraternité Matin Aug. 17 (1987):8.

Biographical background, training and accomplishments of Thiombiano.

1719. Gogui, Désiré. Une nuit de tournage avec Alpha Blondy. Fraternité Matin Aug. 17 (1987):9.

Sidiki Bakaba as director of Guérisseurs.

*1720. Golden, L. Kinematografiia stran tropicheskoi Afiki. Narody Azii i Afriki 3(1981):108-113.

History.

174.

1721. Gomez, René. Jouons le jeu. Le Courrier de Saint-Ex 17(1979):4.

Problems of filmmaking in Gabon.

1722. Gomis, Gabriel Jacques. "Lambaaye," le dernier film de Mahama Traoré. Le Soleil Aug. 12-13 (1972):2. (R)

1723. Gomis, Gabriel Jacques. Mahama J. Traoré: "Il faut revoir la commission de côntrole des films." Le Soleil Jan. 8 (1973):5. (I)

Discussion of SNC, need for national commission to control filmmaking in Senegal.

1724. Gomis, Gabriel Jacques. Sambizanga ou ballade pour un militant. Afrique Nouvelle 1309(1974):22-23. (R)

1725. Gomis, Gabriel Jacques. La Société Nationale de Cinéma est née. Le Soleil Dec. 22 (1972):3.

SNC founded. Need to restrict showing of foreign films in Senegal.

1726. Gomis, Gabriel Jacques. "Touki Bouki" de Djibril Diop Mambety. Le Soleil May 3 (1973):5. (R)

1727. Gonzalez, Alfredo. Nelisita, uma peça importante na filmografia angolana. Novembro 74(1984):55-56. (R)

1728. Goulli, Sophie el. Festival panafricain de Ouagadougou. 7e Art 41(1981):23-24.

1729. Goulli, Sophie el. Oumarou Ganda est mort. 7e Art 41(1981):24.

Obituary.

1730. Goulli, Sophie el. Ousmane Sembène: une trajectoire invariable. SeptièmArt 60(1986):11-12.

Recognition of Sembène's films at J.C.C. Biographical background, themes of his films.

1731. Goulli, Sophie el. Réflexions sur les journées cinématographiques de Carthage. SeptièmArt 52(1984):12-14.

1732. Grah Mel, Frédéric. Un accueil très favorable au film ivoirien "Djéli." Fraternité Matin 4912(1981):16-17. (R)

*1733. Grah Mel, Frédéric. Un classement qui s'annonce difficile. Fraternité Matin Feb. 27 (1981):25.

*1734. Grah Mel, Frédéric. La Côte d'Ivoire arrache le Grand Prix du 7e FESPACO. Fraternité Matin Mar. 2 (1981):28.

1735.  Grah Mel, Frédéric.  La crise.  Fraternité Matin 4912(1981):17.

Absence of national cinema in Côte d'Ivoire.

1736.  Grah Mel, Frédéric.  L'honneur et le devoir.  Fraternité Matin 4906(1981):25.

Films by Fadika Kramo-Lanciné.

1737.  Grall, Xavier.  Soleil O de Med Hondo.  Croissance des jeunes nations 132(1973):34-35.  (R)

1738.  Grant, Jacques.  Lettre paysanne.  Cinéma 77 217(1977):93-94.  (R)

Safi Faye, Kaddu Beykat.

1739.  Greenspun, Roger.  'Mandabi,' bitterly comic film, returns.  New York Times Sept. 30 (1969):41; Mar. 27 (1970):22.  (R)

September review reprinted in March.

1740.  Greenspun, Roger.  Screen: 'Emitai': a tragic vignette from Senegal.  New York Times Feb. 10 (1973):22.  (R)

1741.  Gregor, Ulrich.  Interview with Ousmane Sembene.  Framework 7-8(1978):35-37.  (I)

Functions, production and distribution of African films.

1742.  Grelier, Robert.  Ousmane Sembène.  Revue du Cinéma 322(1977):74-80.  (I)

Discussion of Emitai and Xala.

1743.  Grelier, Robert.  West Indies ou Les nègres marrons de la liberté.  Revue du Cinéma 342(1979):108-109.  (R)

1744.  Gross, Linda.  Africa's 'Xala' and 'Sambizanga.'  Los Angeles Times Sept. 23 (1977): Sect. 4, 14-15.  (R)

1745.  Gross, Linda.  'Amin' follows a violent scenario.  Los Angeles Times Feb. 5 (1983): Sect. 5, 10.  (R)

Sharad Patel, Amin the Rise and Fall.

1746.  Gross, Linda.  'Bush Mama:' a trip to awareness.  Los Angeles Times Apr. 7 (1978): Sect. 4, 20.  (R)

1747.  Gross, Linda.  'Ceddo': an unholy war in Senegal.  Los Angeles Times Apr. 27 (1978): Sect. 4, 20.  (R)

1748.  Gross, Linda.  Decrying the oppressed continent.  Los Angeles Times June 14 (1978): Sect. 4, 18.  (R)

Mahama Johnson Traoré, Njangaan.

1749. Gross, Linda. Fight for Freedom. Los Angeles Times Mar. 12 (1980):Part VI p. 7. (R)

Ola Balogun, Ija Ominira.

1750. Gross, Linda. 'Lovers' film to screen at Nuart. Los Angeles Times Aug. 6 (1983): Sect. 5, 9. (R)

Barney Simon, City Lovers and Manie van Rensburg, Country Lovers.

1751. Un groupe de cinéastes ivoiriens. A propos de CIDC "Bonnet blanc blanc bonnet." Fraternité Matin 5272(1982):24.

Film distribution in Côte d'Ivoire.

1752. Guadarrama, Daniel. Un cinéma sans argent. Croissance des jeunes nations 290(1987):35.

Cheick Oumar Sissoko, Nyamanton shown at Trois Continents film festival.

1753. Guadarrama, Daniel. Le leçon des ordures (Nyamanton) de Cheick Oumar Sissoko. Croissance des jeunes nations 290(1987):39. (R)

1754. Guardian. Clarion calling again. Guardian (Lagos) Oct. 28 (1984):B5.

Clarion Chukwurah, Nigerian actress.

1755. Guardian. Filmmakers urged to rescue Nigeria from moral ruin. Guardian (Lagos) Dec. 21 (1983):11.

1756. Guardian. Films festival begins in Benin today. Guardian (Lagos) Feb. 11 (1985):3.

UNIBEN film festival of Nigerian films.

1757. Guardian. Kongi's Harvest, Things Fall Apart on theatre bill. Guardian (Lagos) Jan. 3 (1987):11.

Francis Oladele, Bullfrog in the Sun and Kongi's Harvest.

1758. Guardian. Late Pa Orlando Martins: a symbol of artistic liberation. Guardian (Lagos) Sept. 28 (1985):13.

Obituary of Nigerian actor includes biographical information.

1759. Guardian. The new Lagos cinematography law. Guardian (Lagos) Sept. 21 (1983):8.

Editorial on new censorship board in Nigeria.

1760. Guardian. Orlando Martins: his world was a stage. Guardian
(Lagos) Oct. 18 (1985):8.

Editorial on significance of Martins's acting career.

1761. Guardian. Pioneer film-maker dreams fresh dreams. Guardian
(Lagos) Feb. 28 (1987):12.

Francis Oladele's plans for making Kongi's Harvest and Bullfrog
in the Sun.

1762. Guardian. Salute to Nigeria's theatre King. Guardian (Lagos)
June 9 (1984):8.

Editorial on Hubert Ogunde's contribution to theater and
potential contribution to film.

1763. Guardian. Supplement on the Nigerian Film Corporation. Guardian
(Lagos) Sept. 11 (1983):5-6, 11-12.

1764. Guardian. Unife film festival begins on Monday. Guardian
(Lagos) Jan. 4 (1986):11.

University of Ife festival of Nigerian films.

1765. Guemriche, Salah. Conte à rebours. Jeune Afrique
1202(1984):70-71.

Ruy Guerra, Erendira.

1766. Guerra, Ruy. Tendres Chasseurs. L'Avant-Scène-Cinéma
112(1971):1-43.

Ruy Guerra, Sweet Hunters, script of film and excerpts from
criticism.

1767. Guetny, Jean-Paul. "Les cinéastes africains, ma famille." Jeune
Afrique 1152(1983):52-53. (I)

Interview with Férid Boughedir.

1768. Guetny, Jean-Paul. Histoire d'une reconquête. Jeune Afrique
1152(1983):52.

History of film as depicted in Férid Boughedir, Caméra d'Afrique.

1769. Guèyé, Sidy Lamine. Baks du Momar Thiam. Le Soleil Feb. 20
(1975):10. (R)

1770. Guèyé, Sidy Lamine. Des droits et devoirs du cinéaste sénégalais
et de son public (le cas de Baks). Le Soleil May 16(1975):2. (R)

Momar Thiam, Baks. Review discusses interaction of filmmaker and
audience.

1771. Guéyé, Sidy Lamine. Point de vue de Njangaane. Le Soleil May 15 (1975):10. (R)

1772. Guido Givet. Aya: le feuilleton sur l'amitie qui a engendre une vraie amitie. Unir Cinéma 136(1987):22. (R)

1773. Guilain, Louis. Côte d'Ivoire: les jeunes loups jouent et gagnent! Africa (Dakar) 155(1983):43-45.

Need for more documentary films in Côte d'Ivoire. Preference for making feature films, prize winning films.

1774. Gupta, Udayan. Banned in Senegal. Seven Days 2,3(1978):25.

Censorship of Sembène Ousmane, Ceddo, in Senegal.

1775. Gupta, Udayan, Deborah Johnson and Nick Allen. Seven Days Interview: Sembene. Seven Days 2,3(1978):26-27. (I)

Discussion of Ceddo.

1776. H.B. Cinéma et télévision. Agecop Liaison 55-56(1980):53.

1777. H.N. Yeelen (La lumière). Positif 317-318(1987):89. (R)

1778. H.Y. Aperçu sur le cinéma africain. Action (Tunis) NS 7272(1976):12-13.

Definition of African film, its themes and traditions.

1779. Hado, Philippe. Le cinéma pour le monde rural. Ehuzu Oct. 24(1984):1,8.

Mobile cinema project for rural areas in Benin.

1780. Hado, Philippe. La mort du Tamarinier. Bingo 348(1982):68-69. (R)

François Sourou Okioh, Odo ti Gban lo.

1781. Haffner, Pierre. L'adolescent africain et le cinéma. Recherche, pédagogie et culture 62(1983):92-96.

Theory of film with a few African examples.

1782. Haffner, Pierre. Une beauté toute africaine. Zone 2 87(1980):15. (R)

Films shown at Locarno film festival: Ben Diogaye Bèye, Seye Seyeti; Ruy Guerra, Mueda and Daniel Kamwa, Notre fille.

1783. Haffner, Pierre. Les cinéastes d'Afrique noire et leurs villes. Unir Cinéma 136(1987):17-20; 137(1987):12-18.

Pioneers since 1960. Urban themes. Problems of distribution.
Cities as an influence on film production.

1784. Haffner, Pierre. Le cinéma, l'argent et les lois. Le mois en
Afrique 198-199(1982):154-166; 203-204(1982-1983):144-154.

Themes of Senegalese films made in 1981.

1785. Haffner, Pierre. Le cinéma (zairois) victime du "funtionnariat."
Le Monde Feb. 25-26(1979):13.

Problems of filmmaking and distribution in Zaire. Filmography
from CinémAction No. 3 reproduced. See No. 45.

1786. Haffner, Pierre. Les cinémas de libération à Tunis. Peuples
Noirs Peuples Africains 44(1985):71-102; 45(1985):56-75.

Themes of films shown at J.C.C.

1787. Haffner, Pierre. Des écrans a la recherche d'une mémoire.
Peuples Noirs Peuples Africains 35(1983):91-102.

FESPACO.

1788. Haffner, Pierre. Edward G-Ray Sugar Robinson, alias Oumarou
Ganda dit: le conteur. 7e Art 42(1981):16-19; 43(1981):16-19. (I)

1789. Haffner, Pierre. Eléments pour un autoportrait magnétique.
Afrique Littéraire 76(1985):20-24; CinémAction 34(1985):20-24.
(I)

Sembène Ousmane discusses his philosophy of filmmaking.

1790. Haffner, Pierre. L'esthétique des films. CinémAction
26(1983):58-71.

1791. Haffner, Pierre. Les films de la différence à Ouagadougou.
Peuples Noirs Peuples Africains 48(1985):97-131.

Day by day record of FESPACO.

1792. Haffner, Pierre. Quatre entretiens avec Paulin Soumanou Vieyra.
Peuples Noirs Peuples Africains 37(1984):88-104; 38(1984):27-49;
39(1984):14-29; 40(1984):26-40; 43(1985):50-68. (I)

History of African film.

1793. Haffner, Pierre. Sandy et Bozambo, entretien avec Jean Rouch sur
Sembène. Afrique Littéraire 76(1985):86-94; CinémAction
34(1985):86-94. (I)

1794. Haffner, Pierre. Sembène Ousmane à Kinshasa. Recherche,
pédagogie et culture. 37(1978):42-48. (I)

Discussion of educational role of film.

1795. Haffner, Pierre. Sénégal in Le tiers monde en film. Guy Hennebelle, ed. Paris: CinémAction Tricontinental, 1982. pp. 157-160.

Films by Djibril Diop, Ababacar Samb, and Paulin Soumanou Vieyra.

1796. Haffner, Pierre. Situation du cinéma négro-africain. Le Mois en Afrique 184-185(1981):127-136.

1797. Haffner, Pierre. Tout ce qu'il faut pour faire du cinéma, mais... Filméchange 6(1979):104-105.

Infrastructure in Zaire. Filmmaking for television documentaries. Audience satisfied with imported films.

1798. Haffner, Pierre. Traditions, roman et cinéma. CinémAction 26(1983):72-75.

Film and literature as means of communication.

1799. Haffner, Pierre. Vous avez dit: publics aliénés? CinémAction 26(1983):149-151.

Audience responses to African and imported films.

1800. Haidara Ipegi, Moulay Boubacar. Les dangers du "Retour de Tiéman." L'Essor Feb. 18 (1971):3. (R)

1801. Hall, Susan. African women on film. Africa Report 22,1(1977):15-17.

1802. Hall, Susan. Last grave at Dimbaza. Film Library Quarterly 9, 1(1976):15-18. (R)

1803. Hamalla, Cheickna. Un cinéaste et son oeuvre. Gros plan sur Diambéré Séga Coulibaly. Sunjata 29(1981):22-24. (I)

1804. Hamalla, Cheickna. Convergences à Ouaga. Sunjata 51/52(1986):37-39. (I)

Manthia Diawara discusses FESPACO.

1805. Hamalla, Cheickna. Le médecin de Gafiré. Jamana 1(1984):37-38. (R)

1806. Hamalla, Cheickna. 1Xe FESPACO. Jamana 3(1985):21-23.

1807. Hamalla, Cheickna. Parler a votre public et le conquérir. L'Essor July 20-21(1985):8. (I)

Cheick Ngaido Ba discusses Xew Xew.

1808. Hamalla, Cheickna. Une rare intensité dramatique mise en valeur par de belles qualités techniques. L'Essor Jan. 14-15 (1984):8. (R)

Mustapha Diop, Médecin de Gafiré.

1809. Hamel, Ian. "L'Etat sauvage" avec Doura Mané. Bingo 302(1978):57. (R)

Acting by Doura Mané.

*1810. Hammer, K. Senegalesisk film. Kosmorama 31(1985):221-227.

1811. Hamou, Salima. Pauvres mais beaux. Jeune Afrique 1351(1986):84. (R)

Cheick Oumar Sissoko, Nyamanton, prize at J.C.C.

1812. Harispe, François-Xavier. Film-maker under duress. South China Morning Post Oct. 22 (1982):2.

Career of Ola Balogun. Problems of film distribution in Nigeria.

1813. Harrow, Kenneth. The Money Order: false treasure or true benefice, in Interdisciplinary Dimensions of African Literature, Kofi Anyidoho, Abioseh M. Porter, Daniel Racine and Janice Spleth, eds. Washington, D.C.: Three Continents Press, 1985. pp. 75-87. (R)

Sembène Ousmane, Mandabi.

1814. Harrow, Kenneth. Sembène Ousmane's Xala: the use of film and novel as revolutionary weapon. Studies in Twentieth Century Literature 4,2(1980):177-188. (R)

1815. Hart, Emmanuel. 'Son of Africa' - a fair start. Daily Times (Lagos) Sept. 2 (1970):11,13. (R)

Funso Adeolu, actor in Son of Africa.

1816. Haustrate, Gaston. L'artisanat prometteur du cinéma africain, in Le guide du cinéma. Paris: Syros, 1985. Vol. 3, pp. 164-169.

Themes of films.

1817. Head, Anne. Africa: towards a national cinema. Screen International 485(1985):16. (I)

Med Hondo discusses need for production funds, lack of African films with international impact.

1818. Hennebelle, Guy. Africains, à vos marks! Jeune Afrique 460(1969):57-58.

Mannheim film festival.

1819. Hennebelle, Guy. Aperçu du cinéma en Afrique anglophone. Afrique-Asie 30(1973):45.

1820. Hennebelle, Guy. "Borom Xam Xam" un guérisseur sénégalais de Maurice Dorès. Afrique-Asie 131(1977):51-52. (I)

1821. Hennebelle, Guy. Cannes 1970: un déluge de 300 films. Jeune Afrique 491(1970):46-47.

1822. Hennebelle, Guy. Cinéma. Jeune Afrique 500(1970):8-9. (R)

Tidiane Aw, Pour ceux qui savent; Sebastien Kamba, Mwana Keba; Gacem Larbi, Contrastes; Seydou Sow, Guereo and Momar Thiam, La malle de Maka Kouli.

1823. Hennebelle, Guy. Le cinéma africain à Ouagadougou. Dénoncer le maraboutisme. Nouvelles Littéraires 2325(1972):25.

1824. Hennebelle, Guy. Le cinéma africain des origines à 1973. Recherche, pédagogie et culture 21(1976):45-46. (BR)

Review of Paulin Vieyra, Le cinéma africain. See No. 74.

1825. Hennebelle, Guy. Le cinéma africain fait irruption. Jeune Afrique 488(1970):27-44.

Review of themes of films, country by country.

1826. Hennebelle, Guy. Le cinéma nigérien, grand vainquer à Ouagadougou. Afrique Littéraire et Artistique 22(1972):98-100.

Nigerien films at FESPACO.

1827. Hennebelle, Guy. Le Ve FESPACO grand rendez-vous du film africain à Ouagadougou. Afrique-Asie 104(1976):43-46.

1828. Hennebelle, Guy. Comment devenir fou. Jeune Afrique 454(1969):53. (I)

Henri Duparc discusses Mouna.

1829. Hennebelle, Guy. Côte d'Ivoire, Haute-Volta, Mali, trois documents sur trois cinémas. Afrique-Asie 271(1982):65. (I)

Victor Bachy discusses his books on African film. See Nos. 8, 10 and 11.

1830. Hennebelle, Guy. Côte-d'Ivoire, Sénégal, Guinée: six cinéastes africains parlent. Afrique Littéraire et Artistique 8(1969):58-70. (I)

Henri Duparc, Désiré Ecaré, Oumarou Ganda, Mohamed Lakhdar Hamina, Sembène Ousmane and Timité Bassori.

1831. Hennebelle, Guy. Courrier. Unir Cinéma 14(1984):9-10.

Brief mention of important books on African film, See Nos. 19, 42, 67, 74 and 77, and major journals: Deux Ecrans, SeptièmArt and Unir Cinéma.

1832. Hennebelle, Guy. Daniel Kamwa: expliquer en amusant. Afrique-Asie 124(1976):51-53. (I)

Discussion of Pousse Pousse.

1833. Hennebelle, Guy. De Carthage à Tachkent: promotion des cinémas du tiers monde. Revue du cinéma international 1(1969):10-14.

J.C.C. and Tashkent film festivals.

1834. Hennebelle, Guy. La dernière tomb a Dimbaza. Ecran 41(1975):62-63. (R)

Nana Mahomo, Last Grave at Dimbaza.

1835. Hennebelle, Guy. Des cinémas d'Afrique noire depuis 1960. Recherche, pédagogie et culture 17-18(1975):3-6.

1836. Hennebelle, Guy. Deux cinéastes noirs. Ousmane Sembène. Jeune Cinéma 34(1968):4-9. (I)

Sembène discusses his films.

1837. Hennebelle, Guy. Deux filmes sénégalais de Ben Diogaye Bèye. Afrique Littéraire et Artistique 41(1976):92-96. (I)

Discussion of Princes noirs de Saint-Germain-des-Prés and Samba Tali; views on Senegalese film.

1838. Hennebelle, Guy. Un "Dur a Cuire" qui vient du Niger. Jeune Afrique 436(1969):38-39. (R)

Oumarou Ganda, Cabascabo.

1839. Hennebelle, Guy. Ecaré: "A nous deux, France" est l'analyse clinique d'un processus d'acculturation. Afrique Littéraire et Artistique 12(1970):76-82. (I)

1840. Hennebelle, Guy. En Afrique noire. Afrique Littéraire et Artistique 52-53(1979):197-202.

Films about migration.

1841. Hennebelle, Guy. Entre lumière et melies. Afrique-Asie 2(1972):46-47. (R)

Mustapha Alassane, F.V.V.A.

1842. Hennebelle, Guy.    Entretien avec Désiré Ecaré.    Cinema 71
152(1971):138-140.  (I)

Discussion of A nous deux France.

1843. Hennebelle, Guy.    Entretien avec Jean-Réné Débrix.    Afrique
Littéraire et Artistique 43(1977):77-89. (I)

History of African film 1930s to mid 1970s.

1844. Hennebelle, Guy.   Entretien avec Mahama Traoré: "Je suis pour le
cinéma politique, contre un cinéma commercial contre un cinéma
d'auteurs."  Afrique Littéraire et Artistique 35(1975):91-99. (I)

1845. Hennebelle, Guy.     Entretien avec Med Hondo.    Cinéma 70
147(1970):39-50. (I)

1846. Hennebelle, Guy.    Entretien avec Sembène Ousmane face a de
nouveaux dangers. Afrique-Asie 83(1975):46-48. (I)

Discussion of Xala.

1847. Hennebelle, Guy.    La femme au couteau.    Jeune Afrique
468(1969):12. (R)

1848. Hennebelle, Guy.    Le festival de "fouilles-les-oies." Jeune
Afrique 499(1970):37.

FIFEF.

1849. Hennebelle, Guy.    Le festival de Tachkent.    Jeune Afrique
416(1968):56-57.

1850. Hennebelle, Guy.    Festival  francophone.    Jeune  Afrique
446(1969):48-50.

FIFEF.

1851. Hennebelle, Guy.    Les films africains en 1975.    Recherche,
pédagogie et culture 17-18(1975):7-9.

Major themes of films.

1852. Hennebelle, Guy.    Gespräch mit Sembène Ousmane (Senegal),
Filmwissenschaftliche Beiträge 21,3(1980):171-198. (I)

1853. Hennebelle, Guy.    Il était un fois CinémAction.    Unir Cinéma
14(1984):10-12.

African coverage in CinémAction.

1854. Hennebelle, Guy. Un immense réservoir d'aventures, d'épopées, de légendes, de mythes. CinémAction 26(1983):4-9.

Themes. Introduction to special issue on African film.

*1855. Hennebelle, Guy. "Je refuse le cinéma de pancartes. Ecran 43(1976):46-49.. (I)

Interview with Sembène Ousmane.

1856. Hennebelle, Guy. Un livre de Paulin Vieyra. Afrique-Asie 96(1975):49-50. (I)

Discussion of Le cinéma africain, See. No. 74, and Senegalese film.

1857. Hennebelle, Guy. Un long métrage congolais: "La Rancon d'une alliance" de Sébastien Kamba. Afrique-Asie 53(1974):50-51. (R)

1858. Hennebelle, Guy. Med Hondo: "Soleil O" est un hurlement de révolte. Afrique Littéraire et Artistique 11(1970):62-69. (I)

1859. Hennebelle, Guy. Un message de Lourenço-Marques: ciné-club au Mozambique. Afrique-Asie 69(1974):46-47.

*1860. Hennebelle, Guy. Mouna ou le rêve d'un artiste, interview Algérie-Actualité June (1969). (I)

1861. Hennebelle, Guy. Un moyen métrage nigerien "Synapse" de Mustapha Diop. Afrique-Asie 87(1975):87-88. (I)

1862. Hennebelle, Guy. Naissance d'un cinéma ivoirien: "Concerto pour un exil" - opus 1 de Désiré Ecaré. Afrique Littéraire et Artistique 4(1969):75-81. (I)

1863. Hennebelle, Guy. Un nouveau cinéaste nigérien: Oumarou Ganda de "Moi un noir" à "Cabascabo." Afrique Littéraire et Artistique 4(1969):70-74. (I)

1864. Hennebelle, Guy. Ou en est le cinéma sénégalais? Africasia 52(1971):47-49.

Major Senegalese filmmakers.

1865. Hennebelle, Guy. Ouagadougou, nouvelle étape pour les cinémas africains. Afrique-Asie 1(1972):42-44.

FESPACO.

1866. Hennebelle, Guy. Ousmane Sembène: "Pour moi le cinéma est un moyen d'action politique, mais..." Afrique Littéraire et Artistique 7 (1969):73-82.

Sembène's philosophy of filmmaking.

1867.  Hennebelle, Guy.  P. Haffner: "En Afrique, le cinéma c'est la
       vie."  Afrique-Asie 198(1979):66-67. (I)

       Discussion of Essai sur les fondements du cinéma africain.  See
       No. 42.

1868.  Hennebelle, Guy.  Panorama des productions africaines et arabes.
       Ecran 30(1974):39-46.

       Country by country survey of themes of recent films.

1869.  Hennebelle, Guy.    Un  petit  "tours."  Jeune  Afrique
       520(1971):43-44.

       Themes of short films.

1870.  Hennebelle, Guy.    Petite planète du cinéma.    Cinéma 70
       142(1970):69-99.

       Themes of North and West African films.

1871.  Hennebelle, Guy.  Pour ou contre un cinéma africain engagé?
       Afrique Littéraire et Artistique 19(1971):87-93. (I)

       Interview with Sarah Maldoror, Sembène Ousmane and Timité
       Bassori.

1872.  Hennebelle, Guy.  Rencontre à Dinard avec des responsables de la
       Fédération Panafricaine des Cinéastes.  Afrique Littéraire et
       Artistique 24(1972):92-97.

       FEPACI meeting at FIFEF.

1873.  Hennebelle, Guy.  "Sambizanga" les premières luttes en Angola.
       Afrique-Asie 25(1973):56-57. (R)

1874.  Hennebelle, Guy.  "Sembène Ousmane cinéaste" de Paulin Soumanou
       Vieyra.  Afrique-Asie 26(1973): 40. (BR)

       See No. 77.

1875.  Hennebelle, Guy.    Sembène Ousmane: "Dénoncer la nouvelle
       bourgeoisie." Afrique-Asie 79(1975):64-65. (I)

1876.  Hennebelle, Guy. Sembène parle de ses films.  Afrique Littéraire
       76(1985):25-29; CinémAction 34(1985):25-29. (I)

1877.  Hennebelle, Guy.  Socially committed or exotic?  Young Cinema and
       Theater 3(1970):23-33.

       Themes of Francophone West African films.

1878.  Hennebelle, Guy.  Tahar Cheriaa "Les cinéastes africains ne sont plus isoles." Afrique-Asie 19(1972):42-43. (I)

Discussion about FEPACI.

1879. Hennebelle, Guy. Themen und stil afrikanischer Film. Afrika Heute supp. to 19(1971):3-7.

1880. Hennebelle, Guy. Le tigre, le chat et la souris. Jeune Afrique 519(1970):47-48.

ACCT sponsored conference on books and film in Dakar.

1881. Hennebelle, Guy. Le 111e festival de Carthage. Afrique Littéraire et Artistique 15(1970):66-72.

1882. Hennebelle, Guy. Le troisième festival panafricain du cinéma de Ouagadougou. Afrique Littéraire et Artistique 22(1972):88-97.

1883. Hennebelle, Guy. Tunisie: l'heure des Bilans. Jeune Afrique 508(1970):54-56.

Themes of films shown in Tunis.

1884. Hennebelle, Guy. Vers un cinéma malien? Afrique-Asie 30(1973):46. (I)

Souleymane Cissé discusses Malian filmmaking.

1885. Hennebelle, Guy. Vers un "tiers cinéma" africain? Jeune Afrique 452(1969):40.

Themes of Nigerien and Senegalese films.

1886. Hennebelle, Guy. Le Wazzou Polygame un film d'Oumarou Ganda contre le mariage forcé. Afrique-Asie 4(1972):49-50. (I)

1887. Hennebelle, Guy. "Zo kwe zo" de Joseph Akouissonne. Afrique-Asie 261(1982):62-63. (I)

1888. Hennebelle, Guy, Abdou Delati, Mohand Ben Salama and Férid Boughedir. Le cinéma de Sembène Ousmane. Ecran 43(1976):41-50. (I)

Interview with Sembène and discussion of his films by the authors.

1889. Hennebelle, Monique. Carthage: un festival ouvert à tous les cinémas. Afrique Littéraire et Artistique 34(1975):79-93.

1890. Hennebelle, Monique. Un "Coup de Fouet" pour le cinéma sénégalais. Afrique-Asie 42(1973):67-68. (I)

Abdoulaye Korka Sow discusses Senegalese film.

1891.  Hennebelle, Monique.  Daniel Kamwa, lauréat du meilleur scénario 1974 décerné par l'agence de coopération culturelle et technique: "Dans Pousse-Pousse, je dénoncerai la pratique de la dot au Cameroun." Afrique Littéraire et Artistique 33(1974):69-73. (I)

1892.  Hennebelle, Monique.  Du cinéma constat au cinéma militant. Afrique-Asie 13(1972):48-50. (I)

Mahama Johnson Traoré discusses development of African filmmaking.

1893.  Hennebelle, Monique.  1974-Les films arabes et africains. Afrique-Asie 63-64(1974):135-138.

Country by country survey of themes of films.

1894.  Hennebelle, Monique.  En Afrique ce ne sont pas les talents qui font défaut. Afrique-Asie 37-38(1973):134-138.

Country by country survey of themes of films.

1895.  Hennebelle, Monique.  Films arabes et africains. Des livres, des thèses, des mémoires. Afrique-Asie 74(1975):48-51. (BR)

Review of books, Nos. 1, 19, 27 and 67.

1896.  Hennebelle, Monique.  "Identité" africaine ou quoi? Afrique-Asie 45(1973):50-51. (I)

Pierre-Marie Dong discusses Identité.

1897.  Hennebelle, Monique.  Une libération sans frontières. Afrique-Asie 152(1978):79-80.

Films on women's liberation.

1898.  Hennebelle, Monique.  Mass média et culture traditionnelle en Afrique noire: le cinéma, un thèse de Mohamed Diop.  Afrique Littéraire et Artistique 33(1974):74-77. (BR)

See No. 19.

1899.  Hennebelle, Monique.  "Muna Moto" un long métrage camerounais. Afrique-Asie 97(1975):51-53. (I)

Jean-Pierre Dikongue-Pipa discusses Muna Moto.

1900.  Hennebelle, Monique.  Un nouveau film témoignage nationalité: immigré.  Afrique-Asie 102(1976):46-48. (I)

Sidney Sokhona discusses Nationalité immigré.

1901.  Hennebelle, Monique.  Ouagadougou: face aux grandes manoeuvres. Africasia 58(1972):46-47. (I)

Tahar Cheriaa discusses FESPACO.

1902. Hennebelle, Monique. Panorama du cinéma arabe et africain en 1975-76. Afrique-Asie 117(1976):149-152.

Country by country survey of themes of films.

1903. Hennebelle, Monique. "Sambizanga": un film de Sarah Maldoror sur les débuts de la guerre de libération en Angola. Afrique Littéraire et Artistique 28(1973):78-87. (R)

1904. Hennebelle, Monique. Sénégal: après "Karim" et "Kodou." Africasia 55(1971):48-49.

Themes of Senegalese films.

1905. Hennebelle, Monique. "Xala" une impuissance sexuelle bien symbolique. Afrique-Asie 79(1975):63-64. (R)

1906. Henri, Charles J.M. Relance au Sénégal. Bingo 369(1983):71.

Attempts to get films shown on Senegalese television.

1907. Henriques, Luis. Algumas observaçoes sobre a música e cinema. Domingo (Maputo) Sept. 28 (1986):6.

Better music needed for films made by INC in Mocambique.

1908. Herald. African films for this year's festival. Herald May 9 (1986):6.

Kine International Film Festival, Harare.

1909. Herald. Film Festival. Herald Apr. 24 (1987):8.

Kine International Film Festival, Harare.

1910. Herald. German film bursary offer. Herald Aug. 30 (1985):6.

Support for Zimbabwean attendance at Mannheim film festival.

1911. Herald. Video craze is invading our space-film industry. Herald Feb. 21 (1985):4.

Influence of video on Zimbabwean film industry's development.

1912. Herald. Zimbabwe symbol of hope -- French film man. Herald May 31 (1985):9.

Development of audiovisual projects.

1913. Herald Reporter. Fund films, African governments urged. Herald June 9 (1986):3. (I)

Ola Balogun discusses need for government support of film.

1914. Herald Reporter. Local voices to be heard on foreign films. Herald May 23 (1986):5.

English narration for film on Mocambiquan independence struggle.

1915. Herald Reporter. Prize-winning photographer tells of Sport Aid odyssey. Herald May 31 (1986):7.

Mohamed Amin's comments on film about Sport Aid.

1916. Herald Reporter. State planning film school for technicians. Herald July 14 (1986):1.

Zimbabwean government plans for film training and approval of scripts for foreign films made in Zimbabwe.

1917. Herald Reporter. Time for Zimbabwean films has come - expert. Herald Feb. 19 (1986):4.

Need for making films that will attract tourists.

1918. Herald Reporter. Zimbabwe may become the 'Hollywood of Africa.' Herald July 26 (1986):5.

Advantages for Zimbabwe of foreign film companies making films there.

1919. Herzberger-Fofana, Pierette. Sembène Ousmane, forgeron de caractères: une interview avec le romancier et cinéaste sénégalais. Komparatistische Hefte 8(1983):55-63. (I)

1920. Hibbin, Sally. Xala, in Magill's Survey of Cinema, Foreign Language Films. Frank N. Magill, ed. Englewood Cliffs, N.J.: Salem Press, 1985. pp. 3443-3447. (R)

1921. Hill, Allan. African film and filmmakers. Essence July (1978):18-24.

Survey of African film as collective effort and national force; focus on Senegal.

1922. Hill, Lyndi. Harvest: 3000 years. Horn of Africa 1,1(1978):59. (R)

1923. Hinxman, Margaret. So many children. Sunday Telegraph July 1 (1973):18. (R)

Sembène Ousmane, Emitai.

1924. Hochart, Philippe. Mozambique, in Le tiers monde en films. Guy Hennebelle, ed. Paris: CinémAction Tricontinental, 1982. pp.

145-146.

Role of INC, Ruy Guerra leading filmmaker.

1925. Holl. Finye. Variety 307, 4(1982):19,24. (R)

1926. Holl. Paweogo. Variety 312,4(1983):23. (R)

HONDO, ABID MOHAMED MEDOUIN, See HONDO, MED.

1927. Hondo, Med. A propos de "West Indies...Les nègres marrons de la liberté." Revue du Cinéma 345(1979):22-26.

Hondo discusses errors in review of West Indies by Robert Grelier. See No. 1743.

1928. Hondo, Med. Les Bicot Nègres Prologue. Framework 7-8(1978):21-22.

Discussion of filmscript and film's meaning.

1929. Hondo, Med. Le cinéaste africain à la conquête de son public, in FESPACO 1983. Paris: Présence Africaine, 1987. pp. 27-32.

Ideals for filmmaking. Discussion of infrastructure.

1930. Hondo, Med. Cinémas africains, écrans colonisés. Le Monde Jan. 21 (1982):12.

Distribution. Failure of French critics to promote African film.

1931. Hondo, Med. Nous aurons toute la morte. Framework 7-8(1978):23-25.

What filmmakers learned in making Nous aurons.

1932. Hondo, Med. What is cinema for us? Jump Cut 31(1986):47-48.

Edited version of No. 2407.

1933. Hoos, Willem. Fest of African pix being planned for Amsterdam in Nov. Variety 328, 1(1987):5, 22.

Amsterdam film festival will include retrospectives on Souleymane Cissé and Sembène Ousmane.

1934. Houédanou, Lucien. A propos de "Pétanqui" des sujets pertinents, une réalisation défaillante. Afrique Nouvelle 1814 (1984):19. (I)

Yeo Kozoloa discusses Pétanqui.

1935. Houédanou, Lucien. L'exemple indien. Afrique Nouvelle 1927(1986):17.

African filmmakers give too much attention to ideology and too little attention to audience response. Ola Balogun's films shown in India.

1936. Houédanou, Lucien.  Le grogne des cinéastes.  _Afrique Nouvelle_ 1931(1986):16-17.

Côte d'Ivoire filmmakers' views of the role of the government in supporting filmmaking.

1937. Houédanou, Lucien.  Ousmane Sembène:  le cinéma africain à l'honneur.  _I.D._ 714(1984):38-40. (R)

Review of Sembène's films.

1938. Howard, Juanita R.  Blacks Britannica: a film review and sociological analysis, in _Journey_ _Across_ _Three_ _Continents_.  Renee Tajima, ed. New York: Third World Newsreel, 1985. pp. 46-49. (R)

1939. Howard, Steve.  A cinema of transformation, the films of Haile Gerima.  _Cinéaste_ 14,1(1985):28-29, 39.

1940. Huannou, Adrien.  Sembène Ousmane: cinéaste et écrivain sénégalais.  _Afrique_ _Littéraire_ _et_ _Artistique_ 32(1974):35-40. (I)

1941. Hughes, David.  High noon in outer space.  _Sunday_ _Times_ (London) Aug. 30(1981):31. (R)

Sharad Patel, _Amin_ _the_ _Rise_ _and_ _Fall_.

1942. Humblot, Catherine.  Le cinéma africain et les ministres.  _Le_ _Monde_ May 6 (1982):17.

FESPACO, CINAFRIC, CIPROFILM.

1943. Humblot, Catherine.  Hollywood sur Volta.  _Le_ _Monde_ May 6 (1982):17.

CINAFRIC production facilities in Ouagadougou.

1944. Hyacinthe, Ya. N.  Pourquoi la S.I.C. _Djassin_ _Foue_ 9(n.d.):31.

1945. I.K. Ablakon.  _Cahiers_ _du_ _Cinéma_ 391(1987):54. (R)

1946. I.S.  A la découverte d'un stand.  _Sidwaya_ Feb. 24 (1987):5.

FESPACO.  Sale of Burkinabe products related to theme of cultural identity.

1947. I.S.  Le ministre Laurent Dona Fologo, "nous sommes venus participer a cette fête du cinéma africain." _Sidwaya_ Feb. 23 (1987):5.

FESPACO.

1948. Ibeabuchi, Aloysius. Problems of film making in Nigeria. Daily Times (Lagos) 278, 169(1985):5.

1949. Ibeabuchi, Aloysius. Why local films are not popular with African audiences. Daily Times (Lagos) Jan. 7(1984):7.

Discussion based on responses to films shown at FESPACO.

*1950. Ibikunle, Supo. Black Goddess: evils of slavery revisited. Lagos Weekend Mar. 30 (1979).

1951. Iboyi, Usman. Pitfalls in the filmed version of Things Fall Apart. Daily Times (Lagos) Oct. 4 (1986):8.

Letter highlights differences between film and novel.

1952. Ibrahim, Abudulkadir A. Cinema houses and delinquents. New Nigerian 5867(1985):9.

Problems in Nigerian theaters.

1953. Ibrahim, Jibo. Teaching Africa through Sembene. Concord Weekly 48(1985):38.

Course at Africa Centre, London, on understanding Africa through film.

1954. ICA Information. Le CIDC et le CIPROFILM ont démarre. ICA Information 11/12(1980):58.

Parallel text in English.

1955. ICA Information. Prix ICA du meilleur film documentaire. ICA Information 13(1981):16.

FESPACO prize for documentary film.

1956. ICA Information. Le Togolais Sanvi Panou vedette du "Sang du Flamboyant." ICA Information 13(1981):20. (R)

Togolese actor in film about Martinique.

1957. ICAM Information. 5e FESPACO. ICAM Information 2(1976):20.

1958. Idah, Emmanuel. The declining popularity of cinema houses. New Nigerian 6238(1986):2.

Problem of bad films shown, censorship and competition from television in Nigeria.

1959. Ido, Emmanuel. Ouagadougou: FESPACO Vlll. Afrika 24,5(1983):26.

1960. Idris, Aya. Rise and fall of Dr. Oyenusi good but... New Nigerian Apr. 8 (1978) Saturday extra pp. 2,4. (R)

1961. Idriss, Z. Ben. Impressions des cinéastes. L'Observateur Feb. 12 (1979):9-10.

Comments on FESPACO by African filmmakers and critics.

1962. Idriss, Z. Ben. Rencontre avec Mme Doura Mané. L'Observateur Feb. 7 (1979):7,9. (I)

Mrs. Doura Mané discusses her role in Bako and gives opinions of Baara and FESPACO.

1963. Idriss, Z. Ben. Vlle FESPACO visite d'un complexe de production. L'Observateur Feb. 24 (1981):1,10-11.

Description of CINAFRIC studios. Filmmakers' views of importance of CINAFRIC.

1964. Idriss, Z. Ben and Azad S. Sawadogo. Vle FESPACO tout a bien commence. L'Observateur Feb. 5 (1979):1,6-9.

Text of speech by Jean Barry on CIDC and CIPROFILM. Filmmakers' impressions of FESPACO.

1965. Ikeakanam, Bosco. Soyinka's film impounded. National Concord 5, 1564(1985):5.

Censorship of Wole Soyinka, Blues for a Prodigal, in Nigeria.

1966. Ikiddeh, Ime. Ozidi: the film, the saga and the play, in Comparative Approaches to Modern African Literature. S.O. Asein, ed. Ibadan: Department of English, Ibadan University, 1982. pp. 46-64.

Tides of the Delta compared with J.P. Clark's play and transcription of the festival.

1967. Ilboudo, Patrick. Ce soir "Lambaaye". L'Observateur. Oct. 19 (1978):6. (I)

Interview with Bernard Yonli, president of Burkinabe film club.

1968. Ilboudo, Patrick. De la double à la simple programmation. L'Observateur. Feb. 8 (1978):6-7. (I)

Interview with Christophe Somé about SONAVOCI.

1969. Ilbuodo, Patrick. De la poule blanche au FESPACO. Revue Africaine de communication 8(1984-1985):37-44; Peuples Noirs/Peuples Africains 44(1985):39-51; Unir Cinéma 16(1985):13-23.

Aims of FESPACO, films shown 1969-1985, definition of an African film, audience responses.

1970. Ilboudo, Patrick and Jacob Olivier. L'autre regard du cinéma. L'Observateur 2525(1983):1,6-7. (I)

Cheick Ngaido Ba's views of African filmmaking.

1971. Ilesanmi, Obafemi. Ogunde: four decades of drama. Guardian (Lagos) June 17 (1984):B1, B4.

Ogunde as theater director and filmmaker, construction of film village in Ososa, example to other theater groups.

1972. Iloegbunam, Chuks. Conversation with Eddie Ugbomah. Guardian (Lagos) Oct. 19 (1983):11. (I)

Discussion of problems in making Death of a Black President.

1973. Iloegbunam, Chuks. Death of a Black President: a review. Guardian (Lagos) Oct. 19 (1983):11. (R)

1974. Independent Film Journal. Emitai. Independent Film Journal Nov. 27 (1972):n.p. (R)

1975. Intrus. FESPACO 87 du festival au carnival. Intrus Feb. 24 (1987):1,3.

1976. Intrus. FESPACO 87 les cinéastes déraillent. Intrus Feb. 25 (1987):1.

Participation of filmmakers in "bataille du rail."

1977. Irungu, John Checkar. African film week. OCIC Info 1-2(1987):17.

African film week in Kenya and conference on future of the African film industry.

1978. Ismail, Carolyn. Long shots and joint ventures. South 69(1986):122.

Ruy Guerra, Opera de Malandro shown at Cannes.

1979. Issec. Philippe Mory: un film sur les dix ans de rénovation. L'Union Dec. 10-11 (1977):2.

On making of film to celebrate 10 years of President Bongo's leadership.

1980. Issec. Qui es-tu, Philippe Mory? L'Union Nov. 11-12(1978):2.

Mory's biographical background and filmmaking experience.

*1981.  Ita, Bassey.  Kongi's Harvest as film.  Sunday Post (Lagos) Apr.
11 (1971):5.

*1982.  Ita, Bassey.  Nigeria joins the film industry.  Morning Post
(Lagos) Aug. 16 (1965).

1983.  Ivoire Dimanche.  Actrice, Younouss Sèye est aussi peintre.
Ivoire Dimanche 75(1972):24.

1984.  Ivoire Dimanche.  Anne Kacou ou "Adjoba": du théâtre au cinéma.
Ivoire Dimanche 542(1981):15.

Ivorian actress.

1985.  Ivoire Dimanche.  Trois questions à Sembène Ousmane.  Ivoire
Dimanche 537(1981):45.  (I)

Discussion of Ceddo.

1986.  Iweriebor, Ifeyinwa.  The image of women in Nigerian films: true
to life?  New Nigerian Nov. 30 (1981):28.

1987.  Iyam, David Uru.  The silent revolutionaries: Ousmane Sembene's
Emitai, Xala and Ceddo.  African Studies Review 29,
4(1986):79-87.

Cultural background of films.  Sembene's use of silence.

1988.  Izeze, Eluem Emeka.  Nigerian film star dies.  New African
220(1986):50-51.

Obituary for Orlando Martins.

1989.  J.B.A.  Un cinéma en zone industrielle.  Fraternité Matin Feb. 24
(1987):12.

New theater in Côte d'Ivoire.

1990.  J.B.K.  La Côte d'Ivoire profonde un hommage à un peuple.
Fraternité Matin 6187 (1985):26.

Agence Ivoire Scribe, La Côte d'Ivoire profonde, shown at
Festival du film publicitaire.

1991.  J.M.  Ce que veulent les cinéastes africains.  Afrique Nouvelle
1216(1970):15.

FEPACI.

1992.  J.M.  Le Festival de Carthage aura-t-il lieu?  Afrique Nouvelle
1171(1970):15.

1993.  J.M.A.  Era uma vez uma bicha de cinema.  Novembro 44(1981):60-61

Theaters.

1994. J.R.Z. Pleins feux sur Cissé Souleymane. 2 écrans
2(1978):18-21. (I)

1995. Jabrane, Khaled. Où vas-tu Koumba? Jeune Afrique 579(1972):54.
(R)

1996. Jacob, Gilles. Tonton Kafka. Nouvelles littéraires
2150(1968):16. (R)

Sembène Ousmane, Mandabi.

*1997. Jacques, J.L. Problèmes et réalisation du cinéma en Afrique.
Entracte 3-4(1961).

1998. James, Emile. Un nouveau film de Sembène Ousmane "Emitai".
Jeune Afrique 539(1971):52-55. (I)

1999. James, Emile. Sembène Ousmane: "Je n'utilise pas de vedettes, ça
coûte trop cher." Jeune Afrique 499(1970):40-41. (I)

2000. Jean-Bart, Anne. Après le 8e FESPACO les questions demeurent.
Le Soleil Feb. 21 (1983):11.

2001. Jean-Bart, Anne. "Certificat d'indigence" de Moussa Yoro Bathily
ou les complexitiés de l'administration. Le Soleil Feb. 21
(1983):11. (I)

2002. Jean-Bart, Anne. Un essai à transformer. Le Soleil Jan. 12
(1984):6. (R)

Cheick Ngaido Ba, Xew Xew.

2003. Jean-Bart, Anne. "Rue Cases nègres" à Dakar. Le Soleil Dec. 13
(1983):5.

SIDEC arrangements for showing Rue Cases nègres; Douta Seck's
role in it.

2004. Jean-Bart, Anne. Seydina Wade: chanson, écriture et... vidéo.
Le Soleil Feb. 4-5 (1984):9.

Wade's music, including that in Xew Xew.

2005. Jensen, Monika. The role of the filmmaker: an interview with
Ousmane Sembene, in Conflict and Control in the Cinema, John
Tulloch, ed. Melbourne: Macmillan Company of Australia, 1977.
pp. 486-491. (I)

Reprint of No. 2006.

2006. Jensen, Monika. The role of the filmmaker: three views -
interview with Ousmane Sembène. Arts in Society

10,2(1973):220-225. (I)

Role of film in society; importance of women in African society; need for filmmaker's commitment.

2007. Jensen, Viggo Holm. Africa, a general dossier. International Film Guide (1975):71-72.

List of films made in Francophone West African countries.

2008. Jensen, Viggo Holm. Ivory Coast. International Film Guide (1974):227.

Films made in 1973.

2009. Jensen, Viggo Holm. Niger. International Film Guide (1974):268.

Films by Moustapha Alassane and Oumarou Ganda.

2010. Jensen, Viggo Holm. Senegal. International Film Guide (1973):289-290.

Distribution problems. Films by Ababacar Samb and Sembène Ousmane.

2011. Jensen, Viggo Holm. Senegal. International Film Guide (1974):293-294.

Distribution problems. Ababacar Samb's role in FEPACI. Sembène Ousmane's film on the Olympics and plans for making Samory.

2012. Jensen, Viggo Holm. Senegal. International Film Guide (1976):317.

Brief review of films made in 1960's; comments on most important recent films.

2013. Jensen, Viggo Holm. Upper Volta. International Film Guide (1974):331.

Nationalization of theaters. Djim Kola, Sang des parias.

2014. Jensen, Viggo Holm and Vibeke Pedersen. Guinea. International Film Guide (1972):158.

Short history of state-supported film industry.

2015. Jensen, Viggo Holm and Vibeke Pedersen. Ivory Coast. International Film Guide (1972):179.

Infrastructure. Recent films by Henri Duparc, Désiré Ecaré and Timité Bassori.

2016. Jensen, Viggo Holm and Vibeke Pedersen. Niger. International

Film Guide (1972):207.

Theaters. Films by Moustapha Alassane and Oumarou Ganda.

2017. Jensen, Viggo Holm and Vibeke Pedersen. Senegal. International Film Guide (1972):233-235.

Infrastructure. Films by Djibril Diop, Momar Thiam, Mahama Johnson Traoré, Sembène Ousmane and Paulin Vieyra.

2018. Jesus, Augusto de. "Lhomulo" passará ao cinema. Domingo (Maputo) Dec. 7 (1986):9. (R)

2019. Jesus, Augusto de. Melhor forma é a televisão. Domingo (Maputo) Apr. 5 (1987):14-15.

President Sankara's address at FESPACO. Comparison of FESPACO and Cannes film festival.

2020. Jesus, Augusto de. Olhai os filmes de Africa! Domingo (Maputo) Mar. 15 (1987):10-11.

FESPACO.

2021. Jesus, Augusto de. Portos abertas ao nosso cinema. Domingo (Maputo) Jan. 20 (1985):16.

Production of Madrugada dos Imbomdeiros with Yugoslavian support.

2022. Jeune Afrique. Ababakar Samb cinéaste africain. Jeune Afrique 573(1972):55.

Georges Sadoul prize for Codou.

2023. Jeune Afrique. Une année qui tiendra ses promesses. Jeune Afrique 574(1972):64-65.

Themes of films made in 1971.

2024. Jeune Afrique. Carthage 1972. Jeune Afrique 605(1972):61.

African films shown at J.C.C.

2025. Jeune Afrique. Un cinéma encore "exile." Jeune Afrique 656(1973):64-65. (R)

Désiré Ecaré, A nous deux France.

2026. Jeune Afrique. Cinéma et politique. Jeune Afrique 616(1972):47.

J.C.C.

2027. Jeune Afrique. Cinéma: une fructueuse patience. Jeune Afrique 658(1973):65.

Films made in Gabon.

2028. Jeune Afrique. Comment dévenir fou. Jeune Afrique 454(1969):53.
(I)

Henri Duparc discusses his acting in films, training as filmmaker
and Mouna.

2029. Jeune Afrique. Désiré Ecaré beaucoup de sympathies et pas
d'argent. Jeune Afrique 386-387(1968):69. (I)

Ecaré's view of filmmaking; support and publicity for Concerto
pour un exil.

2030. Jeune Afrique. Deux cent cinquante cinéastes. Jeune Afrique
520(1970):45. (I)

Ababacar Samb discusses FEPACI.

2031. Jeune Afrique. Emitai ou la résistance collective. Jeune
Afrique 860(1977):90-91. (I)

Sembène discusses Emitai.

2032. Jeune Afrique. Entretien avec Diagne Costades réalisateur et
directeur du cinéma guinéen. Jeune Afrique 416(1968):55. (I)

Discussion of his training as a filmmaker, how he finances his
films and the infrastructure for film in Guinée.

2033. Jeune Afrique. L'événement 66. Jeune Afrique 276(1966):34.

Sembène's La noire de considered for Jean Vigo prize.

2034. Jeune Afrique. La FEPACI à Harlem. Jeune Afrique 649(1973):65.

6 members of FEPACI visit U.S.A.

2035. Jeune Afrique. La FEPACI et Téhéran. Jeune Afrique
600(1972):60.

African films shown at Teheran film festival.

2036. Jeune Afrique. La FEPACI reconnue par l'OAU. Jeune Afrique
605(1972):60-61.

Development of FEPACI and its main concerns.

2037. Jeune Afrique. "L'orphelin de Dieu". Jeune Afrique
583(1982):50. (R)

2038. Jeune Afrique. Les pasionarias n'étaient pas au rendezvous.
Jeune Afrique 792(1976):56. (R)

Safi Faye, Kaddu Beykat shown at Brussels film festival.

2039.  Jeune Afrique. La pellicule, la politique et Med Hondo. Jeune Afrique 654(1973):29. (I)

Hondo discusses his filmmaking philosophy.

2040.  Jeune Afrique. Quatre cinéastes africains: "Nationalisons les salles!" Jeune Afrique 355(1967):43-45.

Distribution discussed by Sembène Ousmane and 3 North African filmmakers.

2041.  Jeune Afrique. Sarah Maldoror nous déclare. Jeune Afrique 469 (1969):45. (I)

Discussion of her films.

2042.  Jeune Afrique. Sébastien Kamba cinéaste congolais nous déclare. Jeune Afrique 509(1970):43. (I)

Discussion of filmmaking in Congo and the documentaries he has made.

2043.  Jeune Afrique. Un secteur en faillite. Jeune Afrique 586(1972):44.

Activities of OCAM.

2044.  Jeune Afrique. Sembène Ousmane pour un congrés des cinéastes africains. Jeune Afrique 386-387(1968):70. (I)

2045.  Jeune Afrique. Toute l'Afrique à Nanterre. Jeune Afrique 371(1968):51-52.

Nanterre film festival.

2046.  Jeune Afrique. Le Wazzou polygame, un film d'Oumarou Ganda. Jeune Afrique 591(1972):60-61.

FESPACO prize.

2047.  Jeune Afrique. Younousse Sèye actrice, artiste, animatrice sénégalaise, nous déclare. Jeune Afrique 513(1970):36. (I)

Senegalese actor discusses how he began acting in Sembène's films and his opinion of theater and film acting.

2048.  Jeune Afrique Magazine. Cinéma infos. Jeune Afrique Magazine 29(1986):9.

New films being made by Ben Diogaye Bèye and Med Hondo. Recent films in which Sidiki Bakaba has roles.

2049.  Jeune Afrique Magazine.  Le sorcier ou le toubib?  Jeune Afrique
       Magazine 23(1986):13. (R)

       Mustapha Diop, Médecin de Gafiré.

*2050.  Jeune Afrique Plus.  [Special issue on film] Jeune Afrique Plus
       6(1984).

2051.  Jeune Cinéma.  Préserver l'esprit du conte, un entretien avec
       Kaboré.  Jeune Cinema 149(1983):15-17. (I)

       Discussion of Wend Kuuni.

2052.  Jeyifo, Biodun.  Cinema, radical will and social consciousness.
       Guardian (Lagos) Jan. 6 (1985):B4. (R)

       Wole Soyinka, Blues for a Prodigal.

2053.  Johnson, Randal.  The Guns (Os Fuzis), in Magill's Survey of
       Cinema, Foreign Language Films.  Frank N. Magill, ed. Englewood
       Cliffs, N.J.: Salem Press, 1985. pp. 1319-1324. (R)

2054.  Johnson, Rudy.  African film makers seek aid here.  New York
       Times May 31(1973):42.

       Members of FEPACI seek financial support in U.S.A.  Differences
       in African and American approaches to filmmaking.

2055.  Johnson, Thomas A.  A film force from Senegal.  New York Times
       Jan. 27 (1978):C5.

       Sembène Ousmane, Ceddo, its censorship in Senegal; reasons why he
       became filmmaker.

2056.  Johnson, Thomas A.  A film maker in Senegal stresses African
       culture.  New York Times Aug. 31 (1974):12. (I)

       Sembène discusses his philosophy of filmmaking.

2057.  Jossais, Lourenço.  O filme como divertimento e também a
       prendizagem.  Domingo (Maputo) Apr. 29 (1984):8-9.

       Films shown to children and their opinions of them solicited, in
       Mocambique.

2058.  Jossais, Lourenço.  Pais devem acompanhar os seus filhos ao
       cinema defende Laura Cardose, do INC.  Domingo (Maputo) Apr. 29
       (1984):8-9.

       Importance of film to children; plans to show films to children
       in Mocambique.

2059.  Jouvet, Pierre.  Emitai.  Cinématographe 27(1977):40.

2060. Jouvet, Pierre. Xala. Cinématographe 18(1976):44. (R)

2061. Jru, I.S. Sourees. Les activités de recherche à l'INAFEC.
Sidwaya Apr. 14 (1987):10.

Objectives, structure and research conducted at INAFEC. Problems
of conducting research and topics on which research needed.

2062. Jules-Rosette, Bennetta. An experiment in African cinema.
International Development Review 3(1976):32-36.

Documentary filmmaking in Zambia.

2063. Jurka, Jan. Rozhovor s režisérem Ousmanem Sembènem. Film a Doba
26, 11(1980):642-644.

2064. Jusu, K.K. Man. Adja-Tio: Le temps du bilan. Fraternité Matin
5086 (1981):15. (R)

2065. Jusu, K.K. Man. L'Afrique pour la 1ère fois répresentée en
competition officielle. Fraternité Matin May 11 (1987):30.

Souleymane Cissé, Yeelen in official competition at Cannes film
festival. Background on Cissé's filmmaking.

2066. Jusu, K.K. Man. Après "Cannes 81". Fraternité Matin
5015(1981):10.

Meeting of Côte d'Ivoire filmmakers.

2067. Jusu, K.K. Man. Une belle initiative de cinéastes ivoiriens.
Fraternité Matin 4936(1981):18.

Film week organized by Côte d'Ivoire filmmakers.

2068. Jusu, K.K. Man. La cérémonie d'ouverture sous les couleurs du
groupe Woya. Fraternité Matin Feb. 24 (1987):11.

Opening ceremony at FESPACO.

2069. Jusu, K.K. Man. Le cinéma africain n'existe pas. Fraternité
Matin 4936(1981):16. (I)

Jean Louis Koula discusses African filmmaking.

2070. Jusu, K.K. Man. Le cinéma vers un nouveau souffle. Fraternité
Matin 6387(1986):10.

Activities of SIDEC and SNPC.

2071. Jusu, K.K. Man. Le 50,000ème spectateur de Djéli. Fraternité
Matin 5206(1982):13. (R)

2072. Jusu, K.K. Man. Un colloque à Niamey sur la production. Fraternité Matin 5208(1982):12.

2073. Jusu, K.K. Man. Un complexe Freudien. Fraternité Matin 5194(1982):18. (R)

Timité Bassori, La femme au couteau.

2074. Jusu, K.K. Man. De la qualité des films africains. Fraternité Matin 5394(1982):10.

Quality of films made in Francophone West Africa.

2075. Jusu, K.K. Man. Des avis partagés sur "Visages de femmes." Fraternité Matin Feb. 27 (1987):9.

Debate about Visages de femmes when shown at FESPACO. FESPACO as source of cultural promotion.

2076. Jusu, K.K. Man. Des films inédits. Fraternité Matin 5212(1982):19.

Ben Diogaye Bèye, Seye Seyeti and Jules Takam, L'appât du gain.

2077. Jusu, K.K. Man. La détaxe des films nationaux. Fraternité Matin 5208(1982):12.

Taxes to support filmmaking in Côte d'Ivoire and other Francophone West African countries.

2078. Jusu, K.K. Man. 2e semaine du cinéma africain ouverture samedi avec "Amok" le film de l'espoir. Fraternité Matin 5213(1982):8.

African film week in Abidjan.

2079. Jusu, K.K. Man. 10ème FESPACO:de nombreuses innovations attendues. Fraternité Matin Jan. 30 (1987):10-11. (I)

Philippe Sawadogo discusses innovation and problems of FESPACO.

2080. Jusu, K.K. Man. "Djéli, ce soir à l'Ivoire, un "gala militant." Fraternité Matin 5006(1981):7. (R)

2081. Jusu, K.K. Man. Djéli, un bilan positif. Fraternité Matin 5220(1982):11. (R)

2082. Jusu, K.K. Man. Djéli: un film de sensibilité. Fraternité Matin 5009 (1981):11. (R)

2083. Jusu, K.K. Man. Ecaré et Bassori...Fraternité Matin 5318(1981):19.

2084. Jusu, K.K. Man. Entre la politique et l'ouverture. Fraternité Matin 6126(1985):25.

FESPACO.

2085. Jusu, K.K. Man. Un festival qui grandit. Fraternité Matin Mar. 8 (1987):1, 12-13.

Importance of actors in films shown at FESPACO. Dynamism of Burkinabe film.

2086. Jusu, K.K. Man. Kitia Touré: de l'écriture au cinéma. Fraternité Matin 6186(1985):11.

2087. Jusu, K.K. Man. Med Hondo: la fin de l'amateurisme. Fraternité Matin Mar. 19 (1987):7. (I)

Hondo's views of FESPACO, roles of films, solutions to infractructural problems.

2088. Jusu, K.K. Man. Les médias au service de la tradition orale. Fraternité Matin Mar. 12 (1987):7.

FESPACO colloquium on oral tradition and the new medias.

2089. Jusu, K.K. Man. N'Dabian Vodio n'est plus. Fraternité Matin Oct. 6 (1986):11.

Obituary reviews his filmmaking career.

2090. Jusu, K.K. Man. Le 9e FESPACO à Ouaga: la liquidation du CIDC-France. Fraternité Matin 6127(1985):26.

2091. Jusu, K.K. Man. Le 9ème FESPACO à Ouagadougou: peu de grands films. Fraternité Matin 6119(1985):29.

2092. Jusu, K.K. Man. 9ème FESPACO. L'originalité des films ivoiriens. Fraternité Matin 6128(1985):26.

2093. Jusu, K.K. Man. Ouagadougou capitale de la culture africaine. Fraternité Matin Jan. 31-Feb. 1 (1987):9-11.

Summary of filmmaking facilities in Ouagadougou.

2094. Jusu, K.K. Man. "Pétanqui" ou le bon exemple de J.L. Koula et Y. Kozoloa. Fraternité Matin 5202(1982):17. (R)

2095. Jusu, K.K. Man. "Pour la liberté" d'Ola Balogun. Le cinéma de libération. Fraternité Matin 5200(1982):15. (R)

Ija Ominira.

2096. Jusu, K.K. Man. Quel avenir pour le cinéma ivoirien? Fraternité Matin 6145(1985):22.

Films by Désiré Ecaré, Roger Gnoan Mbala and Kitia Touré.

2097.  Jusu, K.K. Man.  Rien ne sera plus comme avant.  Fraternité Matin 5021(1981):19.

Newly formed association of filmmakers in Côte d'Ivoire.

2098.  Jusu, K.K. Man.  Roger M'Bala: maître de l'humour.  Fraternité Matin 6141(1985):12.

2099.  Jusu, K.K. Man.  Sidiki Bakaba: le "jusqu'au-boutiste".  Fraternité Matin July 19-20 (1986):20.

Discusses his role in Visages de femmes, why film is beautiful, not obscene, why he chose to be an actor.

2100.  Jusu, K.K. Man.  Timité Bassori: "Faire mieux la prochaine fois."  Fraternité Matin 5220(1982):10.

2101.  Jusu, K.K. Man.  "Yam Daabo" d'Idrissa Ouédraogo: Ah! les hommes.  Fraternité Matin July 28 (1987):9. (R)

2102.  Jusu, K.K. Man.  Yéo Kozoloa: plus de peur que de mal.  Fraternité Matin 6128(1985):26.

2103.  K.K.  "Visages de femmes" projection publique cet après-midi au Palais des Sports.  Fraternité Matin Apr. 1 (1987):9. (R)

2104.  KNA.  Cinema festival draws big crowds.  Daily Nation (Nairobi) Dec. 3 (1986):2.

Kenyan film festival shows African films in Mombasa, Nakuru and Thika.

2105.  KNA.  Festival to 'catalyse Africa's film industry.'  Daily Nation (Nairobi) Dec. 11 (1986):4.

Kenyan film festival to show and promote African films.

2106.  KNA.  'Kolormask' set for 12-day city run.  Daily Nation (Nairobi) Dec. 5 (1986):4. (R)

2107.  KNA.  Nyagah: Take local time.  Daily Nation (Nairobi) Dec. 4 (1986):4.

Jeremiah Nyagah, Kenyan Minister for Environment and Natural Resources discusses role of film in society.

2108.  KNA.  Use of African themes urged.  Daily Nation (Nairobi) Dec. 3 (1986):4.

Francis Lekolool, Kenyan Northeast Provincial Commissioner, discusses need for films to present positive images of Africans.

2109.  Ka, Abdou Anta.  Un acte révolutionnaire: la nationalisation du cinéma sénégalais. <u>Le Soleil</u> Jan. 10 (1974):4.

Plan to control film distribution in Senegal.

2110. Ka, Abdou Anta. Bissine, "La noire de..." 15 ans après. <u>Bingo</u> 335(1980):32-34.

Mbissine Diop, actress in <u>La noire de</u>.

2111. Ka, Abdou Anta. L'oubli...de Paulin Vieyra. <u>Le Soleil</u> 3320(1981):2. (R)

En <u>residence surveillée</u>.

2112. Kaboke, V. L'Accident. <u>Unir Cinéma</u> 23-24(1986):35. (R)

2113. Kaboke, V. Le Certificat d'Indigence. <u>Unir Cinéma</u> 23-24(1986):36. (R)

2114. Kaboke, V. Njages (sic) Noirs. <u>Unir Cinéma</u> 23-24(1986):33. (R)

2115. Kaboke, V. Saitane. <u>Unir Cinéma</u> 23-24(1986):33-34. (R)

2116. Kaboke, V. Le "Wazzou" Polygame. <u>Unir Cinéma</u> 23-24(1986):34. (R)

2117. Kaboré, Gaston J.M. Préserver l'esprit du conte, un entretien avec Kaboré. <u>Jeune Cinéma</u> 149(1983):15-17. (I)

Discussion of <u>Wend Kuuni</u> at press conference at Trois Continents film festival.

2118. Kaboré, Gaston J.M. Qu'est-ce qu'un film africain? <u>Unir Cinéma</u> 20-21(1985):35-36.

2119. Kaboré, Gaston, J.M. and Rasmane Ouédraogo. Irremplacable Fepaci. <u>Afrique-Asie</u> 346(1985):66-67.

2120. Kaboré, Mouni Etienne. Les derniers débats forums. <u>Sidwaya</u> Mar. 2 (1987):9.

Films shown at FESPACO with main attention to Med Hondo, <u>Sarraounia</u>.

2121. Kaboré, Mouni Etienne. Pourquoi ferme-t-on l'INAFEC? <u>Carrefour Africain</u> 975(1987):27-28.

Aims and accomplishments of INAFEC; reasons it was closed.

2122. Kaboré, Mouni Etienne and Sansan Kambou. FESPACO 87 de grandes innovations dans l'organisation. <u>Sidwaya</u> Jan. 23 (1987):4.

2123. Kader, Mehdi. Après Tachkent heureusement, l'Afrique. <u>Afrique-Asie</u> 9(1972):48-49.

Med Hondo, <u>Soleil O</u> and Sembène Ousmane, <u>Emitai</u>.

2124. Kadour, Marie. Les africains à Cannes. <u>Afrique-Asie</u> 6(1972):46-47.

2125. Kadour, Marie. Carthage festival pour toute la ville. <u>Afrique-Asie</u> 16(1972):46-47.

2126. Kadour, Marie. Dinard: le festival des "sous-distribues." <u>Afrique-Asie</u> 10(1972):46-48.

FIFEF.

2127. Kadour, Marie. Ousmane Sembène temoin à Munich. <u>Afrique-Asie</u> 20(1972):94-95. (I)

2128. Kael, Pauline. The current cinema. <u>New Yorker</u> June 11 (1984):106-107. (R)

Ruy Guerra, <u>Erendira</u>.

2129. Kahoun, Joseph. Vllle FESPACO le compte a rebours a commence. <u>Carrefour Africain</u> 763(1983):26.

2130. Kaire, Bara Ndiaye. Reconvertir les mentalités. <u>Le Soleil</u> May 2 (1975):4.

Educational role of film.

2131. Kaissar, Abou. Ou vont les cinémas africains? <u>Ecran</u> 30(1974):36-38.

2132. Kaissar, Abou. Vers une libération totale des cinémas africains. <u>Ecran</u> 30(1974):37-38.

2133. Kajika, Jerome. Le deuxième festival international du film d'expression française. <u>Sentiers</u> 33(1970):31-32.

FIFEF. Problems of film distribution in Africa.

2134. Kakou, Antoine. Les gris-gris d'un conteur. <u>Afrique Littéraire</u> 76(1985):62-65; <u>CinémAction</u> 34(1985):62-65.

Films of Sembène Ousmane.

2135. Kakou, Antoine. La thématique. <u>Afrique Littéraire</u> 76(1985):17-19; <u>CinémAction</u> 34(1985):17-19.

Themes of Sembène's films.

2136. Kalai, Mondher. Consommer notre propre cinéma. <u>SeptièmArt</u> 60(1986):10-11. (I)

Philippe Sawadogo compares J.C.C. and FESPACO.

2137.  Kamal, Mohamed el.   J.C.C. 84 "Ruptures: et "Chant d'automne" de
        l'Algerie, "Zeft" du Maroc et "Rihlat Ouyoune" du Soudan à la
        compétition officielle.   L'Action Oct. 5 (1984):24.

2138.  Kamara, Fodé.   Emitai de d'Ousmane Sembène.   Le Soleil Aug. 11
        (1973):5. (R)

2139.  Kamba, Sébastien.   Les problemes du cinéma en Republique du
        Congo.   Unir Cinéma 12(1984):7.

        Article reprinted from Etumba.

2140.  Kambou, Sansan.   A la découverte du cinéma ivoirien.   Sidwaya
        Feb. 25 (1987):6.

        Ivorian films made since 1972.

2141.  Kambou, Sansan.   L'apartheid au pied du mur.   Sidwaya Feb. 26
        (1987):6.

        FESPACO theme of film and identity.

2142.  Kambou, Sansan.   Conference de presse de la camarade ministre de
        la culture.   Sidwaya Feb. 20 (1987):8.

        Bernadette Sanou discusses FESPACO theme of film and identity.

2143.  Kambou, Sansan.   Ils ont dit... Sidwaya Mar. 2 (1987):9.

        Several government ministers give their opinions of FESPACO.

2144.  Kambou, Sansan.   Zossou Gratien, le héros d'"Ironu," "Mon seul
        souci, m'imposer au niveau africain." Sidwaya Mar. 5 (1987):12.
        (I)

        Beninois actor, musician and playwright discusses his work.

2145.  Kambou, Sansan and Mouni Etienne Kaboré.   La Sécretaire général
        de l'URTNA: "La coopération entre cinéastes est necessaire."
        Sidwaya Feb. 27 (1987):7. (I)

        François Itoua discusses need for cooperation of filmmakers and
        television in interview at FESPACO.

2146.  Kamel, Mohamed.   Q'attendent les cinéastes des J.C.C.?   L'Action
        Oct. 25 (1982):8-9.

        Third World filmmakers' problems different from those in
        capitalist countries.

2147.  Kamissoko, Gaoussou.   Abidjan et "La femme au couteau."
        Fraternité Matin 1619(1970):2. (R)

2148. Kamissoko, Gaoussou. Le cinéma africain: mythe ou réalité? Fraternité Matin 1260(1969):7.

FESPACO. Problems of African filmmakers.

2149. Kamissoko, Gaoussou. Désiré Ecaré, un grand artiste ivoirien. Fraternité Matin 1676(1970):7.

2150. Kamphausen, Hannes. Afrikanische Film und Filmemacher, Ein kleines Lexikon. Afrika heute supp. to 19(1971):24-33.

Biographies and filmography.

2151. Kamphausen, Hannes. Auf dem Weg zu einem afrikanischen Kino. Afrika heute 2(1973):43-45.

FESPACO.

2152. Kamphausen, Hannes. Cinéma in Africa: a survey. Cinéaste 5, 3(1972):28-41.

Films about Africa by African and non-African filmmakers compared. Economics of producing and distributing films.

2153. Kamphausen, Hannes. Ein Festival nicht wie die anderen. Afrika heute 19/20(1972):429-431.

J.C.C.

2154. Kamphausen, Hannes, ed. Filmbeilage, October 1971. Afrika heute supp. to 19(1971):1-34.

Discussion of themes and infrastructure; filmography. See Nos. 1174, 1879, 2150, 3178 and 3831.

2155. Kamphausen, Hannes. Kino in Afrika. Afrika heute 8(1972):152-154.

FESPACO.

2156. Kamwa, Daniel. Comme des arbres à palabres. Le Monde Diplomatique 318(1980):12.

Daniel Kamwa's films. Role of film in Africa.

2157. Kane, A.S. "Touki-Bouki" primé à Moscou. Le Soleil July 26 (1973):5. (R)

2158. Kane, Cheikh. Dépasser la phrase embryonnaire. Le Soleil Apr. 9 (1975):3.

Experimental films made in Senegal. See Nos. 415, 904, 1206, 1327, 1363, 1368, 1369, 1539, 2130, 2162, 2672, 2810, 2837, 3323,

3426 and 3648 for responses to this article.

2159. Kane, K.S. "Table Feraay" premier moyen métrage de Cheikh Ngaido Ba. Le Soleil Mar. 18 (1976):3. (R)

2160. Kane, Oumy Khairy. Films africains primés. Afrique Nouvelle 1414(1976):16.

African films shown at Berlin and Karlov Vary film festivals.

2161. Kane, Samba. Quatre cinéastes ivoiriens "à l'assaut" de Ouaga. Fraternité Matin 2469(1973):7. (I)

Interviews with Henri Duparc, Roger Gnoan-Mbala, Timité Bassori and N'Dabian Vodio.

2162. Kanga, Kinimo and Manjusu Cesti. Aller au fonds des problèmes. Le Soleil Apr. 30 (1975):2. (R)

Momar Thiam, Baks.

2163. Kapalanga Gazungil and Daniel Peraya. Le groupe, essence du spectacle africain? in Caméra Nigra C.E.S.C.A. ed. Brussels: OCIC, 1984. pp. 103-107.

*2164. Kargougou, Emile. Le Cinéma en Haute Volta. Comportements et goûts d'un public africain. Bulletin de Liaison du Centre d'Etudes Economiques et Sociales d'Afrique Occidentale 6(1969):8-12.

2165. Kasji, Nadia. "Monogambée!" cri de révolte en Angola. Africasia 5(1969):45-47. (R)

2166. Kasji, Nadia. La négritude n'est plus un moyen de se libérer. Africasia 25(1970):43-45. (I)

Med Hondo discusses role of African film.

2167. Kasombo, Kumanda. Voir Paris et mourir. Jeune Afrique 914(1979):60. (R)

Cheick Doukouré, Bako.

2168. Katsahnias, Iannis. La politique du zèbre. Cahiers du Cinéma 379(1986):51-52. (R)

Mustapha Diop, Médecin de Gafiré.

2169. Kaunga, Cyril. The role of the Audio-Visual Institute of Dar-es-Salaam on film training in East Africa, in First Mogadishu Pan-African Film Symposium. Pan African Cinema...Which Way Ahead? Ibrahim Awed et al eds. Mogadishu: MOGPAFIS Management Committee, 1983. pp. 39-48.

2170. Keita, Abdoulaye. Les enfants dans les salles de cinéma. L'Essor Aug. 8 (1970):2.

Misbehavior of children in Malian theaters.

2171. Keita, Abdoulaye. Le cinéma A.B.C. une salle qui incite à la révolte. L'Essor Dec. 4 (1972):3.

Poorly run Malian theater.

2172. Keita, Rahmatou. RE-FESPACO: Histoire des femmes. Intrus May 15 (1987):2.

Letter to President Sankara on dissatisfaction with FESPACO.

KEITA BOLIBANA, ABDOULAYE See KEITA, ABDOULAYE

2173. Kelefa. Un fructuex dialogue entre jeunes et cinéastes. Le Soleil Oct. 5 (1970):2.

Conference in Senegal discusses lack of rapport between filmmakers and public.

*2174. Kemer, Sereba Agiobu. First festival of Nigerian films. Lagos Week-end Sept. 30 (1977).

2175. Kernan, Michael. 'Bush Momma': realities. Washington Post Jan. 27 (1977):C9. (R)

2176. Khama, Seretse. The role of the cinema in Botswana. Speech by His Excellency, the President Sir Seretse Khama, on the occasion of the opening of the Capitol Cinema, Gaberone, June 3, 1970. mimeo.

2177. Khayati, Khemais. Namur: présence en force de l'Afrique. Cinéma 78 240(1978):71-73.

2178. Khayati, Khemais and Guy Hennebelle. Nouveaux écrits sur les cinémas afro-arabes. Afrique-Asie 99(1976):46-48. (BR)

Pierre Haffner, Essai sur les fondements du cinéma africain. See No. 42.

2179. Ki-Zerbo, Joseph. Der afrikanische Film und die Entwicklung. Filmwissenschaftliche Beiträge 21,3(1980):17-30.

History of African film.

2180. Kiba, Simon. Le cinéma africain réclame sa place. Afrique Nouvelle 1030(1967):8-9.

Survey of African film, emphasis on themes.

2181. Kieffer, Anne. L'Angola à Amiens. Jeune Cinéma 157(1984):12-14.

2182. Kieffer, Anne. Le choix. Jeune Cinéma 182(1987):34. (R)

Idrissa Ouédraogo, Yam Daabo.

2183. Kieffer, Anne. Cinéma africain anglophone et francophone. Jeune Cinéma 149(1983):13-14.

Trois Continents film festival.

2184. Kieffer, Anne. Cinéma d'Afique noire au Festival des Trois Continents. Jeune Cinéma 149(1983):10-13.

2185. Kieffer, Anne. Flashes sur le cinéma africain: Chartres sur Afrique noire. Jeune Cinéma 157(1984):7-8.

Chartres film festival.

2186. Kieffer, Anne. La maison de la faim de Chris Austin. Jeune Cinéma 157(1984):32-34. (R)

House of Hunger.

2187. Kieffer, Anne. Nantes 1986. Jeune Cinéma 180(1987):34.

2188. Kikassa, Francis. Cinéma congolais. Congo-Afrique 6,7(1966):367.

Films about Zaire shown at FESTAC.

2189. Kitchener, Julie. Africa's poor showing at London Film Festival. New African 208(1985):37-38.

2190. Knaebel, Martial. Désébagato (Le dernier salaire) Unir Cinéma 136(1987):12. (R)

2191. Knaebel, Martial. Deuxième génération. Unir Cinéma 136(1987):7-8.

Differences in themes of first and second generations of African filmmakers.

2192. Knaebel, Martial. L'histoire d'Horokia. Unir Cinéma 136(1987):13. (R)

2193. Knaebel, Martial. Yam Daabo (le choix). Unir Cinéma 136(1987):11. (R)

2194. Knight, Derrick. African films turn on heat. New African 187(1983):42-43.

FESPACO. Themes of films shown, organization of festival.

2195. Kodjo, François. Les cinéastes africains face a l'avenir du cinéma en Afrique. Tiers-Monde 20,79(1979):605-614.

History, colonial period to present.

2196. Koita, P.M. Le CNPC lance "A bana." L'Essor May 31-June 1 (1980):8.

2197. Koita, P.M. Le 8e biennale artistique désormais sur cassettes. L'Essor Aug. 31-Sept. 1 (1985):3.

Need for videocassettes for development in Mali.

2198. Kokore et Brognan. Sidiki Bakaba ou la rage de vaincre. Fraternité Matin 5310(1982):21.

Ivorian actor.

2199. Kola, Djim. Discours introductif par Djim Kola, Secrétaire Général de l'Union National des Cinéastes Voltaiques, in FESPACO 1983. Paris: Présence Africaine, 1987. pp. 23-26.

FESPACO theme, African film and the public; distribution of films.

2200. Konaté, Adam S. L'expérience de la nationalisation des salles de cinéma dans un pays d'Afrique francophone. Afrique Nouvelle 1252(1971):2; 1253(1971):2; 1254(1971):2.

Discussion of nationalization of cinemas and distribution of films in Francophone Africa. Role of SECMA, COMACICO, SONAVOCI and OCINAM.

2201. Konaté, Aminata. Un jeune cinéaste sénégalais, Samb Ababakar pose le problème "des anciens et des modernes." Bingo 153(1965):34-35.

2202. Konde, Hadji. Films and books, in Press Freedom in Tanzania. Arusha: Eastern Africa Publications, 1984. pp. 92-99.

Tanzania Film Company and Audio-Visual Institute; audience primarily Asian.

2203. Kondo, Sidy. Le cinéma pourquoi et pour qui? L'Essor May 6 (1975):3.

Films must educate by focusing on African problems, not just entertaining.

2204. Koruna, Noël. "Obali" à Franceville, une histoire d'amour à la Gabonaise. L'Union Jan. 3 (1976):2. (R)

First Gabonese cooperation between theater and film in Philippe Mory's film of Josephine Bongo's play.

2205. Kotchy, Barthelemy. Grand prix I.D. des arts et des lettres un événement! I.D. 841(1987):38-41.

Désiré Ecaré wins I.D. arts prize.

2206. Kouame, J.B. "Ablakon" aux studios. Le film du peuple. Fraternité Matin 6144(1985):9; 6146(1985):8. (R)

2207. Kouame, J.B. Des exposés enrichissants. Fraternité Matin 6187(1985):27.

Infrastructure in Côte d'Ivoire.

2208. Kouame, J.B. Kitia Touré le défenseur du masque sénoufo. Fraternité Matin 6186(1985):16.

2209. Kouassi, Germain. FESPACO un festival comme les autres. Eburnea 100(1976):28-29.

2210. Kouassi, Germain. M'Bala Gnoan réalisateur ivoirien le cinéma doit répondre aux aspirations du peuple. Bingo 240(1973):32-33.

2211. Kouassi, Guy. "Abusuan" d'Henri Duparc: "Qu'avons-nous fait puor eux?" Fraternité Matin 2430(1972):8. (I)

2212. Kouassi, Guy. "Adja-Tio": du travail bien fait. Fraternité Matin 4957(1981):22. (R)

2213. Kouassi, Guy. "Adja-Tio": un tableau social. Fraternité Matin 4953(1981):19. (R)

2214. Kouassi, Guy. Aujourd'hui: "Abusuan". Fraternité Matin 2435(1972):7. (I)

Henry Duparc discusses his film.

2215. Kouassi, Guy. Le cinéma chez nous. Fraternité Matin 4344(1979):18.

Film distribution in Côte d'Ivoire.

2216. Kouassi, Guy. Le cinéma ivoirien en marche: Henri Duparc tourne "Abusuan." Fraternité Matin 2266(1972):8. (I)

2217. Kouassi, Guy. "Djéli" à la RTL. Fraternité Matin 5398(1982):17.

First Ivorian film shown at RTL theater.

2218. Kouassi, Guy. Lettre paysanne. Fraternité Matin 5372(1982):7. (R)

Safi Faye, Kaddu Beykat.

2219. Kouassi, Guy. Nuages noirs. Fraternité Matin 5389(1982):7. (R)

2220. Kouassi, Guy.   Pour un cinéma africain.   Fraternité Matin 4400(1979):21.

Ideals of what African film should be.

2221. Kouassi, Guy.   Qui fait-on des enfants?   Fraternité Matin Apr. 1 (1987):8.  (R)

Cheick Oumar Sissoko, Nyamanton.

2222. Koumé, Ch. M.   Hommage à Doure Mané.   Afrique Nouvelle 1517(1987):2.

Obituary for Guinean actor.

2223. Koussou, Inama.  Philippe Mory parle du cinéma gabonais.  L'Union Sept. 3-4(1977):2.

Review of 5 of Mory's films.

2224. Kout, Edmond.  La leçon de bureau.  Bingo 379(1984):22.  (R)

Valère Youlou Mingole, Premier bureau, deuxième bureau, troisième bureau.

2225. Kugblenu, John.  Filming Africa's traditional arts.  West Africa 3152(1977):2464-2465.

Filmmakers from Ghana, Liberia and Sierra Leone discuss cooperative project to film arts.

2226. Kugblenu, John.   Filming West Africa's arts.   West Africa 3181(1978):1301.

UNESCO sponsored project to film arts in Anglophone West Africa.

2227. Kumbula, Tendayi.   Stage set for Third Kine film festival. Herald May 23 (1986):13.

Films to be shown at Kine International Film Festival.

2228. Kumm, Bjorn.   African comedy.   Harper's 253, 1519(1976):96-99. (R)

Sembène Ousmane, Xala.

2229. L.A.T.   Une cité, une monument: hommage aux cinéastes africains. Sidwaya Feb. 20 (1985):3.

Burkinabe decision to support FESPACO with cultural activities; film infrastructure located in Ouagadougou.

2230. L.A.T.   FEPACI: Réunion du comité ad hoc.   Sidwaya Feb. 14

(1985):7.

2231. Lajeunesse, Jacqueline. La lumière (Yeelen). Revue du Cinéma 429(1987):50-51. (R)

Souleymane Cissé, Yeelen.

2232. Lambour, M.C. Le festival du Tiers Monde. Afrique 24(1979):24.

2233. Lambour, M.C. Les "Nègres marrons de la liberté." Afrique 29(1979):65. (R)

Med Hondo, West Indies.

2234. Lamien, Watamou. Conférence des ministres africains charges du cinéma Ouagadougou 13 et 14 février 1985 communique final. Sidwaya Feb. 18 (1985):6.

Text of ministers conference at FESPACO dealing with role and support of CIDC and CIPROFILM.

2235. Lamizana, Aboubakar Sangoulé. L'avenir du cinéma africain. Demain l'Afrique 19(1979):79.

FESPACO.

2236. Lampley, James. Cissé's wind of change. South 63(1986):121. (R)

Finyé to be shown in London.

2237. Lampley, James. A fair enough bargain. Africa (London) 85(1978):96-97. (R)

Deji Adefolu, Tryin' Time.

2238. Landy, Marcia. Political allegory and engaged cinema: Sembene's Xala. Cinema Journal 23,3(1984):31-46. (R)

2239. Landy, Marcia. Politics and style in Black Girl. Jump Cut 27(1982):23-25. (R)

Sembène Ousmane, La noire de.

2240. Langlois, Gérard. Bako, l'autre rive. Ecran 76(1979):66-67. (R)

2241. Langlois, Gérard. Brésil. 1.Carlos Diegues et Ruy Guerra. Les Lettres-Françaises July 21 (1971):17. (I)

Discussion of national production, audience and cinema novo in Brazil and the Third World.

2242. Langlois, Gérard. Entretien avec Jacques Champreux, Cheik Doukouré, et Sidiki Bakaba. Ecran 76(1979):67-68. (I)

Discussion about <u>Bako</u>.

2243. Lantran, Cathy. Un court métrage africain tourné à Paris. <u>Bingo</u> 333(1980):1959.

Film being made by Mamadou Kone.

2244. Lardeau, Yann and Serge le Peron. Entretien avec Haile Gerima. <u>2 écrans</u> 50(1982):34-36. (I)

2245. Larson, Charles. The film version of Achebe's Things Fall Apart. <u>Africana Journal</u> 13(1982):104-110. (R)

Francis Oladele, <u>Bullfrog in the Sun</u>.

2246. Laude, Andre. Une révélation: Ababacar Samb. <u>Jeune Afrique</u> 246(1965):30-31.

How Samb's films differ from those of other African filmmakers.

2247. Leahy, James. Ceddo. <u>Monthly Film Bulletin</u> 49(1982):5. (R)

2248. Leahy, James. La Chapelle (The Chapel). <u>Monthly Film Bulletin</u> 54(1987):108-109. (R)

2249. Leahy, James. Kaddu Beykat lettre paysanne (Letter from my village). <u>Monthly Film Bulletin</u> 54(1987):105. (R)

2250. Leahy, James. Tributaries of the Seine. <u>Monthly Film Bulletin</u> 54(1987):106-107.

Problems of African filmmaking in the 1980s; lack of criticism in English.

2251. Leduc, François. Ruy Guerra, Os fuzis. <u>Jeune Cinéma</u> 22(1967):13-16. (R)

2252. Leduc, Jean. Un cinéma trahi.... <u>Cinéma Québec</u> 3,8(1974):30-32.

Themes of films by young filmmakers.

2253. Legrand, Georges. Mali schoolboys shoot their country's first film. <u>UNESCO Features</u> 554/555(1969):26-27.

The making of <u>Bambo</u>.

2254. Lelyveld, Joseph. South Africa on film, as seen by Nadine Gordimer. <u>New York Times</u> May 15 (1983): Sec. 2, 1, 13. (R)

Ross Devenish, <u>Chip of the Glass Ruby</u> and Manie Van Rensburg, <u>Country Lovers</u>.

2255. Lemaire, Charles. Accusé, Med Hondo répond. <u>Afrique Nouvelle</u> 1863(1985):16. (I)

Discussion about CAC.

2256. Lemaire, Charles. L'appât du gain. Unir Cinéma 9(1983):31. (R)

2257. Lemaire, Charles. Architecture et cinéma: le jeu de construction de Moussa Yoro Bathily! Unir Cinéma 13(1984):3.

2258. Lemaire, Charles. Aube noire. SeptièmArt 49(1984):9-10. (R)

2259. Lemaire, Charles. Aucune nouveaute. Afrique Nouvelle 1955(1987):18-19.

No new developments in African film in 1986, reasons why.

2260. Lemaire, Charles, ed. L'aventure ambigue, échoes critiques. Unir Cinéma 13(1984):11-12. (R)

Film of C.H. Kane's novel by Jacques Champreux.

2261. Lemaire, Charles. Un bilan trompeur. Afrique Nouvelle 1921(1986):16-17.

Malian films produced in 1986: Souleymané Cissé, Yeelen; Cheick Oumar Sissoko, Nyamanton; and Falaba Issa Traoré, Kiri kara watita.

2262. Lemaire, Charles. Ceddo. Unir Cinéma 13(1984):9-10. (R)

2263. Lemaire, Charles. Cinéma. Afrique Nouvelle 1901(1985):18.

New films being made in Burkina Faso.

2264. Lemaire, Charles. Cinéma. Afrique Nouvelle 1917(1986):17.

Tiers Monde film festival.

2265. Lemaire, Charles. Cinéma. Afrique Nouvelle 1933(1986):19.

Recent films made in Burkina Faso, Côte d'Ivoire, Guinée, Mauritania, Mali and Niger.

2266. Lemaire, Charles. Le cinéma au Mozambique. Unir Cinéma 6(1983):3-8. (I)

Pedro Pimenta discusses Mocambiquan film.

2267. Lemaire, Charles, ed. Le cinéma au Niger. SeptièmArt 49(1984):5-10.

Review of recent films, crisis in Nigerien film.

2268. Lemaire, Charles. Cinéma et information. Unir Cinéma 23-24(1986):22-24.

Review of _Unir Cinéma's_ attempts to promote African film; role of critics in reviewing and promoting film.

2269. Lemaire, Charles.    Credo libéral.    _Afrique Nouvelle_ 1901(1985):19.

Meeting of UCOA in Dakar.

2270. Lemaire, Charles.    Ecrire et informer.    _Afrique Nouvelle_ 1911(1986):15-17. (BR)

Reveiw article on books and special issues of journals on African film.

2271. Lemaire, Charles.    En attendant le FESPACO.    _Afrique Nouvelle_ 1953(1986):17.

2272. Lemaire, Charles.    Les enfants de la rue.    _Afrique Nouvelle_ 1949(1986):23.

Cheick Oumar Sissoko, _Nyamanton_, prizes et FESPACO and J.C.C.

2273. Lemaire, Charles.    Entretien avec Moussa Kemoko Diakité.    _Unir Cinéma_ 5(1983):14. (I)

Discussion of _Naitou_.

2274. Lemaire, Charles.    ..et le Sénégal en panne.    _Afrique Nouvelle_ 1951(1986):16-17.

SNPC should increase its role in supporting Senegalese film.

2275. Lemaire, Charles.    FEPACI s'unir ou mourir.    _Afrique Nouvelle_ 1863(1985):15-16.

Report on 3rd FEPACI congress.

2276. Lemaire, Charles.    La grande solitude du critique en Afrique. _Unir Cinéma_ 14(1984):12-16.

Criteria for criticism of African films, lack of sources that publish criticism.

2277. Lemaire, Charles.    Ils sont retombes sur la tête.    _Afrique Nouvelle_ 1913(1986):19.

SIDEC criticized for showing _The Gods Are Crazy_ in Senegal.

2278. Lemaire, Charles.    Jom.    _Unir Cinéma_ 1(1982):13-14.    (R)

2279. Lemaire, Charles.    Lemaire de "Unir Cinéma" nous écrit.    _Zone 2_ 249(1984):18.

2280. Lemaire, Charles. Les lutteurs. Unir Cinéma 9(1983):32. (R)

2281. Lemaire, Charles. Moussa Bathily en tournage pour quelques millions de plus! Afrique Nouvelle 1853(1985):20-21. (R)

Petits blancs au manioc et à la sauce gombo.

2282. Lemaire, Charles. 9e Festival panafricain du cinéma de Ouagadougou, histoire d'une rencontre. Afrique Nouvelle 1862(1985):14-17.

2283. Lemaire, Charles. Ouverture. Afrique Nouvelle 1915(1986):21. (R)

Desiré Ecaré, Visages de femmes.

2284. Lemaire, Charles. Paweogo. Unir Cinéma 6(1983):9-10. (R)

2285. Lemaire, Charles. Pluie de récompenses. Afrique Nouvelle 1872(1985):16-17.

Jo Ramaka Gai, Baw Naan, wins prize at Perouse film festival.

2286. Lemaire, Charles. La production en crise. Afrique Nouvelle 1943(1986):16-17.

Problems of film production in Niger.

2287. Lemaire, Charles. La recette magique? Afrique Nouvelle 1899(1985):16-17.

FESPACO seminar on literature and film.

2288. Lemaire, Charles. Sarraounia une reine africaine. Afrique Nouvelle 1941(1986):17. (R)

2289. Lemaire, Charles. Série noire. Afrique Nouvelle 1945(1986):19.

Obituary for Etienne N'Dabian Vodio.

2290. Lemaire, Charles. Si les cavaliers. SeptièmArt 49(1984):8-9. (R)

2291. Lemaire, Charles. Trente ans apres. Afrique Nouvelle 1915(1986):21.

Film festival in Dakar to honor 30 years of African filmmaking.

2292. Lemaire, Charles. Trois inédits, deux déceptions. Afrique Nouvelle 1935(1986):18-19. (R)

Jean-Pierre Dikongue-Pipa, Courte malade and Désiré Ecaré, Visages de femmes.

2293. Lemaire, Charles. "Unir": le rêve devient réalité. Afrique-Asie

349(1985):47.

Importance of Unir Cinéma.

2294.  Lemaire, Charles.  Xew-Xew.  Unir Cinéma 12(1984):11-12. (R)

2295.  Lemaire, Charles and L. Houedanou.  Le même archer bassari?
Afrique Nouvelle 1907(1986):16-17. (R)

Moussa Yoro Bathily's film on Modibo Keita's novel.

2296.  Lemaire, Charles and Seydou Ouattara.  Le Burkina en marche.
Afrique Nouvelle 1951(1986):16.

Idrissa Ouédraogo, Yam Daabo and Emmanuel Sanou, Désébagato,
represent new era in Burkinabe film.

2297.  Lemangoye, Missengué.  Rénovation du cinéma "Akébé."  L'Union May
11 (1978):4.

Renovation of theater in Gabon.

2298.  Len.  Le médecin de Gafiré.  Variety 322, 4(1986):291,295. (R)

2299.  Leo, Robert.  Army captain turned filmstar. Daily Times (Lagos)
Aug. 12 (1986):18.

Babatunde Ishola, Nigerian theater and film actor.

2300.  Léondo.  L'acteur Doura Mané victime d'une accident de voiture.
L'Union July 6 (1978):4.

2301.  LeRoy, Marie-Claire.  Africa's Film Festival - screenings in
Upper Volta's newly nationalized cinemas.  Africa Report
15,4(1970):27-28. (I)

FESPACO, includes short interview with Sembène on importance of
film among other media.

2302.  Lester, Jules.  Mandabi: confronting Africa.  Evergreen Review
78(1970):54-58, 85-90. (R)

2303.  Leup, Beur.  Cinq films sénégalais au festival de Ouagadougou.
Le Soleil Mar. 3 (1972):3.

Senegalese films at FESPACO.

2304.  Leup, Beur.  Je voudrais incarner au cinéma la linguère du temps
passé.  Le Soleil Aug. 31 (1972):2. (I)

Isseu Niang, Senegalese theater and film actress.

2305.  Leup, Beur.  Sarah Maldoror à Dakar pour présenter "Sambizanga."
Le Soleil July 25 (1974):1. (R)

Review includes biographical information on Maldoror.

2306. Levison, Evelyn. Sabela films for black tribes. Variety 291, 1(1978):432.

Simon Sabela, South African film actor.

2307. Leyigny, Guy-Guillaume. Le cinéma "le Mpassa": A l'école de la délinquance juvénile. L'Union 224(1976):3.

Audience misbehavior in theater in Gabon.

2308. Libération Afrique. Cinéma et domination étrangère en Afrique noire. Peuples Noirs Peuples Africains 13(1980):141-144.

Distribution problems.

2309. Lipinska, Suzanne. Cinéma chez les Balantes. Africasia 19(1970):46-49. (R)

Sarah Maldoror, Fusils pour Banta.

2310. Lloyd, Ann, ed. Africa, in The Illustrated History of the Cinema. New York: Macmillan, 1986. pp. 402-403.

Short history focuses on Francophone West Africa.

2311. Lo, Saliou Fatima. Un film-documentaire sur le maraîchage à Koumbédia. Le Soleil Feb. 28(1983):11.

Madick Niang, Maraîchage à Koumbédia.

2312. Loiseau, Yves. Une révélation: la lre Semaine du Cinéma Africain. Afrique Nouvelle 1016(1967):2.

Week of African films shown in Dakar.

2313. Lopes, Arlindo. Poderíamos ter feito melhor. Domingo (Maputo) Sept. 30 (1984):5. (I)

João Costa discusses week of INC films shown in Maputo.

2314. Lory, Georges-Marie. Le Côte-d'Ivoire ne peut encore se prévaloir que d'un modeste florilège cinématographique. Afrique Littéraire 63/64(1982):115-117.

Comparison of 2 generations of Côte d'Ivoire filmmakers.

2315. Louisy, Louis-Georges. Ceddo. Afrique 27(1979):52. (R)

2316. Luapa, Rolf. Touki Bouki, treize ans après. Afrique-Asie 374(1986):78.

European views of <u>Touki Bouki</u>.

2317. Lulle, Thierry.  De la campagne à la ville: exodes et travellings.  <u>Croissance des jeunes nations</u> 259(1984):38.

Films about migration.

2318. Lundkvist, Artur.  La culture au Sénégal.  <u>Le Soleil</u> July 11 (1977):5.

Films of Tidiane Aw, Sembène Ousmane and Mahama Johnson Traoré.

2319. Luntadila Luzolo-Mantwila.  Un aperçu du cinéma au Zaire de 1897 à 1972.  <u>Zaire-Afrique</u> 73(1973):173-183.

History of filmmaking in Zaire.

2320. Luntadila Luzolo-Mantwila.  Le cinéma zairois.  <u>Zaire-Afrique</u> 74(1973):239-250.

2321. Luntadila Luzolo-Mantwila.  Perspectives du cinéma au Zaire.  <u>Zaire-Afrique</u> 75(1973):311-318.

2322. Luo, Martin.  Zambian cinema, in <u>First Mogadishu Pan-African Film Symposium.  Pan African Cinema...Which Way Ahead?</u> Ibrahim Awed et al. eds. Mogadishu: MOGPAFIS Management Committee, 1983. pp. 50-51.

2323. Lutu Mabangu.  S.O.S. pour un cinéma zairois.  <u>Zaire</u> 195(1972):18-19.

Production and distribution problems in Zaire.

2324. Luzolo Mpwati N'tima Nsi.  L'histoire, in <u>Caméra Nigra</u>.  C.E.S.C.A. ed. Brussels: OCIC, 1984. pp. 85-92.

Themes of films.

2325. Lyons, Harriet D.  The use of ritual in Sembene's Xala.  <u>Canadian Journal of African Studies</u> 18,2(1984):319-328. (R)

Comparison of the film and novel.

2326. McCaffrey, Kathleen.  African women on the screen.  <u>Africa Report</u> 26,2(1981):56-58.

Women in films by Sarah Maldoor, Ababacar Samb, Sembène Ousmane and Mahama Johnson Traoré.

2327. McCaffrey, Kathleen.  Images of women in West African literature and film: a struggle against dual colonization.  <u>International Journal of Women's Studies</u> 3,1(1980):76-88.

Women in Sembène's films.

2328. McMullin, Corine. Un regard africain sur la sombre Amérique. Afrique-Asie 212(1980):53-54. (I)

Haile Gerima discusses making films in U.S.A.

2329. M.B. Africa in Berlin. Afrika 20,4(1979):22-23.

African films at Berlin film festival.

2330. M.B. Le cinéma. Agecop Liaison 40(1977):38-39.

Filmmaking in Côte d'Ivoire.

2331. M.C. Cultura. Novembro 86(1985):45.

Activities of national film laboratory in Angola.

2332. M.C. Yam Daabo (Le choix). Positif 317-318(1987):89. (R)

2333. M.D. "Le sang des parias." Le Soleil Apr. 13 (1978):2. (R)

2334. M.J.S. Sexe interdit. Africa (Dakar) 176(1985):49-50. (I)

Désiré Ecaré discusses censorship of Visages de femmes.

2335. M.K. J.C.C. Rétrospective des neuf dernières sessions. L'Action Oct. 11 (1984):11.

J.C.C. prizes 1966-1982.

2336. M.M. Le choix. Cinéma 400(1987):15. (R)

Idrissa Ouédraogo, Yam Daabo.

2337. M.N. Johnny Secka aux U.S.A. pour préparer la venue de J. Brown. Le Soleil Mar. 7 (1974):4.

Senegalese actor aims to make Senegalese film better known.

2338. M.N. Les journées cinématographiques de Carthage un festival indispensable. SeptièmArt 52(1984):6-8.

2339. M.R.B. Ablakon de Gnoan M'Bala. Jeune Afrique Magazine 32(1986):7. (R)

2340. Mabrouki, Azzedine. Baara de Souleymane Cissé. 2 écrans 4(1978):34-35. (R)

2341. Mabrouki, Azzedine. Le cinéma regne a Mogadiscio. SeptièmArt 57(1986):13-14.

Report on MOGPAFIS includes discussion of Le dervich Somali.

2342. Mabrouki, Azzedine.  Cry Freedom de O. Balogun. 2 écrans
35(1981):30-32.  (R)

Ija Ominira.

2343. Mabrouki, Azzedine.  2e Festival International de Rio de Janeiro
21 au 30 Novembre 85.  Seduisante Rio.  SeptièmArt
58(1986):13-15.

Audience responses to African films at Rio de Janeiro film
festival.

2344. Mabrouki, Azzedine.  FESPACO lX les habits neufs du FESPACO.
SeptièmArt 55(1985):3-4.

2345. Mabrouki, Azzedine.  FESPACO 87 scenario d'une passion.
SeptièmArt 62(1987):24-27.

Unusual features of 1987 FESPACO.

2346. Mabrouki, Azzedine.  Le Festival Panafricain de Ouagadougou.  2
écrans 12(1979):8-21.  (I)

Report on FESPACO includes interview with Sembène Ousmane.

2347. Mabrouki, Azzedine.  Un festival sous les tropiques.  SeptièmArt
59(1986):3-4.

Cannes film festival.

2348. Mabrouki, Azzedine.  Littérature-cinéma: aller-retour.  SeptièmArt
55(1985):26-28.

FESPACO colloquium on literature and film.

2349. Mabrouki, Azzedine.  Londres: un hommage à Ousmane Sembène.  2
écrans 35(1981):33-34.

2350. Mabrouki, Azzedine.  Seduisante Rio.  SeptièmArt 58(1986):13-15.

African films shown at Rio de Janeiro film festival.

2351. Mabrouki, Azzedine.  Semaine du Film Africain à Nairobi une
réussite.  SeptièmArt 62(1987):23-24.

Kenyan responses to week of African films; recommendations of
symposium held during film week.

2352. Macame, João C.A.  Co-production moçambicano-cubana.  "Nova
Sifonia" ganha lo prémio de cinema em Espanha.  Domingo (Maputo)
June 19 (1983):24.

Mocambiquan representation at Bilbao film festival.

227.

2353. **Magaji, Mohammed.** Influence of foreign film in Nigeria deplored. New Nigerian May 24 (1978):13.

2354. **Magas.** Cinéma: avec "Backs" (sic) Momar Thiam traite de la délinquance. Le Soleil Sept. 25 (1974):1. (R)

2355. **Maiga, Mohamed.** Le Mali revient à l'écran. Jeune Afrique 990-991(1979-1980):81.

Festival of Malian films in Mali; infrastructure for filmmaking in Mali.

2356. **Maiga, Mohamed.** La nouvelle école du film sénégalais. Jeune Afrique 998(1980):64. (R)

Cheick Ngaido Ba, Kattan.

2357. **Maillat, Philippe.** Le cinéma africain et arabe en plein renouveau. Croissance des jeunes nations. 142(1973):32-34.

Themes of films shown at FIFEF.

2358. **Maillat, Philippe.** Entretien avec Pierre Haffner: pourquoi j'ai écrit "Fondaments du cinéma africain." Afrique Littéraire et Artistique 38(1975):106-109. (I)

2359. **Maillat, Philippe.** Les plus jeunes cinémas du monde se sont rassamblés à Ouagadougou. Croissance des jeunes nations 123(1972):32-33.

FESPACO.

2360. **Maillat, Philippe.** Remue-ménage dans le cinéma africain. Croissance des jeunes nations 104(1970):39-40.

Themes of films shown at several international film festivals in 1970.

2361. **Maillat, Philippe.** République Centrafricaine, in Le tiers monde en films. Guy Hennebelle, ed. Paris: CinémAction Ticontinental, 1982. p. 154. (R)

Joseph Akouissonne, Zo kwe zo.

2362. **Maillat, Philippe.** Le troisième festival de Carthage: le cinéma africain en dévenir. Croissance des jeunes nations 106(1970):38-39.

2363. **Makarius, Michel I.** Kébébe le fou au l'Ethiopie millénaire. Jeune Afrique 807(1976):107. (R)

Haile Gerima, Harvest 3000 Years.

2364. **Makédonsky, Erik.** Route étroite pour le jeune cinéma sénégalais.

Afrique Littéraire et Artistique 1(1968):54-62.

2365. Malal. Un nouveau film de Mahama J. Traoré. "Garga M'Bosse" ou le procès de l'homme. Le Soleil Dec. 27 (1974):1. (R)

2366. Malanda, Ange-Séverin. Le continent cinématographique africain. Peuples Noirs Peuples Africains 6(1978):70-71. (BR)

Guy Hennebelle and Catherine Ruelle, Cinéastes d'Afrique noire. See No. 45.

2367. Malanda, Ange-Séverin. L'exilé et le lointain: Hommage à Oumarou Ganda. Présence Africain 119(1981):170-175; Peuples Noirs Peuples Africains 23(1981):47-51.

Discussion of Ganda's films and his abilities as an actor and filmmaker.

2368. Malawi News. Filming the African dilemma. Atlas 20,5(1971):67. (R)

Francis Oladele, Bullfrog in the Sun.

2369. Malcolm, Derek. Stars over Africa. Guardian (Manchester) July 30 (1987):11.

Taormina film festival.

2370. Malemba, André. Black mic-mac. L'Union June 16 (1986):4. (R)

Isaach Bankolé, actor in Black Mic-Mac.

2371. Malemba, André. Djéli. L'Union Apr. 11 (1986):3. (R)

2372. Malemba, André. Fin de la semaine africaine du cinéma. L'Union Apr. 17 (1986):3.

Jean-Pierre Dikongue-Pipa, Muna Moto shown during week of African films in Libreville.

2373. Malemba, André. "Notre fille": tradition et modernisme. L'Union Apr. 18 (1986):4. (R)

2374. Malemba, André. Semaine africaine à Librevile. L'Union Apr. 9 (1986):2.

Week of African films shown in Libreville, Franceville and Port Gentile.

2375. Malemba, André. Le singe fou. L'Union Apr. 4 (1986):3. (R)

2376. Malemba, André. Wend-Kuni (sic): émourant! L'Union Apr. 14 (1987):3. (R)

2377. Malley, François. Comment mettre le cinéma au service du peuple. Croissance des jeunes nations. 122(1972):33-34.

Summary of Guy Hennebelle, Cinémas africains en 1972. See No. 44.

2378. Malnic, Evelyne. Propos sur le festival de Cannes. Jeune Afrique 806(1976):50-51.

2379. Malu, Kamba. Zaire: la misère dorée. Afrique-Asie 157(1978):56-57.

Survey of Zairois film 1967-1975.

2380. Mamari, K. Kedjo Ebouclé le séducteur. Bingo 391(1985):54-55. (I)

Ivorian actor.

2381. Mamari, K. Silence on tourne. Bingo 390(1985):56. (I)

Roger Gnoan-Mbala discusses Ablakon.

2382. Manaillon. Cinéma pour les jeunes. Le Courrier de Saint Ex 17(1979):6.

Power of film and influence on youth.

2383. Manceau, Jean-Louis. Sarraounia. Cinéma 377(1986):4. (R)

2384. Mandisa. Itumeleng film unit. Medu Art Ensemble Newsletter 6,1-2(1984):23-24.

Film of play, From Maseru, by Wally Serote to be made.

2385. Mangin, Marc. L'Afrique en tournage. Croissance des jeunes nations 275(1985):35.

Films to be released in 1986: Souleymane Cissé, Yeelen; Mustapha Diop, Mami Wata; Med Hondo, Sarraounia and Sembène Ousmane, Samory.

2386. Mangin, Marc. L'Afrique sans fric. Cinéma 386(1987):10-12.

Problems and potentials of filmmaking in Africa.

2387. Mangin, Marc. La colère de Med Hondo. Croissance des jeunes nations 275(1985):30-31. (I)

Discussion of problems of CIDC and FEPACI.

*2388. Mangin, Marc. Entretien avec Safi Faye. Droit et Liberté 389(1980):35-36. (I)

2389. Mangin, Marc. Pour promouvir le cinéma africain. Croissance des jeunes nations 279(1986):35.

Objectives of Association pour la promotion du cinéma africain et tiers monde en Europe.

2390. Mangin, Marc. Vent de sable sur le cinéma africain. Croissance des jeunes nations 271(1985):30-31.

FESPACO.

2391. Mangin, Marc. Wend Kuni (sic) de Gaston Kaboré. Croissance des jeunes nations 271(1985):35. (R)

2392. Mano, Henrique. "O vento sopra do norte" um film de José Cardoso. Tempo 820(1986):48-50. (I)

2393. Mantoux, Thierry. A Madagascar: silence, ou tourne! Afrique Littéraire et Artistique 27(1973):71-75.

Benoit Ramampy, Accident discussed in context of underdevelopment of film in Madagascar.

2394. Manuel, Fernando. Cinema congolês em Maputo. Tempo 786(1985):4. (R)

Youlou, Substituta.

2395. Marchal, Pierre A. "Borom Sarret" un court métrage d'Ousmane Sembène. Afrique Nouvelle 872(1964):19. (R)

2396. Marchal, Pierre A. Le Festival de Venise. Afrique Nouvelle 1002(1966):15.

2397. Marchal, Pierre A. Momar Thiam vainquer à Dinard. Afrique Nouvelle 1252(1971):11.

Karim and other African films shown at FIFEF.

2398. Marcorelles, Louis. L'avenir du cinéma africain. Le Monde Diplomatique 32,376(1985):22.

History and problems of CIDC, CIPROFILM and FEPACI.

2399. Marcorelles, Louis. Ousmane Sembène romancier, cinéaste poète. Les Lettres Françaises Apr. 6 (1967):24. (I)

Discussion of La noire de, its casting, music and reception in Dakar.

2400. Marcorelles, Louis. Les vérités premières de Sembène Ousmane. Le Monde May 7 (1977):1,33. (R)

Emitai and Ceddo compared.

2401. Marquez, Gabriel Garcia. Chronicle of a film foretold. _American Film_ 9,10(1984):12-13, 72.

The making of Ruy Guerra's, _Erendira_.

2402. Martin, Angela. Africa at the London film festival. _Africa Now_ 10(1982):30-31.

2403. Martin, Angela. African cinema. _South_ 4(1981):38-39. (R)

Safi Faye, _Fad jal_, shown at J.C.C.

2404. Martin, Angela. African cinema: the young talent. _Africa Now_ 2(1981):88.

FESPACO prizes.

2405. Martin, Angela. African films at Carthage. _New African_ 162(1981):53.

2406. Martin, Angela. The Carthage prizes. _West Africa_ 3508(1984):2272.

2407. Martin, Angela, ed. Four filmmakers from West Africa: Cissé, Faye, N'Diaye, Hondo. _Framework_ 11(1979):16-21.

2408. Martin, Angela. Home movies could mean 'cultural liberation'. _Africa Now_ 56(1985):60.

Use of super 8 film.

2409. Martin, Angela. Ougadougou (sic). _Framework_ 10(1979):42-43.

FESPACO.

2410. Martin, Angela. Pan-African Festival shows great promise. _New African_ 163(1981):82.

FESPACO.

2411. Martin, Angela. Panafrican film festival. _Educational Broadcasting International_ 12,2(1979):67-68.

FESPACO.

2412. Martin, Angela. Popular African cinema or art-house movies? _Africa Now_ 24(1983):60-61.

FESPACO.

2413. Martin, Françoise and Anne-Marie Engelibert. A propos d'une rétrospective: cinéma africain et domination culturelle. _Aujourd'hui l'Afrique_ 4(1976):40-44.

Themes of films.

2414. Martin, Marcel. Ablakon. Revue du Cinéma 422(1986):31. (R)

2415. Martin, Marcel. Afrique: présence de la vie quotidienne. Revue du Cinéma 374(1982):58-60.

Cannes film festival.

2416. Martin, Marcel. Le choix (Yam daabo). Revue du Cinéma 429(1987):47. (R)

2417. Martin, Marcel. Concerto pour un exil de Désiré Ecaré. Cinéma 68 128(1968):75-76. (R)

2418. Martin, Marcel. Les dieux et les morts. Ecran 32(1975):80-81. (R)

Ruy Guerra, Os deuses e os mortos.

2419. Martin, Marcel. West Indies. Ecran 84(1979):63-64. (R)

2420. Martin, Roland. Afrikas Kino zwischen Kontrolle und Engagement. 3 Welt Magazin 8/10(1976):89.

J.C.C.

2421. Martin, Roland. Le cinéma en allemagne. Afrique-Asie 178(1979):66-67.

Mannheim film festival.

*2422. Martin, Roland. Elfenbeinküste, in Der Afrikanisch-arabische Film. XVlle Filmwoche Mannheim, 1978. pp. 35-43.

*2423. Martin, Roland. Kino in Schwarzafrika: Senegal, in Der Afrikanisch-arabische Film. XXVlle Filmwoche Mannheim, 1978. pp. 19-34.

*2424. Martin, Roland. Nigeria und Ghana in Der Afrikanisch-arabische Film. XXVlle Filmwoche Mannheim, 1978. pp. 70-71.

2425. Marty, Anne. Touki Bouki ou la libération de l'imaginaire. Le Soleil Apr. 25 (1975):2. (R)

2426. Maruma, Olley. Zimbabwe is to be major film making centre. Prize Africa 12, 10(1985):10-11.

Economic advantages of foreign films being made in Zimbabwe.

2427. Maslin, Janet. Film: 'West Indies,' musical history. New York Times Mar. 8 (1985):C10. (R)

2428.  Maslin, Janet.   Screen: Senegalese 'Jom.' New York Times Mar. 28
       (1983):C12. (R)

2429.  Masson, Alain.   Mascarade à Dakar.   Positif 182(1976):54-56. (R)

       Sembène Ousmane, Xala.

2430.  Masters, Reyhana.   Video film series looks at environmental
       problems.  Herald (Harare) June 21 (1987):9.

       Pattie Pink, Road to Survival, its funding and theme.

2431.  Matchet.  African films in Harare.  West Africa 3500(1984):1885.

       African films shown at Zimbabwe Book Fair.

2432.  Matchet.  Cameras roll!  West Africa 3081(1976):1017.

       FESPACO prizes.

2433.  Matchet.  Cameroon in films.  West Africa 3141(1977):1921.

       Jean-Pierre Dikongue-Pipa, Muna Moto and Daniel Kamwa,
       Pousse-Pousse, shown in London.

2434.  Matchet.  "Emitai."  West Africa 3020(1975):535.  (R)

2435.  Matchet.   Film  festival  in  Brussels.   West  Africa
       3483(1984):1058-1059.

2436.  Matchet.  Film maker makes good.  West Africa 3366(1982):360. (R)

       Eddie Ugbomah, Bolus 80.

2437.  Matchet.  Filming SWAPO.  West Africa 3136(1977):1665.

2438.  Matchet.   Films  out  of  West Africa.   West  Africa
       3207(1979):47-48.

       Films by Eddie Ugbomah.

2439.  Matchet.  Matchet's diary.  West Africa 2788(1970):1340-1341.

       Calpenny Films.

2440.  Matchet.  Matchet's diary.  West Africa 3325(1981):851, 853.

       Discussion of claim that Sembène is anti-Islamic; Sembène's views
       on role of film.

2441.  Matchet.  A Nigerian feature film.  West Africa 2946(1973):1657.
       (R)

       Ola Balogun, Alpha.

2442. **Matchet.** Nigerian film. <u>West</u> <u>Africa</u> 3165(1978):501. (R)

Eddie Ugbomah, <u>The</u> <u>Rise</u> <u>and</u> <u>Fall</u> <u>of</u> <u>Dr.</u> <u>Oyenusi</u> shown in London.

2443. **Matchet.** Plastic bags and glass cases. <u>West</u> <u>Africa</u> 2806(1971):332-333. (R)

James Nee-Owoo, <u>You</u> <u>Hide</u> <u>Me</u>.

2444. **Matchet.** Shehu Umar on film. <u>West</u> <u>Africa</u> 3130(1977):1327. (R)

2445. **Matchet.** Traditional Yoruba theater. <u>West</u> <u>Africa</u> 3255(1979):2226-2227. (R)

Ola Balogun, <u>Ija</u> <u>Ominira</u>.

2446. **Mathew, K.M.** "L'autre école" de Nissy Joanny Traoré, au festival du court métrage d'Oberhausen. <u>Sidwaya</u> June 19 (1987):12. (R)

2447. **Mathias, Victor L.** Sidiki Bakaba: un valeur sûre. <u>Bingo</u> 361(1983):58.

Ivorian actor.

2448. **Mathur, Rakesh.** Rough cuts in cut-price Cannes. <u>South</u> 45(1984):85-86.

2449. **Mativo, Kyalo.** Action! Film production gets rolling in Kenya. <u>Weekly</u> <u>Review</u> 579(1986):23-24.

Problems of film production in Kenya.

2450. **Mativo, Kyalo.** Hollywood dominates. <u>Weekly</u> <u>Review</u> 557(1985):16-17.

Absence of African films shown in Kenya attributed to language problem. Sao Gamba discusses Kenya Film Corporation's plans for filmmaking.

2451. **Mativo, Kyalo.** Resolving the cultural dilemma of the African film. <u>UFAHAMU</u> 13,1(1983):134-146.

Films shown at University of California, Los Angeles, film festival.

2452. **Mativo, Kyalo.** 'Rise and Fall of Idi Amin.' <u>Weekly</u> <u>Review</u> 544(1985):16-17. (R)

Sharad Patel, <u>Amin</u> <u>the</u> <u>Rise</u> <u>and</u> <u>Fall</u>.

2453. **Mativo, Kyalo.** Self-image in African films. <u>Third</u> <u>World</u> <u>Affairs</u> (1985):391-394. (R)

King Ampaw, Kukurantumi; Moussa Diakité, Naitou and Sanou Kollo, Paweogo. Review focuses on "is there African film".

2454. Mativo, Wilson. Cultural dilemma of the African film. UFAHAMU 1,3(1971):64-68.

Films of Moustapha Alassane, Henri Duparc, Oumarou Ganda, Sembène Ousmane and Timité Bassori.

2455. Maunick, Edouard J. Charles Mensah. Demain L'Afrique 35(1979):78.

Obali, Ayouma and Ilombé discussed.

2456. Maunick, Edouard. En direct avec Pierre Marie Dong. Demain l'Afrique 25(1979):62-63.

2457. Maupin, Françoise. Entretien avec Safi Faye. Revue du Cinéma 303(1976):75-80. (I)

Discussion of Kaddu Beykat and her role as Africa's first woman filmmaker.

2458. Maurienne, Claude. Premier western africain. Jeune Afrique 273(1976):34-35. (R)

Moustapha Alassane, La Bague du roi Koda.

2459. Mavioga, D. Sé. Une équipe du CENACI en tournage. L'Union Apr. 26-27 (1986):7. (R)

Paul Mouketa, Raphia. Information of its making included in review.

2460. Mawerera, Kay. Liberation film beset by snags. Sunday Mail (Harare) Dec. 30 (1984):5.

Film script by Wilson Katiyo.

2461. Mazda, Sally. Des vampires pour le CIDC CIPROFILM. Intrus May 22 (1987):6.

2462. Mba Nguéma. Le cinéma "Akébé" devrait rouvrir ses portes en août prochain avec une salle entièrement rénovée et de nouveaux gérants. L'Union June 20 (1978):2.

Renovation of theater in Gabon, shortage of theaters.

2463. Mbarga-Abega, Mathieu. Mariama Hima. Bingo 415(1987):62-63. (I)

Discussion of her ethnographic films.

2464. Mbarga-Abega, Mathieu. Momo Joseph, l'homme orchestre à l'américaine. Bingo 376(1984):59-60. (I)

Discussion of his acting and dancing.

2465. **M'bayi Kaninda.** Le héros, le groupe et l'ordre social, in <u>Caméra Nigra</u> C.E.S.C.A. ed. Brussels: OCIC, 1984. pp. 113-136.

Themes of films; filmography.

2466. **Mbeki, Moeletsi.** Vision of Africa's 'man of culture.' <u>Herald</u> (Harare) Sept. 12 (1986):10.

Sembène's attitudes toward literature and film.

2467. **Mbélé, Charles Minko.** Festival de la Francophone: le Gabon remporte le palmier d'or long métrage et le grand prix d'honneur du festival. <u>L'Union</u> Oct. 16 (1979):1,4.

Gabonais films shown at FIFEF.

2468. **Mbélé, Charles Minko.** Le FIFEF, un moyen d'échanges et de communication. <u>L'Union</u> Oct. 17 (1978):2. (I)

Interview with Albert Yangari on FIFEF, response to <u>Ayouma</u> and underdevelopment of African film.

2469. **Mbeuye.** "Le Wazou (sic) polygame" d'Oumarou Ganda. <u>L'Union</u> Feb. 27 (1978):4. (R)

2470. **M'Bodj, Ibrahima.** Des badauds Avenue Clemenceau pour le film de Cheikh Gaidoh Bah: "Arrêt car." <u>Le Soleil</u> Oct. 4 (1973):2.

Problems in making this film for television.

2471. **Mbodji, Moustapha.** Le crise du cinéma sénégalais. <u>Le Soleil</u> 3435(1981):4.

2472. **Mbounja, Francis Emile.** Daniel Kamua a batons rompus. <u>Bingo</u> 274(1975):16-19, 64. (I)

2473. **Mboup, Ibrahima Mansour.** Garga-M'bossé, un film de Mahama Traoré sur les victimes de la sechéresse. <u>Le Soleil</u> Nov. 2 (1973):2. (R)

2474. **Mboup, Ibrahima Mansour.** Je suis incompris dans mon propre pays. <u>Le Soleil</u> 2047(1977):2.

Senegalese and American films in which Johnny Sekka acted.

2475. **Meberka.** Colonne I. <u>Ivoire Dimanche</u> 63(1972):22. (I)

Moustapha Alassane discusses F.V.V.A.

2476. **Meberka.** "Mouna" et "La femme au couteau". <u>Ivoire Dimanche</u> 55(1972):22. (R)

MEDA, JEAN-CLAUDE See MEDA, YIRZAOLA

2477. Meda, Yirzaola. A qui profite la lenteur des travaux? Sidwaya
Feb. 27 (1985):i,iii.

Report on FEPACI meeting.

2478. Meda, Yirzaola. Une bouée de sauvetage pour le CIDC. Carrefour
Africain 988(1987):18-19.

2479. Meda, Yirzaola. Cannes: l'Afrique était présente. Carrefour
Africain 990-991(1987):26-27.

2480. Meda, Yirzaola. Le CIDC doit survivre. Carrefour Africain
988(1987):19.

2481. Meda, Yirzaola. CIDC le ver dans le fruit. Carrefour Africain
981(1987):22-23.

2482. Meda, Yirzaola. Le cinéma burkinabé en quête de souffle.
Carrefour Africain 921(1986):29-32.

Burkinabe films compared to Russian, French and Cuban films; need
for stronger infrastructure.

2483. Meda, Yirzaola. 5ème Conseil Extraordinaire du CIDC/CIPROFILM
sortir de l'impasse. Sidwaya May 6 (1987):3.

2484. Meda, Yirzaola. "Les coopérants", un exemple d'intégration aux
masses? Sidwaya Mar. 1 (1985):i. (R)

2485. Meda, Yirzaola. La cristallisation autour des travaux en
commissions. Sidwaya Feb. 25 (1985):iii.

FEPACI.

2486. Meda, Yirzaola. 10ème FESPACO un grand tournant. Carrefour
Africain 977(1987):8-11.

Problems with FESPACO and suggestions for improvement.

2487. Meda, Yirzaola. En avant pour une Fepaci forte et dynamique.
Sidwaya Feb. 28 (1985):i.

Report on 3rd FEPACI congress.

2488. Meda, Yirzaola. Une expérience à recueillir. Carrefour Africain
900(1985):26-27.

Infrastructure for Burkinabe films.

2489. Meda, Yirzaola. FESPACO et autres festivals, chronique d'un
cheminement. Carrefour Africain 975(1987):8-10.

2490. **Meda, Yirzaola.** Le FESPACO: une dimension internationale. _Carrefour_ _Africain_ 894(1985):55.

2491. **Meda, Yirzaola.** Grande première à Dobao. _Carrefour_ _Africain_ 965(1986):16.

Burkinabe film on development being made.

2492. **Meda, Yirzaola.** Ils ont dit. _Sidwaya_ Feb. 23 (1987):6.

Opinions of 5 participants on FESPACO.

2493. **Meda, Yirzaola.** Ironu ou les intellectuels africains face aux responsibilitiés de leur pays. _Sidwaya_ Feb. 23 (1987):12. (R)

2494. **Meda, Yirzaola.** Le marche du film. _Sidwaya_ Feb. 18 (1987):11.

Arrangements for showing and viewing films at FESPACO.

2495. **Meda, Yirzaola.** "Nous sommmes parvenus à des résultats positifs." _Carrefour_ _Africain_ 988(1987):20-22. (I)

Bernadette Sanou discusses CIDC.

2496. **Meda, Yirzaola.** L'opérateur de son: parent pauvre du cinéma? _Carrefour_ _Africain_ 1002 (1987):20-27. (I)

Issa Traoré, Burkinabe sound recorder, discusses his work.

2497. **Meda, Yirzaola.** Les oubliés du cinéma. _Carrefour_ _Africain_ 983(1987):21-23. (I)

Sékou Ouédraogo, Burkinabe film technician, discusses his work.

2498. **Meda, Yirzaola.** Rétrospective FESPACO. 1985 était une innovation. _Sidwaya_ Jan. 14 (1987):3.

2499. **Meda, Yirzaola.** Les temps forts du FESPACO. _Sidwaya_ Mar. 4 (1985):iii.

2500. **Meda, Yirzaola.** Une thérapeutique à la taille du mal. _Carrefour_ _Africain_ 927(1986):22-24.

Problems of CIDC and CIPROFILM.

2501. **Meda, Yirzaola.** Visages de femmes, vrai ou faux. _Sidwaya_ Feb. 27 (1987):6. (R)

2502. **Meda, Yirzaola.** Une volonté de réussir malgrédes débats houleux. _Sidwaya_ Feb. 22 (1985):5.

Report on 3rd FEPACI congress.

2503. Meda, Yirzaola and Amado Nana. Le FEPACI deux ans après, restaurer la crédibilité. Carrefour Africain 975(1987):29-31.

2504. Meda, Yirzaola and Didier Lézin Zongo. Issaka Thiombiano doyen du cinéma burkinabé. Carrefour Africain 993(1987):17-24. (I)

Burkinabe cameraman discusses his work.

*2505. Medeiros, Carlos Alberto. Ola Balogun o novo cinema africano descobre o Brasil. Afrochambre Dec. (1977).

2506. Medeiros, Richard de. Dialogue a quelques voix. Recherche, pédagogie et culture 17-18(1975):39-43..

Report on 1969 FESPACO roundtable.

2507. Medeiros, Richard de. L'heure des bilans. Le Monde Diplomatique 318(1980):12.

Film production in Benin and other Francophone countries.

2508. Medjigbodo, Nicole. Afrique cinématographiée, Afrique cinématographique. Canadian Journal of African Studies 13, 3(1980):371-387.

History of African film from its capitalist origins through its neocolonial development. Potential of film for education and communication.

2509. Medvedev, Armen. Bookshelf: The cinema in Africa. Young Cinema and Theater 2(1974):41-43. (BR)

Semen Chertok, Nachalo Kino Chornoi Afriki. See No. 20.

2510. Meerapfel, Jeanine. Entretien avec Ruy Guerra. Positif 207(1978):58-60. (I)

Discussion of A Queda.

2511. Méliani, Majid. J.C.C.: le revers de la médaille. SeptièmArt 53(1985):12.

2512. Mendy, Justin. Aprés Carthage et Ouagadougou, les cinéastes africains veulent implanter un troisième festival. Afrique Nouvelle 1283(1972):10-11.

J.C.C., FIFEF and FESPACO.

2513. Mendy, Justin. Et la neige n'était plus. Afrique Nouvelle 967(1966):15. (R)

2514. Mendy, Justin. M. Paulin Vieyra nous expose les difficultés du cinéma africain. Afrique Nouvelle 846(1963):9-10. (I)

2515. Mensah, Charles. Cinéma africain et réalité africain. Le Courrier de Saint-Ex 17(1979):4.

Discussion of filmmaker as witness of his times.

2516. Merzak, M. Entretien avec Med Hondo. 2 écrans 13(1979):24-26. (I)

2517. Meuer, Gerd. Sembène Ousmane - writer and cineast. Afrika 21, 7-8(1980):40-41.

Why Sembène started making films.

2518. Mgbejume, Onyero. The future of television and film in Nigeria. Educational Broadcasting International 12,2(1979):69-71.

2519. Michaud, Paul R. Upper Volta leads black Africa with studio venture. Variety 295,1(1979):244.

CINAFRIC studios.

2520. Mida, Massimo. Uno spiraglio sul cinema africano. Bianco e Nero 37,7-8(1976):132-138.

Films of Alkaly Kaba and Momar Thiam.

2521. Milhomme, Janet. Heritage in a freeze frame. South 50(1984):105.

History of Ghanaian film, colonial period to 1980s.

2522. Milne, Tom. Opera do Malandro. Monthly Film Bulletin 54(1987):247-248. (R)

2523. Milne, Tom. Sweet Hunters. Monthly Film Bulletin 46(1979):54-55. (R)

2524. Ministère de l'Information. Le gouvernement ne se désintéresse pas des cinéastes. Fraternité Matin 4923(1981):5.

Government support of filmmaking in Côte d'Ivoire.

MINKO MBELE, CHARLES, See MBELE, CHARLES MINKO.

2525. Minoun, Mouloud. Peu d'oeuvres authentiques trop de productions hautes entics. 2 écrans 30(1981):11-16.

J.C.C.

2526. Minoun, Mouloud and B. Moulay. Entretien avec Souleymane Cissé. 2 écrans 47-48(1982):20-22. (I)

2527. Moanga-Bygnumba. Ciné-club: Dianka-Bi. Le Courrier de Saint Ex 31(1981):2. (R)

2528. Moha, Farida. La présence africaine au MIP-TV de Cannes. Continent 118(1981):10.

African films shown on French television.

2529. Mohamed, Shehnilla. Couple to shoot local film on teen pregnancy. Herald (Harare) July 13 (1987):3.

Americans to make film in Zimbabwe because of good film processing facilities.

2530. Mohamed, Shehnilla. Focus on rural disabled women. Herald Oct. 11 (1985):5. (R)

Miriam Patsanza, Woman Cry.

2531. Mohamed, Shehnilla. World premier of $39 million Steve Biko movie for Harare. Herald (Harare) July 8 (1987):3.

Foreign films made with Zimbabwean crews and actors.

2532. Mohamed, Shehnilla. Youth completes African film script after struggle. Herald (Harare) Dec. 15 (1986):11.

Joseph Matisi completes script, Sunset at Dawn.

2533. Mojalemotho, Rudolph. Putting Etsha on the map. Zebra's Voice 12,2(1985):15-19.

Film of basketmaking in Botswana.

2534. Mokabe, Max. Mieux qu'à l'école! Afrique-Asie 393(1987):46. (R)

Cheick Oumar Sissoko, Nyamanton.

2535. Mokhtar, Chorfi. Mannheim, un festival qui ouvre la voie aux jeunes talents. L'Action Oct. 22 (1978):13.

2536. Monga, Célestin. Leçon de courage. Jeune Afrique 1229(1984):58-59. (R)

Haile Gerima, Bush Mama.

2537. Moore, Carlos. "Le cinéma n'existe pas encore." Jeune Afrique 1065(1981):66-67. (I)

Ola Balogun discusses Nigerian films in Hausa, Igbo and Yoruba; messages of African films, including his own.

2538. Morakinyo, Dele. Film-makers complain of inadequate government support. Guardian (Lagos) Feb. 12 (1986):11.

Need for filmmaking support and facilities in Nigeria.

2539. Morakinyo, Dele. Kanna-Kanna: another film out. Guardian (Lagos) Nov. 16 (1985):11. (R)

2540. Morakinyo, Dele. 'Ogun Ajaye': another feature film in the yolk. Guardian (Lagos) Mar. 13 (1986):17. (R)

2541. Morakinyo, Dele. Responding to a challenge. Guardian (Lagos) Mar. 18 (1984):B7. (R)

Bayo Aderohunmu, Ireke Onibudo.

2542. Morel Junior, Justin. Entretien Sidikiba Kaba (sic). Zone 2 164(1982):16-17. (I)

Ivorian actor.

2543. Morellet, Jean-Claude. Cannes 1968: foire ou festival? Jeune Afrique 386-387(1968):68-69.

2544. Morellet, Jean-Claude. Carthage 1966:une grande confrontation. Jeune Afrique 312(1967):58-60.

2545. Morellet, Jean-Claude. Carthage 1968. Jeune Afrique 409(1968):58-59.

2546. Morellet, Jean-Claude. Cinéma africain: premiers pas en liberté. Jeune Afrique 373(1968):42-43. (I)

Sembène discusses production and financing of Mandabi.

2547. Morellet, Jean-Claude, ed. La critique et "Le Mandat." Jeune Afrique 418(1968):6-7. (R)

Excerpts from reviews of Sembène Ousmane, Mandabi.

2548. Morellet, Jean-Claude. La farce de Venise. Jeune Afrique 403(1968):54-55.

Sembène Ousmane, Mandabi shown at Venice film festival.

2549. Morellet, Jean-Claude. Le festival de Carthage. Jeune Afrique 404(1968):52.

2550. Morellet, Jean-Claude. Le festival du Leipzig. Jeune Afrique 416(1968):54-55.

2551. Morgenthau, Henry. Guide to African films. Africa Report 13,5(1968):52-54. (R)

Review of 5 catalogues of films about Africa and article on filmmaking by Jean Rouch. See No. 3131.

2552. Morgenthau, Henry. On films and filmmakers. Africa Report

14,5-6(1969):71-75. (R)

Review of 10 films about Africa, 3 are by Sembène: <u>Borom</u> <u>Sarret</u>, <u>Mandabi</u> and <u>La</u> <u>noire</u> <u>de</u>.

2553.  Morin, Jacques.   Vers un marché du film africain?   <u>Cinéma</u> 303(1984):61-62.

Amiens film festival.

2554.  Morineau, Raymond.   L'aide de l'ACCT au cinéma africain.   <u>Demain</u> <u>l'Afrique</u> 19(1979):82-86.

2555.  Morineau, Raymond.   "L'Aventure ambigue."   <u>Africa</u> (Dakar) 164(1984):54-55. (R)

Film of C.A. Kane's novel.

2556.  Morineau, Raymond.   Med Hondo: "Le cinéma africain n'existe pas"... <u>Africa</u> (Dakar) 168(1985):43-44. (I)

Discussion of existence of African filmmakers, but lack of African film; J.C.C., FESPACO, CIPROFILM and audiences.

2557.  Mortimer, Robert A.   Engaged film-making for a new society. <u>Africa</u> <u>Report</u> 15, 8(1970):28-30.

Senegalese films made for the masses.

2558.  Mortimer, Robert A.   Ousmane Sembene and the cinema of decolonization.   <u>African</u> <u>Arts</u> 5,3(1972):64-68.

2559.  Mory, Philippe.   L'impact du cinéma... <u>Le</u> <u>Courrier</u> <u>de</u> <u>Saint-Ex</u> 17(1979):3.

Importance of film in Africa.   Need for use of film and television to reinforce African identity.

2560.  Mosk.  Fad jal. <u>Variety</u> 295,5(1979):22. (R)

2561.  Mosk.  Ija Ominira. <u>Variety</u> 296, 5(1979):22. (R)

2562.  Mosk.  Jom. <u>Variety</u> 307, 4(1982):17. (R)

2563.  Mosk.  Love Brewed in the African Pot.  <u>Variety</u> 302,8(1981):20. (R)

2564.  Mosk.  Sey Seyeti. <u>Variety</u> 300,3(1980):21,34. (R)

2565.  Moto.  African film makers challenge western images.   <u>Moto</u> 28(1984):25.

Report on Southern Africa Regional Film Workshop held in Harare.

2566. Moto. Drama in the House of Hunger. Moto 1,3(1982):37-38. (I)

Chris Austin discusses problems in making House of Hunger, gives opinion on filmmaking in Zimbabwe.

2567. Moto. Swedish Film Institute a lesson to Zimbabwe. Moto 39(1985):30.

Swedish Film Institute a model for government role in establishing film industry.

2568. Moumouni, Madou. En toute liberté quand remonte l'ICEBERG. Sidwaya Feb. 14 (1985):7.

Discussion of CIDC and CIPROFILM activities and problems.

*2569. Moustapha, Mahama Baba. Lettre paysanne de Safi Faye. Cinémarabe 6(1977):36. (R)

Kaddu Beykat.

2570. Mpembele N.M. Sembène Ousmane, le combat par la plume et l'image. Zaire 486(1977):34-35.

Sembène as writer and filmmaker.

2571. Mpembele zi Niangi. "Les routes kinoises." Zaire 358(1975):54.

Debate on film by Zairois filmmakers.

2572. Mpofa, Steve. Zimbabwe to benefit from Cuba's school of film producers. Herald May 19 (1986):4.

Cuban Film Institute training for Zimbabwean film producers.

2573. Mpoyi-Buatu, Th. "Ceddo" de Sembène Ousmane et "West Indies" de Med Hondo. Présence Africaine 119(1981):152-164. (R)

2574. M'pungu Mulenda. Avec les spectateurs du Shaba, in Caméra Nigra. C.E.S.C.A. ed. Brussels: OCIC, 1984. pp. 137-153.

Audience responses to films in Zaire.

2575. Mualabu Mussamba. Ndoma Lwele Mafuta: le cinéma zairois n'est pas encouragé. Zaire 210(1972):35-37. (I)

Discussion of problems of filmmaking.

2576. Mukamabano, Madeleine. FESPACO 85: un essai non transformé. Actuel développement 66(1985):54-58.

2577. Mukamabano, Madeleine. La force et la poésie d'un conte. Actuel développement 60(1984):49-53. (I)

Gaston Kaboré discusses Wend Kuuni.

2578. Mukamabano, Madeleine. Ombres et lumières du film africain. Actuel développement 59(1984):50-51.

Need for promotion of African film. Activities of CIDC and SIDEC.

2579. Mulimbi Zaina. Le cinéma africain, la nouveauté, Zaire 310(1974):52-53.

Themes and quality of films in Congo and Gabon.

2580. Mulimbi Zaina. Le cinéma africain sera-t-il authentique et commercial? Zaire 259(1973):37.

2581. Mulimbi Zaina. Le cinéma des comédiens, pour l'interpretation. Zaire 317(1974):52-53.

Anonymous actors in African films.

2582. Mulimbi Zaina. Le cinéma des réalisateurs, la mise en scène. Zaire 320(1974):61.

2583. Mulimbi Zaina. Le cinéma nigérien. Zaire 304(1974):48-49.

2584. Mulimbi Zaina. Le cinéma spectacle: l'aventure. Zaire 316(1974):52.

Need to improve quality of African films.

2585. Mulimbi Zaina. Le cinéma zairois. Zaire 267(1973):40-41.

2586. Mulimbi Zaina. 10 ans de cinéma africain...et après? Zaire 273(1973):39.

2587. Mulimbi Zaina. Le festival du film africain à Bruxelles, le Sénégal. Zaire 301(1974):48-49.

Senegalese films shown at Brussels film festival.

2588. Mulimbi Zaina. 1er festival du film africain à Bruxelles. Zaire 290(1974):46.

2589. Mulimbi Zaina. Xala "Un réquisitoire contra la bourgeoisie d'affaires". Zaire 355(1975):61. (R)

2590. Murcia-Capel, Pedro. Les caméras de l'Angola. Afrique-Asie 322(1984):56-57.

Activities of Angolan film institute and production of films for television. Ruy Duarte de Carvalho, Nelisita, shown at Amiens film festival.

2591.  Muritala, Sule.  Foreign films and our national survival. National Concord 4,1245(1984):3.

Need for censorship of violent foreign films in Nigeria.

*2592.  Muyiwa, Daniel.  Aiya: a film to watch.  Nationalist Dec. 16 (1979).

Hubert Ogunde, Aiye.

2593.  Mvone-Obiang, Thomas.  Réflexions d'un père de famille sur les films à la télévision.  L'Union June 14 (1979):2.

Need to censor foreign films on television in Gabon; need to show more African films.

2594.  Mwenyekiti, C. Tibakweitira.  Kampuni ya filamu Tanzania.  Dar es Salaam: Kimepigwa Chapa na Kiwanda cha Uchapaji cha, 1982?

Annual report on Tanzania Film Company.

2595.  N.A.P.  Ambrose M'Bia, Bernard Fresson, Robert Liensol et Gilles Segal en tête du générique "De Soleil O".  Dakar Matin Oct. 17 (1969):6.  (R)

Med Hondo, Soleil O completed but not distributed.  Acting and plot discussed.

2596.  N.A.P.  L'angoisse de la jeunesse a l'écran...Moustapha Diop. Nigerama 3(1975?):34.  (R)

Mustapha Diop, Synapse.  Review comments on its structural relationship to oral literature and its dance sequences.

2597.  N.A.P. "Aspirant" et "Sources d'inspiration."  Dakar Matin Oct. 2 (1969):6.  (R)

Two short films made in Moscow by Souleymane Cissé.

2598.  N.A.P.  "Bambo" couronné par le Festival du film du Dinard. Dakar Matin Oct. 6 (1969):6.  (R)

Bambo receives prize at FIFEF.

2599.  N.A.P.  Ben Halima (Tunisie), Momar Thiam (Sénégal) et Oumarou Ganda (Niger) en vedette.  Le Soleil July 9 (1971):6.

Films shown at FIFEF.

2600.  N.A.P. Bientôt des salles de cinéma d'art et d'essai seront crées en Afrique.  Dakar Matin June 26 (1969):4.

Goals of ACNA; participation in meeting with Cinéma d'Art et d'Essai at Cannes.

2601. N.A.P. Une brève histoire d'amour par le Camerounais Urbain Dia Moukori. Dakar Matin May 9 (1966):4. (R)

Point de vue.

2602. N.A.P. La caméra de Med Hondo traque le détective de la misère. Dakar Matin June 28 (1969):4. (R)

Soleil O. Review includes information about the making of the film.

2603. N.A.P. Le cinéma et l'Afrique. Dakar Matin May 13 (1969):4.

About the making of Moustapha Alassane, Contrebandiers; biographical information on Alassane included.

2604. N.A.P. Cinéma quand les nationaux lâchent Hollywood. Le Soleil Mar. 27 (1975):10.

African film dominated by Sembène Ousmane and Med Hondo; problems in development of African film.

2605. N.A.P. La critique française veut prospecter en Afrique Noire. Le Soleil Nov. 16 (1971):6.

Role of Cannes film festival in promoting Third World films and new filmmakers.

2606. N.A.P. Des hommes masques enlevent Lydia Ewande dans "Adam," premier long métrage d'Urbain Dia. Dakar Matin Feb. 3 (1968):6. (R)

2607. N.A.P. Désiré Ecaré tourne un film comique. Dakar Matin Feb. 19 (1969):6. (I)

Discussion of A nous deux France, includes brief comments on Concerto pour un exil.

2608. N.A.P. "En Résidence surveillée" au prochain FESPACO. L'Observateur Edition du nouvel an (1980):10. (R)

2609. N.A.P. "La femme au couteau" oeuvre de cinéaste Ivoirien Timité Bassori. Dakar Matin Oct. 4 (1969):6. (R)

2610. N.A.P. Festival de Carthage: la réalité et la rigueur. Amanié, de Gnoan M'Bala, de nouveau à l'honneur. Fraternité Matin 2378(1972):7. (R)

2611. N.A.P. Le Festival de Dinard ou le bond en avant du cinéma africain. Fraternité Matin 2303(1972):8.

Senegalese films shown at FIFEF.

2612.  N.A.P.  L'Ivoirien Désiré Ecaré.  Dakar Matin July 13 (1968):6.

Reception of Concerto pour un exil at Cannes film festival.

2613.  N.A.P.  James Campbell veut organiser le cinéma africain.  Dakar Matin Feb. 7 (1967):4.

Senegalese actor discusses roles he has played.

2614.  N.A.P.  Le jeune cinéma africain sur les bords de la Seine. Dakar Matin May 24 (1967):6.

Sembène, La noire de and Moustapha Alassane, Retour d'un aventurier shown at African film week in Paris.

2615.  N.A.P.  Un livre sur le cinéma: l'Afrique des caméras.  Dakar Matin Apr. 26 (1968):7.

Summary of No. 1512.

2616.  N.A.P.  Mandabi de Sembène Ousmane est le premier long-métrage africain parlant Ouolof.  Carrefour Africain 336(1968):8.  (I)

Mandabi shown at Venice film festival.  Sembène discusses its making.

2617.  N.A.P.  Moustapha Alassane et "Le retour d'un aventurier."  Dakar Matin May 9 (1966):4.  (R)

2618.  N.A.P.  Le Mvet de Moise Zé est le premier film éthnographique réalisé par un Africain.  Le Soleil Mar. 2 (1973):5.  (R)

Prize at J.C.C. for Moise Zé, Mvet.

2619.  N.A.P.  "Niaye" le nouveau film de l'écrivain sénégalais Sembène Ousmane sera presenté du Festival de Cannes.  Dakar Matin May 17 (1965):4.  (I)

Sembène discusses making Niaye; reasons for making short films and using amateur actors.

2620.  N.A.P.  Le nouveau long-métrage de Sèmbene Ousmane "Mandabi". Dakar Matin Jan. 30 (1969):6.  (R)

2621.  N.A.P.  "Un os pour toi" sera finance par la Haute-Volta et le Niger.  Dakar Matin Oct. 9 (1969):6.  (R)

Os pour toi, tentative title of film made by Moustapha Alassane.

2622.  N.A.P.  Ousmane Sembène en boubou, a représenté l'Afrique au Festival de Cannes.  Dakar Matin May 22 (1967):4.  (I)

Sembène discusses his role on jury for Cannes film festival.

2623.　N.A.P.　Ousmane Sembène nous confie: "Je rentre pour faire des films et écrire." <u>Dakar</u> <u>Matin</u> Aug. 8 (1966):3. (I)

Discussion of finding solutions to economic problems of filmmaking.

2624.　N.A.P.　Participation record de films au prochain festival de Ouagadougou. <u>L'Union</u> 1531(1981):7.

FESPACO.

2625.　N.A.P.　Pour tourner "Codou" Ababacar Samb cherche un co-producer. <u>Le</u> <u>Soleil</u> Nov. 7 (1970):3.

Cost of producing <u>Codou</u>. Samb's aims in filmmaking.

2626.　N.A.P.　"Saitane" d'Oumarou Ganda. <u>Le</u> <u>Soleil</u> Jan. 24 (1973):6. (R)

2627.　N.A.P.　Sékou Amadou Camara avec "Ame Perdue." <u>Dakar</u> <u>Matin</u> May 20 (1969):4. (R)

2628.　N.A.P.　Le Togolais Sanvi Panou vedette du "Sang du flamboyan." <u>Zone</u> <u>2</u> 119(1981):20.

Togolese actor.

2629.　N.A.P.　Toute la Fédération Panafricain des Cinéastes s'est imposée au festival international de Cannes. <u>Le</u> <u>Soleil</u> May 25 (1972):5.

Senegalese participation at Cannes film festival.

2630.　N.G.　Un accord de coproduction tuniso-sénégalais. <u>SeptièmArt</u> 62(1987):18-19. (I)

Mamadou M'Bengue discusses production of <u>Camp</u> <u>de</u> <u>Thiaroye</u>.

2631.　N.Z.　Le vent de l'unité. <u>Sidwaya</u> Feb. 27 (1987):12.

Special edition of <u>Trade</u> <u>Winds</u> for FESPACO.

2632.　Nagbou, Mustapha.　Le capitaine Sankara... et le cinéma. <u>SeptièmArt</u> 55(1985):16-17.

Burkinabe support of film.

2633.　Nagbou, Mustapha.　Les carnets d'un festivalier. <u>SeptièmArt</u> 55(1985):5-8.

FESPACO.

2634.　Nagbou, Mustapha.　Ce qui me gène dans le cinéma africain. <u>SeptièmArt</u> 55(1985):24-26.

*2635. Nagbou, Mustapha.   Ceddo.   Entretien avec Ousmane Sembène.
SeptièmArt 29(1977):9-10. (I)

2636. Nagbou, Mustapha.   C'est encore trop tôt.   SeptièmArt
55(1985):18. (I)

Interview with Kalifa Conde.

2637. Nagbou, Mustapha.   Le FEPACI victime de ses contradictions...et
de son hypocrisie.   SeptièmArt 55(1985):10-11.

2638. Nagbou, Mustapha.   Le FESPACO n'est ni anglophone, ni
francophone, ni arabophone.   SeptièmArt 41(1981):6-8. (I)

Louis Thiombiano discusses FESPACO.

2639. Nagbou, Mustapha.   J'ai dix fleurs à Tachkent.   SeptièmArt
45(1982):10-14.

Films from Angola, Niger and Togo shown at Tashkent film
festival.

2640. Nagbou, Mustapha.   Pour une place au soleil.   Unir Cinéma
14(1984):6-7.

Goals and coverage of SeptièmArt.

2641. Nagbou, Mustapha. Yves Diagne: Le FESPACO est un stimulant, un
catalyseur...et un espoir.   SeptièmArt 41(1981):9-11. (I)

2642. Namakajo, James K.   De-colonising African cinema.   Africa Now
10(1982):32-33.

MOGPAFIS.

2643. Nana, Hamado.   Désébagato "propos" sur la classe ouvrière.
Sidwaya Feb. 24 (1987):5. (R)

2644. Nana, Hamado.   "Les écuelles" de Idrissa Ouédraogo prime en
Allemagne.   Sidwaya July 10 (1985):5. (R)

Les écuelles shown at Oberhausen film festival.   Importance of
Oberhausen festival for Third World filmmakers.

2645. Nana, Hamado.   Formation politique sur écran géant.   Sidwaya Aug.
2 (1985):4.

Political themes of films.

2646. Nana, Hamado.   Nyamanton: un humour dérangeant.   Sidwaya Feb. 26
(1987):5. (R)

2647. Nana, Hamado.   La parole au laureat de la 9ème edition.   Sidwaya

Feb. 23 (1987):10. (I)

Adama Diouf, Senegalese playwright and actor, discusses FESPACO.

2648. Nana, Hamado. Vers un nouvel ordre du cinéma africain. Carrefour Africain 766(1983):15.

FESPACO.

2649. Nana, Hamado and Y. Meda. La contribution de la FEPACI. Sidwaya Feb. 12 (1987):12.

2650. Nana, Hamado and Y. Meda. Le FEPACI présente a plusieurs festivals. Sidwaya Feb. 4 (1987):9.

FEPACI support of MOGPAFIS and film week in Kenya.

2651. Nana, Hamado and Zakara Yeye. Interview express a propos de "Visages de femmes." Sidwaya Mar. 2 (1987):9. (R)

7 members of the audience give their opinions of Ecaré's film.

2652. Nana, Hamado and N. Zongo. "Je viens decouvrir la révolution burkinabé" déclare Fela Anikulapo Kuti en arrivant hier dans notre pays. Sidwaya Feb. 27 (1987):7.

Kuti's impressions of FESPACO.

*2653. Nargo, Fat. CENAI: regarder gabonais. Mbile-Nzambi 13(Sept. 15-30)1985.

2654. Nass. "Je ne milite dans aucun parti, je milite à travers mon oeuvre" nous affirme Ousmane Sembène. Dakar Matin Apr. 11-12 (1966):1. (I)

2655. Nation Reporter. Kenya praised for initiating film week. Daily Nation (Nairobi) Dec. 6 (1986):4.

2656. National Concord. UN panel gets film script on apartheid. National Concord 6, 1662(1985):1,15.

Film script by Harry Akande.

2657. Nave, Bernard. Ceddo. Jeune Cinéma 104(1977):43-44. (R)

2658. Nave, Bernard. Emitai. Jeune Cinéma 103(1977):34-36. (R)

2659. Ndaw, Aly Kheury. A propos de deux films. Le Soleil Mar. 3 (1979):2. (R)

Cheick Doukouré, Bako and Pierre-Marie Dong, Demain un jour nouveau.

2660. Ndaw, Aly Kheury. A propos du FIFEF 75. Le Soleil July 17

(1975):8.

FEPACI initiatives to include Anglophone countries.

2661.  Ndaw, Aly Kheury.  L'Afrique reste en rade.  Zone 2 82(1980):21.

Films shown at FIFEF.

2662.  Ndaw, Aly Kheury.  Après la rencontre de Saint-Vincent intérêt accru de l'Italie pour le cinéma francophone de l'Afrique.  Le Soleil Jan. 27-28 (1979):2.

UNICEF conference on African film.

2663.  Ndaw, Aly Kheury.  "Baara" de Souleymane Cissé un film malien sur nos écrans.  Le Soleil Sept. 29-30 (1979):3.  (R)

2664.  Ndaw, Aly Kheury.  Badou Boy un film à sketches de Djibril Diop.  Le Soleil Oct. 8 (1970):3.  (R)

2665.  Ndaw, Aly Kheury.  Black Mic-Mac sera tourné à Paris et en Afrique.  Le Soleil Mar. 25 (1985):7.

Sidiki Bakaba, Cheick Doukouré, Gerald Essomba, Doura Mané and Joseph Momo, actors.

2666.  Ndaw, Aly Kheury.  Cannes 86 succès de Lakhdar-Hamina.  Le Soleil May 14 (1986):8.

2667.  Ndaw, Aly Kheury.  Carthage et après! Le Soleil Nov. 18 (1974):4; Nov. 19 (1974):4; Nov. 20 (1974):7.

Criticism of J.C.C. jury.

2668.  Ndaw, Aly Kheury.  Carthage: les neuvièmes rencontres du cinéma afro-arabe.  Le Soleil Nov. 16 (1982):20-21.

2669.  Ndaw, Aly Kheury.  Carthage: notre cinéma à l'honneur.  Le Soleil Oct. 20 (1970):2.  (R)

Djibril Diop, Badou Boy, receives prize at J.C.C.

2670.  Ndaw, Aly Kheury.  Le cinéma africain a Ouagadougou.  Le Soleil Feb. 19 (1976):8.

Themes of films shown at FESPACO.

2671.  Ndaw, Aly Kheury.  "Le cinéma africain doit être utile à nos sociétiés".  Le Soleil May 4 (1974):3.  (I)

Férid Boughedir discusses FESPACO conference on role of African filmmaker, SIDEC, SONACI and need for authentic representations of Africa.

2672. **Ndaw, Aly Kheury.** Cinéma: après Dinard 72 un FIFEF 73 a Beyrouth. Le Soleil June 15 (1973):5.

2673. **Ndaw, Aly Kheury.** Cinéma: bientôt dans nos salles deux nouveaux films sénégalais "Badu Boy" et "Contrast city." Le Soleil Jan. 11 (1972):6. (R)

2674. **Ndaw, Aly Kheury.** Cinéma: la session du FIFEF à Dakar compromise... Le Soleil Oct. 18 (1979):2.

2675. **Ndaw, Aly Kheury.** Le cinéma sénégalais au Festival de Carthage. Le Soleil Oct. 24 (1974):7.

2676. **Ndaw, Aly Kheury.** Le cinéma sénégalais repart. Le Soleil June 11 (1979):2.

SNC support of Senegalese film.

2677. **Ndaw, Aly Kheury.** Le cinéma sénégalais se porte bien. Mais... Le Soleil Feb. 8 (1975):10.

Need for Senegalese government support of film. Censorship of **Xala**.

2678. **Ndaw, Aly Kheury.** Un colloque sur le critique. Le Soleil Mar. 6 (1979):2.

Report on FESPACO colloquium on the role of film critics.

2679. **Ndaw, Aly Kheury.** Le consortium de distribution de films en voie de création. Le Soleil Apr. 8 (1977):3. (I)

Kalifa Conde discusses CIDC and distribution problems.

2680. **Ndaw, Aly Kheury.** "La création de la SIDEC doit ouvrir des perspectives nouvelles aux cinéastes sénégalais" nous déclare Mahama Traoré. Le Soleil Apr. 11 (1974):4. (I)

2681. **Ndaw, Aly Kheury.** De 4 au 11 mars Ouagadougou sera le rendez-vous des cinéastes africains. Le Soleil Feb. 8 (1972):3.

FESPACO.

2682. **Ndaw, Aly Kheury.** "Demain un jour nouveau." Le Soleil Mar. 5 (1979):2. (R)

2683. **Ndaw, Aly Kheury.** Désaffection des auteurs africains. Le Soleil July 29 (1980):2.

FIFEF compared to FESPACO and J.C.C.; African films shown.

2684. **Ndaw, Aly Kheury.** 2 sénégalais primés à Carthage. Le Soleil Nov. 24 (1980):1,9.

Safi Faye, Fad jal and Ousmane Mbaye, Domu Ngac shown at J.C.C.

2685.  Ndaw, Aly Kheury. "Diègue-Bi" ou la vie d'un couple dernier film de Johnson Traoré. Le Soleil Feb. 3 (1971):2. (R)

2686.  Ndaw, Aly Kheury. Dinard première capitale. Le Soleil July 28 (1980):2.

FIFEF.

2687.  Ndaw, Aly Kheury. Dinard prochain rendez-vous des cinéastes francophones. Le Soleil June 10 (1974):2.

FIFEF.

2688.  Ndaw, Aly Kheury. Xe FESPACO. La visite impromptue de Thomas Sankara. Le Soleil Feb. 27 (1987):8.

2689.  Ndaw, Aly Kheury. Djibril Diop: "Je vais présenter mon film au festival de Cannes." Le Soleil Mar. 21 (1972):2. (I)

Discussion of Touki-Bouki, aims in filmmaking.

2690.  Ndaw, Aly Kheury. Doura Mané succomba à ses blessures. Le Soleil July 11 (1978):1, 8.

Review of Mané's career.

2691.  Ndaw, Aly Kheury. Du 11 au 18 octobre, au 3ème festival de Carthage 4 cinéastes sénégalais essaieront de faire aussi bien qu'Ousmane Sembène en 1969. Le Soleil Oct. 5 (1970):3.

Films of Tidiane Aw, Djibril Diop, Momar Thiam and Mahama Johnson Traoré shown at J.C.C.

2692.  Ndaw, Aly Kheury. Elargir l'horizon. Le Soleil July 30 (1980):2.

Value of FIFEF for African filmmakers.

2693.  Ndaw, Aly Kheury. Emergence de jeunes talents. Le Soleil Mar. 2 (1979):2.

FESPACO prize-winning films.

2694.  Ndaw, Aly Kheury. En avant première du film "Diankha-Bi." Dakar Matin Apr. 19 (1969):3. (I)

Mahama Johnson Traoré discusses Diankha-Bi, lack of infrastructure.

2695.  Ndaw, Aly Kheury. Entretien avec Ecaré: "Nous venons apporter au cinéma le langage de l'homme noir." Le Soleil Dec. 12 (1973):3. (I)

Why Ecaré does not participate in film festivals, his goals in filmmaking.

2696. Ndaw, Aly Kheury.   Entretien avec Paulin S. Vieyra à propos de son nouveau livre "Ousmane Sembène cinéaste." Le Soleil Feb. 21 (1973):5. (I)

Discussion of Sembène and book Vieyra wrote about him.   See No. 77.

2697. Ndaw, Aly Kheury.   Faire du cinéma pas de la politique. Le Soleil Nov. 11 (1980):1,4. (I)

Mahama Johnson Traoré discusses activities of FEPACI, his opinion of J.C.C.

2698. Ndaw, Aly Kheury. Le FEPACI à Alger pour son congrès. Le Soleil Dec. 31-Jan. 1 (1974-1975):1,3.

Report on FEPACI congress.   Role of Senegalese filmmakers in FEPACI.

2699. Ndaw, Aly Kheury.   Festival de Cannes.   "Chronique d'une mort annoncée" en compétition. Le Soleil May 11 (1987):9. (R)

Background on making Yeelen by Souleymane Cissé, included in review.

2700. Ndaw, Aly Kheury.   Festival de Cannes.   L'entrée de Souleymane Cissé. Le Soleil May 9-10 (1987):10.

2701. Ndaw, Aly Kheury.   Festival de Cannes.   Et voici "Pierre et Djemila..." Le Soleil May 12 (1987):10.

2702. Ndaw, Aly Kheury.   Festival de Cannes.   Tout est redevenu comme avant. Le Soleil May 14 (1987):7.

2703. Ndaw, Aly Kheury.   Festival du film francophone à Dakar. Le Soleil July 20 (1979):4.

FIFEF to be held in Dakar.   FESPACO becoming more important.

2704. Ndaw, Aly Kheury.   Festival Panafrican de Ouagadougou. Le Soleil Feb. 7 (1973):5; Feb. 10 (1973):5; Feb. 12 (1973):5; Feb. 13 (1973):5; Feb. 15 (1973):5; Feb. 16 (1973):5.

Detailed report on FESPACO.   Organizational problems, comparison to J.C.C.

2705. Ndaw, Aly Kheury.   Un festival vraiment populaire. Le Soleil Mar. 1 (1979):2.

FESPACO.

2706.  Ndaw, Aly Kheury.  Le fils de qui? de Maguette Diop.  Le Soleil
       Mar. 16 (1980):2. (R)

2707.  Ndaw, Aly Kheury.  Fin du Xe FESPACO.  L'etalon du Yennenga à Med
       Hondo.  Le Soleil Mar. 2 (1987):10.

2708.  Ndaw, Ali Kheury.  Le fisc est trop gourmand.  Le Soleil Sept. 6
       (1977):2.

       Film distribution in Senegal before SIDEC.  Evaluation of SIDEC's
       activities.

2709.  Ndaw, Aly Kheury.  Un gouffre a argent.  Le Soleil Sept. 5
       (1977):2.

       Films assisted by SNC.  Activities of SIDEC.

2710.  Ndaw, Aly Kheury.  Un homme des femmes de Ben Diogaye Bèye.  Le
       Soleil Apr. 3-7 (1980):6. (R)

       Seye Seyeti.

2711.  Ndaw, Aly Kheury.  Les J.C.C. ont dix ans.  Le Soleil Nov. 10
       (1976):6.

2712.  Ndaw, Aly Kheury.  Les jeunes cinéastes africains se lancet à
       l'assaut des monopoles.  Le Soleil Sept. 11 (1972):5.

       Problem of financing films.  Role of FEPACI.

2713.  Ndaw, Aly Kheury.  Johnny Sekka sera Bilal au cinéma.  Le Soleil
       Jan. 16 (1975):3.

       Film roles of Senegalese actor.

2714.  Ndaw, Aly Kheury.  "Jom," prochain film d'Ababacar Samb.  Le
       Soleil May 27 (1980):2.

       On production of Jom.

2715.  Ndaw, Aly Kheury.  Les lampions sont allumes à Ouaga.  Le Soleil
       Feb. 23 (1987):10.

       FESPACO.

2716.  Ndaw, Aly Kheury.  La liberté au bout de la cinéma.  Le Soleil
       Feb. 23-24 (1985):7.

       FESPACO.

2717.  Ndaw, Aly Kheury.  Lionel N'Gakane (A.N.C.-Afrique du Sud): "Je
       fais des films pour combattre l'Apartheid."  Le Soleil Mar. 1
       (1973):5. (I)

2718. Ndaw, Aly Kheury. Un lourd héritage légué par la SECMA et la COMACICO. Le Soleil Feb. 6 (1977):3.

Film distribution in Senegal.

2719. Ndaw, Aly Kheury. Moins d'état dans la production tunisienne. Le Soleil Jan. 6 (1986):8.

Senegal and Tunisia pioneers in African filmmaking.

2720. Ndaw, Aly Kheury. "La nationalisation des salles a multiplié par dix notre chiffre d'affaires" déclare le directeur de la SONAVOCI (Haute-Volta). Le Soleil Mar. 14 (1973):5. (I)

Gaston Kaboré discusses Burkinabe attempts to control film distribution.

2721. Ndaw, Aly Kheury. "N'Diagane" l'oublié de Carthage. Le Soleil Nov. 27 (1974):2. (R)

Criticism of failure of J.C.C. jury to award prize to N'Diangane.

2722. Ndaw, Aly Kheury. Ne pas détruire...Carthage. Le Soleil Nov. 12 (1976):6.

Review of J.C.C. benefits to African film.

2723. Ndaw, Aly Kheury. Un nouveau cinéma est en train de naître. Le Soleil Sept. 21 (1973):7.

FIFEF.

2724. Ndaw, Aly Kheury. Un nouveau départ pour la FEPACI. Le Soleil Nov. 13-14 (1976):8.

2725. Ndaw, Aly Kheury. Ouaga: un festival aux dimensions nouvelles. Le Soleil Mar. 12 (1985):12-13.

FESPACO.

2726. Ndaw, Aly Kheury. L'Ours d'Or pour un film canadien. Le Soleil July 9 (1974):1, 7.

African films shown at Berlin film festival.

2727. Ndaw, Aly Kheury. Point de vue sur...Coudou (d'Ababacar Samb) L'universe de la folie. Emitai (d'Ousmane Sembène). Loin des poncifs habituels. Le Soleil Jan. 22-23 (1972):6. (R)

2728. Ndaw, Aly Kheury. Pousse-Pousse de Daniel Kamwa. Le Soleil Dec. 11 (1975):8.

Pousse-Pousse to be shown in Dakar. Kamwa has acted in Safi

Faye, La passante.

*2729. Ndaw, Aly Kheury. Projections à Paris du film "Demain un jour nouveau." L'Union Apr. 6 (1979).

2730. Ndaw, Aly Kheury. Quand la politique s'en mêle. Le Soleil Nov. 11 (1976):6.

Films shown at J.C.C.

2731. Ndaw, Aly Kheury. 95 millions de plus sur l'année 1975. Le Soleil Feb. 5 (1977):3.

Activities of SIDEC.

2732. Ndaw, Aly Kheury. Quelle solution pour l'avenir? Le Soleil Sept. 8 (1977):5.

Crisis in Senegalese film production; little benefit from SNC.

2733. Ndaw, Aly Kheury. Une quinzaine du cinéma du Tiers-monde à Alger. Le Soleil Aug. 27 (1973):3.

Report on FEPACI conference.

2734. Ndaw, Aly Kheury. Quinze nouveaux films africains au festival de Ouaga qui ouvre aujourd'hui ses portes. Le Soleil Feb. 3 (1973):5.

FESPACO.

2735. Ndaw, Aly Kheury. Les raisons profondes d'une faillite. Le Soleil Sept. 7 (1977):2.

Problems of production and distribution in Senegal. Activities of SNC and SIDEC.

2736. Ndaw, Aly Kheury. Une rencontre francophone à la Nouvelle-Orléans. Le Soleil Jan. 3 (1977):6.

FIFEF.

2737. Ndaw, Aly Kheury. Rétrospective du cinéma africain et arabe. Le Soleil Nov. 13 (1979):2. (R)

Moustapha Alassane, F.V.V.A. and Retour d'un aventurier shown in Dakar.

2738. Ndaw, Aly Kheury. Semaine du cinéma organisée par le Club des Atlantes. Le Soleil Sept. 28 (1970):3.

Senegalese films to be shown and discussed by film club.

2739. Ndaw, Aly Kheury. Sembène Ousmane tourne "Le camp de Thiaroye."

Le Soleil Mar. 24 (1987):10.

Script preparation and production of Camp de Thiaroye.

2740. Ndaw, Aly Kheury.  Sidney Sokhona: un cinéaste de l'immigration.
Le Soleil June 3 (1977):4. (R)

Review of Karamokho, Nationalité: immigré and Safrana includes
information from an interview with Sokhona.

2741. Ndaw, Aly Kheury.  S.N.C. un bilan non négligeable.  Le Soleil
Sept. 9 (1977):2.

Seminar and films supported by SNC.

2742. Ndaw, Aly Kheury.  Un société mort-née.  Le Soleil Sept. 3
(1977):2.

SNC's activities.

2743. Ndaw, Aly Kheury.  Tachkent: un festival pour le Tiers-Monde.  Le
Soleil June 28 (1976):5; June 29 (1976):7.

2744. Ndaw, Aly Kheury.  "Tago" dernier né du cinéma sénégalais.  Le
Soleil July 16 (1975):2. (R)

2745. Ndaw, Aly Kheury.  "Thiaroye": une affaire de professionnels.  Le
Soleil Apr. 22 (1987):13.

Cast and production of Camp de Thiaroye.

2746. Ndaw, Aly Kheury.  Trois structures mises en question.  Le Soleil
Mar. 14 (1985):12.

Activities of FEPACI, CIDC and CAC.

2747. Ndaw, Aly Kheury.  Trois tendance nouvelles du cinéma arabe et
africain.  Le Soleil Nov. 29-30 (1980):12.

Themes of films shown at J.C.C.

2748. N'Diaye, A. Entretien avec Tahar Cheriaa.  Le Soleil Feb. 20
(1973):5. (I)

Discussion of FESPACO and themes of films shown there.

2749. N'Diaye, Catherine.  La parole retrouvée.  Jeune Afrique
1212(1984):59. (R)

Gaston Kaboré, Wend Kuuni.

2750. N'Diaye, Malal.  Abusuan d'Henri Duparc.  Le Soleil June 21
(1973):2. (R)

2751. N'Diaye, Malal. "Cinéma et tradition orale" un conférence de l'A.N.J.S. donnée verdredi par Paulin Vieyra. Le Soleil Mar. 19 (1973):3.

Report on conference on relationship of film to oral tradition.

2752. N'Diaye, Malal. Cinéma: les prix augment aux guichets de nos salles. Le Soleil Jan. 23 (1975):1.

Ticket prices in Senegal too high.

2753. N'Diaye, Malal. L'O.R.T.F. à la recherche de la vérité de la coopération. Le Soleil Apr. 18 (1972):3.

Problems in obtaining cooperation in film training for Africans.

2754. N'Diaye, Malal. Un Sénégalais diplômé de l'Institut indien de cinéma. Le Soleil Aug. 4-5 (1973):7.

Baidy Dia, Senegalese filmmaker trained in India, plans to make television films.

2755. N'Diaye, Malal. La ville en effervescence: "M. Pot de vin" est dans les murs. Le Soleil Dec. 7 (1971):4.

Plans of Mahama Johnson Traoré to make Lambaaye.

2756. Ndiaye, Ousmane Altine. A propos de "Sey Seyeti." Le Soleil 3240(1981):2. (R)

2757. Ndiaye, Tabara. "Xew-Xew": précisions de Tabara Ndiaye. Zone 2 222(1983):18.

Senegalese actor.

2758. Ndiaye, Vieux Doro. Rénovation des salles de cinéma. Le Soleil Sept. 21 (1982):7.

New theater in Senegal. Plans to improve sound in theaters.

2759. Ndiaye-Thiasse, Henri. Cinema africano in Italia. Nigrizia 97,3(1979):14.

UNICEF Conference on African film.

2760. Ndibe, Okey. Protecting the film industry. African Guardian 2,5(1987):28.

Need indigenization decree in Nigeria to stimulate film production.

2761. Ndoye, Ousmane. Groupes eléctrogènes de secours pour les cinémas. Le Soleil 3424(1981):6.

Improved electric supply needed for Senegalese theaters.

2762.  Ndoye, Papa Massar.  Rompre avec le cinéma patronage.  Le Soleil Apr. 30 (1975):2.

Sembène Ousmane and Momar Thiam as revolutionary filmmakers.

2763.  Nduka, Bernard.  All films must be censored.  New Nigerian May 14 (1977):4.

Need for constructive film policy in Nigeria to keep out bad films and insure supply of good films.

2764.  Ndutum, Patrick-Paulin.  CENACI.  Constitution du nouveau bureau du l'Association des cinéastes gabonais.  L'Union July 9 (1985):3.

Meeting of ACG to discuss expenditure of funds provided by President Bongo.

2765.  Ndutum, Patrick-Paulin.  CENACI.  Des tests pour recenser les comédiens.  L'Union July 11 (1985):3.

CENACI course on film production; 1986 budget for filmmaking. Need for better press coverage on film.

2766.  Ndutum, Patrick-Paulin.  Entretien avec Henri-Joseph Koumba, réalisateur du "Singe fou".  L'Union Mar. 26 (1986):3. (I)

2767.  Ndutum, Patrick-Paulin.  "Le singe fou" ...enfin... L'Union Mar. 21 (1986):3. (R)

2768.  Ndzanga, Alphonse.  "La Chapelle," prix de l'originalité africaine.  Bingo 342(1981):48-51. (I)

Jean-Michel Tchissoukou discusses his film.

2769.  Ndzanga, Alphonse.  "Les lutteurs" tradition et allégorie.  Bingo 354(1982):53-54. (I)

Jean-Michel Tchissoukou discusses his film.

2770.  Nefzi, Tahar.  J.C.C.: Pouvoir et servitudes d'un forum arabo-africain.  L'Action Nov. 16 (1980):32.

2771.  Negriolli, Maria Luisa.  Africa sul Reno.  Nigrizia 104, 12(1986):41.

Mannheim film festival.

2772.  Negriolli, Maria Luisa.  L'angelo de focolare.  Nigrizia 101, 10(1983):4-5.

Venice film festival.

2773. Negriolli, Maria Luisa.  I dimenticati del Lido.  _Nigrizia_ 102,
9(1984):44-45.

Venice film festival.

2774. Negriolli, Maria Luisa.  Verona chiama Tunisi.  _Nigrizia_
103,1(1985):44-45.

J.C.C.

2775. Negriolli, Maria Luisa.  Voglia di decollare.  _Nigrizia_
105,1(1987):50-52.

Angolan and Camerounian films shown at Verona film festival.

2776. Nepoti, Roberto.  Sembene Ousmane, in _Dizinario universale del
cinema_.  Fernaldo Di Giammatteo, ed.  Rome: Editori Riuniti,
1985, Vol. 2. pp. 1211-1212.

Biographical information and a short description of each of
Sembène's films.

2777. Network Africa.  Segun Oyekunle.  _Network Africa_ 2,
9(1985):18,20.

Oyekunle's aims as a filmmaker, _Malama_, a screenplay he's written
and _Broken Cells_, a film he is producing.

2778. New African.  Africa must make films.  _New African_ 134(1978):108.

Comments made by Sembène at U.S. symposium on cinema and society.
Africans must make films that raise people's consciousness.

2779. New African.  Brutal censorship.  _New African_ 142(1979):73-74.

Censorship of _Blacks Britannica_.

2780. New African.  Film that fights for political consciousness.  _New
African_ 130(1978):64. (R)

Sidney Sokhkona, _Safrana_.

2781. New African.  Forbidden relationship.  _New African_ 155(1980):70.
(R)

Kwaw Ansah, _Love Brewed in the African Pot_.

2782. New Culture.  The film industry in Nigeria.  _New Culture_
1,5(1979):1-3.

2783. New Nigerian.  Award for African cinema.  _New Nigerian_ Mar. 14
(1973):12.

OCIC award to be given at FESPACO.

2784.  New Nigerian.  Bendel cinema embarks on ₦5m project.  New
       Nigerian Oct. 23 (1976):16.

       Theaters to be built in Nigeria for FESTAC.

2785.  New Nigerian.  Challenge of film industry.  New Nigerian Aug. 18
       (1973) Saturday extra, p. 2.

       Problems of training personnel and running theaters in Nigeria.

2786.  New Nigerian.  Cinema houses for Rivers L G headquarters soon.
       New Nigerian June 30 (1978):7.

       Theaters to be built in rural areas of Nigeria.

2787.  New Nigerian.  Cinematographic Act for amendment.  New Nigerian
       Apr. 25 (1987):2.

       Need for stricter control of films imported into Nigeria.

2788.  New Nigerian.  Film producer mourns Umara Ladan's death.  New
       Nigerian Jan. 7 (1978) Saturday extra, n.p.

       Ladan dubbed Hausa version of Ola Balogun, Animata.

2789.  New Nigerian.  France hails Mauritanian film.  New Nigerian Mar.
       7 (1973):12. (R)

       Med Hondo, Soleil O.

2790.  New Nigerian.  Government donates ₦1,000 to indigenous film
       industry.  New Nigerian May 17 (1978):10.

       Oyo State government support for Nigerian film production.

2791.  New Nigerian.  Ija Ominira: new film on Nigerian screen.  New
       Nigerian Apr. 8 (1978) Saturday extra, p. 2. (R)

2792.  New Nigerian.  Kwara develops ₦ .5m film unit.  New Nigerian Nov.
       4 (1981):25.

       Description of Nigerian film production unit.

2793.  New Nigerian.  Need for ban on importation of feature films
       stressed.  New Nigerian 6150(1985):9.

       Things Fall Apart to be filmed for Nigerian television.

2794.  New Nigerian.  "Things Fall Apart" to show at National Theater.
       New Nigerian May 19 (1979) Saturday extra, p. 1. (R)

       Francis Oladele, Bullfrog in the Sun.

2795. New York Times. Films of 33 nations seen at Tunis fete. New York Times Oct. 20 (1970):73.

J.C.C.

2796. New York Times. 'Xica' and African films. New York Times Aug. 12 (1983):C3. (R)

Sembène Ousmane, Ceddo and La noire de.

2797. New Yorker. Ousmane Sembene. New Yorker Sept. 25 (1971):37-39. (R)

Emitai, Mandabi and Tauw.

2798. Newswatch. 'Blues for a prodigal.' Newswatch 1,3(1985):11-13.

Cast and production of Soyinka's film.

2799. Newswatch. Curtain falls on Orlando Martins. Newswatch 2,16(1985):37.

Review of Martins's acting career.

2800. Ngakane, Lionel. African films get a wider screen. Africa (London) 147(1983):70-71.

MOGPAFIS.

2801. Ngakane, Lionel. Cinema and the liberation of people. Africa (London) 164(1985):88-89.

Report on FESPACO and third FEPACI congress.

2802. Ngakane, Lionel. The cinema in South Africa. Présence Africaine 80(1971):131-133.

Film censorship in South Africa.

2803. Ngakane, Lionel. Decolonizing films. Africa (London) 125(1982):62-63.

Report on MOGPAFIS, including recommendations for improving film production and distribution.

2804. Ngakane, Lionel. Enfin un festival pour le Commonwealth. Afrique 43(1981):36.

Commonwealth film festival in Nicosia.

2805. Ngakane, Lionel. Filmmakers focus on African problems. Africa (London) 116(1981):70-71.

Films shown at FESPACO.

2806. Ngakane, Lionel. From Hollywood to Tunis. _Africa_ (London) 135(1982):77-78. (R)

Souleymane Cissé, _Finyé_.

2807. Ngakane, Lionel. Old script, new spirit. _Africa_ (London) 177(1986):97-98.

Old problems and new directions for FEPACI.

2808. Ngakane, Lionel. The role of films in the liberation struggle, in _First_ _Mogadishu_ _Pan-African_ _Film_ _Symposium._ _Pan_ _African_ _Cinema...Which_ _Way_ _Ahead?_ Ibrahim Awed et al eds. Mogadishu: MOGPAFIS Management Committee, 1983. pp. 22-26.

History of liberation films in South Africa, problems of their production and distribution.

2809. Ngara, John. Xala-an allegory on celluloid. _Africa_ (London) 64(1976):51. (R)

2810. Ngom, Assane. A nos cinéastes. _Le_ _Soleil_ May 17 (1987):5.

Ideals for filmmaking in Senegal. Role of SNC and SIDEC.

2811. Ngom, Moustapha. Mahama Johnson Traoré commence le tournage de son film "Diegue-Bi". _Dakar_ _Matin_ May 15 (1970):2.

2812. Ngouah-Beaud, C.W. "Demain un jour nouveau" le tournage a repris. _L'Union_ July 12 (1987):4.

2813. Ngouah-Beaud, C.W. "Demain, un jour nouveau," les dernièrs séquences. _L'Union_ July 27 (1978):4.

2814. Ngouah-Beaud, C.W. Doura Mané est mort samedi. _L'Union_ July 10 (1978):6.

Death of Guinean actor.

2815. Ngouah-Beaud, C.W. L'équipe de Pierre-Marie Dong prépare un nouveau film. _L'Union_ May 20-21(1978):4. (R)

_Demain_ _un_ _jour_ _nouveau_.

2816. Ngouah-Beaud, C.W. Pierre-Marie Dong parle de son futur film: "Demain un jour nouveau." _L'Union_ May 22 (1978):4. (R)

2817. Ngouah-Beaud, C.W. Sancho Castor: "Le rire d'autrui me fait rire." _L'Union_ 764(1978):4.

Actor in Pierre-Marie Dong, _Identité_.

2818. Nguéma, Samuel Minko.  Le cinéma "le Ntem" fait peu neuve. L'Union Aug. 13-14 (1983):2.

Poor conditions in Gabon theaters.

2819. N'Guessan, Raphael.  Des frustrations?  Fraternité Matin 6187(1985):28.

Jury for Festival du film publicitaire, Côte d'Ivoire.

2820. Ng'weno, Hilary.  The potential for local film production in Kenya.  Weekly Review 544(1985):14-15.

2821. Niandou, Harouna.  "L'acteur doit avoir du sang froid," déclare Issa Bagna, acteur.  Nigerama 3(1975?):29.  (I)

Nigerien actcr discusses his career and plans for organizing travelling theater with Moustapha Alassane.

2822. Niandou, Harouna.  Le cinéma nigerien.  Nigerama 3(1975?):5,9,11-12.

History of film in Niger 1957 to mid 1970s.

2823. Niandou, Harouna.  Le cinéma nigérien: un instrument de lutte pour l'éveil d'une conscience nationale.  Nigerama 7(1977):43-45.

Same article as No. 2822.

2824. Niandou, Harouna.  Claude François: de la photographie au cinéma. Nigerama 3(1975?):26.  (I)

Discussion of Qui est fou?, Tambours et violins de la mort and future filmmaking plans.

2825. Niandou, Harouna.  Damoure Zika, le doyen de nos acteurs. Nigerama 3(1975?):25.  (I)

Nigerien actor discusses his career from 1954 to mid 1970s; problems of coproducing films with Jean Rouch.

2826. Niandou, Harouna.  Devant ou derrière la caméra avec Djingarey Abdoulaye Maiga.  Nigerama 3 (1975?):27,31,36.  (I)

Discussion of his training, acting, filmmaking and needed improvements for Nigerien film.

2827. Niandou, Harouna.  La distribution et l'exploitation des films dans notre pays.  Nigerama 3(1975?):14, 16.  (I)

Theater owner discusses distribution problems in Niger.

2828. Niandou, Harouna.  Editorial.  Nigerama 3(1975?):3.

Importance of film in Niger.

2829.  Niandou, Harouna.  M.Mounkaila Yacouba (SONEXI): quelques difficultés de distribution.  Nigerama 3(1975?):24.  (I)

Theater owner discusses distribution problems, shortage of Nigerien films to show.

2830.  Niandou, Harouna.  Moussa Alzouma, les dieux noirs en images. Nigerama 3(1975?):37.

Casse-gueule voyou, Conflit des dieux nous and Alzouma's training as filmmaker.

2831.  Niandou, Harouna.  Moussa Hamidou, les difficultes d'etre technicien.  Nigerama 3(1975?):20,28,30.  (I)

Film technician discusses his work with Jean Rouch and sound recording for films.

2832.  Niandou, Harouna.  Le Niger remporte deux des principaux prix. Nigerama 3(1975?):9.

FESPACO prizes for Nigerien films.

2833.  Niandou, Harouna.  Oumarou Ganda: "Le cinéma c'est le livre qui se lit par excellence de tout le monde."  Nigerama 3(1975?):13, 17-18, 22.  (I)

Ganda discusses his training and career, cultural immportance of film.

2834.  Niandou, Harouna.  Un pionnier: Moustapha Alassane.  Nigerama 3(1975?):7,  10,  12;  Recherche,  pédagogie  et  culture 17-18(1975):55-56.  (I)

Discussion of Alassane's career and ways to improve Nigerien film production.

2835.  Niandou, Harouna.  Succès du cinéma nigérien.  Nigerama 3(1975?):4.

Films by Oumarou Ganda and Yaya Kossoko.

2836.  Niandou, Harouna.  Zalika Souley devant la caméra.  Nigerama 3(1975?):19.

Nigerien actress, her career and attendance at film festivals.

2837.  Niang, Mamadou Leye.  Le fond et la forme.  Le Soleil May 2 (1975):4.  (R)

Sembène Ousmane, Xala.

2838. Nibe, Soro A. Cinéaste et écrivain de renom, Kitia Touré: revaloriser la culture sénoufo avec "Comédie exotique." Fraternité Hebdo 1354(1985):24-27. (I)

2839. Nicolas, Marcel. 7e Festival International du Cinéma de la Havane. SeptièmArt 58(1986):15.

African representation at Havana film festival; sale of Angolan, Burkinabe, Ghanaian and Mocambiquan films; plans for Cuban coproductions.

2840. Nicolini, Elisabeth. Un grand débat sur le septième art africain. Jeune Afrique 1318(1986):64-65. (I)

Daouda Diallo discusses low production of films in Niger in last 5 years.

2841. Nicolini, Elisabeth. Sarraounia de Med Hondo. Jeune Afrique Magazine 32(1986):8. (R)

2842. Nigerama. Le première quinzaine nigerienne du cinéma organisée par l'association des cinéastes nigeriens. Nigerama 3(1975?):6,8.

Meeting of Nigerien filmmakers, themes of films shown.

2843. Nigrizia. Cinema africano: il più giovane. Nigrizia 99,4(1981):25-40.

Special section provides overview of African film.

2844. Nikiéma, R. Festival en Haute-Volta. Jeune Afrique 421(1969):50.

FESPACO.

2845. Njama, Kaleb. How serious is the video cassette threat? Weekly Review 544(1985):17-18.

Impact of videocassettes on film production in Kenya.

2846. Nkoulou Nguéma and Alain Dickson. Réponses à l'article: "Reflexions d'un père de famillie sur les film à la télévision." L'Union June 20 (1979):2.

Relation of films shown on television in Gabon to delinquent behavior. Reply to No. 2593.

2847. Nogueira, Rui. Entretien avec Ruy Guerra. Revue du Cinéma 291(1974):67-71. (I)

Discussion of Os Deuses e o Mortos.

2848. Nogueira, Teresa Sá. Artur Torohate cineasta guerriheiro. Tempo

830(1986):44-45.

Films of Mocambiquan history made by Torohate.

2849. Nogueira, Teresa Sá. Camilo da Sousa "Aqui nao há cinema sobre a guerra." Tempo 822(1986):43-46.

Sousa's filmmaking career.

2850. Nogueira, Teresa Sá. Cinema Moçambicano. Tempo 827(1986):41-45. (R)

José Cardoso, O Vento Sopra do Norte.

2851. Nogueira, Teresa Sá. Cinema Moçambicano (2) Como era antigamente. Tempo 828(1986):46-48.

Documentaries shown at retrospective of Mocambiquan film.

2852. Nogueira, Teresa Sá. Cinema Moçambicano (VI) Cinema móvel. Tempo 836(1986):48-50.

Mobile film units. Production of Tempo dos Leopardos with Yugoslavian assistance.

2853. Nogueira, Teresa Sá. Cinema Moçambicano (VII) Kanemo um projecto de cinema. Tempo 841(1986):44-45.

Film production by Kanemo, a Brazilian company, and INC compared.

2854. Nogueira, Teresa Sá. Cinema Moçambicano (VIII) Desenhos animados, um cinema que desapareceu. Tempo 845(1986):43-45.

Animated films made by INC for adults and children.

2855. Nogueira, Teresa Sá. Cinema Moçambicano (X) Entrevista com Samuel Matola. Tempo 856(1987):42-45. (I)

Discussion of history of INC and second Mocambiquan film festival.

2856. Nogueira, Teresa Sá. Cinema Moçambicano sintese de um percurso. Tempo 859(1987):40-43; 860(1987):43-46.

History of Mocambiquan filmmaking based on interviews with persons involved. Major INC films reviewed.

2857. Nogueira, Teresa Sá. O cinema para mostrar Moçambique. Tempo 814(1986):42-43. (I)

Rodrigo Gonçalves discusses his work and financial risks of filmmaking.

2858. Nogueira, Teresa Sá. Cinema: uma prioridade para Mocambique.

270.

Tempo 850(1987):36-38. (I)

Licinio de Azevedo, Brazilian journalist, discusses priorities for filmmaking in Mocambique.

2859.  Nogueira, Teresa Sá.  Crónicas à margen de um festival.  Tempo 819(1986):49-50; 820(1986):53-55.

Mocambiquan films at Aveiro film festival.  Comments on Ruy Guerra's films made in Brazil included.

2860.  Nogueira, Teresa Sá.  Ismael Vuvo "O comboio da vida."  Tempo 834(1986):45-48. (R)

Review includes biographical background on Vuvo.

2861.  Nogueira, Teresa Sá.  Kanemo "Um projecto de cinema" vozes de discordãncia.  Tempo 843(1986):49-53.

Report on roundtable on films produced by Kanemo (Brazilian Company) in Mocambique.  Production by Kanemo and INC compared.

2862.  Nogueira, Teresa Sá.  Moçambique um troféu de ouro e duas mençoes honrosas.  Tempo 818(1986):40-41.

Camilo de Sousa, Tempo dos Leopardos shown at Aveiro film festival.

2863.  Notre Bureau Parisien.  Premier film d'un amour franco-africain.  Le Soleil Aug. 9 (1970):8. (R)

Mustapha Diop, Synapse.

2864.  Novicki, Margaret A.  Burkina Faso: a revolutionary culture.  Africa Report 32, 4(1987):57-60.

Support of FESPACO as part of cultural revival for building Burkinabe nationalism.

2865.  Novicki, Margaret A.  Interview with King Ampaw.  Africa Report 32,4(1987):53-56. (I)

Ampaw's training, filmmaking, acting and ideals for filmmaking.

2866.  Nvula.  Le cinéma africain doit partir de l'authenticité africaine.  Zaire 236(1973):32-33. (I)

Mulimbi Zaina discusses Zairois filmmaking.

2867.  Nwagboso, Maxwell.  Africa joins 'Third Cinema' bandwagon.  Africa Now 65(1986):39-40.

African films at Edinburgh film festival.  Infrastructure of African film.

2868. Nwagboso, Maxwell. West African film festival Sembene Ousmane rides high. Africa Now 50(1985):63.

2869. Nwagboso, Maxwell. Wole Soyinka speaks out on the opportunists. Africa Now 50(1985):64. (R)

Censorship of Blues for a Prodigal.

2870. Nwosu, Nduka. Blues for a prodigal. Daily Times (Lagos) Jan. 19 (1985):5. (R)

2871. Nyakunu, Tendayi. Anti-apartheid film starts shooting. Herald (Harare) Aug. 30 (1987):4.

Michael Raeburn, Soweto, some scenes being shot in Zimbabwe.

2872. Nycz, Benicjusz. Nuovi talenti. Nigrizia 102, 2(1984):44-45.

African representation at Trois Continents film festival.

2873. O.D.T. Ousmane Sembène, la polygamie, une pratique irritante. Bingo 211(1970):35-36. (R)

Mandabi.

2874. O.Z. Niger semaine Ganda Oumarou. Unir Cinéma 23-24(1986):17-18.

Film week in Niger features Ganda's films.

2875. Obiagwu, Kodilinye. Cultural heritage and the survival of the film industry. Daily Times (Lagos) July 18 (1987):12.

Problems with films being made in Nigeria. Films based on Yoruba theater most successful.

2876. Obiang, Bogass Pascal. Fête à Bitam pour l'inauguration du cinéma Ntem. L'Union 151(1976):3.

New theater opens in Gabon.

2877. Observateur. Assemblée constitutive du CIPROFILMS et du CIDC. L'Observateur Jan. 24 (1978):4-6,10.

Report on meeting held in Ouagadougou.

2878. Observateur. Le capital du CIDC est fixe a 300 millions. L'Observateur Jan. 30 (1978):3-4.

Final communique of meeting held in Ouagadougou.

2879. L'Observateur. Le C.I.D.C. L'Observateur 2035(1981):11-13.

2880. Observateur. CIDC-CIPROFILM. L'Observateur Jan. 29 (1979):7,9.

Final communique of meeting held in Ouagadougou.

2881. Observateur. CIDC-CIPROFILM. L'Observateur June 6 (1980):6-7.

Report on ministers conference.

2882. Observateur. Le CIDC deux ans après. L'Observateur Feb. 23 (1981):1, 11-12.

Recent activities of CIDC; its relationship to UAC.

2883. Observateur. Cinafric ou'est-ce-que c'est? L'Observateur Feb. 23 (1981):1, 6-10. (I)

Fernand Yougbare discusses objectives and potentials of CINAFRIC; Burkinabe film production in the context of CINAFRIC.

2884. Observateur. CINAFRIC une contribution voltaique a'l'éssor du cinéma africain. L'Observateur Apr. 3 (1979):7-8.

Description of facilities to be built; advantages to Burkina Faso.

2885. Observateur. Ciné-club. L'Observateur Feb. 2 (1980):5.

Film club opens in Ouagadougou.

2886. Observateur. Conclave des ministres africains charges du cinéma. L'Observateur Jan. 24 (1979):1, 6-7, 9-10.

Text of speech by Sydney Moutia on CIDC, CIPROFILM and OCAM activities in support of African film.

2887. Observateur. FESPACO cinq jours après. L'Observateur Feb. 26 (1981):1, 8, 12.

Discussion of Daniel Kamwa, Notre fille and Idrissa Ouédraogo, Poko.

2888. Observateur. FESPACO jour J-2. L'Observateur Feb. 2 (1981):11.

2889. Observateur. FESPACO un nouveaux prix. L'Observateur June 18 (1981):5.

Jean Débrix prize to be given to Oumarou Ganda at FESPACO.

2890. Observateur. Vllle FESPACO. L'Observateur Feb. 2 (1983):10-12, 14. (I)

Mustapha Ky discusses CINAFRIC and FESPACO.

2891. Observateur. Vlle FESPACO jour J-1. L'Observateur Feb. 20-22 (1981):1, 8, 11, 13.

2892. Observateur. Vlle FESPACO le palmarès. L'Observateur Mar. 3 (1981):1, 12-13.

FESPACO groups giving prizes, list of prizes.

2893. Observateur. Vle FESPACO l'image et le son au service de l'Afrique. L'Observateur Feb. 2-4 (1979):1, 5, 7.

2894. Observateur. SONAVOCI. L'Observateur Feb. 29, Mar. 1-2 (1984):9.

2895. OCIC Info. African and Asian films in festival at Quito. OCIC Info 7, 2-3(1986):15.

2896. OCIC Info. Sudan: Video as an alternative. OCIC Info 7,1(1986):9.

2897. OCIC Info. Syrian film awarded prize at Carthage. OCIC Info 7,5(1986):8.

2898. OCIC Info. Yeelen (Light) by Souleymane Cissé. OCIC Info 8,3(1987):4-5. (R)

2899. Octavio, Ruy. As guerras de Ruy Guerra. Novembro 33(1980):60-62.

2900. Odamo, Samuel. Who is Jewo's father? Daily Times (Lagos) May 16 (1986):18. (R)

Ola Balogun, Ajani Ogun. Actors discussed at length.

2901. Odemwingie, Tommy. Don deplores seizure of Soyinka's film. Guardian (Lagos) Mar. 20 (1985):3.

Censorship of Blues for a Prodigal in Nigeria.

2902. Odou, René. Charles Foster: après "Amok" je souhaite faire carrière au cinéma. Afrique Nouvelle 1764(1983):20-21. (I)

Senegalese actor discusses his work.

2903. Odou, René. Xew-Xew un incroyable voyage. Afrique Nouvelle 1802(1984):19. (R)

2904. Odunfa, Sola. Has Soyinka found a new medium in film acting? Daily Times (Lagos) Apr. 10 (1971):7.

Soyinka as actor in Kongi's Harvest.

2905. Odunjo, Lekan. Boost for film industry. New Nigerian Oct. 1 (1979):2.

Plans for building a film village in Nigeria.

2906.  Ogan, Amma.  Ola Balogun's Black Goddess revisited.  <u>Daily Times</u>
(Lagos) May 5 (1979):9.  (I)

Balogun discusses his film, responses of Nigerian audiences,
criticism that it is about Brazil.

2907.  Ogan, Amma.  Pa Orlando's last bow.  <u>Guardian</u> (Lagos) Oct. 20
(1985):B1, B4.

Review of Orlando Martins's acting career.  Nigerian actors'
comments about his career.

2908.  Ogun, Sam.  Orlando stars in 3m-dollar film.  <u>Daily Times</u> (Lagos)
Sept. 2 (1970):10.

International fame of Orlando Martins, Nigerian actor.

2909.  Ogun, Sam.  Use tapes of FESTAC '77 on TV rather than foreign
films.  <u>Daily Times</u> (Lagos) Aug. 8 (1987):12.

More African films needed on Nigerian television.

2910.  Ogunbambo, Sina.  Councillor Balogun: drama is my hobby.
<u>Guardian</u> (Lagos) June 2 (1986):11.

Roles of Nigerian actor in television and feature films.

2911.  Ogundipe, Moyo.  Films: getting the act together.  <u>Guardian</u>
(Lagos) Feb. 2 (1985):7.

Activities of Nigerian Film Corporation, problems it needs to
solve.

2912.  Ogundipe, Moyo.  The Nigerian film industry: in search of an
ideology.  <u>Guardian</u> (Lagos) May 12 (1984):7.

2913.  Ogunleye, S.A.  Whither the film censorship board?  <u>New Nigerian</u>
Jan. 25 (1980):4.

Need for more rigorous censorship of foreign films in Nigeria.

2914.  Ogunmade-Davies, Akin.  'Dinner with the devil.'  <u>New Nigerian</u>
June 5 (1976) Saturday extra, n.p.  (R)

2915.  Ogunwale, Oye.  A new approach to film industry in Nigeria.  <u>New
Nigerian</u> June 27 (1973):16.

Vision International Film Corp., new Nigerian production company.

2916.  Okeke, Eric.  Film industry hit by economic squeeze.  <u>Guardian</u>
(Lagos) Jan. 3 (1985):10.

Lack of facilities for film production in Nigeria and lack of foreign exchange for overseas services.

2917. Okioh, François Sourou. Problems of African cinema. Young Cinema and Theater 3(1982):24-30.

Excerpts from manuscript of Okioh's book. See No. 61.

2918. Okoba, G.S.J. 1986 World film festival. Daily Times (Lagos) May 20 (1986):3.

Yoruba and Hausa films to be shown at Tashkent film festival.

2919. Okon, Ita. Filmmakers close rank. Daily Times (Lagos) April 25 (1986):5.

Meeting of Filmmakers Association of Nigeria to draft constitution.

2920. Okwuwa, Chuks. Fresh hope for Nigerian film producers. Nigerian Observer 8, 2325(1976):7. (R)

Ola Balogun, Ajani Ogun.

2921. Oladele, Francis A. Film as an educational medium in development: the case of Nigeria. International Development Review 16,4(1974):31-32.

Activities of Calpenny Films.

2922. Olaniyan, M.L.O. 'Ajani Ogun' film is faultless. New Nigerian July 10 (1976) Saturday extra, n.p. (R)

2923. Olapade, Femi. The cinema industry in Nigeria. New Academy 1,2(1985):39-40.

2924. Ollo-Mombey. Le directeur du CENACI "Contribuer à la promotion du cinéma gabonais." L'Union Apr. 5 (1985):7.

2925. Olojede, Dele, Chuks Iloegbunam and George Otiono. The World of Chinua Achebe. Newswatch 3, 12(1986):11-17.

David Orere, Things Fall Apart.

2926. Olusola, Segun. Film-television and the arts: the African experience. New Culture 1,4(1979):9-12.

Need for films to reflect audience sentiment.

2927. O'Meara, Patrick. Films of South Africa. Jump Cut 18(1978):7-8. (R)

Nana Mahomo, Last Grave at Dimbaza.

2928. Omotoso, Kole. Blues for the Prodigal. Sunday Concord

5,200(1985):7. (R)

2929. Omotoso, Kole. Film maker Bello breaks new ground. _Africa_
(London) 126(1982):80, 85. (R)

Efunsetan Aniwura.

2930. Omotunde, Dele. The artist as an activist. _Newswatch_
1,3(1985):14-15.

Soyinka's reasons for making Blues for a Prodigal.

2931. Omotunde, Soji. Women on the sidewalks. _Newswatch_
1,11(1985):36. (R)

Gold Oruh, Away from the Sidewalk.

2932. Ondobo Ndzana. Le cinéma en Afrique. _Zaire_ 195(1972):12-13.

Film distribution.

2933. Oni, Alex. Dispute over Mirror in the Sun: NTA, firm asked to
settle out of court. _Guardian_ (Lagos) Apr. 30 (1986):2.

2934. Onobrakpeya, Ejiro. Burkina Faso hosts film festival. _Guardian_
(Lagos) Mar. 10 (1985):3.

FESPACO.

2935. Onwuchekwa, Charles. Falling into place with Things Fall Apart.
_Guardian_ (Lagos) July 26 (1986):14. (R)

2936. Opapé, Gervais. Un film sur la promotion féminine. _L'Union_
84(1976):3.

Film produced by CENACI.

2937. Opapé, Gervais. Un long métrage en cours de réalisation sur la
province. _L'Union_ Mar. 30 (1981):3.

Gabon filmmakers assist in making film on missionaries.

2938. Orishayomi, Rufus. Screen test for Nigeria. _Africa_ (London)
172(1985):60-65.

Need for training facilities for Nigerian film technicians and
actors.

2939. Osborne, Robert. The fight for freedom. _Hollywood Reporter_
260,43(1980):23. (R)

Ola Balogun, Ija Ominira.

*2940. Ostor, Akos. Cinema and society in India and Senegal: the films

277.

of Satyajit Ray and Ousmane Sembene.  <u>Cinewave</u> 7(1984-1985):8-18.

2941.  Osunbor, Onoise.  Nigerian film lab under way.  <u>Sunday</u> <u>Concord</u> 5, 190(1984):13.

2942.  Osundare, Niyi.  Comedian and churchman.  <u>West</u> <u>Africa</u> 3537(1985):1172-1173. (I)

Moses Olaiya discusses his acting.

2943.  Osundare, Niyi.  Following in 007's footsteps.  <u>West</u> <u>Africa</u> 3302(1980):2178-2179. (R)

Eddie Ugbomah, <u>Mask</u>.

2944.  Osundare, Niyi.  A grand escape into metaphysics.  <u>West</u> <u>Africa</u> 3277(1980):826-828. (R)

Ola Balogun, <u>Aiye</u>, and discussion of Balogun's other films.

2945.  Osundare, Niyi.  The king of laughter.  <u>West</u> <u>Africa</u> 3388(1982):1821. (R)

Moses Olaiya, <u>Orun</u> <u>Mooru</u>.

2946.  Osundare, Niyi.  The Mask is a very rough film.  <u>West</u> <u>Africa</u> 3290(1980):1487-1489. (R)

2947.  Otiono, George and Joyce Osakwe.  Newsliners.  <u>Newswatch</u> 4,14(1986):54.

Nigerian audience responses to Eddie Ugbomah's films.

2948.  Ouattara, N. Ollivier.  A propos de la critique de Désébagato. <u>Sidwaya</u> Feb. 26 (1987):5. (R)

2949.  Ouédraogo, Alassane K.  Sur le chemin de la réconciliation. <u>Carrefour</u> <u>Africain</u> 588(1974):5-6. (R)

Review includes biographical information about René Bernard Yonli.

2950.  Ouédraogo, B. Wole René.  Grand prix du public ou le miroir du FESPACO. <u>Sidwaya</u> Feb. 26 (1985):iii.

2951.  Ouédraogo, B. Wole René.  Symposium "Cinéma africain cinéma afro-americain." <u>Sidwaya</u> Feb. 26 (1985):i.

FESPACO symposium aims to bring rapprochement between African and Afro-American filmmakers.

2952.  Ouédraogo, Hamadou.  Les Africains sur la croisette.  <u>Bingo</u> 368(1983):66-67.

Cannes film festival.

2953. Ouédraogo, Hamadou. Carthage: le festival du Tiers monde. _Bingo_ 313(1979):63.

2954. Ouédraogo, Hamadou. Un Ivoirien couronné. _Bingo_ 344(1981):36.

Fadika Kramo-Lanciné, _Djéli_ receives prize at FESPACO.

2955. Ouédraogo, Hamadou. Kitia Touré: la confiance d'un privé. _Bingo_ 386(1985):48. (I)

2956. Ouédraogo, Hamadou. Pelé roi de Cannes. _Bingo_ 295(1977):54-56. (R)

Sembène Ousmane, _Ceddo_.

2957. Ouédraogo, Isaac Rogomnoma. Cinéma et littérature (aspects juridiques). _Carrefour Africain_ 873(1985):22.

Report on FESPACO symposium.

2958. Ouédraogo, Isaac Rogomnoma. Les problems juridiques et fiscaux du cinéma en Afrique Subsaharienne. _Carrefour Africain_ 870(1985):26-30.

2959. Ouédraogo, Michel. Conference de presse de M. Jack Lang, ancien ministre français. _Sidwaya_ Feb. 25 (1987):10. (I)

Lang's reasons for attending FESPACO, opinions on FESPACO and African filmmaking.

2960. Ouédraogo, Michel. La sortie des masques. _Sidwaya_ Feb. 23 (1987):11.

Cultural performance at FESPACO.

2961. Ouédraogo, Michel. Voici la rue marchande. _Sidwaya_ Feb. 6 (1987):11.

Innovations at FESPACO.

2962. Ouédraogo, Michel and Elisabeth Sougue. Xème FESPACO un monument-symbole. _Sidwaya_ Jan. 8 (1987):4.

Monument to African filmmakers built in Ouagadougou.

2963. Ouédraogo, Omer Ousmane. Si le FESPACO m'était conté: 1973-le 4ème rendez-vous. _Sidwaya_ Feb. 27 (1985):iii.

2964. Ouédraogo, Omer Ousmane. Si le FESPACO m'était conte: seconde period: 1972 à nos jours. _Sidwaya_ Feb. 26 (1985):ii.

2965. Ouédraogo, Omer Ousmane. Si le FESPACO m'était conte 6ème et

7ème FESPACO. Sidwaya Mar. 1 (1985):ii.

Comparison of FESPACO participation and prizes 1979 and 1981.

2966. Ouédraogo, Oumar.   Un monument pour les cinéastes africains.
Bingo 414(1987):58-59. (I)

Ignace Sawadogo discusses monument to African filmmakers in
Ouagadougou, films shown at FESPACO.

2967. Ouédraogo, Oumar.   Ouagadougou capitale du cinéma.   Bingo
409(1987):54-55. (I)

Philippe Sawadogo discusses FESPACO.

2968. Ouédraogo, P.P. Claver.   Quand le sextuor de jazz de l'Université
de Howard s'en mêle. Sidwaya Feb. 25 (1987):9.

Cultural activities at FESPACO.

2969. Ouédraogo, P.P. Claver.   Un séjour bien rempli au Burkina.
Sidwaya Mar. 5 (1987):10.

Music performances at FESPACO.

2970. Oumara, Magatte.   Sembène Ousmane ou le peintre d'une société.
Le Soleil Oct. 2 (1974):3.

2971. Our Correspondent. Festival cinema. Afriscope 7,3(1977):11-12.

FESTAC.

2972. Our Film Correspondent.   First feature film in a Nigerian
language. New Nigerian Mar. 29 (1975) Saturday extra, pp. 2-3.
(R)

Ola Balogun, Amadi.

2973. Our Film Correspondent.   Nigerian film-maker calls for film
industry.  New Nigerian Apr. 19 (1975) Saturday extra, p. 2.

Ola Balogun calls for government support of filmmaking.

2974. Our Reporter.   'FESTAC films must restore dignity of black race.'
New Nigerian June 24 (1976):16.

2975. Ousseini, Inoussa.   L'évolution du marché cinématographique
africain, in FESPACO 1983. Paris: Présence Africaine, 1987. pp.
61-70.

Film distribution.

2976. Ousseini, Inoussa.   Vers un économie affranchie.   Le Monde
Diplomatique 300(1979):29.

Efforts to improve distribution of African films in Africa.

2977. Ousseini, Inoussa, Moustapha N'Diaye and Pierre Marlange. La fiscalité cinématographique en Afrique noire francophone. Filméchange 17(1982):37-49.

Production and distribution of films.

2978. Ovurevu, Agidi. Face-to-face with Ola Balogun. New Nigerian June 14 (1975) Saturday extra, pp. 2-3. (I)

Balogun's training, views on filmmaking and films he's made.

2979. Owomoyela, Oyekan. Candles and Incense, an excerpt from a film script. Journal of the New African Literature and the Arts 3(1967):73-79.

2980. Oyekunle, Segun. Africans in Hollywood. West Africa 3459(1983):2728-2729.

African filmmakers visit Hollywood.

2981. Oyekunle, Segun. A challenge to African film-makers. Africa Now 37(1984):32-33.

Filmmakers should use concepts from oral tradition not from Hollywood.

2982. Oyekunle, Segun. Films for the future. West Africa 3423(1983):725-726.

FESPACO.

2983. Oyekunle, Segun. The promises of Mogadishu. West Africa 3462(1983):2938-2940.

MOGPAFIS.

2984. Oyeleye, Tunde. Film industry: the Ososa experiment. Daily Times (Lagos) Aug. 1 (1987):5.

Hubert Ogunde's film village where Ayanmo is being made.

2985. Oyono, Jean-Philippe. Une reprise cinématographique: Obali, l'appel des générations. L'Union Oct. 3 (1977):2. (R)

Pierre-Marie Dong, Obali.

2986. P.C. Deux festivals africains a Paris. Jeune Afrique 380(1968):46.

Festival of Moroccan film and films about Africa, including La noire de.

281.

2987. P.J. Le cinéma africain, des origines à 1973 de Paulin Soumanou Vieyra. Cinématographe 18(1976):47. (BR)

Review of No. 74.

2988. P.J. Xala d'Ousmane Sembène. Cinématographe 18(1976):44. (R)

2989. PANA. Journée africaine du cinéma. Le Soleil Feb. 28 (1985):8.

Report on meeting of FEPACI at FESPACO.

2990. Pâquet, André. Ababacar Samb, "Codou" et le cinéma au Sénégal. Cinéma Québec 1,10(1972):28-31. (I)

2991. Pâquet, André. L'avance des cinémas arabes. Cinéma Québec 4,2(1974):34-39.

Senegalese films shown at J.C.C.

2992. Pâquet, André. The 'Fespaco' of Ouagadougou--Towards unity in African cinema. Cinéaste 6,1(1973):36-38.

2993. Pâquet, André. Lionel N'Gakane: "L'Afrique anglophone doit rattraper son retard." Afrique-Asie 30(1973):44-45. (I)

2994. Pâquet, André. Ouagadougou. Cinéma Québec 3,1(1973):38-39.

Films shown at FESPACO.

2995. Pare, B. Hubert. Débats forum: un intérêt de plus en plus manifeste. Carrefour Africain 977(1986):12-13.

Discussion by filmmakers of films shown at FESPACO.

2996. Pare, B. Hubert. Les débats ont baissé d'intensité. Sidwaya Mar. 1 (1985):ii.

Discussion about films and their production: Kwami Mambu Zinga, N'gambo; Jean-Claude Tchuilen, Suicides; and Kitia Touré, Comédie exotique.

2997. Pare, B. Hubert. Clôture du 8ème FESPACO. Le sacre de Souleymane Cissé réalisateur de Finyé. Carrefour Africain 766(1983):10-11.

2998. Pare, B. Hubert. Un départ encourageant. Sidwaya Feb. 25 (1985):i,iv.

Opening session of FESPACO.

2999. Pare, B. Hubert. Le Directeur général de la SONACIB "L'autodiscipline pour une meilleur service". Sidwaya Feb. 11 (1987):9. (I)

Yacouba Traoré discusses theaters and audience responses to films in Burkina Faso.

3000. Pare, B. Hubert. Un festival charnière. Sidwaya Mar. 4 (1985):i-iv.

FESPACO.

3001. Pare, B. Hubert. Hier, c'était Pétanqui, les Coopérants et Refus. Sidwaya Mar. 1 (1985):iv. (R)

3002. Pare, B. Hubert. 8ème FESPACO: Symbole de l'unité africaine. Carrefour Africain 765(1983):23.

3003. Pare, B. Hubert. Ironu-Duel sur la falaise-Mosebolatan - Moulin. Sidwaya Feb. 26 (1987):6. (R)

3004. Pare, B. Hubert. Michel Zabeline. Sidwaya Mar. 1 (1985):iii. (I)

Soviet delegate discusses FESPACO and Russian film festivals.

3005. Pare, B. Hubert. Programmation: nette amélioration. Carrefour Africain 873(1985):23.

FESPACO.

3006. Pare, B. Hubert. Quatre films passes au crible. Sidwaya Feb. 25 (1987):5-6. (R)

King Ampaw, Juju; Idrissa Ouédraogo, Yam Daabo; and Nissi Joanny Traoré, Autre école.

3007. Pare, B. Hubert. 15 salles de projection a Ouagadougou. Sidwaya Jan. 30 (1987):12.

New theaters built in Burkina Faso.

3008. Pare, B. Hubert. Trois films a la barre. Sidwaya Feb. 27 (1985):i,iv. (R)

Kalifa Conde and Daouda Keita, Quelques pages de la vie de Toussaint L'Overture; Orlando Fortunato, Memoire d'une journée Angola; and Paul Zoumbara, Jours de tourmente.

3009. Passek, Jean-Loup. Dinard. Cinéma 169(1972):29-31.

FIFEF.

3010. Patraquin, Luis. Cinema: Mineiro moçambicano. Tempo 558(1981):54-55. (R)

Moira Forjaz.

3011. Paul, Leandro.  Que caminhos para o cinema africano?  Tempo
542(1980):52-55.

Films of Med Hondo.

3012. Paulhan, Jean.  A la recherche du cinéma de l'Afrique
francophone.  French Review 55,6(1982):912-914.

Themes of films by West and North African filmmakers.

3013. Paulus.  "Djéli" de Fadika Kramo Lanciné.  Ivoire Dimanche
526(1981):42.  (R)

3014. Paulus.  Grand prix I.D. des arts et des lettres des premiers pas
bien assurés...  I.D. 841(1987):36-37.

I.D. film prize to Désiré Ecaré.

3015. Paulus.  Jean-Louis Koula: Adjatio, 18 mois après.  Ivoire
Dimanche 609(1982):33.  (R)

3016. Pearson, Lyle.  Four years of African film.  Film Quarterly
36,3(1973):42-47.

Themes of films the author has seen at film festivals in the
early 1970s.

3017. Pearson, Lyle.  Senegal.  International Film Guide
(1983):265-266.

3018. Pelegri, Pierre.  , Entretien avec Ruy Guerra.  Positif
86(1967):3-15.  (I)

Discussion of Os cafajestes, Os fuzis and cinema novo.

3019. Pelletier, Renee.  Sembène Ousmane ou le defi.  Africa (Dakar)
113(1979):33-34.

Ceddo.

3020. Perez, Michel.  "Femme nue, femme noire."  Combat (Paris) Dec. 3
(1970):13.  (R)

Désiré Ecaré, A nous deux France.

3021. Perez, Michel.  Pousse-Pousse de Daniel Kamwa.  Nouvelles
Littéraires 2532 (1976):25.  (R)

3022. Perret, Jacques G.  Tendres Chasseurs.  Avant-Scène Cinéma
112(1971):10-38.

Film script of Sweet Hunters.  Biographical information and
filmography of Ruy Guerra.

3023. Perry, G.M. and Patrick McGilligan.  Ousmane Sembene.  Film Quarterly 36,3(1973):36-42.

3024. Perry, George.  African adventures.  Times (London) Apr. 21 (1972):10. (R)

Michael Raeburn, The Grass Is Singing.

3025. Peters, Alaba.  Film and TV in Africa.  Africa Report 15,8(1970):21.

Need for feasibility study to expand film and television, which are essential for development.

3026. Peters, C. Geo Leo.  Blood and beauty.  New Nigerian 172(1982):49. (R)

Ola Balogun, Ija Ominira.

3027. Peters, Jonathan.  Aesthetics and ideology in African film: Ousmane Sembene's Emitai, in African Literature in its Social and Political Dimensions. Eileen Julien, Mildred Mortimer and Curtis Schade, eds.  Washington, D.C.: Three Continents Press, 1986. pp. 69-75. (R)

3028. Peters, Jonathan.  Nancy J. Schmidt, Sub-Saharan African Films and Filmmakers: A Preliminary Bibliography.  Research in African Literatures 18,2(1987):256-258. (BR)

Review of No. 69.

3029. Peterson, Maurice.  Ousmane Sembene.  Essence March (1973):8. (I)

Review of Emitai and interview with Sembène.

3030. Peyrière, Marie-Christine.  Ouagadougou. Le creux de la vague. Cinéma 317(1985):52.

FESPACO.

3031. Peyrière, Marie-Christine.  Un réalisateur à tout faire.  Jeune Afrique 1166(1983):50-51.

Work of Souleymane Cissé.

3032. Pfaff, Françoise.  Ceddo, in Magill's Survey of Cinema, Foreign Language Films.  Frank N. Magill, ed. Englewood Cliffs, N.J.: Salem Press, 1985. pp. 492-496. (R)

3033. Pfaff, Françoise.  Cinema in Francophone Africa.  Africa Quarterly 22,3/4(1983):41-48.

History, with emphasis on Sembène's films.

285.

3034. Pfaff, Françoise.   De quelle moisson s'agit-il.   _Positif_
198(1977):53-56. (I)

Haile Gerima discusses _Harvest 3000 Years_.

3035. Pfaff, Françoise.   Entretien avec Ousmane Sembène à propos de
Ceddo.  _Positif_ 235(1980):54-57. (I)

3036. Pfaff, Françoise.   Films of Med Hondo.   _Jump Cut_ 31(1986):44-46.

3037. Pfaff, Françoise.   Myths, traditions and colonialism in Ousmane
Sembène's Emitai.  _CLA Journal_ 24,3(1981):336-346. (R)

3038. Pfaff, Françoise.   Ousmane Sembene: his films, his art.   _Black
Art_ 3,3(1979):29-36.

Films and posters that advertise them.

3039. Pfaff, Françoise.   Researching Africa on film.   _Jump Cut_
31(1986):50,57.

French journals that include articles on African film.

3040. Pfaff, Françoise.   Three faces of Africa: women in Xala.   _Jump
Cut_ 27(1982):27-31. (R)

3041. Pheto, Molefe.   Black film-makers.   _Index on Censorship_
10,4(1981):34.

Reasons why there is little filmmaking by blacks in South Africa.

3042. Pieterse C. Geo.   Film images of the leader who drenched himself
in violence.  _New African_ 169(1981):62-63. (R)

Sharad Patel, _Amin the Rise and Fall_.

3043. Pimenta, Pedro.   FESPACO em Ouagadougou.   Que futuro para o
cinema africano?  _Domingo_ (Maputo) Mar. 6 (1983):8-9.

3044. Pimenta, Pedro.   Para quando uma cinemateca em Moçambique?
_Domingo_ (Maputo) Aug. 21 (1983):22-23.

Need for film archive in Mocambique; what should be preserved and
how.

3045. Pina, Marie-Paule de.   Sarah Maldoror: après "Sambizanga"
"Velada".  _Afrique-Asie_ 62(1974):49. (R)

3046. Pinel, Vincent.   Ciné club qu'est-ce que c'est?   _Unir Cinéma_
17(1985):45-47.

Activities of film clubs.

3047. Pires, Jean.   Interview Cheikh Tidiane Diop.   Zone 2
      121(1981):18-19. (I)

      Discussion of Bataxal, adaptation of Miriama Ba's, Un si longue
      lettre.

3048. Placca, Jean-Baptiste.   La consécration d'un non-conformiste.
      Jeune Afrique 1278(1985):60-61. (R)

      Désiré Ecaré, Visages de femmes.

3049. Placca, Jean-Baptiste.   Qu'il est ingrat d'être femme! Jeune
      Afrique 1274-1275(1985):38-39.

      Censorship of Désiré Ecaré, Visages de femmes.

3050. Pokam, Pierre Nguewa.   L'évocation du sacré.   CinémAction
      26(1983):113-117.

      Religious themes.

3051. Pommier, Pierre.   Africa: overcoming a colonial heritage.   Atlas
      23,3(1976):37.

      Problems of filmmaking.  Edited version of No. 3052.

3052. Pommier, Pierre.   Movies of the people, by the people, for the
      people.  Development Forum 3,6(1975):6-7.

      History and problems of filmmaking in Africa.

3053. Potts, Jim.   Film production course in Ethiopia.   Educational
      Broadcasting International 6,2(1979):102-106.

3054. Potts, Jim.   Film training: a Kenyan perspective.   Educational
      Broadcasting International 9,4(1976):171-174.

3055. Potts, Jim.   A pioneer talks.   Educational Broadcasting
      International 13,3(1980):144-148. (I)

      Sam Aryeetey discusses his career, ideals for filmmaking, and
      problems of filmmaking.

3056. Pouillaude, Jean-Luc.   L'emblème sur "Ceddo".   Positif
      235(1980):50-53. (R)

3057. Poussaint, Renee.   African film: the high price of division.
      UFAHAMU 1,3(1971):51-63.

      Film criticism, language in which films made, problems of
      financing films.

3058. Powell, Dilys.   Rage for freedom.   Sunday Times (London) Feb. 17
      (1974):37. (R)

Ross Devenish, Boesman and Lena.

3059. Prédal, Réne. Deux cinéastes noirs: Désiré Ecare. Jeune Cinéma 34(1968):4-9. (I)

Discussion of Concerto pour un exil.

3060. Prédal, Réne. Jean Rouch, un griot gaulois. CinémAction 17(1982):1-190.

Includes comments by African filmmakers influenced by Rouch.

3061. Prédal, René. La noire de...premier long métrage africain. Afrique Littéraire 76(1985):36-39; CinémAction 34(1985):36-39. (R)

3062. Prelle, François. Ousmane Sembène à bâtons rompus. Bingo 222(1971):56-60. (I)

3063. Prelle, François. Touki-Bouki de Djibril Diop. Le rire de l'hyène. Bingo 247(1973):64-65. (R)

3064. Prosper, Séka, J. La situation des cinéastes africains. Djassin Foue 7(1971):21-22.

Problems of distribution, legislation needed.

3065. Pulleine, Tim. Africa's box office art. South 47(1984):102.

African films shown on British television.

3066. Quam, Michael D. Harvest: 3000 years. Sowers of maize and bullets. Jump Cut 24/25(1981):5-7. (R)

3067. R.L.M. "Ceddo" de Sembène Ousmane. Le Courrier de Saint Ex 22(1980):3. (R)

3068. R.N. Festival du film publicitaire. 21 films primés. Fraternité Matin 6187(1985):25.

3069. Raeburn, Michaël. Absent de Ouagadougou: le cinéma ghanéen va-t-il décoller? Afrique Littéraire et Artistique 23(1972):88-98. (I)

Interview with Sam Aryeetey, Lionel Ngakane, James Nee-Owoo and Bernard Odjidja.

3070. Ralison, Lalao. Filmemacher aus Kamerun. Afrika Heute 23/24(1972):533.

Films of Daniel Kamwa.

3071. Ralison, Lalao. Freiheitskampf in Angola "Sambizanga". Afrika

Heute 21/22(1972):482-483. (R)

3072. Ralph-Bowman, Mark. A special delivery. West Africa
3422(1983):860-861. (R)

Segun Oyekunle, Parcel Post.

3073. Ramaroson, Patricia. "Certificat d'indigence" ou la lourdeur de
l'administration. Le Soleil July 7 (1983):2. (R)

3074. Ramonet, Ignacio. Un bilan africain. Le Monde Diplomatique
300(1979):29.

FESPACO.

3075. Ramonet, Ignacio. Marasme africain. Le Monde Diplomatique
318(1980):12.

Film production.

3076. Ramonet, Ignacio. "Sëy Sëyëti," ou l'obsession de la polygame.
Le Monde Diplomatique 318(1980):12. (R)

3077. Randal, Jonathan C. An African director reaching the people.
Washington Post June 12 (1976):B1,4.

The making of Sembène's Ceddo and his goals in filmmaking.

3078. Ranvaud, Dan. African dossier. Framework 7-8(1978):20.

Themes.

3079. Ranvaud, Dan. Interview with Med Hondo. Framework
7-8(1978):28-30. (I)

Discussion of militant films.

3080. Ranvaud, Dan. Nous aurons. Framework 7-8(1978):26-28. (R)

3081. Rauss, Raymond. L'art et le récit: un pont entre deux cultures.
A propos du film de Moustapha Diop "Le médecin de Gafiré."
Peuples Noirs Peuples Africains 52(1986):116-126.

Film is discussed in the context of European-African dialogue,
European understanding of Africa and the ability of film to
facilitate this understanding.

3082. Rayfield, J.R. The use of films in teaching about Africa. Film
Library Quarterly 17,2-4(1984):34-52.

Types of films by non-Africans, marginal Africans and Africans;
background on films and information about how some were made.

3083. Reid, Mark. Med Hondo interview. Jump Cut 31(1986):48-49. (I)

1982 interview on his filmmaking and the Niamey conference on film production.

3084. Reis, Maria Fernanda. Fad jal. <u>Celuloide</u> 291(1980):17. (R)

3085. Relich, Mario. African filmmakers. <u>West Africa</u> 3439(1983):1617-1618. (BR)

Review of <u>Jeune Cinéma</u> March 1983. Films of Kwaw Ansah, Bankole Bello and Gaston Kaboré.

3086. Relich, Mario. Africa's women film makers. <u>West Africa</u> 3385(1982):1650.

Sarah Maldoror and Selma Baccar.

3087. Relich, Mario. Chronicle of a student. <u>West Africa</u> 3393(1982):2212. (R)

Safi Faye, <u>Man Sa Yay</u>.

3088. Relich, Mario. Films of struggle. <u>West Africa</u> 3495(1985):1632-1633.

Films on Namibia and South Africa.

3089. Relich, Mario. From glitter to gore in the film world. <u>West Africa</u> 3358(1981):2907-2911.

African films at the London film festival.

3090. Relich, Mario. Ghana's documentary tradition. <u>West Africa</u> 3511(1984):2457-2458.

3091. Relich, Mario. Heroes and critics. <u>West Africa</u> 3517(1985):106-107.

Films shown at the London film festival.

3092. Relich, Mario. Lessons from children. <u>West Africa</u> 3616(1986):2651-2652. (R)

Ross Devenish, <u>Happy Valley</u> and Cheick Oumar Sissoko, <u>Nyamanton</u>.

3093. Relich, Mario. Ousmane Sembene in London. <u>West Africa</u> 3325(1981):861-865.

Review of Sembène's films.

3094. Relich, Mario. Sembène Ousmane as film-maker in <u>African fiction and film</u>. Angus Calder et al. Milton Keynes: Open University Press, 1983. pp. 28-33.

*3095.  Renaudin, Nicole.  Kaddu Beykat (Lettre paysanne).  Films et
         Documents 309(1975):27. (R)

3096.  Ricard, Alain.  Le cinéma popular nigérian.  Recherche, pédagogie
        et culture 58(1982):65-69.

3097.  Ricard, Alain.  Du théâtre au cinéma yoruba: le cas nigérian.
        CinémAction 26(1983):160-167.

        Nigerian films of Yoruba theater productions.

3098.  Rich.  Sarraounia.  Variety 324,7(1986):19. (R)

3099.  Richard, Moussa M.  Arthur Si Bita réalisateur du film Les
        Coopérants.  Kazel 15(1985):6-9. (R)

        Review includes biographical information on Si Bita.

3100.  Richter, Erika.  Gespräch mit Afework Manna und Deribew Temesgen.
        Filmwissenschaftliche Beiträge 21,3(1980):138-142. (I)

        Discussion of film in Ethiopia.

3101.  Richter, Erika.  Safi Faye (Senegal) -Dem afrikanischen Baurern
        eine Stimme geben.  Filmwissenschaftliche Beiträge
        21,3(1980):212-221.

3102.  Richter, Rolf.  Gespräch mit Armando de Carmo Guinapo.
        Filmwissenschaftliche Beiträge 21,3(1980):134-137. (I)

        Film in Angola.

3103.  Richter, Rolf.  Gespräch mit Djalma Martins Fettermann.
        Filmwissenschaftliche Beiträge 21,3(1980):143-148. (I)

        Film in Guinea Bissau.

3104.  Richter, Rolf.  Gespräch mit José Pedro Pimenta.
        Filmwissenschaftliche Beiträge 21,3(1980):149-154. (I)

        Film in Mocambique.

3105.  Richter, Rolf.  Ich will mit meinem Volk reden.  Film und
        Fernsehen 2(1978):32-34. (I)

        Sembène Ousmane discusses his work.

3106.  Richter, Rolf.  "Mueda" der erste moçambiquanische Spielfilm.
        Filmwissenschaftliche Beiträge 21,3(1980):155-156. (R)

3107.  Richter, Rolf.  Der Schriftsteller und Filmemacher Sembène
        Ousmane.  Filmwissenschaftliche Beiträge 21,3(1980):199-211.

        Xala.

3108.   Richter, Rolf.   Souleymane Cissé-Gesellschaftsanalyse als
        notwendige Selbstverständigung.   Filmwissenschaftliche Beiträge
        21,3(1980):164-169.

3109.   Rivel, Moune de.   Alkaly Kaba écrivain cinéaste malien.   Bingo
        263(1974):76-77. (I)

3110.   Rivel, Moune de.   Un mauritanien tourne l'histoire des Antilles.
        Bingo 319(1979):35-37. (I)

        Med Hondo discusses West Indies.

3111.   Rivel, Moune de.   Le premier long métrage africain en couleur.
        Bingo 299(1977):77. (R)

        Souelymane Cissé, Den Muso.

3112.   Robinson, Cedric.   Domination and imitation: Xala and the
        emergence of the black bourgeoisie.   Race and Class
        22,2(1980):147-158. (R)

3113.   Robinson, David.   Boesman and Lena.   Times (London) Feb. 15
        (1974):11. (R)

3114.   Robinson, David.   History as weapon in symbolic struggle.   Times
        (London) Aug. 28 (1981):13. (R)

        Sharad Patel, Amin the Rise and Fall.

3115.   Robinson, David.   The nasty spell of success.   Times (London)
        Nov. 5 (1976):9. (R)

        Sembène Ousmane, Xala.

3116.   Robinson, David.   Subverting the conventions in tough realism.
        Times (London) June 13 (1986):19. (R)

        Ruy Guerra, Erendira.

3117.   Robinson, David.   Visionary quality survives.   Times (London) May
        27 (1981):15. (R)

        Michael Raeburn, The Grass Is Singing.

3118.   Roditi, Edouard.   L'Afrique donne le ton.   Jeune Afrique
        550(1971):41-43.

        African films shown at the Berlin film festival.

*3119.  Roitfeld, Pierre.   Afrique noire francophone.   Unifrance Film
        Sept. (1980):16-32.

3120.   Rol.   From outcast to superstar of the African continent.   Afrika

25,11(1984):24-25.

Censorship of Sembène's films in Senegal.

3121. Rolland, Béatrice.  Alger, juillet 1969:  1er festival panafricain.  Positif 113(1970):87-92.

3122. Rolot, Christian and Francis Ramirez.  Problèmes et perspectives du cinéma en Afrique noire et à Madagascar.  Africa-Tervuren 25,4(1979):103-112.

Potential of film as a medium of communication in Africa.

3123. Ropars-Wuilleumier, M.C.  A propos du cinéma négro-africain: la problématique culturelle de La Noire de.  Recherche, pédagogie et culture 17-18(1975):10-15;  in Colloque sur littérature et esthétique négro-africaines.  Dakar:  Nouvelles Editions Africaines, 1979. pp. 291-299. (R)

3124. Ross, René.  L'Afrique noire ouvre le feu a Dinard.  Africasia 21(1970):68-70.

FIFEF.

3125. Rouch, J.  Codou par Ababakar Samb.  Jeune Afrique 565(1971):62-63. (R)

3126. Rouch, Jane.  Cannes a révèle le cinéma noir.  Bingo 40(1986):43-45.

3127. Rouch, Jane.  Hip hop Cannes! Bingo 378(1984):47-49.

3128. Rouch, Jane.  Les jurés éblouis par la "lumière" de Souleymane Cissé.  Bingo 414(1987):52-57. (R)

3129. Rouch, Jane.  Momar Thiam et les autres.  Jeune Afrique 551(1971):34.

FIFEF.

3130. Rouch, Jane.  Tarzan raconte son épopée africaine.  Bingo 382(1984):26.

Venice film festival.

3131. Rouch, Jean.  The awakening African cinema.  Unesco Courier 15,3(1962):10-15.

History of African film 1950-1962, most about films by non-Africans.

3132. Rouch, Jean.  Cartes postales de Niamey-Ouagadougou.  CinémAction 26(1983):10-13.

Rouch's recollections of African filmmakers he's known.

3133.  Rouch, Jean.  Situation et tendances du cinéma en Afrique, in
Films ethnographiques sur l'Afrique noire.  Paris: UNESCO, 1967.
pp. 374-408.

History, mainly about European films about Africa and
documentaries made by African governments.

3134.  Roy, Amit.  Film of Amin dedicated to 500,000 dead.  Daily
Telegraph Aug. 3 (1979):3.

Cast of Sharad Patel, Amin the Rise and Fall.

3135.  Ruelle, Catherine.  Une Afrique du cinéma?  Afrique-Asie
185(1979):50-52.  (I)

Inoussa Ousséini discusses CIDC and CIPROFILM.

*3136.  Ruelle, Catherine.  Black Goddess.  Happy Home Oct. (1978).

3137.  Ruelle, Catherine.  Le "come-back" du cinéma sénégalais.  Actuel
développement 32(1979):49-51.

3138.  Ruelle, Catherine.  Les écrans africains convoités.  Actuel
développement 30(1979):56-58.

Activities of CIDC and CIPROFILM.

3139.  Ruelle, Catherine.  FIFEF à Dakar la fin des complexes.  Actuel
développement 34(1980):47-48.

3140.  Ruelle, Catherine.  "Lettre paysanne" de Safi Faye.  Afrique-Asie
171(1978):48-49.  (I)

Discussion of Kaddu Beykat.

3141.  Ruelle, Catherine.  Ouagadougou: dixième anniversaire.
Afrique-Asie 183(1979):72-74.

FESPACO.

3142.  Ruelle, Catherine.  La place de la femme.  Afrique Littéraire
76(1985):80-83; CinémAction 34(1985):80-83.

Women in Sembène's films.

3143.  Ruelle, Catherine.  Que retiendrons nous de Cannes?  Agecop
Liaison 53(1980):23-25.

3144.  Ruelle, Catherine.  La rentrée tiers monde une saison chargée.
Actuel développement 39(1980):38-40.

Films to be shown at international festivals in 1980-1981.

3145. Ruelle, Catherine. Souleymane Cissé, grand prix du FESPACO "Finyé est une étape." Ivoire Dimanche 628(1983):44-45. (I)

3146. Ruelle, Catherine. Super 8 et superproduction. Actuel développement 43(1981):43-44.

3147. Ruelle, Catherine. Le tiers monde dédaigné. Actuel développement 31(1979):42-43.

Cannes.

3148. Ruelle, Catherine. Le triomphe des géants. Actuel développement 29(1979):54-55.

FESPACO.

3149. Ruelle, Catherine. Visages de femmes: chanter l'Afrique. Actuel développement 68(1985):61. (R)

3150. Ruelle, Catherine. West Indies Story: une superproduction noire. Actuel développement 30(1979):59. (R)

3151. Ruelle, Catherine and Andrée Tournes. Gespräch mit Souleymane Cissé (Mali). Filmwissenschaftliche Beiträge 21,3(1980):157-163. (I)

*3152. Ruf, Wolfgang, Ousmane Sembene: Die Postanweisung. Medium 12(1973):77-78.

3153. S.B. "Bako", l'ésclave du 20e siècle. Bingo 305(1978):55-56. (R)

3154. S.B. Un concours de scénario pour déceler des talents. Fraternité Matin Jan. 3-4 (1987):14.

Report on UCOA colloquium on film production held in Dakar.

3155. S.K. Ceddo ou l'homme du refus. Jeune Afrique 812(1976):60-61. (R)

3156. S.K. Le cinéma sénégalais sort du tunnel. Bingo 395(1985):69.

Insufficient financial support for filmmaking in Senegal.

3157. S.K. Thiaroye 44 devient le camp de Thiaroye. Bingo 413(1987):11.

Differences between two scripts for Camp de Thiaroye.

3158. S.S.T. En marge du cinéma, les forum. Sidwaya Feb. 2 (1987):10.

FESPACO seminars, 1974-1987.

3159.  S.X.S.  L'idée d'un forum africain.  <u>Carrefour</u> <u>Africain</u>
       977(1987):20.

       Text of FESPACO anti-apartheid declaration.

3160.  Saakana, Amon Saba.  Third eye looks at African cineastes'
       problems.  <u>Africa</u> <u>Now</u> 32(1983):80-81.

       Third Eye film festival, London.

3161.  Sada, Niang.  Njangaan, in <u>Dictionnaire</u> <u>des</u> <u>ouevres</u> <u>littéraires</u>
       <u>négro-africaines</u> <u>de</u> <u>langue</u> <u>française</u>.  Ambroise Kom, ed.
       Sherbrooke: Editions Naaman, 1983. pp. 394-395. (R)

       Review of film script by Chérif Adramé Seck, of Mahama Johnson
       Traoré's film.

3162.  Sagara, Abdoulaye.  "Den muso" le film qui fait courir tout
       Bamaka.  <u>Afrique</u> <u>Nouvelle</u> 1530(1978):19. (R)

3163.  Said, Abdulkadir Ahmed.  A perspective on African cinema, in
       <u>First</u> <u>Mogadishu</u> <u>Pan-African</u> <u>Film</u> <u>Symposium.</u> <u>Pan</u> <u>African</u>
       <u>Cinema...Which</u> <u>Way</u> <u>Ahead?</u>  Ibrahim Awed et al eds.  Mogadishu:
       MOGPAFIS Management Committee, 1983. pp. 32-36.

       Need for new film language related to African culture.

3164.  Sail, Noureddine.  La question du public dans la problématique du
       cinéma africain, in <u>FESPACO</u> <u>1983</u>. Paris: Présence Africaine,
       1987. pp. 71-82.

       Roles of critics, film clubs, radio, television and governments
       in promoting film.

3165.  Saint-Lot, Emile.  Audio-Visual techniques and Africa.  <u>Présence</u>
       <u>Africaine</u> 50(1964):266-268.

       Algiers film festival.  Educational roles of film.

3166.  Saivre, Denyse de.  Le cinéma de l'Afrique au sud du Sahara:
       quelques propositions paradoxicales.  <u>Französische</u> <u>Heute</u>
       2(1982):157-165.

       Audience, distribution problems, themes of films.

3167.  Saivre, Denyse de.  Entretien avec Charles Mensah, cinéaste
       <u>Recherche,</u> <u>pédagogie</u> <u>et</u> <u>culture</u> 56(1982):83-84. (I)

       Discussion of Mensah's training, films he's made and his ideals
       for filmmaking.

3168.  Saivre, Denyse de.  Entretien avec Dicongue Pipa.  <u>Recherche,</u>
       <u>pédagogie</u> <u>et</u> <u>culture</u> 23-24(1976):54-57. (I)

Discussion of <u>Muna</u> <u>Moto</u>.

3169. Sajoux, Thérèse. Démarriage malgache. <u>Jeune</u> <u>Afrique</u> 629(1973):37. (R)

Benoît Ramampy, <u>L'accident</u>.

3170. Sajoux, Thérèse. Itinéraire d'un déraciné. <u>Jeune</u> <u>Afrique</u> 901(1978):73. (R)

Cheick Doukouré, <u>Bako</u>.

3171. Sajoux, Thérèse. "Que nos films ne dorment plus dans les tiroirs." <u>Jeune</u> <u>Afrique</u> 899(1978):62-63. (I)

Helder Camara discusses <u>Chagrin</u>, actors and film distribution.

3172. Salama, A. Ben. Festival de Carthage l'âge de l'adolescence. <u>Actuel</u> <u>développement</u> 27(1978):6-8.

3173. Salama, Mohand Ben. Cinquième Fespaco. <u>Recherche,</u> <u>pédagogie et culture</u> 23-24(1976):58-59.

3174. Salia, Issaka. La nationalisation des salles de spectacle en Haute-Volta. <u>Ciné</u> <u>Qua</u> <u>Non</u> 2(1972):7-10.

3175. Salif, Diaby. 2e Festival de films publicitaires. Ouverture sur l'international. <u>Fraternité</u> <u>Matin</u> 6184(1985):2.

3176. Salif, Diaby. Festival international du film publicitaire. 100 films seront présentés. <u>Fraternité</u> <u>Matin</u> 6181(1985):2-3. (I)

Roland Roux discusses Festival du film publicitaire.

3177. Salif, Diaby. La publicité un outil de développement. <u>Fraternité</u> <u>Matin</u> 6186(1985):2.

Festival du film publicitaire.

3178. Samb, Ababacar. Schutz für den afrikanischen Film. <u>Afrika</u> <u>Heute</u> supp. to 19(1971):8-10.

Problems of production and distribution.

*3179. Samb, Ababacar. Tout artiste est une projection dans le futur. <u>7e</u> <u>Art</u> 27(1976):5,6,18.

3180. Samb, Abdoulaye and Thiaroye S. Mer. Notre cinéma sauvé. <u>Le</u> <u>Soleil</u> Jan. 14 (1986):10.

Alioune Badara Bèye, <u>Maba,</u> <u>laisse</u> <u>le</u> <u>sine</u>, a positive film. Films of Moussa Yoro Bathily and Sembène Ousmane are negative.

3181. Samb, Abdourahamane. La cinémathèque nationale a commencé ses activitiés. Le Soleil Dec. 9 (1976):2.

Activities of SIDEC.

3182. Samb, Boubacar. La créativité des jeunes en image. Le Soleil Jan. 16 (1986):8. (R)

D'Ameth Diallo, Fowukaay.

*3183. Samson, Anne. Le Haute Volta mise sur le cinéma. Africéchos Apr.-May (1981):58.

3184. Sané, Julien K. Xala l'Afrique par Sembène. Afrique Nouvelle 1341(1985):16-17. (R)

3185. Sanga-Kanku, Bertin. L'importance du cinéma dans les pays en voie de développement. Congo Magazine Aug. (1970):5-6.

3186. Sangare, Abdel Kader. Cinq jours d'une vie. L'Essor Apr. 14 (1971):1,4. (R)

3187. Sangare, Abdel Kader. "5 jours d'une vie." L'Essor May 1 (1971):1,3. (I)

Souleymane Cissé discusses background, symbolism and plot of his film.

3188. Sango, J. Pakebo. Où en est le cinéma camerounais? Bingo 298(1977):62,67.

3189. Sangre Scinfoma, Sidi. Le festival du cinéma à Tachkent. L'Essor June 17 (1974):1,4; June 22-23 (1974):4.

Same article on both dates.

3190. Santos, Arnaldo. Cinema e tv: concorrência ou complementaridade? Novembro 39(1980):62-63.

J.C.C.

3191. Santos, Arnaldo. O festival de cinema pela paz, o progresso social e liberdade dos povos. Novembro 55(1982):58-60.

Tashkent film festival.

3192. Santos, Arnaldo. As jornadas cinematográficas de Cartago. Novembro 41(1981):60-61.

J.C.C.

3193. Sarbois, M. Un art ignoré: le cinéma. Le courrier de Saint-Ex 14(1979):1-2.

Film as a business and art. Basic themes of films.

3194. Sartor, Freddy. Filmen in Mozambique. Film en Televisie 288/289(1981):25. (I)

3195. Saturia, Dominique. "Den Muso" de Souleymane Cissé. Le Soleil Jan. 22 (1976):8. (R)

3196. Saturia, Dominique. Entretien avec la réalisatrie Safi Faye. Le Soleil Dec. 5 (1975):12. (I)

Discussion of Kaddu Beykat and her views of ethnographic films.

3197. Savané, Vieux. Patrice Toto: "Si, j'avais eu un droit de regard." Waraango 6(1984):14-15. (I)

How he became interested in film, promotion of Xew Xew, plans to make Le feu dans le sang.

3198. Savané, Vieux and Idy-Caras Niane. Ce que les cinéastes africains disent. Unir Cinéma 17(1985):48-50. (I)

Moussa Yoro Bathily discusses her role as a Senegalese filmmaker, films she is working on.

3199. Savitskii, N.V. Pravda iskusstva--pravda bor'ba (k itogam vii Mezhdunarodnogo Kinofestivalia stran Azii, Afriki i Latinskoi Ameriki v Tashkente) in, Kinoiskusstvo Azii i Afriki. A.V. Karaganov, ed. Moscow: Izdvo Nauka, Glav red vostochnoi lit-ry, 1984. pp. 21-35.

African participation in Tashkent film festival.

3200. Sawadogo, Azad S. Le director général de CIDC et de CIPROFILM raconte. L'Observateur Feb. 15 (1979):1,6-7, 10.

Inoussa Ousseini discusses CIDC and CIPROFILM.

3201. Sawadogo, Azad S. FESPACO Au travail pour le rendez-vous de 1981? L'Observateur Feb. 12 (1979):1,8-9.

3202. Sawadogo, Azad S. VIe FESPACO Le cinéma une industrie? L'Observateur Feb. 8 (1979):1, 6-8. (I)

Interview with Paul Michaud about INAFEC and new initiatives in film production. General comments on FESPACO.

3203. Sawadogo, Philippe. Xème session des journées cinématographiques de Carthage. Sidwaya Nov. 30 (1984):5.

3204. Sawadogo, Philippe. L'esprit de Tachkent. Carrefour Africain 837(1984):20-21.

Tashkent film festival.

3205. Sawadogo, Philippe.    FESPACO information.    Unir Cinéma
23-24(1986):12-16.

3206. Sawadogo, Philippe.    Maquette du moment de la place des cinéastes
africains au Burkina Faso.    SeptièmArt 60(1986):13.

3207. Sawadogo, Philippe.    3ème symposium du cinéma de Mogadiscio.
Carrefour Africain 908(1985):25-27.

MOGPAFIS.

3208. Sawadogo, Philippe.    3ème Symposium du cinéma de Mogadiscio.
Unir Cinéma 20-21(1985):24-29.

MOGPAFIS.

3209. Sayre, Norma.    'Sambizanga', new film about Angola, tells of
oppression and determination.    New York Times Nov. 22 (1973):50.
(R)

3210. Schaaf.    Cabascabo.    Afrika Heute 9(1973):47. (R)

3211. Schaaf.    Et la neige n'était plus.    Afrika Heute 10/11(1973):52.
(R)

3212. Schaaf.    Femme noir-Femme nu.    Afrika Heute 4-8(1974):83. (R)

Désiré Ecaré, A nous deux France.

3213. Schaaf.    Silence et feu de brousse.    Afrika Heute 12(1973):47.
(R)

3214. Schaaf.    Wazzou.    Afrika Heute 3(1974):47. (R)

Oumarou Ganda, Wazzou polygame.

3215. Scheinfeigel, Maxime.    Borom Sarret, la fiction documentaire.
Afrique Littéraire 76(1985):32-34; CinémAction 34(1985):32-34.
(R)

3216. Scheinfeigel, Maxime.    Borom Sarret, un film de Ousmane Sembène.
Avant-Scène-Cinéma 229(1979):35-42.

Background on Sembène's films and selected dialogue from Borom
Sarret.

3217. Scheinfeigel, Maxime.    Cabascabo un film de Oumarou Ganda.
Avant-Scène-Cinéma 265(1981):39-50.

Biographical information about Ganda and selected dialogue from
Cabascabo.

3218. Schideler, Jack.    Kenya tries moviemaking.    Christian Science
Monitor Jan. 17 (1968):3.

Activities of Kenya Film Corporation.

3219. Schissel, Howard. Among the peasants. New African 132(1978):73. (R)

Safi Faye, Kaddu Beykat.

3220. Schissel, Howard. Kicking karate out of the cinema. New African 192(1983):43-44.

Soleymane Cissé's training, problems in making Finyé, success of his films.

3221. Schissel, Howard. People's film-maker. West Africa 3481(1984):973-974. (I)

Souleymane Cissé discusses how he became interested in filmmaking, his training, Baara, Finyé and lack of understanding of film by African leaders.

3222. Schissel, Howard. Sembène Ousmane: film-maker. West Africa 3440(1983):1665-1667.

Review of Sembène's films.

3223. Schmidt, Hannes. The cinema in the Third World. Afrika 19,7(1978):22-23.

Oberhausen film festival.

3224. Schmidt, Hannes. Films from Africa on Africa. Afrika 19,6(1978):25.

Berlin film festival.

3225. Schmidt, Hannes. Safi Faye...first African woman film maker needs the roots of home. Afrika 19,10(1978):25.

Faye's appearance on German television.

3226. Schmidt, Nancy J. African filmmaking, country by country. African Studies Review 28,1(1985):111-114. (BR)

Victor Bachy, Le cinéma au Mali, Le cinéma en Côte d'Ivoire and Le Haute-Volta et le cinéma; Rik Otten, Le cinéma dans les pays des grands lacs; and Paulin Vieyra, Le cinéma au Sénégal. See Nos. 8, 10, 11, 64 and 75.

3227. Schmidt, Nancy J. African literature on film. Research in African Literatures 13,4(1982):518-531.

Films of African novels and plays.

3228. Schmidt, Nancy J. African Literature on film: a preliminary bibliography/filmography. Research in African Literatures 17,2(1986):261-266.

3229. Schmidt, Nancy J. Africa's foremost filmmaker. Africa Today 33,1(1986):55-56. (BR)

Francoise Pfaff, The Cinema of Ousmane Sembene. See No. 66.

3230. Schmidt, Nancy J. Conference Report, Colloque sur la littérature et le cinéma africaine. African Literature Association Bulletin 12,2(1986):16-17. (BR)

FESPACO. See No. 30.

3231. Schmidt, Nancy J. Ethnographic film in Angola. SVA Newsletter 3,1-2(1987):5. (BR)

Ruy Duarte de Carvalho, O Camarada e a Camera. See No. 28.

3232. Schmidt, Nancy J. Victor Bachy, Le cinéma au Gabon. African Studies Review 30(1987). (forthcoming) (BR)

See No. 7.

3233. Schmitt, Jean-Louis. Le verdict du public en fait un succès. Fraternité Matin 4936(1981):17. (R)

Jean-Louis Koula, Adja Tio.

3234. Schork, Erika. Ousmane Sembène. Afrika 18,11(1977):18-19. (I)

3235. Seck, Ibrahima. Aurions-nous un cinéma vraiment africain? Afrique Nouvelle 856(1964):19.

Need for technicians, actors and production facilities.

3236. Secka, Mamadou Johnny. Le Johnny Secka sénégalais repond. Le Soleil Feb. 12 (1974):4.

Distinction between Johnny Sekka and Johnny Secka.

3237. Segal, Aaron. Film review, Sambizanga. Africa Today 21,1(1974):67. (R)

3238. Seguin, Louis. A nous deux, France. Positif 118(1970):42-43. (R)

3239. Seguin, Louis. Les Africains. Positif 47(1962):66-67.

Cannes film festival.

3240. Seiler-Deitrich, Almut. Der film, in Die Literaturen Schwarzafrikas. Munich: C.H. Beck, 1984. pp. 133-135.

About Sembène Ousmane.

3241.  Seitz, Michael H.  Lit flicks.  The Progressive 48,8(1984):40-41.
(R)

Ruy Guerra, Erendira.

3242.  Sekka, Johnny.  Le vrai Johnny Sekka nous écrit.  Le Soleil Feb.
7 (1974):4.

Distinction between Johnny Sekka and Johnny Secka.

3243.  Sembène, Carrie D.  Cinema in Africa: the Senegalese experience.
International Development Reviw 17,2(1975):32-35.

Political and apolitical films in Senegal.  Censorship of
Sembene's films.

3244.  Sembène Ousmane.  African cinema seeks a new language.  Young
Cinema and Theater 3(1983):26-28. (I)

Interview with Sembène at UNESCO conference in Mexico.

3245.  Sembène Ousmane.  Film-makers and African culture.  Africa
(London) 71(1977):80. (I)

3246.  Sembène Ousmane.  Filmmakers have a great responsibility to our
people, in The Cineaste Interviews. Dan Georgakas and Lenny
Lubenstein, eds.  Chicago: Lake View Press, 1983. pp. 41-52. (I)

Sembène discusses Emitai, use of music in film, distribution of
films.

3247.  Sembène Ousmane.  Jukkut pour Ibou Camara.  Le Soleil Aug. 11
(1973):5.

Ibou Camara, actor in Emitai.

3248.  Sembène Ousmane.  Lettre ouverte.  Africa (Dakar) 163(1984):41.

Censorship of Ceddo in Senegal.

3249.  Sembène Ousmane.  "Retrouver l'identité africaine."  Le Monde
Diplomatique 300(1979):29.

African history in Sembène's films.

3250.  Sembène Ousmane.  Situation du cinéma africain.  Aujourd'hui
l'Afrique 6(1976):33-39.

History, infrastructure, censorship and themes of films.

3251.  Sene, M'Backé.  Ce soir première de "Karim" prix spécial du festival de Dinard. Le Soleil Aug. 3 (1971):3. (R)

Momar Thiam discusses his Karim and other films· he's made.

3252. Sene, Birakane. Avec "la malle de Maka Kouli" Momar Thiam présente un conte qui rappelle les fables de La Fontaine. Le Soleil Oct. 9 (1970):3. (R)

3253. Senga, Jean-François. L'aventure était ambigue. Jeune Afrique 1226(1984):49-50.

Film of C.H. Kane's novel shown in Dakar.

3254. Senghor, Blaise. Les conditions préalables à un authentique cinéma africain. Afrique Nouvelle 874(1964):10-11.

History, infrastructure and audience.

3255. Senghor, Blaise. Pour un authentique cinéma africain. Présence Africaine 49(1964):104-110.

3256. Sentiers. Le Mandat prix spécial Festival de Venise 1968. Sentiers 26(1969):30-31. (R)

3257. SeptièmArt. Accuse, levez vous! SeptièmArt 55(1985):19-23. (I)

Yves Diagne discusses infrastructure in Senegal.

3258. SeptièmArt. Cinéma africain: espoirs... SeptièmArt 55(1985):12-13. (I)

Interview with Abdoulaye Ascofare.

3259. SeptièmArt. Nous n'avons pas le choix. SeptièmArt 55(1985):14-15.

Work of Paul Zoumbara.

3260. SeptièmArt. Les palmarès. SeptièmArt 55(1985):9.

FESPACO prizes.

3261. Serceau, Daniel. Ceddo, la barbarie à visage divin. Afrique Littéraire 76(1985):54-57; CinémAction 34(1985):54-57. (R)

3262. Serceau, Daniel. Un "inconnu" nommé Sembène Ousmane. Afrique Littéraire 76(1985):5-7; CinémAction 34(1985):5-7.

3263. Serceau, Daniel. La recherche d'un écriture. Afrique Littéraire 76(1985):66-72; CinémAction 34(1985):66-72.

Social and political themes of Sembène's films. Sembène as a social critic.

3264. Serceau, Michel. Du masque au mandat; tradition et modernité. Afrique Littéraire 76(1985):72-79; CinémAction 34(1985):72-79.

Islamic themes in Sembène's films.

3265. Serceau, Michel. Emitai, l'échec d'une transposition dramatique. Afrique Littéraire 76(1985):43-45; CinémAction 34(1985):43-45. (R)

3266. Serceau, Michel. Le Mandat, un film catalyseur des relations sociales. Afrique Littéraire 76(1985):40-42; CinémAction 34(1985):40-42. (R)

3267. Serceau, Michel. Naiye, l'Afrique sans masque. Afrique Littéraire 76(1985):35; CinémAction 34(1985):35. (R)

3268. Serceau, Michel. Xala, une fable sur la bourgeoisie africaine. Afrique Littéraire 76(1985):46-50; CinémAction 34(1985):46-50. (R)

3269. Sérémé, Daba. Une comparison toute simple. L'Essor Jan. 5 (1971):4.

Theater accommodations and ticket prices in Mali.

3270. Sérgio, Paulo. Para filme sobre Africa Austral. Tempo 848(1987):51-52.

Jose Mucavele, Mocambiquan musician, makes soundtrack for Brazilian film.

3271. Servet, Michel. Le bon, la brute et le révolté. Jeune Afrique 1244(1984):72. (R)

Souleymane Cissé, Baara.

3272. Service Commercial du Groupe Fraternité Matin. Festival du film publicitaire. La fête de la pub. Fraternité Matin 6185(1985):13-20.

3273. Service de Psychologie et de Sociologie. Qu'est-ce qui fait courir nobila ou la psychologie du spectateur, in FESPACO 1983. Paris: Présence Africaine, 1987. pp. 83-89.

Impact of films on audience. Audience preferences in Burkina Faso. Weaknesses of African films compared to those preferred by audiences.

3274. Sevastakis, Michael. Neither gangsters nor dead kings. Film Library Quarterly 6,3(1973):13-23, 40-48. (R)

Sembène Ousmane, Borom Sarret, Emitai, La noire de, Mandabi and Tauw.

3275. Seydou, Ouattara.  Sidiki Bakaba: jouer pour les autres me frustrait.  _Bingo_ 408(1987):53. (I)

Bakaba's acting in Europe and Africa, view of the "star system."

3276. Seyni, Abdoulkarim.  Communiqué de presse.  _Sidwaya_ Mar. 1 (1985):ii.

FESPACO program dedicated to Oumarou Ganda.

3277. Shaibu, Samson Alhaji.  Establishing a film industry.  _New Nigerian_ Aug. 2 (1981):12.

Reasons Nigerians should invest in film industry.

3278. Shakur, Nyisha Mbalia and John Downing.  Selected Third World classic films.  _Film Library Quarterly_ 16,4(1983):53-67. (R)

Nana Mahomo, _Last Grave at Dimbaza_ and Sembène Ousmane, _La noire de_ and _Xala_.

3279. Sharma, Yojana.  African cinema in Brussels.  _Afrika_ 25,6(1984):24-25.

Filmmakers' roundtable at Brussels film festival.

3280. Shaw, Angus.  Epic film of suffering produced.  _Herald_ June 8 (1986):9. (R)

Mohamed Amin, _African Calvary_.

3281. Sheikh, Mohamed Aden.  Opening speech, in _First Mogadishu Pan-African Film Symposium. Pan African Cinema...Which Way Ahead?_ Ibrahim Awed et al. eds.  Mogadishu: MOGPAFIS Management Committee, 1983. pp. 6-9.

Aims of MOGPAFIS. Overview of filmmaking in Somalia.

3282. Shirazi, Manny.  Film festival host.  _West Africa_ Mar. 23 (1987):558-559.

Films shown at FESPACO.

3283. Shungu, Ekanga.  Sidiki Bakaba un prince en proie au démon du théâtre.  _Jeune Afrique Magazine_ 6(1984):14-15.

Bakaba's theater and film acting.

*3284. Si Bita, Arthur.  Sous le signe de la fraternité.  _CinémArabe_ 10/11(1978):40-42.

Locarno film festival.

3285. Si Bita, Arthur, et al.  Le sacré par ceux qu'il inspire, in

Caméra Nigra. C.E.S.C.A. ed. Brussels: OCIC, 1984. pp. 77-83.
(I)

Comments on themes of sacred by Mahamane Bakabé, Richard de
Medeiros, Jean-Pierre Ossin, Arthur Si Bita and Augustine Taoko.

3286. Sice, A. di-Djilène. Après "Diankha-Bi": un nouveau film de
Johnson Traoré. Dakar Matin June 5 (1969):3. (R)(I)

Traoré discusses Enfer des innocents.

3287. Sice, A. di-Djilène. Le film "Diankha-Bi de Johnson Traoré: un
coup d'essai qui annonce un Maître. Dakar Matin Apr. 21
(1969):3. (R)

3288. Sicé, A. di-Djilène. Der Film im Senegal. Afrika Heute.
14-15(1971):292-297.

Film in Senegal, focus on Sembène.

3289. Sidibé, Kara. La rivalité ville et campagne est-ce fini. Bingo
346(1981):68-70. (I)

Interview with Kalifa Dienta.

3290. Sidibé, Ladji. Les cinéastes ivoiriens déclarent: "nous en
sommes pas aidés." Fraternité Matin 4910(1981):5.

FESPACO prizes.

3291. Sidwaya. Assemblée générale de la FEPACI, Le bilan de deux ans
de redressement. Sidwaya Feb. 25 (1987):8.

Review of 1985 FEPACI meeting and subsequent activities.

3292. Sidwaya. Benin-Burkina. Sidwaya June 28 (1985):7.

Watamou Lamine in Benin to discuss CIDC and CIPROFILM.

3293. Sidwaya. Cérémonies d'inauguration du monument des cinéastes
africains et de la rue marchande. Sidwaya Feb. 23 (1987):11.

Monument to filmmakers in Ouagadougou.

3294. Sidwaya. Le cinéma au Bénin. Sidwaya Feb. 23 (1987):12.

Nationalisation of theaters, major filmmakers.

3295. Sidwaya. Colloque sur tradition orale et nouveaux média, des
communications importants. Sidwaya Feb. 25 (1987):7.

Excerpts from communications of FESPACO colloquium on oral
tradition and the media.

3296. **Sidwaya.** Dans les coulises du FESPACO. *Sidwaya* Feb. 27 (1987):11.

3297. **Sidwaya.** Des directeurs généraux et représentants d'organismes de télévisions africaines à la 10ème édition de FESPACO. *Sidwaya* Feb. 27 (1987):10.

Press communique by representatives of URTNA at FESPACO.

3298. **Sidwaya.** Discours de clôture du Ministre de la Culture, la camarade Bernadette Sanou. *Sidwaya* Mar. 2 (1987):6.

Text of FESPACO closing address.

3299. **Sidwaya.** Discours de la camarade Bernadette Sanou Ministre de la Culture a l'occasion de l'ouverture de la Xè edition du FESPACO. *Sidwaya* Feb. 23 (1987):5.

Text of FESPACO opening address.

3300. **Sidwaya.** Donner une orientation nouvelle au cinéma africain. *Sidwaya* Feb. 25 (1985):1.

FESPACO theme: film and liberation.

3301. **Sidwaya.** Exposition de mets burkinabé. *Sidwaya* Feb. 23 (1987):11.

Burkinabe products displayed and sold at FESPACO.

3302. **Sidwaya.** FESPACO 87: un parti gagne. *Sidwaya* Feb. 23 (1987):1.

3303. **Sidwaya.** FESPACO une trentaine de films en compétition. *Sidwaya* Feb. 13 (1985):4.

3304. **Sidwaya.** Les festivals ou Fespaco 85. *Sidwaya* Mar. 4 (1985):iv.

Non-African film festivals in which Africans participated.

3305. **Sidwaya.** La fête commence demain. *Sidwaya* Feb. 22 (1985):1.

Announcement about FESPACO opening ceremony.

3306. **Sidwaya.** La grogne de Idrissa Ouédraogo. *Sidwaya* Mar. 1 (1985):iii.

Short films shown at FESPACO. Ouédraogo's objections to how Burkinabe films chosen for FESPACO competition.

3307. **Sidwaya.** Palmarès du 10ème FESPACO du 21 au 28 février 1987. *Sidwaya* Mar. 2 (1987):6-7.

3308. **Sidwaya.** Palmarès officiel 9ème FESPACO. *Sidwaya* Mar. 4 (1985):ii.

Press releases on FESPACO prizes.

3309.    Sidwaya.   Prix Air Afrique FESPACO 87.   Sidwaya Feb. 25 (1987):7.

3310.    Sidwaya.   Une réelle volonté de redressement du CIDC-CIPROFILM.
         Sidwaya Feb. 18 (1985):6.

Opening of ministers conference at FESPACO.

3311.    Sidwaya.   Résumés de quelques films en programmation.   Sidwaya
         Feb. 26 (1985):ii.  (R)

Abdoulaye Ascofare, M'sieur Fane; Ruy Duarte de Carvalho,
Nelisita; and Emmanuel Sanou, Doba.

3312.    Sidwaya.   Le sacré de Souleymane Cissé.   Sidwaya Mar. 4
         (1985):ii.

FESPACO prizes and attendance.  Need for additional prizes.

3313.    Sidwaya.   "Sarraounia" grand prix FESPACO 87.   Sidwaya Mar. 2
         (1987):1,6.

Jury's principles for selecting films for prizes.

3314.    Sidwaya.   Une séquence érotique du film "Visages de femmes"
         polarise l'attention.   Sidwaya Feb. 27 (1987):8.  (R)

Désiré Ecaré, Visages de femmes and Paul Mouketa, Raphia.

3315.    Sidwaya.   Si le FESPACO m'était conte: 1969-1970: les premières
         manifestations.   Sidwaya Feb. 25 (1985):ii, iv.

3316.    Sidwaya.   "Touki-Bouki" une séance pour servir une juste cause.
         Sidwaya Feb. 26 (1987):9.  (R)

3317.    Sidwaya.   Vu et entendu.   Sidwaya Feb. 23 (1987):6.

FESPACO.  Audience responses and radio commentary on films.

3318.    Sidwaya.   Vu et entendu.   Sidwaya Feb. 25 (1987):9.

FESPACO.  Impact of Nyamanton.

3319.    Sidwaya.   Yam Daabo (Le choix) au ciné Burkina.   Sidwaya June 26
         (1987):6.  (R)

3320.    Siegfried, Shula.   Avec "Sambizanga" Sarah Maldoror continue le
         combat.   Afrique-Asie 11-12(1972):118-119.  (R)

3321.    Silombert.   Le cinéphile dérouté.   Le Soleil 3320(1981):2.  (R)

Paulin Vieyra, En residence surveillée.

3322. Siminoski, Ted. Mandabi, in Magill's Survey of Cinema, Foreign Language Films. Frank N. Magill, ed. Englewood Cliffs, N.J.: Salem Press, 1985. pp. 1945-1949. (R)

3323. Sine, Allé. A propos de "Baks." Le Soleil Apr. 15 (1975):2. (R)

3324. Sine, Babacar. Audio-visuel et extra-version culturelle. Ethiopiques 10(1977):19-28.

Functions of visual media.

3325. Sine, Babacar. Les techniques de communication et notre destin culturel. Revue africaine de communication 6(1981):13-22.

Section on film pp. 20-22.

3326. Singou-Basseha, Appolinaire. Le cinéma africain en question. Bingo 412(1987):44-45. (I)

Interview with Makala Kadima-Nzuji on FESPACO colloquium on oral tradition and the new media.

3327. Siskel, Gene. 'Xala' a potent Senegalese film. Chicago Tribune June 11 (1976):sect. 3, p. 3. (R)

3328. Sissoko, M. Le prix des journalistes et de la critique internationale de cinéma 1972. L'Essor Oct. 23 (1972):1,4.

J.C.C. prize for Souleymane Cissé, Cinq jours d'une vie.

3329. Sitoe, Ernesto Eugénio. Cine-clube de Maputo uma iniciativa para aplaudir. Domingo (Maputo) Feb. 13 (1983):3.

Aims and organization of film club in Maputo.

3330. Smart, Christopher. In Mali, cultural life defies hardships. Christian Science Monitor June 17 (1986):34.

Infrastructure and films of Souleymane Cissé.

3331. Smith, Grahame. Film, Africa and the great hall. Baraza 1(1983);11-14.

State of film in black Africa; will Malawi be able to participate in these developments.

3332. Smith, Henry. Le FESPACO 81 évoqué à Berlin. Afrique Nouvelle 1660(1981):19.

3333. Smith, Stephen. Xe FESPACO "Le choix" crève l'écran. Le Soleil Feb. 28-Mar. 1 (1987):9. (I)

Interview with President Sankara about FESPACO and Burkinabe film.

3334. Smith, Stephen. Xe FESPACO Marché télévisuel. <u>Le Soleil</u> Feb. 25 (1987):8.

Sale of films and cassettes at FESPACO. FESPACO as opportunity for exchange between filmmakers and television producers.

3335. Snoussi, Rafy. Clôture des Xèmes Journées Cinématographiques de Carthage. <u>L'Action</u> Oct. 23 (1984):24.

J.C.C. prizes.

3336. Snoussi, Rafy. Colloque: Le cinéma africain, sa mission et ses responsibilitiés. <u>L'Action</u> Oct. 29 (1982):10.

U.S. African Studies Association symposium on African film.

3337. Snoussi, Rafy. Coup d'envoi des XIe Journées cinématographiques de Carthage. <u>L'Action</u> Oct. 16 (1986):7.

3338. Snoussi, Rafy. Entretien avec l'actrice camerounaise Nicole Okala. <u>L'Action</u> Nov. 20 (1980):10. (I)

Actress in <u>Notre fille</u>.

3339. Snoussi, Rafy. Etablir de nouveau contact avec le cinéma arabo-africain. <u>L'Action</u> Oct. 10 (1984):24.

J.C.C.

3340. Snoussi, Rafy. VIIIèmes journées cinématographiques de Carthage du 15 au 23 novembre 1980. <u>L'Action</u> Nov. 12 (1980):7.

3341. Snoussi, Rafy. Les J.C.C. consacrent "L'homme de cendres" meilleur film de la onzième session. <u>L'Action</u> Oct. 28 (1986):13.

Summaries of prize-winning films.

3342. Snoussi, Rafy. Les J.C.C. 80 ou le réveil du cinéma tunisien. <u>L'Action</u> Dec. 6 (1980):9.

Sub-Saharan African films at J.C.C. of poorer quality than Maghrebian films.

3343. Snoussi, Rafy. J.C.C. 82 la chasse aux tanits est ouverte. <u>L'Action</u> Oct. 23 (1982):13.

3344. Snoussi, Rafy. J.C.C. 84 le tournant. <u>L'Action</u> Oct. 12 (1984):24.

3345. Snoussi, Rafy. J.C.C. "West Indies." <u>L'Action</u> Nov. 23 (1980):110. (R)

3346. Snoussi, Rafy. Ouverture ce soir des VIIIème journnées cinématographiques de Carthage. L'Action Nov. 15 (1980):8.

J.C.C. program and film jury.

3347. Snoussi, Rafy. Ouverture des 9èmes Journées Cinématographiques de Carthage. L'Action Oct. 24 (1982):7.

J.C.C. address by Bechir Ben Slama on role of film in national and cultural struggles.

3348. Snoussi, Rafy. Le rendez-vous du cinéma arabo-africain. L'Action Oct. 17 (1984):12.

J.C.C.

3349. Snoussi, Rafy. Retrospective: J.C.C. quatorze ans après. L'Action Oct. 18 (1980):12-13.

Review of J.C.C. since 1966.

3350. Snoussi, Rafy. Tunis, capitale du cinéma arabo africain. L'Action Oct. 14 (1986):24.

J.C.C.

3351. Snoussi, Rafy. 25 pays arabes et africains au rendez-vous des IXèmes J.C.C. L'Action Oct. 21 (1982):12.

3352. Sodofi, David. Jeunes cinéastes africains des idées plein la tête. Afrique Nouvelle 1806(1984):14-16. (I)

Interview with Nestor Ahamada, Christian Moukala and Samuel Wilson.

3353. Sohouenou, Epiphane. In the steps of a pioneer. OCIC Info 7,1(1986):13.

Association of Beninois filmmakers.

3354. Sokhona, Sidney. Notre cinéma. Cahiers du cinéma 285(1978):55-57.

Infrastructural problems.

3355. Soleil. Annette M'Baye et A. Samb obtiennent le prix "Georges Sadoul" avec leur film "Codou". Le Soleil Dec. 20 (1971):6. (R)

3356. Soleil. L'association des cinéastes sanctionne. Le Soleil 3432(1981):6.

Ababacar Samb, Jom; Thierno Sow, L'oeil; and Momar Thiam SaDagga.

3357. Soleil. L'association des critiques a un nouveau bureau. Le

Soleil Mar. 12-13 (1983):2.

History of ASSECCI since 1977, current officers.

3358. Soleil. Au Festival de Dinard. Le Soleil July 13-14 (1970):3.
(I)

Blaise Senghor and Sembène Ousmane discuss FIFEF, need for film criticism in the African press.

3359. Soleil. "Badou Boy" de Djibril Diop Medaille d'or à Milan. Le Soleil May 12 (1971):3.

Prize at MIFED.

3360. Soleil. Bientôt sur l'écran "Le fils d'Agatha Moudio." Le Soleil Aug. 21 (1975):8.

Film script completed, Louis Balthazar Amadangoleda seeking financing for his film.

3361. Soleil. "Caméra d'Afrique" ou la problématique du 7e art africain. Le Soleil May 14-15 (1983):22.

Discussion of film on the history of African film shown at Cannes film festival.

3362. Soleil. Une charte du cinéma africain. Le Soleil Jan. 25 (1975):10.

Excerpts from FEPACI charter.

3363. Soleil. Les cinéastes du Tiers-Monde réunis à Alger. Le Soleil Dec. 10 (1973):6.

Sembène participates in filmmakers conference in Algiers.

3364. Soleil. Cinéastes sénégalais. Le Soleil May 17 (1978):2.

Meeting of ACS.

3365. Soleil. "Le cinéma africain se porte bien." Le Soleil Feb. 12 (1976):6.

FESPACO.

3366. Soleil. Collaboration entre télé et cinéma encouragée. Le Soleil Aug. 1 (1979):1,6.

Meeting of national audiovisual council in Senegal.

3367. Soleil. Confirmation du cinéma africain. Le Soleil Oct. 29 (1982):18.

J.C.C.

3368.  Soleil.  Consécration des cinémas malien et voltaique.  Le Soleil
       Nov. 2 (1982):19.

       J.C.C. Comments on Souleymane Cissé, Finyé and Gaston Kaboré,
       Wend Kuuni.

3369.  Soleil.  Coopération télévision-ciné décide le Conseil national
       de l'audio-visuel.  Le Soleil Jan. 31 (1976):3.

       Senegalese national audiovisual council approves plan for
       cooperation between television and filmmaking.

3370.  Soleil.  Décoloniser les écrans.  Le Soleil Dec. 16-18 (1983):21.

       Report on CIDC meeting in Ouagadougou.

3371.  Soleil.  Le dernier film de Johnson Traoré "Diègue-bi" sur les
       écrans ivoiriens.  Le Soleil Aug. 12 (1971):2.

       Common problems of filmmakers in Côte d'Ivoire and Senegal.

3372.  Soleil.  Deux films mauritaniens cet après-midi.  Le Soleil June
       22 (1977):4.

       Sidney Sokhona, Nationalité: immigré and Safrana to be shown in
       Dakar.

3373.  Soleil.  250 millions pour la relance du cinéma sénégalais.  Le
       Soleil Dec. 4-5 (1982):3.

       Problems of Senegalese film production and suggested solutions.

3374.  Soleil.  Dinard: Palmarès du Festival du film francophone.  Le
       Soleil July 16 (1974):6.

       FIFEF prizes.

3375.  Soleil.  Djelli (sic) de l'Ivoirien Kramo remporte "l'étalon du
       Yatenga".  Le Soleil 3261(1981):7. (R)

3376.  Soleil.  Edition et cinéma.  Deux sociétés nationales créées
       prochainement.  Le Soleil May 13 (1971):1,3.

       Proposed structure for national film production society in
       Senegal.

3377.  Soleil.  Le festival de Dinard début aujourd'hui.  Le Soleil July
       4-5 (1970):3.

       Senegalese production in FIFEF.

3378.  Soleil.  Festival du cinéma africain au cours Sainte-Marie.  Le

<u>Soleil</u> 3336(1981):2.

African films shown in Senegal.

3379. **Soleil.** Un festival du film sénégalais à New York. <u>Le Soleil</u> Mar. 17 (1978):7.

Senegalese films shown at Museum of Modern Art, New York.

3380. **Soleil.** Un film africain à Paris: "Sambizanga" de Sarah Maldoror. <u>Le Soleil</u> Apr. 26 (1973):5. (R)

3381. **Soleil.** Le film "Lettre Paysanne" de Safi Faye gagne le prix Sadoul. <u>Le Soleil</u> Dec. 13 (1975):6. (R)

<u>Kaddu Beykat</u>.

3382. **Soleil.** Un film malien favorablement accueilli. <u>Le Soleil</u> Sept. 16-17 (1986):13. (R)

Souleymane Cissé, <u>Baara</u>.

3383. **Soleil.** Henri Duparc le réalisateur d'"Abusuan" aujourd'hui à Dakar. <u>Le Soleil</u> June 18 (1973):5. (R)

3384. **Soleil.** L'ICA offrira un prix du meilleur film documentaire. <u>Le Soleil</u> Oct. 4-5 (1980):4.

FESPACO prize for documentary film.

3385. **Soleil.** Johnny Secka veut devenir producteur de films. <u>Le Soleil</u> Oct. 23-24 (1971):4.

Secka wants to create African film production society. Contribution of film to progress in African nations.

3386. **Soleil.** Une journée d'étude sur le cinéma. <u>Le Soleil</u> Mar. 7 (1986):8.

SNPC to hold meeting on problems in quality of film production.

3387. **Soleil.** Journées d'études sur le cinéma. <u>Le Soleil</u> Apr. 2 (1986):8.

Senegalese minister of communications to hold seminar on film production and distribution.

3388. **Soleil.** "Karim" de Momar Thiam. <u>Le Soleil</u> July 10-11 (1971):2. (R)

3389. **Soleil.** Large participation africaine au festival de cinéma de Dinard. <u>Le Soleil</u> May 29-30 (1971):5.

Films to be shown at FIFEF.

3390.  Soleil.  Le lauréat de Dinard a des soucis.  <u>Le Soleil</u> Sept. 30 (1970):3.

Ababacar Samb, <u>Codou</u> wins FIFEF prize.

3391.  Soleil.  M. Salzgeber du festival cinématographique de Berlin à Dakar.  <u>Le Soleil</u> Nov. 12 (1982):6.

Berlin film festival.  Possibility of German-Senegalese cooperation in production.

3392.  Soleil.  Le Malien Cissé primé à Ouagadougou.  <u>Le Soleil</u> Feb. 14 (1983):1, 19.

FESPACO.

3393.  Soleil.  Med Hondo (Soleil O) va tourner un film sur l'apartheid. <u>Le Soleil</u> Mar. 30 (1973):5.

Production of <u>Soleil O</u>.

3394.  Soleil.  "Mon beau pays" premier film de Thierno Faty Sow.  <u>Le Soleil</u> June 23 (1972):2. (R)

3395.  Soleil.  Morosité artistique sur fond de fête.  <u>Le Soleil</u> Feb. 28 (1985):8.

FESPACO.

3396.  Soleil.  Myriam Niang au Festival de Cannes.  <u>Le Soleil</u> Apr. 30 (1976):2.

Roles of Senegalese actress.

3397.  Soleil.  9e FESPACO grand prix.  <u>Le Soleil</u> Mar. 4 (1985):6.

3398.  Soleil.  Le nouveau film d'Ola Balogun fait rimer amour et humour...en langue ibo.  <u>Le Soleil</u> July 4 (1975):10. (R)

<u>Amadi</u> compared to <u>Alpha</u>. Balogun's view of Nigerian audiences.

3399.  Soleil.  Nouveau film sénégalais en chantier.  <u>Le Soleil</u> Aug. 20 (1980):5. (R)

Akhya Alpha Dia, <u>Allahou</u> <u>Akbar</u>.

3400.  Soleil.  Ouverture du 8ème festival panafricain de cinéma.  <u>Le Soleil</u> Feb. 7 (1983):17.

FESPACO, summary of address at opening ceremony.

3401.  Soleil.  Ouverture du 7ème festival panafricain à Ouagadougou. <u>Le Soleil</u> 3254(1981):13.

3402.  Soleil.  Première ce soir de "Karim".  Le Soleil May 26 (1971):3.
        (R)

3403.  Soleil.  Pour Ousmane Sembène Munich a commencé hier à Dakar.  Le
        Soleil July 6 (1972):2.

        Film festivals Sembène has attended.  Reasons for making film on
        Olympics.

3404.  Soleil.  Pour son deuxième film Tidiane Aw est réalisateur mais
        aussi...actionnaire.  Le Soleil Sept. 24 (1973):7.  (R)

        Bracelet de bronze.

3405.  Soleil.  Projection de "Agit Rewo" de Ngaido Ba.  Le Soleil Oct.
        9 (1979):15.  (R)

3406.  Soleil.  Le réalisateur de "Amok" dénonce les distributeurs
        africains.  Le Soleil Oct. 27 (1982):17.

3407.  Soleil.  Les réalisateurs: "Les acteurs ne comprennent rien au
        cinéma."  Le Soleil Aug. 31 (1971):1, 3.

        Comments on actors and actresses by Yves Diagne, Djibril Diop and
        Sembène Ousmane.

3408.  Soleil.  Rétrospective africaine.  Le Soleil Mar. 29 (1985):21.

        Retrospective of 48 African films to be held in Dakar.

3409.  Soleil.  Rôle accru de SIDEC.  Le Soleil June 21-22 (1986):6.

3410.  Soleil.  Séminaires du livre et du film francophones à Dakar fin
        novembre.  Le Soleil Aug. 14-16 (1970):1,2.

        ACCT seminar to be held in Dakar.

3411.  Soleil.  Le Sénégal invité au festival du film de Berlin.  Le
        Soleil Nov. 15 (1982):9.

        Senegalese participation at Berlin film festival.

3412.  Soleil.  Silence...on ne toune plus pourquois?  Le Soleil
        3308(1981):2.

        Reasons for lack of film production in Senegal.

3413.  Soleil.  [Souleymane Cissé].  Le Soleil May 15 (1987):17.

        Cannes prize for Yeelen.  Brief comments on Baara and Finyé.

3414.  Soleil.  Tidiane Aw reçoit un prix pour le "Bracelet de bronze."
        Le Soleil Jan. 8 (1975):1.  (R)

Prize at Karlov Vary film festival.

3415. Soleil. Toujours Sembène. Le Soleil Dec. 31-Jan. 1 (1985-1986):12.

Sembène is always making films, but is there opportunity for young filmmakers?

3416. Soleil. 30 films à l'affiche du cinéma franco-africain. Le Soleil Feb. 13 (1979):1.

African films to be shown in Dakar.

3417. Soleil. 35e Festival de Cannes. Le Soleil May 15-16 (1982):19.

Films nominated for prizes.

3418. Soleil. Le troisième festival panafricain des cinéastes se tiendra à Dar-es-Salaam déclare Ababacar Samb à l'A.P.S. Le Soleil Oct. 8 (1973):7.

Planned meeting of FEPACI in Dar es Salaam.

3419. Soleil. "Xala" et "Mercedès". Le Soleil Feb. 19 (1974):2.

Use of Mercedes car in Xala.

3420. Soleil. "Xala" sur les écrans de Washington. Le Soleil Dec. 23 (1976):7.

Xala shown in U.S.A.

3421. Somé, Sylvestre. L'après FESPACO 1981. Carrefour Africain 712-713(1981):13-14.

3422. Somé, Sylvestre. 9ème FESPACO: cinéma et libération des peuples. Carrefour Africain 873(1985):20-21.

3423. Somé, X.S. Le MBRAP organise des jeux concours. Sidwaya Feb. 16 (1987):11.

Anti-apartheid activities at FESPACO.

3424. Sonuga, Gbenga. 'From Alpha to Black Goddess', film-maker in search of an idiom. New Culture 1,5(1979):37-42.

Discussion of Ola Balogun's films.

3425. Sougue, Elisabeth. 10è FESPACO. Entretien avec le camarde Yonli Alain responsable de la commission accueil. 350 invités attendus. Sidwaya Jan. 15 (1987):4; Jan. 16 (1987):5. (I)

Travel and housing arrangements for FESPACO invited guests. Same article printed twice.

3426. Souillac, Pierre. De la nécessaire éducation du public. Le Soleil May 17 (1975):5. (R)

Djibril Diop, Touki Bouki.

3427. Souillac, Pierre. "Emitai" vu par un vieil Européen. Le Soleil Feb. 1 (1972):2. (R)

3428. Souillac, Pierre. Lettre ouverte de M. Dupont à O. Sembène. Le Soleil Apr. 10 (1975):2. (R)

Xala.

3429. Soulié, Christophe. Med Hondo: "En France nous sommes exclus." Croissance des jeunes nations 290(1987):34-35. (I)

3430. Source-In-Press. Sarraounia, exemple de cinéma national africain. Sidwaya Apr. 13 (1987):9. (R)

3431. Sourwema, Issaka. FESPACO 87, la fête est finie. Sidwaya Mar. 2 (1987):10.

Overview and closing address.

3432. Souza, Koami. Sidiki Bakaba: le cinéma africain se trouve dans un cercle vicieux. Bingo 402(1986):40-42. (I)

Bakaba discusses source of his success as actor and problems with West African film.

3433. Sow, B. Le Sénégal à la recherche du second souffle. Bingo 329(1980):48.

Film production.

3434. Sow, Bachir el. "Le FEPACI n'est pas l'attachée de presse des JCC." Zone 2 95(1980):21. (I)

Mahama Johnson Traoré discusses FEPACI activities.

3435. Sow, Bachir el. Kodjo Conçalvès "Faire du film un outil de recherche." Zone 2 91(1980):15.

Togolese journalist discusses possibilities of super 8 film and need for educational films.

3436. Sow, Bachir el. Option pour la coopération sud-sud dans la production de films. Le Soleil Mar. 15 (1985):13. (I)

Mahama Johnson Traoré discusses SNPC activities and problems of non-Senegalese who want to make films in Senegal.

3437. Sow, Bachir el. Seydina Wade "Je veux etre libre." Zone 2 229(1984):17.

Senegalese actor discusses his work.

3438. Sow, Dieudonné A.A. Un film par soirée: la fin des navets? L'Essor May 17-18 (1979):8.

Film distribution in Mali.

3439. Sow, Dieudonné A.A. Ouverture de l'exposition "Trois photo-romans." L'Essor June 27-28 (1981):3.

Film training program by CNPC and Centre Français in Mali.

SOW, E.B. See SOW, BACHIR EL.

3440. Sow, Sadio Lamine. Le fétiche et le bistouri. Jeune Afrique 1162(1983):68-69. (R)

Mustapha Diop, Médecin de Gafiré.

3441. Spass, Lieve. Female domestic labor and Third World politics in La Noire de. Jump Cut 27(1982):26-27; in Journey Across Three Continents. Renee Tajima, ed. New York: Third World Newsreel, 1985. pp. 33-36.

3442. Special correspondent. Cinema in Africa. Africa (London) 42(1975):54-56.

Films shown at J.C.C. and filmmakers in attendance; activities of FEPACI; nationalization of theaters in Burkina Faso.

3443. Springer, Claudia. Black women filmmakers. Jump Cut 29(1984):34-37.

Ruby Bell-Gam, My Child, Their Child; Ijeoma Iloputaife, African Woman USA; and Anne Ngu, Little Ones.

3444. Srour, Heiny. Coup d'oeil critique sur le cinéma africain. Africasia 2(1969):51-52.

African films at Mannheim film festival.

3445. Ssali, Ndugu Mike. Apartheid and cinema. UFAHAMU 13, 1(1983):105-133.

Film production and projection in South Africa.

3446. Stam, Robert. The Fall (A Queda), in Magill's Survey of Cinema, Foreign Language Films. Frank N. Magill, ed. Englewood Cliffs, N.J.: Salem Press, 1985. pp. 1039-1041. (R)

3447. Stam, Robert. Formal innovation and radical critique. Jump Cut

22(1980):20-21. (R)

Ruy Guerra, A queda.

3448.  Standa, E.M.  The role of film in African development.  Busara 6,2(1974):73-77.

Role of film to promote and strengthen national unity and possible dysfunctions.

3449.  Statt, Bruno.  Ceddo de Sembène Ousmane.  Revue africaine de communication 1(1981):36-42. (I)

Article based on transcript of 1977 interview in which Sembène discusses Ceddo and films as vehicles of ideology.

3450.  Stern, Yvan.  L'âme des peuples qu'on assasine.  Unir Cinéma 17(1985):30-31.

Importance of film in Third World and infrastructural problems.

3451.  Stern, Yvan.  Difficile rentabilité.  Unir Cinéma 136(1987):9-10.

Problems in functioning of CIDC.

3452.  Stern, Yvan.  Festival de films du Tiers-Monde.  Unir Cinéma 23-24(1986):26-29.

3453.  Stern, Yvan.  A festival of Third World films favourizes dialogue between cultures.  OCIC Info 7,1(1986):14.

Gaston Kaboré, Wend Kuuni wins prize at film festival in Switzerland.

3454.  Stern, Yvan.  Nigeria: le cinéma féérique.  Unir Cinéma 136(1987):13.

Comedy and dreams in Nigerian films.  Excerpt from article in Ciné Feuilles 115.

3455.  Stern, Yvan.  Yeelen (La lumière).  Unir Cinéma 136(1987):21-22. (R)

3456.  Sterritt, David.  Where are those '60s radicals?  Christian Science Monitor Nov. 20 (1975):11. (R)

Sembène Ousmane, Xala.

3457.  Stuart, Jay.  'White' cinemas will fade out in South Africa. Variety 323,4(1986):1,98.

Theater segregation in South Africa.

3458.  Suchet, Simone.  Hommage au FESPACO.  2 écrans 47-48(1982):10.

Films by Moustapha Alassane, Souleymane Cissé and Fadika Kramo-Lanciné.

3459.   Sultan, René.   "Pousse-Pousse" film de Daniel Kamuwa. (sic) L'Union 209(1976):4. (R)

3460.   Sultan, René.   "Xala"...ou les formes de l'impuissance.   L'Union 193(1976):4. (R)

3461.   Sumo, Honoré de.   Genèse et avenir du cinéma camerounais. Afrique Littéraire et Artistique 39(1976):59-62.

        History from colonial period.   Films made in 1960s and early 1970s.   Infrastructure for production and distribution.

3462.   Sunday Concord.   Nigeria launches a 'Jihad' movie.   Sunday Concord 4, 153(1984):Mag xi. (R)

3463.   Sunday Mail.   'Cinema sows seeds of hope.' Sunday Mail (Harare) June 2 (1985):3.

        Film festival in Zimbabwe to raise money for local filmmakers.

3464.   Sunday Mail.   Film-maker wins U.S. scholarship.   Sunday Mail (Harare) June 30 (1985):5.

        Albert Chimedza, first Zimbabwean to win Fulbright fellowship for film.

3465.   Sunday Mail.   Film message is family planning.   Sunday Mail (Harare) Dec. 15 (1985):14.

        Documentary by Zimbabwe National Family Planning Council.

3466.   Sunday Mail.   Film that explores racial attitudes in changing times.   Sunday Mail (Harare) Apr. 7 (1985):9. (R)

        Albert Chimedza, Chameleon.

3467.   Sunday Mail.   'Harare can be new film hub.' Sunday Mail (Harare) June 9 (1985):3.

        Zimbabwe can be center for SADCC filmmaking.

3468.   Sunday Mail.   Hopes for birth of local film industry.   Sunday Mail (Harare) Mar. 17 (1985):9.

        Development of infrastructure in Zimbabwe.

3469.   Sunday Mail.   Hundreds turn out for film premiere.   Sunday Mail (Harare) Jan. 13 (1985):1. (R)

        Ola Balogun, Ija Ominira.

3470. Sunday Mail. Mines film is his big break. Sunday Mail (Harare)
March 17 (1985):11.

Film on mining by Alfregio Muronda.

3471. Sunday Mail. Minister: we're out to develop industry. Sunday
Mail (Harare) Sept. 1 (1985):9.

Foreign film companies that make films in Zimbabwe must help
local film development.

3472. Sunday Mail Reporter. Film training aids discussed. Sunday Mail
(Harare) Dec. 1 (1985):4.

Support for documentary filmmaking in Zimbabwe.

3473. Sunday Mail Reporter. Soweto film set for December. Sunday Mail
(Harare) Sept. 20 (1987):3.

Scenes from Michael Raeburn, Soweto, to be made in Zimbabwe.

3474. Sunday Mail Reporter. State has role in film-making says
director. Sunday Mail (Harare) Oct. 27 (1985):10.

Government support for filmmaking in Zimbabwe.

3475. Sunday Mail Reporter. 'Struggle' film date set - Shamuyarira.
Sunday Mail (Harare) Dec. 29 (1985):1.

Charles Ndlovu, Struggle for Zimbabwe to be completed in 1987.

3476. Sunday Mail Reporter. Two American films taken off screens.
Sunday Mail (Harare) Oct. 13 (1985):1.

Censorship in Zimbabwe.

3477. Sunjata. Dikongué Pipa: un cinéma de dénonciation. Sunjata
16(1979):36-37. (I)

Discussion of his film training and ideology, relationship of
theater and film, Prix de la liberté and plans for La cicatrice.

3478. Sunjata. Marie-Thérèse Badjel: "le cinéma n'est pas une
aventure." Sunjata 16(1979):37. (I)

Camerounian actress discusses her film career and role in Prix de
la liberté.

3479. Suret-Canale, Jean. Sarraounia un film de Med Hondo.
Aujourd'hui l'Afrique 33(1986):27-28. (R)

3480. Sweet, Louise. Finyé (The Wind). Monthly Film Bulletin
52(1985):377-378. (R)

3481. Sy, Moulaye Abdoul Aziz. Lecture du film: "Touki-Bouki" de Djibril M. Diop. Unir Cinéma 16(1985):27-29; 18(1985):14-15. (R)

3482. Sy, Moulaye Abdoul Aziz. Les nationalisations. Waraango 4(1983):8,14.

Theaters nationalized in Burkina Faso and Mali.

3483. Sy, Moulaye Abdoul Aziz. Réflexion critique sur le cinéma africain. Waraango 4(1983):6-8.

Distribution. Adaptations of literature in film.

3484. Sy, Sidi Abd Allah. Autour d'un festival. Afrique Nouvelle 1302(1974):24-25.

African films at Tashkent film festival.

3485. Sylla, Papa Mor. "Ceddo" prochain film de Ousmane Sembène. Le Soleil June 4 (1975):4.

3486. Taal, Lune. Du théâtre au cinéma "Bac ou mariage" de Tam-Sir Niane sera tourne by Jean Rouch. Le Soleil Feb. 14-15 (1987):11.

Jean Rouch to make film of Senegalese play with Senegalese actors, will be a Senegalese/French coproduction.

3487. Table ronde Chartres. Table ronde des Africains. Jeune Cinéma 157(1984):8-12. (I)

Films shown at Chartres film festival. Short interviews with Souleymane Cissé and Arthur Si Bita about role of film in Africa and film production.

3488. Taconet, Catherine. Wend Kuuni de Gaston Kaboré. Cinéma 304(1984):57. (R)

3489. Tahar, Aicha. La diffusion du film africain en Europe: quelques espoirs... Agecop Liaison 83(1985):19-22.

Discussion of film distribution, role of CIDC at Amiens film festival.

3490. Tahar, Aicha. Khouribga: à la découverte du cinéma africain. Agecop Liaison 73(1983):34-37.

Report on second meeting on film in Morocco.

3491. Tahar, Aicha. Images africaines et arabes. Agecop Liaison 81(1985):32-37. (R)

Désiré Ecaré, Visages de femmes.

3492. Tahar, Aicha. Les journées cinématographiques de Carthage. L'heure des bilans. <u>Agecop Liaison</u> 78(1984):11-14.

J.C.C.

3493. Tahar, Aicha. 9e FESPACO: une fête populaire. <u>Agecop Liaison</u> 80(1985):20.

3494. Tahar, Aicha. 3e Congrès de la FEPACI un nouveau depart. <u>Agecop Liaison</u> 80(1985):21-22.

3495. Taifour, Kaba. L'avis d'un cinéaste ivoirien: T. Bossory (sic). <u>Eburnea</u> 17(1968):15.

Views on film of Timité Bassori.

3496. Taifour, Kaba. "Rêve d'un artiste," de Henri Duparc. <u>Eburnea</u> 19(1968):14-17. (I)

Discussion of <u>Mouna</u>.

3497. Tains, S. Le soleil noir. <u>Afrique Nouvelle</u> 1165(1969):15.

Ambroise Mbia, Camerounian actor's role in Russian produced film.

3498. Tajima, Renee. A selected filmography of films from Africa and the black diaspora, in <u>Journey Across Three Continents</u>. Renee Tajima, ed. New York: Third World Newsreel, 1985. pp. 63-66.

56 films listed by country.

3499. Tamo, Claude. L'Histoire d'un peuple. <u>Bingo</u> 407(1986):50. (I)

Med Hondo discusses the production of <u>Sarraounia</u>.

3500. Tamo, Claude. Kitia Touré: il faut savoir cibler. <u>Bingo</u> 392(1985):56-57. (I)

3501. Tamo, Claude. La passionné oublié. <u>Bingo</u> 393(1985):66-67. (I)

Jean-Baptiste Tiémélé, Côte d'Ivoire actor discusses his film and theater roles.

3502. Tapsoba, Clément. Aminata Zouré, première maquilleuse burkinabé de cinéma. <u>Sidwaya</u> Feb. 27 (1987):10. (I)

Burkinabe costumer discusses films she's worked on and problems of creating historical costumes.

3503. Tapsoba, Clément. Bientôt un structure permanante pour un success de la 11ème edition. <u>Sidwaya</u> Mar. 5 (1987):4.

President Sankara's comments on past success and future needs of FESPACO.

3504. Tapsoba, Clément. "Black Mic-Mac" sur nos écrans, une image dévalorisante du noir. Sidwaya Feb. 4 (1987):6. (R)

Reasons Sidiki Bakaba refused to act in Black Mic Mac.

3505. Tapsoba, Clément. Le Burkina sur la co-production. Afrique Nouvelle 1960(1987):16-17.

Coproduction of films supported by Burkinabe government.

3506. Tapsoba, Clément. Une cascade prix. Sidwaya Feb. 26 (1987):7.

FESPACO prizes and film jury.

3507. Tapsoba, Clément. Ce qu'en pense le public. Carrefour Africain 766(1983):16.

Audience views of films shown at FESPACO.

3508. Tapsoba, Clément. "Le choix" un regard optimiste sur les problemes de développement. Sidwaya Feb. 25 (1987):16. (R)

Idrissa Ouédraogo, Yam Daabo.

3509. Tapsoba, Clément. CIDC-CIPROFILM grands maux grands remèdes. Carrefour Africain 871(1985):24-26.

3510. Tapsoba, Clément. CIDC et CIPROFILM, la conférence de la dernière chance. Carrefour Africain 975(1987):25-26.

Crisis in functioning of both CIDC and CIPROFILM, suggested solutions.

3511. Tapsoba, Clément. Les cinéastes à la bataille du rail. Sidwaya Mar. 1 (1985):i,iii. (I)

Sidiki Bakaba and Cheick Oumar Sissoko comment on symbolism of FESPACO participation in Burkinabe battle of the rail.

3512. Tapsoba, Clément. Cinéma et libération des peuples. Carrefour Africain 871(1985):16-17.

FESPACO theme.

3513. Tapsoba, Clément. Le cinéma, un instrument de développement. Carrefour Africain 963(1986):12.

UCOA seminar on film production and development held in Dakar.

3514. Tapsoba, Clément. Concilier le public africain et son cinéma. Carrefour Africain 767(1963):19-20.

FESPACO seminar on African film and its audience.

3515. Tapsoba, Clément. La co-production, seule voie viable. Carrefour Africain 975(1987):12-17.

Improved production quality of FESPACO films, importance of coproduction of films in recent years.

3516. Tapsoba, Clément. D'Alger à Ouagadougou: temps difficiles pour les cinémas arabe et africain. Carrefour Africain 870(1985):22-23.

FEPACI activities.

3517. Tapsoba, Clément. Deux prix de l'UNICEF. Sidwaya Feb. 16 (1987):11.

FESPACO prizes for films for children, youth and women; jury composed of women and children.

3518. Tapsoba, Clément. 10ème FESPACO: Conference de presse du Président du Faso. "Le FESPACO est avant tout l'affaire des cinéastes..." Sidwaya Mar. 3 (1987):1-3.

President Sankara's comments on importance of film in Africa and film activities in Burkina Faso.

3519. Tapsoba, Clément. Emmanuel Sanou, cinéaste burkinabé, réalisateur de "Doba" ou "Heritage perdu." Sidwaya Mar. 1 (1985):iii. (I)

3520. Tapsoba, Clément. FEPACI, un an après, credibilité assurée. Carrefour Africain 939(1986):14-18.

3521. Tapsoba, Clément. FESPACO 85 un succes politique les objectifs ont ete largement atteints. Carrefour Africain 873(1985):18-19.

3522. Tapsoba, Clément. FESPACO 87: les grandes innovations. Carrefour Africain 971(1987):8-10.

3523. Tapsoba, Clément. FESPACO 87 plus de 150 films attendus. Sidwaya Jan. 21 (1987):11.

3524. Tapsoba, Clément. FESPACO 87 un enjeu ne laisse plus indifferent. Carrefour Africain 978(1987):22-25.

3525. Tapsoba, Clément. Les films burkinabé selectionnes pour la compétition. Sidwaya Feb. 20 (1987):9.

Burkinabe films in competition at FESPACO.

3526. Tapsoba, Clément. 8ème edition du FESPACO. La Haute-Volta en sort auréolée. Carrefour Africain 766(1983):13-15.

3527. Tapsoba, Clément. 8ème FESPACO pari pour Cinafric. Carrefour

Africain 765(1983):25-27. (I)

Moustapha Ky discusses activities of CINAFRIC.

3528. Tapsoba, Clément. Idrissa Ouédraogo: les cinéastes africains doivent être modestes. Carrefour Africain 874(1985):26-28. (I)

3529. Tapsoba, Clément. Ils ont dit... Sidwaya Feb. 26 (1987):10.

FESPACO, Sembène's presence since 1969, UCOA and production problems.

3530. Tapsoba, Clément. Les jeunes comediennes voltaique du cinéma. Carrefour Africain 765(1983):27-28. (I)

Interview with actors and actresses: Marie-Claire Coeffé, Djénéba Dao, Sali Samaké and Simone Tapsoba.

3531. Tapsoba, Clément. Un lieu de rencontre multi-culturel à l'occasion du FESPACO. Sidwaya Feb. 20 (1987):11.

Cultural activities at FESPACO.

3532. Tapsoba, Clément. 9ème journees cinématographiques de Carthage (22-30 Octobre). Carrefour Africain 753(1982):23.

Gaston Kaboré, Wend Kuuni shown at J.C.C.

3533. Tapsoba, Clément. Pour l'amitie entre les peuples. Sidwaya Feb. 27 (1985):ii.

Summary of comments made about FESPACO by Jean Pierre Garcia and Philippe Sawadogo.

3534. Tapsoba, Clément. Le président du Faso rencontre les organisateurs appel à la courtoisie dans la dignité. Sidwaya Feb. 6 (1987):11.

Plans for FESPACO.

3535. Tapsoba, Clément. Quel avenir pour le cinéma africain? Beaucoup reste a faire. Carrefour Africain 765(1983):24-25.

FESPACO.

3536. Tapsoba, Clément. Samori Touré bientôt immortalisé à l'écran par Sembène Ousmane. Carrefour Africain 853(1984):22.

Sembène Ousmane to make Samory.

3537. Tapsoba, Clément. Sidiki Bakaba, acteur de cinéma: un homme en plusieurs morceaux. Carrefour Africain 743(1982):24-25.

3538. Tapsoba, Clément. Sidiki Bakaba, comedien de cinéma. Carrefour

Africain 966(1986):18-21. (I)

Discussion of role in Désébagato, roles he is willing to play, training for actors and themes of films.

3539.  Tapsoba, Clément.  Souleymane Cissé: nous, cinéastes et africains, ne devons pas fuir nos responsabilités.  Carrefour Africain 766(1983):18-19. (I)

3540.  Tapsoba, Clément.  "Suicide" (sic) de J.C. Thuilen, (sic) l'autre face cachée du vécu quotidien des africains en Europe.  Sidwaya Mar. 1 (1985):i. (R)

3541.  Tapsoba, Clément.  Vers la fin du mégotage?  Carrefour Africain 934(1986):24-27.

New Burkinabe films, Idrissa Ouédraogo, Yam Daabo, and Emmanuel Sanou, Désébagato.  Factors that inhibit film development.

3542.  Tapsoba, Clément and M. Etienne Kaboré.  Les nouvelles actrices du cinéma burkinabé.  Sidwaya Feb. 27 (1987):9. (I)

Interview with Miriam Yago.  Information about roles played by Djénéba Dao, Awa Guiro, Claire Koeffe and Simone Tapsoba.

3543.  Tapsoba, Clément and Hamado Nana.  Entretien Med Hondo.  Carrefour Africain 980(1987):22-23. (I)

Problems in making Sarraounia.  Need for historical films.

3544.  Tarbagdo, Sita.  A la découverte du cinéaste Bernard Menyo.  Sidwaya Feb. 27 (1985):i,iii. (I)

Burundian filmmaker resident in Ghana discusses Whose Fault?

3545.  Tarbagdo, Sita.  Au revoir et au rendez-vous prochain.  Sidwaya Mar. 4 (1985):i.

FESPACO.

3546.  Tarbagdo, Sita.  "Le Choix" d'Idrissa Ouédraogo, prix du CICT.  Sidwaya May 27 (1987):5. (R)

Yam Daabo receives prize at Cannes film festival.

3547.  Tarbagdo, Sita.  CIDC-CIPROFILMS (sic) un conseil d'administration salvateur? Sidwaya Feb. 11 (1985):4.

3548.  Tarbagdo, Sita.  Colloque: "Littérature et cinéma africains" deux termes d'un même combat.  Sidwaya Feb. 19 (1985):5.

Report on FESPACO colloquium.

3549.  Tarbagdo, Sita.  Colloque littérature et cinéma africains, quel mariage? <u>Sidwaya</u> Feb. 25 (1985):iii.

Report on FESPACO colloquium includes list of films of African literature.

3550. Tarbagdo, Sita. Concours d'affiche au FESPACO "85". <u>Sidwaya</u> Sept. 26 (1984):4.

CIPROFILM meeting at FESPACO. ICA to offer prize.

3551. Tarbagdo, Sita. Conférence des ministres des pays membres du CIDC-CIPROFILM haro sur les assassins. <u>Sidwaya</u> Feb. 18 (1985):7.

3552. Tarbagdo, Sita. Désiré Ecaré a propos de son film "Visages de Femmes" "C'est n'est pas la scene d'amour qui a attiré le monde..." <u>Sidwaya</u> Mar. 12 (1987):11. (I)

Reasons why <u>Visages de femmes</u> attracts large audiences, use of music in film, purpose of film.

3553. Tarbagdo, Sita. Faire du CIDC-CIPROFILM un instrument efficace et viable. <u>Sidwaya</u> Feb. 18 (1985):6.

Report on conference at FESPACO includes excerpts from official communique and statement by Watamou Lamien on role of CIDC.

3554. Tarbagdo, Sita. "Le FESPACO c'est quoi ça..." <u>Sidwaya</u> Feb. 18 (1985):6.

International impact of FESPACO.

3555. Tarbagdo, Sita. "Le FESPACO 85, une grande victoire des peuples africains" déclare le Dr. Manthia Diawara de l'Université de Californie. <u>Sidwaya</u> Mar. 12 (1985):4. (I)

3556. Tarbagdo, Sita. FESPACO le prix ICA du meilleur film documentaire. <u>Sidwaya</u> Sept. 27 (1984):6.

3557. Tarbagdo, Sita. Festival de Cannes. Les lauréats. <u>Sidwaya</u> May 22 (1987):12.

3558. Tarbagdo, Sita. Festival panafricain du cinéma de Ouagadougou (FESPACO) un atout considérable pour notre pays. <u>Sidwaya</u> Jan. 10 (1985):5. (I)

Philippe Sawadogo discusses purposes of FESPACO, why Burkina Faso supports it and value to Burkina.

3559. Tarbagdo, Sita. La fièvre du "Zouk Machine." <u>Sidwaya</u> Feb. 23 (1987):10.

Musical performances at FESPACO.

3560. Tarbagdo, Sita. Fin de séminaire sur la presse, cinéma et revolution. *Sidwaya* Feb. 6 (1985):3, 6.

Activities of CIDC, CIPROFILM and INAFEC; text of primary motions included.

3561. Tarbagdo, Sita. Ils n'ont pas deçu. *Sidwaya* Mar. 2 (1987):8.

Cultural performance at FESPACO.

3562. Tarbagdo, Sita. L'Institute ferme ses portes après dix ans d'existence. *Sidwaya* June 29 (1987):9.

Review of 10 years of INAFEC activities.

3563. Tarbagdo, Sita. Le message de l'ONU a la FEPACI. *Sidwaya* Feb. 20 (1985):3.

Address to FEPACI congress by Marcel Diouf on issues to be considered.

3564. Tarbagdo, Sita. La renaissance d'une institution. *Sidwaya* Feb. 20 (1985):3.

Review of FEPACI activities since 1970 and report on opening session of third congress.

3565. Tarbagdo, Sita. Séminaire national sur les médias "Cinéma presse et revolution." *Sidwaya* Feb. 4 (1985):7.

Discussion by Fidélè Toé of need to promote press and film.

3566. Tarbagdo, Sita. "Tradition orale et nouveau média" un nouveau départ. *Sidwaya* Feb. 27 (1987):6.

Report on FESPACO colloquium on oral tradition and the new media.

3567. Tarbagdo, Sita. Les Woya à l'ouverture. *Sidwaya* Feb. 18 (1987):11.

Musical performance at FESPACO.

3568. Tarbagdo, Sita, Hubert Pare and J.C. Meda. Que pense les cinéastes présents au congrès de la FEPACI? *Sidwaya* Feb. 21 (1985):6. (I)

Filmmakers express views of FEPACI: Souleymane Cissé, Abdoul Karim, Kouam, Simao Maki Makiadi and Sembène Ousmane.

3569. Tarbagdo, Sita and Zakaria Yeye. Colloque: tradition orale et nouveau média, richesses fécondes. *Carrefour Africain* 977(1987):15-17.

Report on FESPACO colloquium on oral tradition and the new media.

3570.  Tarratt, Margaret.    The Money Order.    <u>Films</u> <u>and</u> <u>Filming</u>
       20,4(1974):45,48. (R)

       Sembène Ousmane, <u>Mandabi</u>.

3571.  Taylor, Clyde.    Africa, in <u>World</u> <u>Cinema</u> <u>since</u> <u>1945</u>.    William
       Luhr, ed. New York: Ungar, 1987. pp. 1-21.

       History from colonial period, infrastructural problems, themes of
       films by internationally known filmmakers.

3572.  Taylor, Clyde.    Africa, the last cinema, in <u>Journey</u> <u>Across</u> <u>Three</u>
       <u>Continents</u>.    Renee Tajima, ed. New York: Third World Newsreel,
       1985. pp. 50-58.

       Relation of film to politics, infrastructural problems and
       attempted solutions, major themes of films by internationally
       known filmmakers.

3573.  Taylor, Clyde.    Film reborn in Mozambique.    <u>Jump</u> <u>Cut</u>
       28(1983):30-31. (I)

       Pedro Pimenta discusses filmmaking in Mocambique.

3574.  Taylor, Clyde.    Haile Gerima: firestealer.    <u>Africa</u> <u>Now</u>
       32(1983):81-82.

       Short review of Gerima's films.

3575.  Taylor, Clyde.    Two women, in <u>Journey</u> <u>Across</u> <u>Three</u> <u>Continents</u>.
       Renee Tajima, ed. New York: Third World Newsreel, 1985. pp.
       28-31. (R)

       Comparison of heroines in Sembène Ousmane, <u>La</u> <u>noire</u> <u>de</u> and Julia
       Dash, <u>Illusions</u>.

3576.  Taylor, Elyseo J.    Film and social change in Africa south of the
       Sahara.    <u>American</u> <u>Behavioral</u> <u>Scientist</u> 17,3(1974):424-438.

       Brief mention of films by African filmmakers in discussion of
       films about Sub-Saharan Africa.

3577.  Tchernova, G.    Le cinéma sénégalais vu par les soviétiques. <u>Dakar</u>
       <u>Matin</u> Sept. 15 (1967):3.

       Ababacar Samb, <u>Et</u> <u>la</u> <u>neige</u> <u>n'était</u> <u>plus</u> and Sembène Ousmane, <u>La</u>
       <u>noire</u> <u>de</u>.

3578.  Tchibinda, Claude Abdon.    Le film nigérian "Ajani Ogun" a drainé
       les foules au Komo. <u>L'Union</u> July 16 (1978):4. (R)

3579.  Tempo.    No cinema, o factor decisivo é o homem.    <u>Tempo</u>
       513(1980):53-55. (I)

Cuban filmmakers discuss Mocambiquan/Cuban cooperation in film production.

3580. Tempo. Que cinema? <u>Tempo</u> 471(1979):34-38.

Problems of film distribution.

3581. Tempo. Sahara agonia de um rei fantoche. <u>Tempo</u> 567(1981):54-55. (R)

Camilo de Sousa, <u>Sahara agonia de um rei fantoche</u>.

*3582. Tempo. "Sambizanga" - a repressao colonial. <u>Tempo</u> 217(1974):38-43. (I)

Luandino Vieira discusses film of his novel, <u>A vida verdadeira de Domingos Xavier</u>.

3583. Tenaille, Frank. Samory Toure à l'écran. <u>Afrique Nouvelle</u> 1939(1986):18-19.

Budget, historical sources used in <u>Samory</u> and background on Sembène's filmmaking.

3584. Terrell, Angela. 'No more Tarzan and Jane.' <u>Washington Post</u> June 16 (1972):B13. (R)

Francis Oladele, <u>Kongi's Harvest</u>.

3585. Terres, Dominique. Mozambique: communiquer en "Super 8". <u>Afrique-Asie</u> 200(1979):59.

Filmmaking in Maputo.

3586. Tessier, Danièle. Oumarou Ganda la nostalgie d'un poète. <u>Actuel développement</u> 40(1981):45-46.

Biographical background, experience with Jean Rouch and other French filmmakers, films he made.

3587. Tessier, Max. A nous deux, France. <u>Cinéma 70</u> 147(1970):21-22. (R)

3588. Tesson, Charles. Critique- "Yeelen." <u>Unir Cinéma</u> 137(1987):25-26. (R)

Excerpt from No. 3589.

3589. Tesson, Charles. Genèse. <u>Cahiers du Cinéma</u> 397(1987):10. (R)

Souleymane Cissé, <u>Yeelen</u>.

3590. Tesson, Charles. Lorsque l'enfant parle. <u>Cahiers du Cinéma</u> 358(1984):44-45. (R)

Gaston Kaboré, Wend Kuuni.

3591. Tetteh-Lartey, Alex. Lessons from the villains. New African 129(1978):133. (R)

Eddie Ugbomah, The Rise and Fall of Dr. Oyenusi.

3592. Thepe, Charles. Few African documentaries at the Leipzig Festival. Africa Now 10(1982):35.

3593. Thiam, Bebeč. Sidiki Bakaba a Bako. Ivoire Dimanche 416(1979):22-23.

3594. Thiam, Momar. Carthage ou un certain refus des valeurs africaines. Le Soleil Nov. 13 (1974):4.

Reply to No. 1209 on view of J.C.C.

3595. Thiam, Momar. "Sa Dagga" Momar Thiam aime son film. Zone 2 225(1983):18. (R)

3596. Thiombiana, D. Louis. FESPACO une volonte voltaique. L'Observateur Nov. 16 (1978):9-10.

3597. Thirard, Paul. La plage du désir. Cinéma 64 90(1964):123-124. (R)

Ruy Guerra, Os Cafajestes.

3598. Thirard, Paul-Louis. Sur "La femme au couteau." Positif 109(1969):44-47. (I)

Timité Bassori discusses his film.

3599. Thomas, Kevin. African film's exciting evolution. Los Angeles Times Aug. 12 (1984):C21-22.

Short history.

3600. Thomas, Kevin. 'Erendira': fable of truth and illusion. Los Angeles Times June 9 (1984):V8. (R)

3601. Thoraval, Yves. Carthage a vingt ans! Cinéma 377(1986):9.

J.C.C. being held despite reduced budget.

3602. Thoraval, Yves. Le cinéma en Afrique du Sud. CinémAction 26(1983):44-47.

Comparison of South African films made for blacks and whites.

3603. Tiao, Luc Adolphe. A bâtons rompus avec Sembène Ousmane. Carrefour Africain 710-711(1981):7-8. (I)

3604. Tiao, Luc Adolphe. Brahim Babai président sortant de la FEPACI explique. Sidwaya Feb. 21 (1985):6. (I)

3605. Tiao, Luc Adolphe. Le C.A.C. mis en cause. Sidwaya Feb. 22 (1985):4.

CAC and FEPACI are complimentary, not in competition.

3606. Tiao, Luc Adolphe. Distribution: malgré le goulot d'étranglement. Carrefour Africain 710-711(1984):5.

3607. Tiao, Luc Adolphe. Med Hondo: Le cinéma est une matière première de civilisation. Carrefour Africain 710-711(1981):6. (I)

3608. Tiao, Luc Adolphe. Reflexion Fespaco: Autre arme de la liberation des peuples. Sidwaya Mar. 4 (1985):i.

3609. Tiao, Luc Adolphe. 11lème congrès FEPACI: redynamiser une arme de combat du cinéma africain. Carrefour Africain 870(1985):19-20.

3610. Tiao, Luc Adolphe. La victoire des peuples africains. Sidwaya Mar. 1 (1985):iii.

Need to revive FEPACI and restore confidence in it.

3611. Tiao, Luc Adolphe and Sylvestre Somé. CINAFRIC: une grande première. Carrefour Africain 710-711(1981):4,6.

3612. Tiao, Luc Adolphe, Sylvestre Somé and Gaston Kaboré. Le CIDC est dans sa phase opérationnelle. Carrefour Africain 710-711(1981):5-6. (I)

Inoussa Ousseini discusses CIDC.

3613. Tiéfing. En avant-première. Tiefing a vu "Le Retour de Tiéman." L'Essor Sept. 19 (1970):3. (R)

3614. Tiéfing. Existe-t-il un cinéma malien? L'Essor 7502(1976):4; 7507(1976):4.

Themes of Malian films.

3615. Tiéfing. Les salles de cinéma privées sont fermées. L'Essor Jan. 5 (1971):1,4.

Theaters nationalized in Mali.

3616. Tilly, Beverley. Film industry promising in Zimbabwe. Spotlight on Zimbabwe 6,1(1986?):21-23.

Zimbabweans will gain film production experience from working on feature films directed by non-Africans.

3617. Timité Bassori.   Un cinéma mort-né?   Présence Africaine
      49(1964):111-115.

      Problems in growth of African film industry.

3618. Timité Bassori.   Le festival du cinéma africain de Ouagadougou.
      Eburnea 35(1970):17.

      First FESPACO did not reach international stature.

3619. Timité Bassori and Antoine Kacou.   Ce que veulent les cinéastes
      ivoiriens.   I.D.   817(1986):38-40.

      Summary of document, "De la creation et de la réglementation de
      l'industrie cinématographique en Côte d'Ivoire."

3620. Timossi, Jorge.   Produire des films pour qui? demande Sembène
      Ousmane. Africasia 15(1970):48-49.

3621. Tine, Alioune.   Wolof ou français le choix de Sembène.   Notre
      Librarie 81(1985):43-54.

      Discussion of Sembène's fiction and films.

3622. Tinga.   Avec Irono ou irons-nous?   Intrus Feb. 23 (1987):2.   (R)

      François Sourou Okioh, Ironu.

3623. Tingo, Felisberto.   O cinema é para mim uma arma.   Tempo
      713(1984):46-47. (I)

      François Sourou Okioh discusses his work.

3624. Toe, Al. comp. FESPACO '87.   Trade Winds 5,4(1987):1-6.

      Aims of FESPACO, opening ceremony speeches, cultural displays and
      Paul Robeson award.

3625. Toï, R.   Débat autour du film "Visages de Femmes."   Ehuzu June 17
      (1987):8. (R)

3626. Tomaselli, Keyan.   The cinema in South Africa today.   Cinéaste
      15,2(1986):13-15.

      Films made for blacks; films made about blacks by filmmakers in
      exile.

3627. Tomaselli, Keyan G.   Class and ideology: reflections in South
      African cinema.   Critical Arts 1,1(1980):1-13.

      Themes of films made for blacks.

3628. Tomaselli, Keyan G. ed.   Ideological negotiations in 'black'

South African films. Unir Cinéma 10/11(1984):1-24.

3629. Tomaselli, Keyan G. Racism in South African cinema. Cinéaste 13,1(1983):12-15.

Black characters in films made by Afrikaners.

3630. Tomaselli, Keyan G. Seige mentality. Index on Censorship 10,4(1981):35-37.

Censorship of films in South Africa.

3631. Tomaselli, Keyan G. The teaching of film and television production in a Third World context: the case of South Africa. Journal of the University Film and Video Association 34,4(1982):3-12.

3632. Tomaselli, Keyan G. Visual images of South African communities. Johannesburg: University of Witwatersrand, African Studies Institute, 1984.

Seminar paper. Themes of 25 films discussed, two by Nana Mahomo included.

3633. Tomoloju, Ben. Africa's first movie star to be buried today. Guardian (Lagos) Oct. 18 (1985):1-2.

State funeral for Orlando Martins, Nigerian actor.

3634. Tomoloju, Ben. Baba Sala: 25 years of comedy. Guardian (Lagos) May 12 (1985):B1-B2.

Moses Olaiya as actor and filmmaker for television.

3635. Tomoloju, Ben. 'Mirror in the Sun' bows out for new documentary. Guardian (Lagos) Jan. 11 (1986):10. (R)

3636. Tomoloju, Ben. 'Mirror in the Sun' gets new producer. Guardian (Lagos) June 30 (1985):1,12.

Problems in production of Mirror in the Sun.

3637. Torcato, Maria de Lourdes. Um cinema em lingua portugesa. Domingo (Maputo) June 3 (1984):4.

Mocambiquan films produced since 1981 shown in Maputo, along with Angolan, Brazilian and Portuguese films.

3638. Torcato, Maria de Lourdes. 80 films moçambicanos em busca de espectador. Domingo (Maputo) Oct. 7 (1984):2.

Film festival in Mocambique of locally made documentaries.

3639. Touati, Lotfi. Clôture aujourd'hui des J.C.C. L'Action Nov. 25

(1978):18.

Films shown at J.C.C.

3640. Touati, Lotfi. J.C.C. 78: Le tanit d'or ne devra pas entre une fin de soi.. L'Action Nov. 16 (1978):9.

J.C.C. schedule, jury and list of previous prizewinning films.

3641. Touil, Hatem. Perugia, città aperta. Nigrizia 103,6 (1985):44.

Perugia film festival.

3642. Touré, A. A propos d'exploitation de films. Le Soleil June 8 (1977):3.

Discussion of error about SIDEC in interview reported in No. 1298.

3643. Touré, Al Hassane. Djibo Kâ installe le comité d'enterprise. Le Soleil Jan. 23 (1985):9.

Plans to reorganize SIDEC to make it more effective.

3644. Touré, Fabou. Nyamanton le leçon des ordures. Jamana 8 (1986):44-46. (R)

3645. Touré, H. "Nos films ne sont pas compétitifs" déplore Djibril Kouyaté. L'Essor Aug. 15(1975):1,4; Aug. 16-17 (1975):1,5. (I)

Discussion of Drapeau noir and Retour de Tiéman. Same article printed both days.

3646. Touré, H. Le souffle de la révolution sur l'écran du Cinéma Vog. Le Soleil July 27 (1974):2. (R)

Sarah Maldoror, Sambizanga.

3647. Touré, Kitia. Une dramaturgie dominée par une volonté de didactisme. CinémAction 26(1983):78-83.

Critique of kinds of action depicted in African films.

3648. Touré, Tapha. Momar mal compris? ...Le Soleil Apr. 14 (1975):2. (R)

Momar Thiam, Baks.

3649. Toureh, Fantah. Nature et décors. CinémAction 26(1983):131-135.

Depiction of space, including nature, buildings and structure interiors, in African films.

3650. Tournès, Andrée. A festival foisonnant, bonheur du spectateur, dilemme critique. <u>Jeune Cinéma</u> 182(1987):20.

Cannes film festival.

3651. Tournès, Andrée. Entretien avec Souleymane Cissé. <u>Jeune Cinéma</u> 119(1979):16-17. (I)

3652. Tournès, Andrée. Mannheim 1986. <u>Jeune Cinéma</u> 180(1987):31.

3653. Touti, Moumen. Etat du cinéma dans quelques pays arabo-africains. <u>SeptièmArt</u> 52(1984):33-36.

Films shown in African countries.

3654. Trabelsi, Hechmy. Cabascabo (Niger) de Oumarou Ganda. <u>L'Action</u> Oct. 16 (1970):7. (R)

3655. Trabelsi, Hechmy. Le cinéma arabo-africain à travers les discussions. <u>L'Action</u> Oct. 20 (1970):5.

Summary of discussions of films shown at J.C.C.

3656. Trabelsi, Hechmy. De "Nous sommes tous Fidayins" à "Diegue-Bi": les bonnes intentions prévalent. <u>L'Action</u> Oct. 18 (1970):5. (R)

3657. Trabelsi, Hechmy. Les discussions du Festival. <u>L'Action</u> Oct. 15 (1970):7.

Discussion of national production of films at J.C.C.

3658. Trabelsi, Hechmy. Interview de Oumara Ganda. <u>L'Action</u> Oct. 20 (1970):5. (I)

Discussion of source of inspiration for and making of <u>Cabascabo</u>.

3659. Trabelsi, Hechmy. Pourquois les journées cinématographiques de Carthage? <u>L'Action</u> Oct. 18 (1974):5.

Aims of J.C.C.

3660. Trabelsi, Hechmy. Qu'y a-t-il en marge du festival? <u>L'Action</u> Oct. 27 (1974):7.

Importance of J.C.C. discussions and round tables.

3661. Trabelsi, Hechmy. Retrospectives des Journées Cinématographiques de Carthage. <u>L'Action</u> Oct. 29 (1974):8; Nov. 3 (1974):12.

Summary of films shown at J.C.C.

3662. Traoré, Abdou. Nyamanton au dela du succès. <u>Jamana</u> 10(1986):43. (R)

Review discusses importance of film for Malian society.

3663.  Traoré, Biny.  Le cinéaste Ousmane Sembène a Biny Traoré "L'artiste a le devoir de donne a reflechir..." Sidwaya Mar. 25 (1987):5. (I)

1979 interview with Sembène about role of artist/filmmaker in society.

3664.  Traoré, Biny.  Cinéma africain et développement.  Peuples Noirs Peuples Africains 33(1983):51-62; L'Observateur Aug. 1 (1983); Aug. 2 (1983):6-7,12.

Films on social, economic and political development.  Limitations of film as an instrument of development.

3665.  Traoré, Biny.  Djéli ou le mariage impossible?  L'Observateur Feb. 27-28, Mar. 1 (1981):6-8. (R)

3666.  Traoré, Biny.  Entretien de Monsieur Biny Traoré avec le cinéaste Sembène Ousmane, in Aspects socio-politiques et techniques dans le roman africain d'aujourd'hui: l'exemple de Xala de Sembène Ousmane.  Ouagadougou: Centre National de la Recherche Scientifique et Technologique, 1981. pp. 169-172. (I)

3667.  Traoré, Biny.  L'Exilé d'Oumarou Ganda.  Peuples Noirs Peuples Africains 23(1981):54-93. (R)

Detailed analysis of Exilé, which is compared with other African films.

3668.  Traoré, Biny.  Les films africains.  L'Observateur Feb. 26 (1981):1,4-5,9.

Discussion of films in relation to strength of their ideological expression.

3669.  Traoré, Biny.  "Jom" et "Money Power".  L'Observateur 2525(1983):1,4-5,10. (R)

3670.  Traoré, Biny.  La prix de la liberté, le film vu par un critique. L'Observateur Oct. 11 (1979):1,6-7; Oct. 12 (1979):1,9; Oct. 17 (1979):7. (R)

Detailed analysis of Dikongue-Pipa's film and comment on audience responses in Burkina Faso.

3671.  Traoré, Biny.  VIe FESPACO projections et forums se succedent. L'Observateur Feb. 6 (1979):1,4-7. (I,R)

Review of Pierre-Marie Dong, Demain un jour nouveau and Sembène Ousmane, Ceddo.  Interview with Sembène about Ceddo, focus on its imagery.

3672.  Traoré, Issa.  A propos du film voltaique "Sur le chemin de la reconciliation." Afrique-Asie 114(1976):72. (R)

3673. Traoré, Mahama J.  Notes on the cinema and oral tradition, in Cinema and Society, International Film and Television Council, ed. Paris: IFTC, 1981. pp. 27-29.

3674. Traoré, Mahama J.  Towards a new strategy for African cinema, in First Mogadishu Pan-African Film Symposium. Pan African Cinema...Which Way Ahead? Ibrahim Awed et al eds.  Mogadishu: MOGPAFIS Management Committee, 1983. pp. 29-31.

Problems of production and distribution.  Nationalization of theaters has not brought decolonization of screens.

3675. Traoré, Mamadou.  L'Afrique des marginaux.  Bingo 401(1986):50-51. (R)

Patrice Toto, Feu de le sang.

3676. Traoré, Mamadou.  Avis aux prétendus cinéastes... Bingo 396(1986):50-51. (I)

Louis Balthazar Amadangoleda discusses film production in Cameroun.

3677. Traoré, Mamadou.  Une compléte harmonie.  Bingo 398(1986):56.

Cheick Doukoure's role in Black Mic Mac.

3678. Traoré, Mamadou.  Le debat s'anime autour de FESPACO.  Bingo 407(1986):52-53. (I)

Idrissa Ouédraogo and Kitia Touré discuss FESPACO.

3679. Traoré, Mamadou.  Désiré Ecaré l'affirme le cinéma africain est rentable.  Bingo 404(1986):27-29. (I)

Discussion of problems of financing and producing films.

3680. Traoré, Mamadou.  Une grande fresque africaine.  Bingo 398(1986):54.

Cheick Doukoure's acting in Black Mic Mac.

3681. Traoré, Mamadou.  Mustapha Diop: le cinéma africain doit dépasser le stade du bricolage.  Bingo 397(1986):52-54. (I)

Discussion of Médecin de Gafiré and political role of film in Africa.

3682. Traoré, Mamadou.  La passion du cinéma.  Bingo 394(1985):72. (I)

Salahou Ismael discusses his first film.

3683. Traoré, Mamadou.   La  passion  pour  l'Afrique.   <u>Bingo</u> 398(1986):56-57. (I)

Monique Annaud discusses Cheick Doukoure's acting.

3684. Traoré, Mory.   Le 10ème FESPACO ou la fin d'un rêve.   <u>Fraternité Matin</u> Mar. 1 (1987):19.

3685. Traoré, Mory.   Pour une cinématographie de l'ignorance.   <u>Afrique</u> 42(1980):72.

Ideals for content of films.

3686. Traoré, Moussa.   Burkina:  capitale  du  cinéma.   <u>Bingo</u> 401(1984):52-53.

Burkinabe feature filmmakers.

3687. Traoré, Moussa.   La  passion  selon  Safi  Faye.   <u>Bingo</u> 319(1979):28-29. (I)

3688. Traoré, Yacouba.   Le cinéma: un moyen de communication de masse par excellence.   <u>Sunjata</u> 19(1980):27-28.

3689. Traoré, Yacouba.   Les cinémas négro-africains sont-ils aux abois.   <u>Sunjata</u> 18(1979):26-28.

Unique aspects of African films; problems of distribution.

3690. Trzaska, Pawel.   African films at the 23rd Karlov Vary Festival.   <u>Young Cinema and Theater</u> 4(1982):3-7.

3691. Tshishi Bavuala Matanda.   Discours  filmique  africain  et communication  traditionelle, in <u>Caméra Nigra</u>. C.E.S.C.A. ed. Brussels: OCIC, 1984. pp. 157-174.

Momar Thiam, <u>Sarzan</u>. Criticism of African films.

3692. Turvey, Gerry.   'Xala' and the curse of neo-colonialism.   <u>Screen</u> 26,3-4(1985):75-87. (R)

3693. UNESCO.   Africa, in <u>World Communications</u>. Paris: UNESCO, 1975. pp. 35-113.

Statistics on theaters, seating capacity, attendance, number of films produced and source of imported films listed country by country.

3694. UNESCO Features.   African cinema seeks a new language.   <u>UNESCO Features</u> 776-777(1982):6-10. (I)

Interview with Sembène Ousmane.

3695. UPI.   "Femme  nue  femme  noire" de Désiré Ecaré expose les problèmes de l'exil africain. Le Soleil Dec. 5-6(1970):3. (R)

Summary of review of A nous deux France from Combat Dec. 14, 1970.

3696. Undenwa, Chuzzy. Jagua: I want to be a film-maker. Guardian (Lagos) July 14 (1985):B5.

Career of Afolabi Afolayan, Nigerian television actor who wants to make films.

3697. Unegbu, Clement. Violent films -- 'major cause of crime, robbery in our society.' New Nigerian Apr. 26 (1987):4.

Nigerian censorship board has failed to keep harmful foreign films off the screens.

3698. Union. L'Afrique ne veut plus être le parent pauvre. L'Union 211(1976):2.

Malian and Senegalese films shown at Venice film festival.

3699. Union. Association des cinéastes gabonais. M. Simon Augé élu président. L'Union May 17 (1984):3.

3700. Union. Aujourd'hui à Cannes "Demain un jour nouveau." L'Union May 23 (1979):5.

3701. Union. "Ayouma" remporte le prix de la ville de Ouagadougou. L'Union Feb. 12 (1979):1.

3702. Union. Une charte du cinéaste africain. L'Union Feb. 21 (1975):6.

Growth and development of FEPACI.

3703. Union. Les cinéastes africains au palais Rénovation. L'Union 1211(1980):1.

Gabonais filmmakers meet with President Bongo.

3704. Union. Cinéma: fin du 7ème FESPACO. Le Gabon devra abriter le 4ème Congrès. L'Union Mar. 5 (1981):4.

3705. Union. Le cinéma Ougooué fermé pour une semaine par la deputé-maire de Port-Gentil. L'Union Feb. 15 (1979):3.

Theater closed in Gabon.

3706. Union. Une délégation gabonaise à la conference de Ouagadougou (Haute Volta). L'Union Jan. 25 (1979):3.

Philippe Mory and Samuel Lambert Ondo attend CIPROFILM meeting.

3707.  Union.  "Demain, un jour nouveau" le premier tour de manivelle. L'Union June 2 (1978):5.

3708.  Union.  Festival de Ouagadougou.  Le bilan.  L'Union 46(1976):2.

FESPACO.

3709.  Union.  Fin du festival du film francophone à Brest.  L'Union 1359(1980):7.

FIFEF.

3710.  Union.  Grand première d'Ayouma le second film de Mme. Bongo. L'Union Jan. 7-8(1978):1.

3711.  Union.  La grand prix d'honneur obtenu à Nice présenté au chef de l'Etat.  L'Union Nov. 5 (1979):3.

Pierre Marie Dong, Demain un jour nouveau shown at FIFEF.

3712.  Union.  M. Paulin Vieyra: "Revoir les statuts de la FEPACI." L'Union Mar. 20 (1981):7. (I)

3713.  Union.  "Muna Moto" du camerounais Dikongue Pipa grand prix du Festival panafricain de Ouagadougou.  L'Union 40(1976):2.  (R)

3714.  Union.  La relance du cinéma gabonais est bien partie.  L'Union Oct. 5-6(1985):12.

Activities of CENACI.

3715.  Unir.  Prix de l'O.C.I.C. au Vllle Festival panafricain de Ouagadougou (FESPACO).  Unir NS103(1983):17.

3716.  Unir.  Prix de l'O.C.I.C. au lXe Festival panafricain de Ouagadougou (FESPACO) 1985.  Unir NS110(1985):34.

3717.  Unir. Le Vlle FESPACO à Ouagadougou.  Unir 96(1981):12-13.

Prizes to be given.

3718.  Unir. Session de la Sous Commission Cinéma-CERAO.  Unir NS110(1985):32-33.

Origin of Unir Cinéma.

3719.  Unir Ciné-Média. La sous-commission du cinéma.  Unir Cine-Média 7(1985):11-14.

Activities of national offices of OCIC.

3720.  Unir Cinéma.  A l'intention des cinéastes africains: comment distribuer les films aux Etats Unis.  Unir Cinéma 13(1984):5-6.

3721. Unir Cinéma. Ablakon: Unir Cinéma 27(1986):15-16. (R)

3722. Unir Cinéma. "Le camp de Thiaroye." Unir Cinéma 135(1987):25-26.

Summary of article in Soleil. See No. 2739.

3723. Unir Cinéma. Le cinéma au Mali. Unir Cinéma 2(1982):7-10.

3724. Unir Cinéma. Colloque "Tradition orale et nouveaux médias" Ouagadougou. Unir Cinéma 136(1987):4-6; 137(1987):5-8.

List of participants. Brief review of film about Africa before independence, characteristics of oral tradition, variety and influence of new media.

3725. Unir Cinéma. Conférence de presse. Unir Cinéma 12(1984):8-10.

Activities of ACS.

3726. Unir Cinéma. Culture cinématographique. Unir Cinéma 27(1986):18-20.

Film clubs in Benin, Côte d'Ivoire and Senegal.

3727. Unir Cinéma. Dossier Niamey. Unir Cinéma 1(1982):3-8.

Report on conference on film production.

3728. Unir Cinéma. FESPACO cérémonie d'ouverture du festival. Unir Cinéma 135(1987):5-6.

3729. Unir Cinéma. Le FESPACO, podium d'éveil culturel. Unir Cinéma 27(1986):3-5.

Summary of interview with Philippe Sawadogo in Sidwaya, Dec. 9, 1986.

3730. Unir Cinéma. Fespaco 83. Unir Cinéma 5(1983):3-12.

3731. Unir Cinéma. FESPACO 87 programme. Unir Cinéma 135(1987):7-13.

3732. Unir Cinéma. Finyé. Unir Cinéma 23-24(1986):43-45. (R)(I)

Souleymane Cissé discusses Finyé, including its differences from Baara.

3733. Unir Cinéma. Info FEPACI. Unir Cinéma 19(1985):15-16.

3734. Unir Cinéma. Info FEPACI. Unir Cinéma 23-24(1986):19-21.

3735. Unir Cinéma. Manifeste de Carthage pour l'information. Unir Cinéma 15(1984):15-17.

Joint communique to J.C.C. from SeptièmArt and Unir Cinéma on problems of African filmmaking.

3736.  Unir Cinéma.  Le médecin de Gafiré.  Unir Cinéma 22(1986):32. (R)

3737.  Unir Cinéma.  Mogadishu Panafrican film symposium.  Unir Cinéma 9(1983):3-10.

3738.  Unir Cinéma.  Mozambique.  Unir Cinéma 12(1984):3-6.

Films produced by INC 1981-1983.

3739.  Unir Cinéma.  Le peuple grogne.  Unir Cinéma 14(1984):23-28.

Reprinted articles from Sidwaya, Aug. 1984, on SONAVOCI.

3740.  Unir Cinéma.  Sarraounia de Med Hondo.  Unir Cinéma 27(1986):12-14. (R)

3741.  Uzoma, Chidi.  Pa Orlando's last stage: let's mourn the living. Daily Times (Lagos) Oct. 26 (1985):5.

Orlando Martins, Nigerian actor, honored at National Theater.

3742.  V.M.  L'Afrique anglophone parente pauvre du cinéma africain. Bingo 244(1973):83.

Film infrastructure in Anglophone Africa.

3743.  Valentinetti, Claudio.  Os cafejestes, in Dizinario universale del cinema.  Fernaldo Di Gaiammatteo, ed.  Rome: Editori Riuniti, 1985. Vol. 1, pp. 160-161. (R)

3744.  Valentinetti, Claudio.  Os fuzis, in Dizinario universale del cinema.  Fernaldo Di Giammatteo, ed. Rome: Editori Riuniti, 1985. Vol. 1, pp. 398. (R)

3745.  Valentinetti, Claudio.  Sweet Hunters, in Dizinario universale del cinema.  Fernaldo Di Giammatteo, ed. Rome: Editori Riuniti, 1985. Vol. 1, pp. 985-986. (R)

3746.  Van Espen, Daniel.  French-speaking Africa, planning and projects.  OCIC Info 7,6(1986):16.

Report on OCIC meeting in Lome.  OCIC plans and problems of CIDC.

3747.  Van Gelder, Lawrence.  "Harvest: 3000 Years" is elementary film. New York Times April 6 (1976):27. (R)

3748.  Van Goor, André.  Festival "Sembène Ousmane" cinéaste sénégalais à Kinshasa.  Zaire-Afrique 121(1978):59-60.

Ceddo, Emitai and Xala shown in Zaire.

3749.  Van Wert, William F.  Ideology in the Third World cinema: a study of Sembene Ousmane and Glauber Rocha.  Quarterly Review of Film Studies 4,1(1979):207-226.

3750. Variety.  Africa making 80-100 feature films annually.  Variety 273,9(1974):90,94.

3751. Variety.  "Soweto" music pic rolling in Nigeria.  Variety 327,5(1987):24.

Soweto to be filmed in Nigeria and Zimbabwe.

3752. Vast, Jean.  Cinéma africain.  Unir NS105(1983):8-9.

Unir activities in support of film in Senegal 1968-1983.

3753. Vast, Jean.  Le cinéma africain et le sacre.  Unir Cinéma 23-24(1986):3-4.

Editorial on how the sacred is communicated.

3754. Vast, Jean.  Cinéma et video.  Unir Cinéma 137(1987):3-4.

Film and video theaters in Senegal.  (Unir Cinéma stopped numbering separately from Unir in 1987 which accounts for the numbering discrepancy with the preceding citation.)

3755. Vast, Jean.  Communique de presse.  Unir NS103(1983):18.

OCIC meeting regarding FESPACO prizes.

3756. Vast, Jean.  Culture cinématographique.  Unir Cinéma 23-24(1986):31-32.

Need to discuss language and themes of films and promote film clubs.

3757. Vast, Jean.  Editorial.  Unir Cinéma 135(1987):3-4.

Value of FESPACO.

3758. Vast, Jean.  Formation et information ciné-club.  Unir Cinéma 17(1985):43-44.

3759. Vast, Jean.  Ouagadougou FESPACO 1983.  Unir Ciné Média 2-3(1982-1983):9-12.

3760. Vast, Jean.  Ousmane Sembène et Maxence van der Meerech: même combat pour la justice.  Unir Cinéma 18(1985):4-5; Unir NS111(1985):21-22.

Culture week at Centre Culturel Africaine de Saint-Louis on works of Sembène.

3761. Vast, Jean.  Le Père Daniel Brottier patron des cinéastes et des journalists. <u>Unir</u> NS107(1984):3-4.

3762. Vast, Jean.   Prix de la critique de cinéma.   <u>Unir</u> <u>Cinéma</u> 135(1987):21-22.

What goals of criticism should be.   Decision to establish Association Panafricaine de la Critique de Cinéma.

3763. Vast, Jean.   "Sarraounia."   <u>Unir</u> <u>Cinéma</u> 135(1987):14-17. (R)

Includes excerpts from reviews in <u>Cinéma</u>, <u>Jeune</u> <u>Afrique</u> and <u>Jeune</u> <u>Cinéma</u>.

3764. Vast, Jean.   La sous-commission cinéma.   <u>Unir</u> <u>Ciné-Média</u> 4(1984):25-32.

Annual report on OCIC activities.

3765. Vast, Jean.      Sous-commission cinéma.   <u>Unir</u> <u>Ciné-Média</u> 5(1984):3-4.

Annual report on OCIC activities.

3766. Vast, Jean.      Sous-commission cinéma.   <u>Unir</u> <u>Ciné-Média</u> 6(1985):5-10.

Annual report on OCIC activities.

3767. Vast, Jean.   La sous-commission du cinéma.   <u>Unir</u> <u>Ciné-Média</u> 2-3(1982-1983):27-35.

Annual report on OCIC activities.

3768. Vast, Jean.   Xala.   <u>Unir</u> <u>Cinéma</u> 20-21(1985):37-83. (R)

Includes comments excerpted from <u>CinémAction</u> No. 34, see No. 70.

3769. Vast, Jean.   Yam Daabo "Le choix."   <u>Unir</u> <u>Cinéma</u> 135(1987):18-20. (R)

3770. Vast, Jean et. al.   Sous commission du cinéma.   <u>Unir</u> <u>Ciné-Média</u> 8(1986):17-25.

Annual report on OCIC activities.   Role of <u>Unir</u> <u>Cinéma</u>.

3771. Vaugeois, Gérard.   Lettre Paysanne.   <u>Ecran</u> 53(1976):65. (R)

Safi Faye, <u>Kaddu</u> <u>Beykat</u>.

3772. Vauthier, René.   L'autre oeil la caméra.   <u>Jeune</u> <u>Afrique</u> 275(1966):supp. xv-xviii.

Films shown at FESTAC.

3773. Vauthier, René. Special 1975 cinéma: "Et le mot frère et le mot camarade." Jeune Afrique 730-731(1975):92-93.

Activities in 1975: Algiers congress; films about Africa, focus on those by Jean Rouch; films by African filmmakers the author considers ethnographic.

3774. Venegas, Cristina. Erendira, in Magill's Cinema Annual 1985. Frank N. Magill, ed. Englewood Cliffs, N.J.: Salem Press, 1985. pp. 181-185. (R)

*3775. Vernon, Mariel. A nous deux, France. Republique Matin Apr. 23 (1970). (R)

3776. Veysset, Marie-Claude. Un film, deux visions. Jeune Cinéma 34(1968):10-11.

Different responses of European and African audiences to Sembène Ousmane's, La noire de.

3777. Vieyra, Paulin Soumanou. Africa: the images that must not fade. Unesco Courier 37,8(1984):7-8.

About showing films in Africa.

3778. Vieyra, Paulin Soumanou. "Afrika am Rhein." Présence Africaine 143(1987):203-204. (R)

3779. Vieyra, Paulin Soumanou. L'Afrique au 30e Festival de Cannes. Afrique Nouvelle 1458(1977):16-17.

3780. Vieyra, Paulin Soumanou. L'agonie du cinéma africain. Le Soleil Feb. 9-10 (1985):10.

Problems of African film discussed at FESPACO.

3781. Vieyra, Paulin Soumanou. Après Ouaga: vaincre ou mourir. Africa (Dakar) 171(1985):40-42.

FESPACO. Films shown. Meetings of CAC, CIDC and FEPACI.

3782. Vieyra, Paulin Soumanou. L'argent détermine la nationalité d'un film. Zone 2 74(1980):19.

How can enough films be produced to meet African demand.

3783. Vieyra, Paulin Soumanou. Au rendez-vous de Mogadiscio. Afrique Nouvelle 1794(1983):15-16.

MOGPAFIS.

3784. Vieyra, Paulin Soumanou. Bilan de l'année 82. Africa (Dakar) 147(1983):80-83.

FESPACO, J.C.C., MOGPAFIS. Films made in Mali, Nigeria and Senegal.

3785. Vieyra, Paulin Soumanou. Cannes, Cannes, Cannes. *Africa* (Dakar) 173(1985):43-45.

3786. Vieyra, Paulin Soumanou. Cannes et Tachkent: deux festivals au service du cinéma. *Présence Africaine* 91(1974):147-151.

3787. Vieyra, Paulin Soumanou. Cannes fête ses 35 ans. *Le Soleil* May 6 (1982):13.

3788. Vieyra, Paulin Soumanou. Cannes 1975 et le cinéma africain. *Le Soleil* June 12 (1975):8.

3789. Vieyra, Paulin Soumanou. Cannes 81 et l'Afrique. *Afrique Nouvelle* 1665(1981):14-15.

3790. Vieyra, Paulin Soumanou. Cannes 79 peu de films africains. *Afrique Nouvelle* 1513(1978):16-17, 24.

3791. Vieyra, Paulin Soumanou. Carthage 1984 18 ans déjà. *Afrique Nouvelle* 1844(1984):18-19.

3792. Vieyra, Paulin Soumanou. Carthage 78. *Présence Africaine* 110(1979):159-166.

3793. Vieyra, Paulin Soumanou. "Chronique..." en tête. *Africa* (Dakar) 165(1984):50-52.

10 best African films.

3794. Vieyra, Paulin Soumanou. Cinéma africain ou africain du cinéma. *Zone 2* 75(1980):19.

Distribution problems.

3795. Vieyra, Paulin Soumanou. Cinéma africain et pédagogie de l'image. *Recherche, pédagogie et culture* 17-18(1975):16-22.

3796. Vieyra, Paulin Soumanou. Le cinéma au 1er festival culturel panafricain d'Alger. *Présence Africaine* 72(1969):190-201.

Report on all aspects of Algiers film festival: the symposium, roundtables, films shown and discussion of films.

3797. Vieyra, Paulin Soumanou. Le cinéma au Sénégal en 1976. *Présence Africaine* 107(1978):207-216.

3798. Vieyra, Paulin Soumanou. Le cinéma et la communication en Afrique. *Revue africaine de communication* 4(1984):43-44.

Economic and cultural problems in the development of African film.

3799. Vieyra, Paulin Soumanou. Le cinéma et la révolution africaine. Présence Africaine 34-35(1960-1961):92-103.

3800. Vieyra, Paulin Soumanou. Cinéma et raison d'Etat. Africa (Dakar) 156(1983):73.

   Ineffectiveness of SIDEC.

3801. Vieyra, Paulin Soumanou. The cinema in Senegal. Benin Review 1(1974):10-16.

   Short history.

3802. Vieyra, Paulin Soumanou. Cinéma: le festival de Cannes. Le Soleil May 16 (1975):6.

3803. Vieyra, Paulin Soumanou. Cinéma: les films africains à Cannes et à Oberhausen. Le Soleil 2129(1977):7.

3804. Vieyra, Paulin Soumanou. Le cinquième FESPACO. Présence Africaine 98(1976):187-192.

3805. Vieyra, Paulin Soumanou. Le 5es journées cinématographiques de Carthage. Présence Africaine 93(1975):208-214.

3806. Vierya, Paulin Soumanou. Circoncision réussie! Africa International 181(1986):44. (R)

   Sana Na N'hada, Fanado.

3807. Vieyra, Paulin Soumanou. Considerations of African cinema, in First Mogadishu Pan-African Film Symposium. Pan-African Cinema...Which Way Ahead? Ibrahim Awed et al eds. Mogadishu: MOGPAFIS Management Committee, 1983. pp. 13-21.

   Film festivals, distribution problems, state of production, need for film archive and African critics.

3808. Vieyra, Paulin Soumanou. La création cinématographique en Afrique. Présence Africaine 77(1971):218-232.

   History of film from 19th century including context in which films are being made in Africa in the 1960s.

3809. Vieyra, Paulin Soumanou. Critères critiques. Le Monde Diplomatique 300(1979):29.

3810. Vierya, Paulin Soumanou. "David Diop: Poète d'Amour." Présence Africaine 143(1987):198. (R)

3811. Vieyra, Paulin Soumanou. Le deuxième congrès de la FEPACI. Présence Africaine 97(1976):165-174.

3812. Vieyra, Paulin Soumanou. Le 2e Festival Cinématographique de Tachkent. Présence Africaine 83(1972):86-91.

3813. Vieyra, Paulin Soumanou. Dinard 1971 ou le cinéma, fait politique. Présence Africaine 80(1971):139-142.

African films at FIFEF.

3814. Vieyra, Paulin Soumanou. Xe anniversaire des Journées Cinématographiques de Carthage. Présence Africaine 101-102(1977):231-235.

3815. Vieyra, Paulin Soumanou. Le 10e Festival cinématographique de Moscou. Le Soleil Aug. 9 (1977):5.

3816. Vieyra, Paulin Soumanou. D'un festival à un autre. Le Soleil Nov. 29-30 (1980):12.

J.C.C. Overview of past festivals, films shown in 1980.

3817. Vieyra, Paulin Soumanou. FESPACO: brilliant...et utile? Africa International 193(1987):41-43.

3818. Vieyra, Paulin Soumanou. Fespaco 1979. Présence Africaine 111(1979):101-106.

3819. Vieyra, Paulin Soumanou. FESPACO 83 au tournant de l'histoire. Afrique Nouvelle 1756(1983):20-21.

3820. Vieyra, Paulin Soumanou. FESPACO 83, avant première. Afrique Nouvelle 1751(1983):18-19.

3821. Vieyra, Paulin Soumanou. FESPACO 87. Présence Africaine 143(1987):190-194.

3822. Vieyra, Paulin Soumanou. Le Festival cinématographique de Cannes et l'Afrique. Afrique 2(1977):73-77.

3823. Vieyra, Paulin Soumanou. Le Festival cinématographique de Cannes et l'Afrique. Présence Africaine 104(1977):143-151.

Small African representation at Cannes film festival. Most of the article is about general aspects of the festival.

3824. Vieyra, Paulin Soumanou. Festival de Cannes et ce sera un nouveau départ. Afrique Nouvelle 1720(1982):18-19.

3825. Vieyra, Paulin Soumanou. Le festival de Cannes et la présence africaine. Afrique Nouvelle 1874(1985):14-17.

3826. Vieyra, Paulin Soumanou. Festival de Cannes 84 l'Afrique mal représentée faute de moyens. Afrique Nouvelle 1823(1984):11,16-17.

3827. Vieyra, Paulin Soumanou. Festival de Moscou rencontre avec Alimata Salembéré. Afrique Nouvelle 1780(1983):18-19. (I)

Comparison of juries at J.C.C. and Moscow; how Moscow jury functions.

3828. Vieyra, Paulin Soumanou. Le festival du cinéma à Moscou. Le Soleil Sept. 17 (1979):12; Sept. 18 (1979):10.

3829. Vieyra, Paulin Soumanou. Festival du film de Moscou 1971. Présence Africaine 80(1971):143-149.

3830. Vieyra, Paulin Soumanou. Le film africain. African Arts 1,3(1968):60-69.

Films from Francophone Africa.

3831. Vieyra, Paulin Soumanou. Film in Afrika: Das erste Jahrzehnt. Afrika Heute supp. to 19(1971):11-18.

Organization of film industry reviewed country-by-country.

3832. Vieyra, Paulin Soumanou. "Gorée l'Ile de Grand-Père." Présence Africaine 143(1987):201-202. (R)

Film by Tunisian filmmaker made with Senegalese support.

3833. Vieyra, Paulin Soumanou. Hommage à Oumarou Ganda: cinéaste nigérien. Présence Africaine 119(1981):165-169.

3834. Vieyra, Paulin Soumanou. Le 8e Festival cinématographique de Moscou. Présence Africaine 89(1974):234-242.

3835. Vieyra, Paulin Soumanou. Les lauriers de Carthage. Africa (Dakar) 166(1984):51-53.

3836. Vieyra, Paulin Soumanou. Les nouveaux films d'Afrique noire pour deux festivals. Le Soleil July 3 (1978):2.

Differences between J.C.C. and FIFEF, African films shown at both.

3837. Vieyra, Paulin Soumanou. "Nyamanton" (ou "La leçon des ordures"). Présence Africaine 143(1987):199-200. (R)

3838. Vieyra, Paulin Soumanou. L'olympiade du cinéma. Le Soleil May 31 (1977):6.

Cannes, films shown and prizes.

3839. Vieyra, Paulin Soumanou. Où en sont le cinéma et le théâtre africains? Présence Africaine 13(1957):143-146.

3840. Vieyra, Paulin Soumanou. Ouagadougou capitale du cinéma africain. Le Soleil Jan. 27 (1983):21.

Recent activities of CIDC, CIPROFILM and CINAFRIC. Attendance at FESPACO.

3841. Vieyra, Paulin Soumanou. Ouagadougou, mon amour. Africa (Dakar) 169(1985):35-38.

J.C.C. 1984 and FESPACO 1985. Third FEPACI congress.

3842. Vieyra, Paulin Soumanou. Ousmane Sembène réalisateur de télévision vient d'effectuer une enquête sur le couple au Sénégal. Dakar Matin June 18 (1969):3.

Sembène making films for Swiss television in Senegal.

3843. Vieyra, Paulin Soumanou. Participation africaine aux techniques audio-visuelles à Vancouver. Présence Africaine 101-102(1977):227-230.

African filmmakers' participation in film workshop in Vancouver.

3844. Vieyra, Paulin Soumanou. Présence africaine. Le Soleil June 24 (1982):19.

African films shown at Cannes film festival, 1960-1982.

3845. Vieyra, Paulin Soumanou. Propos sur le cinéma africain. Présence Africaine 22(1958):106-117.

3846. Vieyra, Paulin Soumanou. Les quatre Journées Cinématographiques de Carthage. Présence Africaine 86(1973):178-187.

Short description of films shown at J.C.C.

3847. Vieyra, Paulin Soumanou. Le 4e festival cinématographique panafricain du Ouagadougou. Présence Africaine 88(1973):218-227.

Important new films shown at FESPACO.

3848. Vieyra, Paulin Soumanou. Réflexions sur la diffusion du film africain en Europe. Africa International 181(1986):43-44.

Problems of film distribution.

3849. Vieyra, Paulin Soumanou. Refléxions sur le premier concours international du film d'Outre-Mer. Présence Africaine 17(1957-8):118-122.

Africans on FIFEF jury, but no African films in competition.

3850. Vieyra, Paulin Soumanou. Un rendez-vous a la Havane. Africa International 180(1986):33-35.

African attendance at International Festival of New Latin American Cinema.

3851. Vieyra, Paulin Soumanou. Responsabilités du cinéma dans la formation d'une conscience nationale africaine. Présence Africaine 27-28(1959):303-313.

3852. Vieyra, Paulin Soumanou. Le rôle du critique et de l'historien africains dans le processus de développement de la productions cinématographique en Afrique, in FESPACO 1983. Paris: Présence Africaine, 1987. pp. 43-48.

Role of film criticism in development of African film. Relationship between audience preferences and criticism.

3853. Vieyra, Paulin Soumanou. Sauver le film africain. Africa (Dakar) 149(1983):45-48, 154.

Mediocre films at FESPACO, prizes, language of films, important new films.

3854. Vieyra, Paulin Soumanou. Scusi, dove va? Nigrizia 102, 1(1984):42-43.

MOGPAFIS.

3855. Vieyra, Paulin Soumanou. La semaine de la critique. Le Soleil June 24 (1982):19.

African films acclaimed at Cannes film festival.

3856. Vieyra, Paulin Soumanou. Si "Liberté 1" m'était conté... Africa (Dakar) 161(1984):57-58. (R)

Film based on Leopold Senghor's, Liberté, made by UCINA in 1960, still a classic.

3857. Vieyra, Paulin Soumanou. Silence, on (de) tourne! Africa (Dakar) 178(1985):36-38.

History and activities of SNPC.

3858. Vieyra, Paulin Soumanou. 6e Festival International de Films d'expression française. Présence Africaine 92(1974):190-195.

*3859. Vieyra, Paulin Soumanou. Suggestions pour le développement du cinéma en AFO, in Rencontres internationales: Le cinéma et l'Afrique au Sud du Sahara. Brussels: 1958, pp. 95-97.

3860. Vieyra, Paulin Soumanou. Le symposium panafricain de Mogadiscio. Afrique Nouvelle 1688(1981):24-25.

MOPAFIS.

3861. Vieyra, Paulin Soumanou. Le 35 Festival de Cannes une ouverture inhabituelle. Fraternité Matin 5292(1982):19.

3862. Vieyra, Paulin Soumanou. 36e festival de Cannes. Le Soleil May 3 (1983):20.

African films to be shown.

3863. Vieyra, Paulin Soumanou. Triomphe du cinéma africain à Genève. Le Soleil Nov. 13 (1975):8.

Films awarded prizes at FIFEF: Ben Diogaye Bèye, Samba Tali; Jean-Pierre Dikongue-Pipa, Muna Moto; and Safi Faye, Kaddu Beykat.

3864. Vieyra, Paulin Soumanou. Le 3e Festival cinématographique de Dinard. Présence Africaine 84(1972):109-116.

FIFEF.

3865. Vieyra, Paulin Soumanou. Le 3e Festival panafricain de Ouagadougou. Présence Africaine 82(1972):120-130.

FESPACO prizes. FEPACI activities.

3866. Vieyra, Paulin Soumanou. 25 ans après... 1. Les promesses. Africa (Dakar) 168(1985):45-46.

Three generations of African filmmakers: 1960-1972, 1972-1981, since 1981.

3867. Vieyra, Paulin Soumanou. 25 ans après... 11. La moisson. Africa (Dakar) 169(1985):38-39.

Aesthetics of African films.

3868. Vieyra, Paulin Soumanou. 25 pays et 60 films à l'affiche. Africa (Dakar) 148(1983):69-71.

FESPACO.

3869. Vieyra, Paulin Soumanou. Le 25e Festival International du Film de l'Ensemble francophone. Présence Africaine 108(1978):166-172.

African films shown at FIFEF.

3870. Vieyra, Paulin Soumanou. Voyage à Tokyo. Africa (Dakar) 174(1985):45-47.

African films shown at Tokyo film festival.

3871. Vokouma, François. Du rôle de nos cinéastes pour perpétuer nos valeurs. Carrefour Africain 975(1987):18-19.

FESPACO colloquium on oral tradition and the new media.

3872. Voyles, Marc. Le cinéma africain... Où? Quand? Comment? Afrique Nouvelle 846(1963):10-11.

Problems of filmmaking.

3873. Warren, Herrick and Anita Warren. The film artist in a developing nation: Ethiopia. Horn of Africa 1,1(1978):57-58.

3874. Watrigant, R. Cabascabo. Afrique Nouvelle 1142(1969):15. (R)

3875. Watrigant, R. "Concerto pour un exil." Afrique Nouvelle 1093(1968):14. (R)

3876. Watrigant, R. "Concerto pour un exil." Afrique Nouvelle 1105(1968):15. (R)

Contains basically the same information as No. 3875.

3877. Watrigant, R. Le Mandat. Afrique Nouvelle 1150(1969):11. (R)

3878. Watrigant, R. La Semaine du Jeune Cinéma d'Afrique Noire Paris: 14-22 Avril 1967. Afrique Nouvelle 1050(1967):10-11.

Conference of African filmmakers held in Paris.

3879. Watts, Ian. African films making impact at festival. Africa (London) 174(1986):66.

London film festival. Most commentary on Désiré Ecaré, Visages de femmes.

3880. Wauthier, Claude. "Sarraounia" de Med Hondo, l'épopée africaine. Le Monde Nov. 26 (1986):16. (R)

3881. Weaver, Harold. Film-makers have great responsibility to our people. Cinéaste 6,1(1973):26-31. (I)

Sembène Ousmane discusses role of African filmmaker in his society.

3882. Weaver, Harold. Interview with Ousmane Sembène. Issue 2,4(1972):58-64. (I)

Discussion of Borom Sarret, Emitai, and La noire de.

3883. Weaver, Harold. The politics of African cinema, in Black Cinema Aesthetics, Gladstone L. Yearwood, ed. Athens: Ohio University Center for Afro-American Studies, 1982. pp. 83-92.

Political themes of African films. Obstacles in exhibition, distribution and production.

3884.  Weekly Review.  Cinemas sold.  Weekly Review 559(1986):17.

Theaters in Kenya.

3885.  Weekly Review.  Feature film to be made of Ogot play.  Weekly Review 363(1982):43.

Seth Adagala, The White Veil.

3886.  Weekly Review.  Film symposium in Mogadishu.  Weekly Review 346(1981):42-43.

MOGPAFIS.

3887.  Weekly Review.  Ghanaian film of star-crossed lovers.  Weekly Review 328(1981):59. (R)

Kwaw Ansah, Love Brewed in the African Pot.

3888.  Weekly Review.  Hard road ahead for African cinema.  Weekly Review 449(1983):35-36.

MOGPAFIS.

3889.  Weekly Review.  Kenya passed over.  Weekly Review 563(1986):15-16.

Biko film to be made in Zimbabwe despite Kenya's adequate facilities.

3890.  Weekly Review.  Lessons of film week.  Weekly Review 608(1986):44-45.

Problems in organization of Kenya film week.  More government support needed for filmmaking.

3891.  Weekly Review.  Mama plans her family.  Weekly Review Sept. 4 (1987):47.

Hilary Ng'weno, Mama Binga, television film series in Swahili.

3892.  Weekly Review.  New guidelines.  Weekly Review 535(1985):24-25.

Guidelines for foreign films made in Kenya to include minimum number of Kenyan staff.

3893.  Weekly Review.  President supports local film industry.  Weekly Review 567(1986):27.

Film training facilities of the Kenya Institute of Mass Communication.

3894.  Weiler, A.H.  Screen: 2 from Senegal.  New York Times Jan. 13 (1969):31. (R)

Borom Sarret and La noire de.

3895. Welsh, Henry. Bako, l'autre rive. Jeune Cinéma 117(1979):46-47.
(R)

3896. Welsh, Henry. Safi Faye: Lettre paysanne. Jeune Cinéma
99(1976-1977):8-12. (I)

Discussion of Kaddu Beykat.

3897. West, Dennis. A film school for the Third World. Cinéaste 15, 3
(1987):37, 57.

School of Three Worlds, an international film and television
school in Havana.

3898. West, Hollie I. 'Kongi's Harvest.' Washington Post June 17
(1973):E7. (R)

3899. West Africa. African films at the Cannes Film Festival. West
Africa 3279(1980):918-919.

3900. West Africa. Film festival award. West Africa 3321(1981):656.
(R)

Kwaw Ansah, Love Brewed in the African Pot.

3901. West Africa. Film for FESTAC. West Africa 3096(1976):1646. (R)

Poor quality of Ovonremuen Nogbaisi, based on Ola Rotimi's play.

3902. West Africa. Film prize. West Africa 3047(1975):1393. (R)

FIFEF prize for Jean-Pierre Dikongue-Pipa, Muna Moto.

3903. West Africa. People. West Africa 2796(1971):43.

Cast and crew for Bullfrog in the Sun.

3904. West Africa. People. West Africa 2799(1971):121.

Johnny Sekka, Senegalese actor in Bullfrog in the Sun.

3905. West Africa. People. West Africa 2821(1971):775.

Wole Soyinka's complaints about soundtrack for Kongi's Harvest.

3906. West Africa. People. West Africa 2830(1971):1047.

Films by Med Hondo and Sembène Ousmane.

3907. Willemen, Paul. Interview with Haile Gerima on 3000 year
harvest. Framework 7-8(1978):31-35. (I)

3908. Wilson, David. Boesman and Lena. Monthly Film Bulletin 41(1974):43-44. (R)

3909. Wilson, Julius. African films top on agenda. Daily Times (Lagos) Aug. 23 (1987):20.

Importance of Moscow film festival to African filmmakers.

3910. Wilson, Melba. When love triumphed over class. Africa (London) 148(1983):61,63. (R)

Kwaw Ansah, Love Brewed in the African Pot, shown at Third Eye film festival.

3911. Wolfers, Michael. Where cinema opposes escapism. Africa Now 46(1985):40.

Mocambique's first film festival.

3912. Wright, Ramond. Establishment of a cinematographic unit. Ikoro 5,1-2(1984):36-42.

Film unit at Institute of African Studies, University of Nigeria, Nsukka.

3913. Wuilleumier, Marie-Claire. Naissance d'un cinéma. Esprit 35,7-8(1967):135-140. (R)

Sembène Ousmane. La noire de. Documentaries by other African filmmakers mentioned.

3914. Xalifa, Ababacar. A la recherche d'un souffle nouveau. Wal Fadjri 50(1986):8-9.

SOFIDAK discussion of quantity and quality of films in Senegal.

3915. Xalifa, Ababacar. La fronde des jeunes. Wal Fadjri 45(1986):20-21.

Goals of young Senegalese filmmakers.

3916. Y.L. A la recherche d'un cinéma national. Afrique Nouvelle 1328(1974):22.

Brief review of 10 years of film production in Senegal. Need for a national cinema supported by legislation.

3917. Yacouba, Kébé. La publicité en "liberté surveillée." Fraternité Matin 6186(1985):3.

Festival du film publicitaire.

3918. Yameogo, R. Med Hondo, biographie et filmographie. Carrefour

Africain 977(1987):14.

3919. Yangari, Albert. Le cinéma gabonais au Festival de Ouagadougou (FESPACO). L'Union Feb. 9 (1979): 1,5.

Gabonais participation in FESPACO as filmmakers and jury member.

3920. Yao, Djédjé. S.O.S. pour le cinéma ivoirien. Fraternité Matin 5282(1982):20.

Too few films being produced in Côte d'Ivoire.

3921. Yao, Henri. Doura Mané: que penser de "L'Etat sauvage." Bingo 306(1978):50-54.

Mané's view of Francis Girod's film on colonialism.

3922. Yao, Henri. Une révélation nommée Viviane Mariam Touré. Bingo 293(1977):52-53. (I)

Ivorian actress discusses her work.

3923. Yao, Henri. Sarah Maldoror le pionnier. Bingo 301(1978):59-61. (I)

Discussion of Sambizanga.

3924. Yao, Henri. Sept films africains à Paris. Bingo 308(1978):53-56.

Films from Benin, Mali, Niger and Senegal shown.

3925. Yao, Jules. Le Festival du film publicitaire organisé par l'UNIDA et l'INSET. Fraternité Hebdo 1257(1983):5.

YASBACK, ASSANE See YAZBACK, HASSANE.

3926. Yattara, Mohamed Soudha. Le réalisature Souleymane Cissé a été fait chevalier de l'ordre national. L'Essor June 13-14(1987):8.

Cissé given Chevalier de l'Ordre National following receipt of Cannes prize for Yeelen. Other talented Malian filmmakers; problems of financing films.

3927. Yazback, Hassane. Le cinéma et les temps modernes. Le Soleil July 9 (1975):2.

Necessity of film for education.

3928. Yazback, Hassane. Point de vue arabe sur le film sénégalais. Le Soleil Aug. 22 (1975):2.

Polygamy as theme in Senegalese films.

3929. Yédagne, Honorat de. Des élèves cinéastes au lycée de Sassandra. Fraternité Matin 6132(1985):9.

Teaching filmmaking in Côte d'Ivoire.

3930. Yédagne, Honorat de. Festival du film publicitaire. Les spots primés: des choix judicieux. Fraternité Matin 6187(1985):28. (I)

Interview with Ali Coulibaly and Claude Marin.

3931. Yédagne, Honorat de. Festival du film publicitaire. Un forum utile. Fraternité Matin 6187(1985):25.

3932. Yédagne, Honorat de. Sidiki Bakaba dans l'écriture d'Art Média. Fraternité Matin Sept. 4 (1986):8-9.

Films in which Bakaba has acted, actors he has worked with. Wrote script for Art Média, the first film he has made.

3933. Yelizarov, Yuri. The Tashkent Festival is in a class of its own. Asia and Africa Today 6(1984):56-59.

YETI, K.M. BIM, See BIM YETI, K.M.

3934. Yeye, Zakaria. Colloque: "Tradition orale et nouveaux médias" la griologie et la drummologie au centre de débats. Sidwaya Feb. 26 (1987):9.

Report on FESPACO colloquium.

3935. Yeye, Zakaria. La rue marchande. "La moisson était bonne, nous avons tisse des relations!!" Sidwaya Mar. 2 (1987):10.

Sale of Burkinabe products at FESPACO.

3936. Yoboue, Koffi. Gnoan M'Bala (l'auteur d'Amanié): une récompense? Une responsabilité? Fraternité Matin 2330(1972):7. (R)

FIFEF prize.

3937. Youbi, Matthieu X. 20 ans de 7e art camerounais. Bingo 394(1985):75.

Best-known Camerounian films. Government support for filmmaking.

3938. Youn. "L'OCINAM ne decevra pas son public." L'Essor July 6 (1971):1,3-4. (I)

Samba Sall discusses theaters in Mali.

3939. Young, Colin. Introduction to the work of CILECT, in First Mogadishu Pan-African Film Symposium Pan African Cinema...Which Way Ahead? Ibrahim Awed et al eds. Mogadishu: MOGPAFIS Management Committee, 1983. pp. 61-65.

Training provided by CILET, an international organization of film and television schools.

3940. Young, Deborah. Confusion and controversy mark 11th edition of Carthage days. Variety 325, 3(1986):5,32.

Désiré Ecaré, Visages de femmes, censored at J.C.C.

3941. Young Cinema and Theater. Final communique of the first film colloquy on film production in Africa. Young Theater and Cinema 1(1983):16-20.

Niamey 1982 conference on film production.

3942. Yung. L'Appât du Gain. Variety 309, 3(1982):20. (R)

3943. Yung. En Residence Surveillee. Variety 309, 3(1982):20. (R)

3944. Yung. Jours de Tourments. Variety 319, 13(1985):17. (R)

3945. Yung. Les Lutteurs. Variety 309,3(1982):20. (R)

3946. Yung. Nelisita. Variety 318,8(1985):18. (R)

3947. Yung. Ntturudu. Variety 325,8(1986):29. (R)

3948. Yung. Nyamanton. Variety 325,8(1986):27,29. (R)

3949. Yung. La vie est belle (Life is Rosy). Variety 327,5(1978):18. (R)

3950. Yung. Wend Kuuni. Variety 309,3(1982):26. (R)

3951. Yung. Yam Daabo (The Choice). Variety 327,5(1987):45. (R)

3952. Yung. Yeelen (Brightness). Variety 327,3(1987):137. (R)

3953. Z Promotions. 1986 Audio Visual Zimbabwe. Harare: Z Promotions, 1986.

Includes information on infrastructure for filmmaking and the Zimbabwe Film and Video Association.

3954. Z Promotions. Audio-visual Zimbabwe 1987. Harare: Z Promotions, 1987.

Film in focus p. 4; film finance p. 5; list of feature films made in Zimbabwe in 1987.

3955. Zaire. Le cinéma africain à séduit bonn. Zaire 233(1973):35-36.

Bonn film festival.

3956. Zaire. Un cinéma africain pour les Africains. _Zaire_ 342(1975):59-60.

Brussels film festival.

3957. Zaire. Les films qu'il faut. _Zaire_ 339 (1975):10-11.

Educational role of films. Too few films shown on television in Zaire.

3958. Zaire. L'image de l'aube. _Zaire_ 437(1976):45. (R)

Group of filmmakers at Voix de Zaire make _Le hazard n'existe pas_.

3959. Zaire. "Le mandat" de Ousmane Sembène. _Zaire_ 354(1975):66-67. (R)

3960. Zaire. Un metteur en scène et un film africain remportent des prix américains. _Zaire_ 502(1978):34.

Film by Mahama Johnson Traoré.

3961. Zaire. "Sambizanga" de Sarah Maldoror. _Zaire_ 255(1973):34. (R)

3962. Zanotelli, Alessandro. A difesa dell'uomo. _Nigrizia_ 100,5(1982):8-11. (I)

Interview with Med Hondo.

3963. Zanotelli, Alessandro. Non ci avete mai visti. _Nigrizia_ 99,5(1981):6-7.

First Rome festival of African film.

3964. Zele, Van. Os fuzis. _Image et son_ Nov. (1969):121-130. (R)(I)

Ruy Guerra discusses the making of his film, music in it, the characters, and editing. Review provides detailed plot summary.

3965. Zeni, Moulaye. De l'objective cinématographique. _L'Essor_ July 18 (1975):3.

Need for films suited to Malian, not Hollywood's interests.

3966. Zerbo, Salia. A propos du film Ironu, quelle methode de lutte pour nos peuples? _Sidwaya_ Feb. 24 (1987):5. (R)

3967. Zerbo, Salia. Une ambiance de fête populaire. _Sidwaya_ Feb. 23 (1987):7.

Opening session of FESPACO.

3968. Zerbo, Salia. La camarade Yassalam Sessouma du CNC explique. _Sidwaya_ Feb. 26 (1987):10.

General discussion of different kinds of film (16mm, 35mm, feature, etc.), relation of images and sound, synchronization and subtitling.

3969. Zerbo, Salia. Le début des grandes innovations 1985. Sidwaya Feb. 26 (1987):7.

Review of FESPACO 1985.

3970. Zerbo, Salia. L'ère des premières compétitions 1972-1973. Sidwaya Feb. 23 (1987):6.

Review of FESPACO 1973.

3971. Zerbo, Salia. Ils ont dit. Sidwaya Feb. 23 (1987):10. (I)

Bernard Mathonnat discusses Burkinabe/French cooperation.

3972. Zerbo, Salia. Interview de Philippe Sawadogo secrétaire général du FESPACO. Sidwaya Feb. 20 (1987):8-9. (I)

3973. Zerbo, Salia. Marche de soutien aux cinéastes de l'inédit dans le FESPACO. Sidwaya Feb. 25 (1985):ii.

3974. Zerbo, Salia. Mes premiers pas: 1969-1970. Sidwaya Feb. 20 (1987):9.

First FESPACO and countries that provided support for it.

3975. Zerbo, Salia. Les periodes charnieres 1981-1983. Sidwaya Feb. 25 (1987):5.

FESPACO prizes 1981 and 1983.

3976. Ziana Adn. Local film commended in Leipzig. Sunday Mail (Harare) Nov. 24 (1985):5.

Zimbabwean documentary on literacy made by B. Tuwaya and R. Moyo.

3977. Ziane, Farrah. "Thiaroye 44": histoire d'un massacre de Sénégalais. Afrique-Asie 358(1985):64.

Plans to film original Bèye script of film which has subsequently become Camp de Thiaroye by Sembène and Sow.

3978. Zika, Damouré. Damouré Zika: mon patron Jean Rouch. Bingo 382(1984):26-28.

Nigerien film technician discusses his work.

3979. Zone 2. Un Ceddo gagnant. Zone 2 254(1984):19. (R)

3980. Zone 2. Festival du film africain au Japan. Zone 2

271(1984):15.

Tokyo film festival.

3981. Zone 2. Journées cinématographiques de Carthage. Zone 2
269(1984):15.

3982. Zone 2. Nécessité d'une muilinationale africaine de production.
Zone 2 2(1979):18.

CIDC and CIPROFILM.

3983. Zone 2. 1Xe Journées de Carthage. Souleymane Cissé. La moisson
du vent. Zone 2 165(1982):18. (R)

Finyé.

3984. Zone 2. Précisions à propos du film "Samory". Zone 2
271(1984):15.

Sembène's plans for making Samory.

3985. Zone 2. Le retour de Sembène. Zone 2 280(1985):15. (R)

Ceddo.

3986. Zone 2. Trois films pour s'imposer. Zone 2 178(1983):18.

Ceddo, Sa Dagga and Sarax-si.

3987. Zongo, Calliste. Sous le signe de la maturité. Afrique Nouvelle
1961(1987):12-13.

FESPACO.

3988. Zoungrana, Ben Idriss. "Désébagato" ou le dernier salarie.
Carrefour Africain 954(1986):23-29. (R)

Review includes information on actors and technicians.

3989. Zoungrana, Marc-André. Le 5ème FESPACO: moins qu'hier et demain?
Carrefour Africain 616(1976):3.

3990. Zoungrana, Seydou. Dans les coulisses du FESPACO. Sidwaya Feb.
25 (1985):iii.

Vignettes about Sembène, Aventure ambique and Centre Culturel
Africain.

3991. Zoungrana, Seydou. Dans les coulisses du FESPACO. Sidwaya Feb.
27 (1985):iv.

Vignettes about invited guests, equipment installed by CINAFRIC,
music and other cultural activities.

3992.  Zoungrana, Seydou and Clément Tapsoba.   Le MOBRAP au rendez-vous.
        _Sidwaya_ Mar. 1 (1985):iii-iv.

        MOBRAP activities related to FESPACO theme of liberation.

3993.  Zyl, John van.   A reeling industry film in South Africa.
        _Leadership_ 4,4(1985):102-106.

        Includes brief information on films for blacks.

# ACTORS AND ACTRESSES INDEX

## SUB-SAHARAN AFRICAN FILMS

Imoudu, Daniel, 113

Ishola, Babatunde, 2299

Joseph, Momo, 353, 470, 2464, 2665

Kacou, Anne, 1984

Kamwa, Daniel, 669, 2728

Kelani, Tunde, 168

Koeffe, Claire, 3542

Kolly, Natou, 1376

Koto, Sidney, 1230, 1270

Kouyaté, Sotigui, 857

Lemoine, Joy, 166

Maiga, Djingarey, 2826

Mané, Doura, 200, 681, 1208, 1301, 1310, 1344, 1531, 1809, 2222, 2300, 2665, 2690, 2814, 3921

Mané, Mme. Doura, 1962

Martins, Orlando, 38, 670, 1758, 1760, 1988, 2799, 2907, 2908, 3633, 3741

Mbali, Sophie, 684

M'bia, Ambroise, 684, 3497

Mory, Philippe, 684

Moutouari, Pierre, 692

M'Pongo, Love, 692

Ndiaye, Lamine, 524

Ndiaye, Ndiaye Mour, 524

Ndiaye, Tabara, 2757

Niang, Isseu, 2304

Niang, Myriam, 3396

Obriango, Melville, 114

Okala, Nicole, 1483, 3338

Olaiya, Moses, 2942, 3634

Ouédraogo, Rasman, 1560

Pamelo, Monka, 692

Sabela, Simon, 2306

Samaké, Sali, 3530

Sanvi, Panou, 1956, 2628

Sarr, Ismaila, 1499

Seck, Douta, 2608

Seck, Ibrahima, 662, 684

SECK, LAMINE, see Sekka, Johnny

Seck, Oumar, 524

Secka, Johnny, 2337, 3236, 3242, 3904

Sekka, Johnny, 407, 2474, 2713, 3236, 3242, 3904

Senghor, Nanette, 684

Sèye, Khoudia, 663

Sèye, Yonousse, 1983, 2047

Sidibé, Moussa, 703, 1604

Sikirou, Ogounjobe Adéboyé, 682

Souaré, Bama, 1478

Souley, Zalika, 1714, 2836

Soyinka, Wole, 2904

Sy, Maurice, 407

Talla, André Marie, 692

Tapsoba, Simone, 3530, 3542

Thiam, Kesso, 684

FESPACO (continued)
2301, 2303, 2344-2346,
2359, 2390, 2404, 2409-2412,
2432, 2477, 2485-2487, 2489,
2490, 2492, 2494, 2498, 2499,
2502, 2506, 2512, 2554, 2568,
2576, 2624, 2631, 2633, 2637,
2638, 2641, 2647-2649, 2652,
2659, 2670, 2678, 2681, 2682,
2688, 2693, 2704, 2705, 2707,
2715, 2716, 2725, 2734, 2748,
2783, 2801, 2805, 2807, 2832,
2835, 2844, 2864, 2887-2893,
2934, 2950, 2951, 2954, 2957,
2959-2969, 2975, 2982, 2989,
2992, 2994-3000, 3002, 3004,
3005-3007, 3030, 3043, 3074,
3141, 3148, 3158, 3159, 3164,
3173, 3201, 3202, 3205, 3230,
3260, 3273, 3276, 3282, 3290,
3293, 3295-3319, 3326, 3332-3334,
3365, 3375, 3384, 3392, 3395,
3397, 3400, 3401, 3421-3423,
3425, 3431, 3458, 3493, 3503,
3506, 3507, 3511, 3512, 3514,
3517, 3518, 3521-3526, 3529,
3531, 3533-3535, 3545, 3547-3549,
3551, 3553-3556, 3558, 3559,
3561, 3563, 3564, 3566-3569,
3596, 3604, 3605, 3608, 3610,
3618, 3624, 3668, 3671, 3678,
3684, 3701, 3704, 3708, 3713,
3715-3717, 3724, 3728-3731,
3757, 3759, 3780, 3781, 3784,
3804, 3811, 3817-3821, 3840,
3841, 3847, 3852, 3853, 3865,
3868, 3871, 3919, 3934, 3935,
3967, 3969-3975, 3987, 3989-3992

FESTAC, 234, 1124, 1136, 1137, 1144,
2188, 2971, 2974, 3772

Festival du Film de la Jeunesse, 81

Festival du Film Publicitaire, 1990,
2819, 3068, 3175, 3272

FIFEF, 95, 215, 231, 313, 314, 362,
373, 517, 600, 607, 614, 731, 739,
775, 789, 850, 880, 908, 936, 972,
979, 1034, 1113, 1123, 1138, 1152,
1323, 1494, 1637, 1661, 1684-1687,
1708, 1712, 1848, 1850, 1872, 2126,
2133, 2357, 2397, 2467, 2468, 2512,

FIFEF (continued)
2598, 2599, 2611, 2660, 2661,
2672, 2674, 2683, 2686, 2687,
2692, 2703, 2723, 2736, 3009,
3124, 3129, 3139, 3358, 3374,
3377, 3388, 3389, 3405, 3711,
3813, 3836, 3849, 3858, 3863,
3864, 3869, 3902, 3936

Fort de France, 1591

Geneva International Television,
1632

Giffoni Valle Piana, 1595

Havana, 2839, 3850

Hyères, 2029

INTERNATIONAL FESTIVAL OF NEW
LATIN AMERICAN CINEMA,
see Havana

JCC, 125, 127, 129-131, 133, 135,
137, 139-146, 148, 149, 152,
157, 159, 180, 196, 214, 218,
232, 233, 248, 335, 372, 375,
389, 420, 529, 530, 573, 577,
604, 638, 714, 717, 722, 724-727,
737, 741, 744, 745, 765, 768,
771, 776, 777, 802, 814, 829,
834-837, 839, 841-843, 849,
906, 928, 949, 970, 971, 973,
1004, 1008, 1103, 1151, 1173,
1209, 1231, 1240, 1265, 1381,
1493, 1524, 1526, 1666-1668,
1690, 1700, 1703, 1716, 1730,
1731, 1786, 1833, 1881, 1889,
1992, 2024, 2026, 2125, 2136,
2137, 2146, 2153, 2335, 2338,
2362, 2403, 2405, 2406, 2420,
2511, 2512, 2525, 2544, 2545,
2549, 2610, 2667-2669, 2684,
2691, 2711, 2722, 2730, 2747,
2770, 2774, 2795, 2806, 2897,
2953, 2991, 3172, 3190, 3192,
3203, 3328, 3335, 3337,
3339-3344, 3346-3351, 3367,
3368, 3434, 3442, 3492, 3532,
3594, 3601, 3639, 3640, 3655,
3657, 3659-3661, 3735, 3784,
3791, 3792, 3805, 3814, 3816,
3827, 3835, 3836, 3846, 3940,

# FILM TITLE INDEX

A Banna, 1528, 2196

A nous deux France, 310, 968, 1444,
1633, 1635, 1839, 1842, 2025, 2607,
3020, 3212, 3238, 3587, 3695, 3775,

Ablakon, 132, 438, 439, 446, 451,
489, 634, 640, 868, 1012, 1945,
2206, 2214, 2339, 2381, 2414, 3721

Abusuan, 324, 325, 966, 1376, 1439,
1534, 2211, 2216, 2750, 3383

Accident, 2112, 2393, 3169

Adam, 2606

Adja Tio, 79, 452, 453, 1273,
2064, 2212, 2213, 3015, 3233

Adjoba, 1984

African Calvary, 185, 3280

African Fever, 115

African Woman U.S.A., 3443

Afrika am Rhein, 3778

Agit Rewo, 3405

Aiye, 2592, 2944

Ajani Ogun, 519, 967, 1040, 1522,
1693, 2900, 2920, 2922, 3578

Alimentaire face à la dépendance
alimentaire, 105

Allahou Akbar, 1202, 3399

Alpha, 292, 854, 2441

Amadi, 1453, 1550, 1554, 2972, 3398

Amanie, 2610, 3936

Ambassades nourricières, 540

Ame perdue, 2627

Amin the Rise and Fall, 877, 1745,
1941, 2452, 3042, 3114, 3134

Animata, 2788

Anvil and the Hammer, 1027

Appât du gain, 126, 2076, 2256, 3942

Archer bassari, 2295

Arrêt car, 2470

Arusi ya Mariamu, 190

Ashes and Embers, 292

Aspirant, 2597

Aube noire, 141, 2258

Autre école, 2446, 3006

Awake the Morning, 178

Away from the Sidewalk, 273, 2931

Aya, 1772

Ayanmo, 1454, 2984

Ayouma, 138, 1162, 1419, 1420, 3701, 3710

Baara, 311, 579, 1021, 1038, 1163, 1182,
1345, 1571, 1664, 2340, 2663, 3271, 3382

Badou Boy, 558, 1128, 2664,
2669, 2673, 3359

Bague du roi Koda, 413, 2458

Bako, 199, 258, 1018, 1210, 1228,
1459, 1665, 2167, 2240, 2659,
3153, 3170, 3593, 3895

Baks, 609, 904, 1068, 1769, 1770,
2162, 2354, 2675, 3323, 3648

Bambo, 665, 1051, 1347, 1495,
1501, 2253, 2598

Bataxal, 3047

## SUB-SAHARAN AFRICAN FILMS

## SUB-SAHARAN AFRICAN FILMS

Henriques, Carlos, 913

Hima, Miriama, 623, 2463

Hondo, Med, 52, 143, 150, 158,
292, 376, 396, 477, 499, 501,
542, 625, 735, 868, 961, 969,
974, 992, 1010, 1017, 1020,
1045, 1074, 1178, 1181, 1183,
1323, 1335, 1393, 1428, 1435,
1489, 1509, 1569, 1629, 1640,
1649, 1737, 1743, 1817, 1845,
1858, 1927-1932, 2039, 2048,
2087, 2120, 2123, 2166, 2233,
2255, 2288, 2383, 2385, 2387,
2407, 2419, 2427, 2516, 2556,
2558, 2573, 2595, 2602, 2789,
2841, 3011, 3036, 3079, 3080,
3083, 3098, 3110, 3142, 3150,
3313, 3345, 3393, 3429, 3430,
3479, 3499, 3543, 3607, 3740,
3763, 3880, 3906, 3918, 3962

Iloputaife, Ijeama, 3443

Ismael, Salahou, 3682

Jacob, Sou, 2192

Kaba, Alkaly, 1044, 1666, 2520,
3109, 3698

Kaboré, Gaston, 37, 580, 589,
719, 763, 827, 878, 1281,
2051, 2117-2119, 2376, 2391,
2577, 2720, 2749, 3453,
3488, 3532, 3590, 3950

Kamba, Sebastien, 154, 1822,
1857, 2042, 2139

Kamwa, Daniel, 13, 181, 472,
669 767, 813, 1015, 1041, 1295,
1630, 1782, 1832, 1891, 2156,
2373, 2433, 2472, 2728, 3021,
3070, 3459

Karim, Abdoul, 3568

Keita, Daouda, 3008

Keseruani, Alalade, 1815

KONDE, KHALIFA, see Conde,
Kalifa

Koita, Abdoulaye, 105

Kola, Djim, 1025, 2199, 2333

Kollo, Daniel Sanou, 141, 1926,
2284, 2453

Kone, Mamadou, 2243

Kouam, 3568

Koula, Jean-Louis, 79, 452, 453,
1273, 1984, 2064, 2069, 2094,
2212, 2213, 3015, 3233

Koumba, Henri-Joseph, 926, 1461,
1462, 1715, 2375, 2766, 2767

Kouyaté, Djibril, 703, 704, 1046,
1604, 1800, 3613, 3645

Kozoloa, Yéo, 477, 497, 552, 638,
711, 1082, 1934, 2094, 2102,
3001

Kramo-Lanciné, Fadika, 381, 549,
1076, 1077, 1241, 1251, 1297,
1519, 1732, 1736, 2071, 2080-
2082, 2217, 2371, 2954, 3013,
3375, 3458, 3665

Kwami Mumbu Nzinga, 1610, 2996

LANCINE, FADIKA KRAMO, see
Kramo-Lanciné, Fadika

Larbi, Gacem, 1822

Mahomo, Nana, 328, 329, 1003, 1075,
1416, 1433, 1599, 1613, 1802,
1834, 2927, 3278

Maiga, Dingarey, 141, 490, 493,
1309, 1692, 2114, 2219, 2258,
2826

Makiadi, Simao, 3568

Oliveira, Mendes do, 1595

Onwenu, Onyeka, 1632

Orere, David, 189, 272, 1508,
1517, 1951, 2793, 2925, 2935

Oruh, Gold, 273, 2931

Ossin, Jean-Pierre, 3285

Ouédraogo, Hamadou, 116, 1479,
2952-2956

Ouédraogo, Idrissa, 398, 468,
581, 622, 623, 1105, 1560,
1563, 2101, 2182, 2193, 2332,
2336, 2416, 2644, 3306, 3319,
3508, 3528, 3546, 3678, 3769,
3951

Ousseini, Inoussa, 945, 1689,
1711, 2975-2977, 3135, 3200,
3612

Oyekunle, Segun, 183, 708, 1415
2777, 2980-2983, 3072

Patel, Sharad, 877, 1745,
1941, 2452, 3042, 3114, 3134

Patraquim, Luis, 315, 3010

Patsanza, Miriam, 2530

Pimenta, Pedro, 2266, 3043,
3044, 3573

Pink, Pattie, 2430

Raeburn, Michael, 840, 1063, 2871,
3024, 3069, 3117, 3473, 3751

Rahaga, Jean-Claude, 143, 1458

Ramampy, Benôit, 2112, 2393, 3169

Rasco, Segun, 267

SALA, BABA, see Olaiya, Moses

Samb, Ababacar, 78, 223, 278,
551, 559, 596, 976, 1115,
1129, 1130, 1150, 1203, 1254,

Samb, Ababacar (continued)
1641, 1666, 1795, 2022, 2030,
2201, 2246, 2278, 2326, 2428,
2513, 2562, 2625,2714,2727,2990,
3125, 3178, 3179, 3211, 3355,
3356, 3390, 3577, 3669

SAMB MAKHARAM, ABABACAR, see Samb,
Ababacar

SANON, EMMANUEL, see Sanou,
Emmanuel

Sanou, Emmanuel, 696, 2190, 2643,
2948, 3311, 3519, 3988

Sarr, Mamadou, 689

Seck, Alioune Badara, 3778

SECK, PAPE, see Seck, Alioune
Badara

Sembène, Ousmane, 3,24,36,37,43,
46, 52, 54, 60, 62, 66, 70, 77,
99, 102, 106, 107, 109, 121,
123, 124, 182, 191, 208, 226-
229, 249, 292, 295, 298, 308,
309, 312, 322, 331, 332, 343,
346, 348, 368, 385, 388, 402,
408, 409, 412, 465, 476, 531,
541, 561, 599, 618, 633, 655,
675, 685, 686, 697, 706, 709,
710, 716, 767, 809, 820, 855,
861, 864, 875, 879, 893, 910,
921-923, 929, 930, 934, 935,
947-949, 960, 989, 994, 1009,
1013, 1026, 1028, 1030-1032,
1037, 1050, 1073, 1074, 1091,
1110, 1115, 1117, 1119, 1134,
1141, 1146, 1149, 1158, 1185,
1186, 1189, 1198, 1201, 1215,
1227, 1232-1234, 1262, 1272,
1274, 1278, 1366-1368, 1418,
1427, 1443, 1451, 1470, 1472,
1535, 1537, 1555, 1560, 1564,
1566, 1567, 1583, 1594, 1597,
1598, 1602, 1612, 1619, 1622,
1627, 1629, 1642, 1649, 1699,
1730, 1739-1742, 1744, 1747,
1774, 1775, 1789, 1793, 1794,
1813, 1814, 1836, 1846, 1852,
1855, 1866, 1871, 1874-1876,
1888, 1905, 1919, 1920, 1923,

# SUB-SAHARAN AFRICAN FILMS

Traoré, Mahama Johnson, 36, 279, 286,
602, 671, 688, 1052, 1067, 1069,
1070, 1074, 1075, 1138, 1152, 1179,
1190, 1242, 1252, 1253, 1256, 1320,
1627, 1722, 1723, 1748, 1771, 1844,
1892, 2318, 2326, 2365, 2473, 2527,
2675, 2680, 2685, 2694, 2697, 2721,
2724, 2755, 2811, 3161, 3286, 3287,
3371, 3434, 3436, 3656, 3673, 3674,
3960, 3986

Traoré, Mory, 466, 627, 1192, 3684,
3685

Traoré, Nissy Joanny, 2446

Tuwaya, B., 3976

Ugbomah, Eddie, 118, 173, 237, 285,
403, 1960, 1972, 1973, 2436, 2438,
2442, 2943, 2946, 2947, 3591

U'kset, Umbam, 3947

Van Rensburg, Manie, 876, 1750, 2254

Vieyra, Paulin Soumanou, 73-77, 349,
382, 412, 465, 689, 1014, 1031,
1140, 1313, 1342, 1402, 1480,
1795, 1824, 1856, 1874, 2111,
2514, 2608, 2986, 3321, 3777-3870,
3943

Vodio, Etienne N'Dabian, 16, 327, 445,
1377, 2089, 2161, 2289

Vuvo, Ismael, 2860

Wilson, Samuel, 3352

Yonli, Bernard, 1679, 1967, 2949, 3672

Youlou, 2394

Zé, Moise, 2618

Zoumbara, Paul, 590, 3008,
3259, 3944

SUB-SAHARAN AFRICAN FILMS

Togo, 1084, 1956, 2628, 2639

Togo-Infrastructure, 277

UPPER VOLTA, see Burkina Faso

Western Sahara, 205

Zaire, 26, 47, 55, 56, 64, 65,
   701, 827, 859, 911, 1166, 1456,
   1610, 2188, 2320, 2321, 2571,
   2585, 2866, 2996, 3226, 3568,
   3949, 3958

Zaire-Audience, 2574

Zaire-Distribution, 1523, 2323,
   3957

Zaire-History, 1282, 2319, 2379

Zaire-Infrastructure, 721, 1785,
   1797, 2575

Zaire-Production, 1282, 2323

Zaire-Themes, 1609

Zambia, 6, 2062

Zambia-Infrastructure, 2322

Zimbabwe, 964, 2186, 2430, 2431,
   2530, 2532, 2565-2567, 2871,
   3464-3466, 3470, 3473, 3475,
   3751, 3976

Zimbabwe-Audience, 963

Zimbabwe-Censorship, 3476

Zimbabwe-Infrastructure, 1655,
   1910-1912, 1914, 1916, 1918,
   2426, 2460, 2529, 2531, 2572,
   3463, 3467, 3468, 3471, 3472,
   3474, 3616, 3953, 3954

SUB-SAHARAN AFRICAN FILMS

Infrastructure (continued)
3617, 3653, 3693, 3702, 3706, 3712,
3718, 3719, 3733-3735, 3742,
3746, 3750, 3755, 3758, 3759,
3762, 3764-3767, 3770, 3773,
3777, 3780-3782, 3787, 3798,
3807, 3840, 3841, 3865, 3872,
3878, 3883, 3897, 3939, 3941,
3968, 3982

Production, 39, 440, 560,
938, 1943, 2500, 2977, 3178,
3674

Theaters, 1171, 1993

Themes, 1, 6, 15, 18, 20, 24,
27, 30, 44, 45, 49, 52, 71,
100, 352, 377, 390-392, 421,
433, 500, 535, 578, 643, 646,
648-654, 656-661, 747, 766,
773, 791, 801, 909, 946, 950,
955, 995, 996, 1033, 1046,
1064, 1180, 1225, 1330, 1357,
1403, 1413, 1446, 1527, 1532,
1616, 1653, 1669, 1673, 1778,
1783, 1786, 1798, 1801, 1816,
1819, 1825, 1840, 1851, 1854,
1868-1870, 1877, 1879, 1883,
1893-1895, 1897, 1902, 1969,
2023, 2135, 2154, 2178, 2180,
2191, 2194, 2226, 2252, 2260,
2270, 2317, 2324, 2327, 2357,
2360, 2366, 2377, 2413, 2465,
2509, 2555, 2645, 2747, 2843,
2957, 3012, 3016, 3050, 3078,
3079, 3082, 3085, 3089, 3119,
3142, 3144, 3166, 3227, 3249,
3250, 3253, 3285, 3422, 3490,
3512, 3571, 3576, 3647, 3649,
3664, 3753, 3773, 3793, 3830,
3883